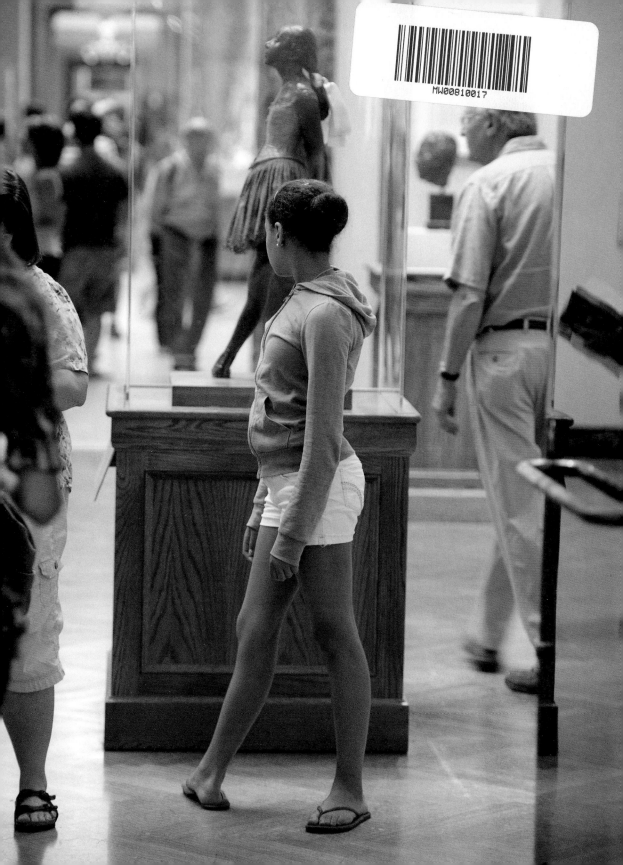

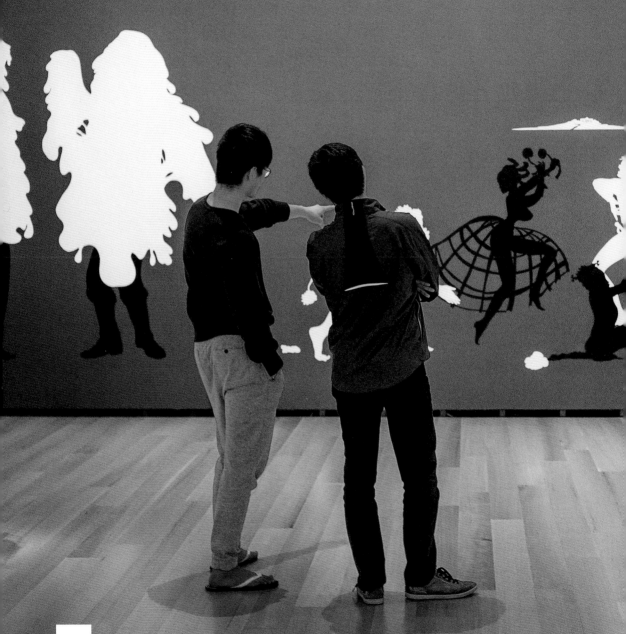

mfa
BOSTON

MFA PUBLICATIONS *Museum of Fine Arts, Boston*

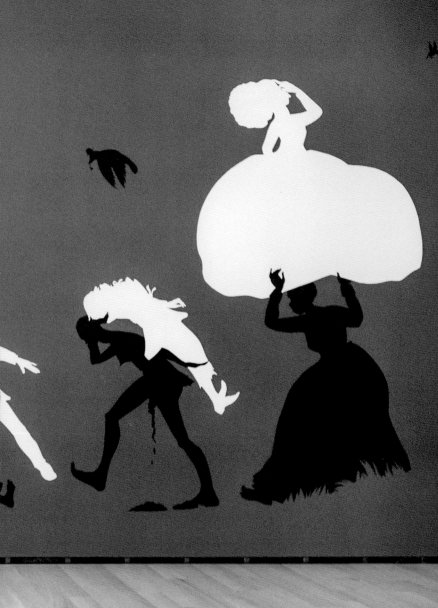

MUSEUM OF FINE ARTS, BOSTON

a guide to the collections

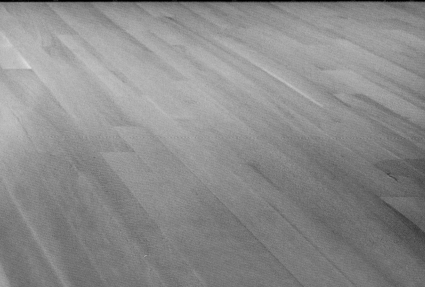

Entries by

Gilian Shallcross and **Adam Tessier**

Introduction by

Matthew Teitelbaum

A Brief History of the MFA by

Maureen Melton

MFA Publications
Museum of Fine Arts, Boston
465 Huntington Avenue
Boston, Massachusetts 02115
www.mfa.org/publications

The Museum of Fine Arts, Boston, is a nonprofit institution
devoted to the promotion and appreciation of the creative arts.
The Museum endeavors to respect the copyrights of all authors
and creators in a manner consistent with its nonprofit educational mission. If you feel any material has been included in this
publication improperly, please contact the Department of Rights
and Licensing at 617 267 9300, or by mail at the above address.

While the objects in this publication necessarily represent only a
small portion of the MFA's holdings, the Museum is proud to be
a leader within the American museum community in sharing the
objects in its collection via its website. Currently, information
about approximately 400,000 objects is available to the public
worldwide. To learn more about the MFA's collections, including
provenance, publication, and exhibition history, kindly visit
www.mfa.org/collections.

For a complete listing of MFA publications, please contact the
publisher at the above address, or call 617 369 4233.

Generous support for this publication given in loving memory
of Ellen Fallon and Judy Keyes, tireless MFA volunteers,
by their husbands Peter Fallon and Jonathan Keyes.

Edited by Hope Stockton
Copyedited by Patty Bergin and Theresa Duran
Proofread by Kathryn Blatt
Typesetting and layout by Matt Mayerchak and Laura Glassman
Series design by Lucinda Hitchcock
Production by Terry McAweeney
Production assistance by Jessica Altholz Eber
Printed on 150 gsm Gardamatte
Printed and bound at Verona Libri, Verona, Italy

Distributed in the United States of America and Canada by
ARTBOOK | D.A.P.
75 Broad Street, Suite 630
New York, New York 10004
www.artbook.com

Distributed outside the United States of America and Canada by
Thames & Hudson, Ltd.
181A High Holborn
London WC1V 7QX
www.thamesandhudson.com

REVISED EDITION
Printed and bound in Italy
This book was printed on acid-free paper.

Contents

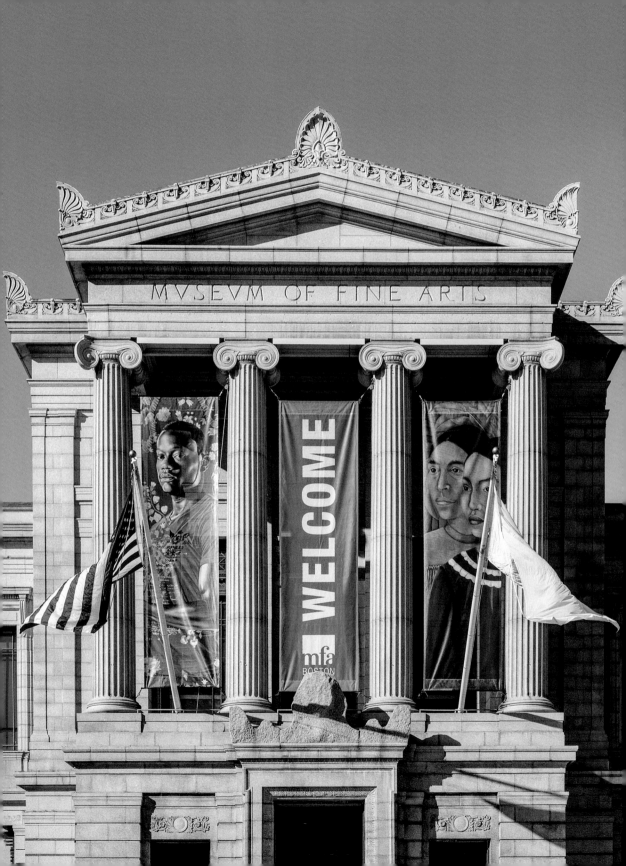

The Art of Collecting

Matthew Teitelbaum, *Ann and Graham Gund Director*

We all collect something: memories, travel experiences, associations
through friendships. When we collect material objects—flowers for our
garden, seashells for our windowsills, books for our shelves—we move
into a world in which the critical mass of things allows us to compare and
contrast. We begin conversations about what is important to us, why we like
some things rather than others, what distinguishes one object from another
that looks similar. At the very least, collections strengthen our powers of
discernment and judgment.

Perhaps there is more. On another level, our collections of objects and
images allow us to realize the world we create for ourselves. And that is a
key motivating aspect of collecting—it is an essentially creative act that
gives us a form of expression. Collections lead us to material understanding,
cataloging of knowledge, and a personal stamp on sequence and display.
How do we order things to understand them better? Think of photo albums:
collections of photographs we gather and sequence to create narratives
filled with meaning through associations.

And what of museum collections, repositories of knowledge through the
preservation of works of art—are they different? At the core of the museum
are collections held together in trust for future generations. Professionals in various disciplines, using their training and continually refreshed
knowledge, work to build collections in direct response to the mission and
purpose of the institution. Curators work within departments and categories—of place, time, medium, and type—and their collecting systematically
orders thoughts and objects and images. And so, over time, collections grow
to represent established narratives, but also to reflect new understandings
and refined knowledge. As we learn more and begin to challenge long-held
assumptions, museum collections come to represent their world differently. In some cases, collections are extended with an urge to completeness;
in other cases, to question whether the boundaries we put around things
might be usefully opened and experiences deepened. Think of the personal
photo album again. Sometimes we add to it simply because it is another
photograph of our parents in youth, and other times because we have just
identified our grandfather's sister, and it is the first photograph of her
we have ever seen.

To state it differently, we collect personally to create a cherished
understanding and, likely, to satisfy a personal urge to order. We collect

The Huntington

Avenue Entrance

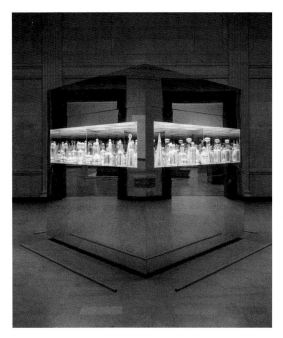

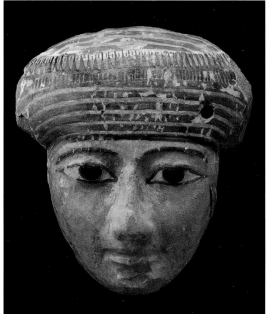

institutionally to create and reflect history. And if we assume that history is always shifting to some degree, as new questions are asked and new facts are established, it is evident that collections shift too. Their contours change, or explorations lead to particular areas of depth. New media are engaged, new categories introduced, new cultures and communities included. It is exciting and challenging to be both *of* history and alive and open *in* the moment. It is exciting to build collections, for they are living things.

In collecting for history, institutions constantly ask, When is enough, enough? When do we know we must keep going? If we are collecting for future generations, what do words like "definitive," "complete," or "iconic" mean? Don't such words stop time and place collections in a deep freeze? When do we have the instinct and courage to try something new? When do we decide we need "just one more" work by an artist whose achievement is already represented in depth?

And here the evolution of the Museum of Fine Arts, Boston, matters. We were founded in 1870 with the generalized ambition that a great city needed a great art museum. More specifically, our charter directs us "to make, maintain and exhibit collections of works of art, and to afford Instruction in the Fine Arts."

Leading citizens gathered, representing family and institutional interests (institutional representatives included Harvard University, Massachusetts

Left

Josiah McElheny, *Endlessly Repeating Twentieth Century Modernism*, 2007

Right

Egyptian Face from mummiform coffin, 1070–660 B.C.

Institute of Technology, the Boston Athenaeum, the Boston Public Library, and the Lowell Institute; ex officio representatives such as the mayor and school superintendent also attended). They began collecting work and combining collections already formed in the community. In the framing documents, one of the founders, Charles Callaghan Perkins, wrote: "Nations as well as individuals should aim at that degree of aesthetic culture which, without passing the dividing line between general and special knowledge, will enable them to recognize and appreciate the beautiful in nature and in art." Among our first works were a biblical painting by antebellum Boston's favorite artist, Washington Allston, two lush landscapes by Rococo master François Boucher, and bountiful collections of archaeological objects from Cyprus and ancient Egypt.

The idea of a collection was central to the conception of the Museum. Indeed the Museum was formed as a home for objects, with an ambition to represent many world cultures and, through their presentation, to educate and excite the Boston community. At its founding, the MFA was emblematic of an America poised to lead the world and establish its own narratives by placing itself in the center of discussion and reflection. American art was to be seen within that kaleidoscopic mix, in the context of a nation creating a sense of itself, at the center of a world order. And so it was that the Museum's collections began to be formed under the direction of a small staff and members of a wealthy philanthropic community, whose gifts and bequests very much mirrored themselves and their understanding of the world.

Quickly the Museum became home to the greatest public art holdings in America. Superb collections were formed and given in early European art, specifically French painting of the nineteenth century; Egyptian art, largely through the joint archaeological excavations with Harvard University; art from Japan and China, collections still thought to be unsurpassed outside Asia; and Classical art. In all cases, these were collections and objects that could teach values and beliefs worthy of a museum that had a civic role to educate the public and to affirm America's leadership in the world.

In the early days of the Museum, comprehensiveness mattered. Collections were meant to be broad, deep, and preeminent in areas of interest. Many examples were sought to reinforce the educational value of comparing and contrasting. Celebrating connoisseurship, the Museum encouraged its visitors to develop a capability for refined judgment. Words like "definitive" and "complete" were part of the drive to be both a museum of international consequence and an effective forum for teaching and leadership.

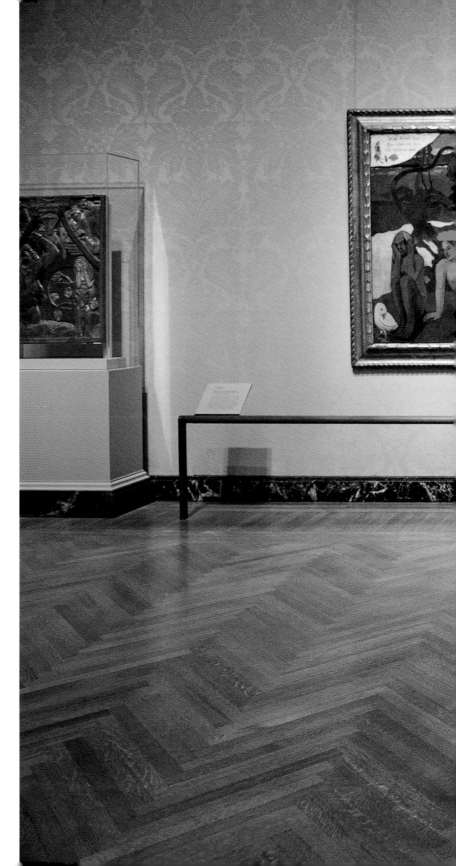

Visitors engage with
Paul Gauguin, *Where Do We
Come From? What Are We?
Where Are We Going?*, 1897–98

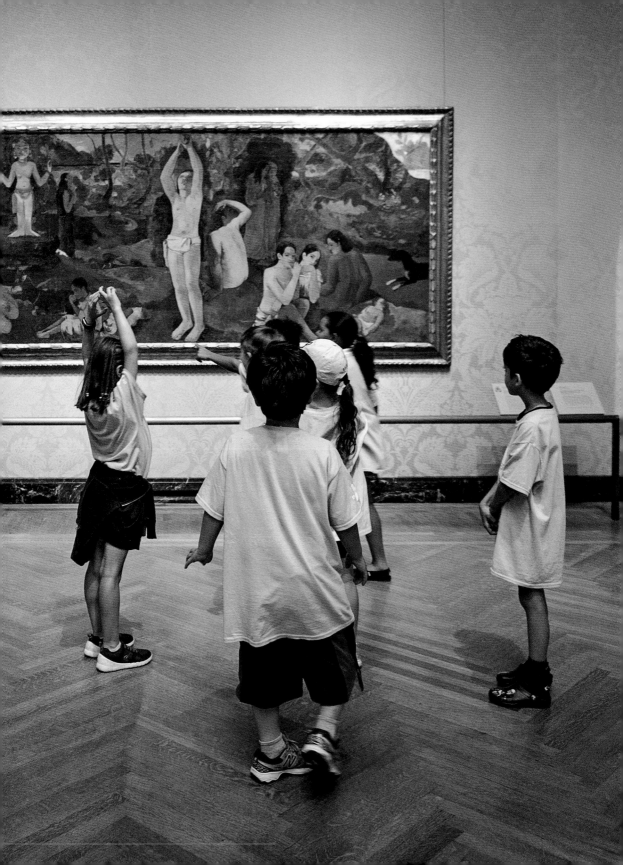

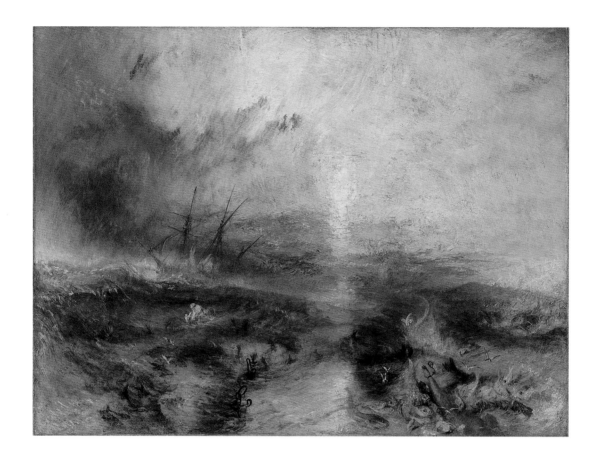

In all of this, befitting its mission to serve the community as an educational institution and to reflect the values of its founders, the Museum
assumed an early and sustained research agenda. Publications, learned
display, and careful determination of loans to other institutions were
sequenced to create knowledge and to base emerging understanding on
academic rigor. The Museum had an early bulletin, which shared writings
on the collections of the MFA and those of other institutions. Lectures were
held, classes given. Shortly after its founding, the Museum established the
School of the Museum of Fine Arts, specifically to encourage a generation
of amateur (and sometimes professional) artists to share the values of art
and its making in their communities. Offering of art classes was seen by
Museum leadership as a key part of creating an enlightened community of
museumgoers, those who could become advocates for the civilizing importance of a museum. Collections fit into this paradigm, for while they were
gathered for aesthetic pleasure, they served a purpose for scholarly pursuit
as well, constituting a repository of knowledge tethered to material things.

Joseph Mallord William Turner,
Slave Ship, 1840

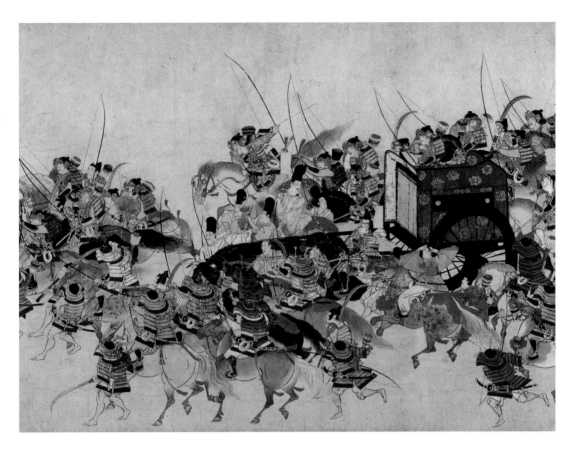

From the outset, "iconic" or singularly important works were sought
in order to create stronger narratives of art history. Sometimes they were
purchased directly by the Museum, or were solicited from private collectors
in and around Boston. Singular works, those against which a whole category
of related objects could be measured—such as J. M. W. Turner's *Slave Ship*,
Paul Gauguin's *Where Do We Come From? What Are We? Where Are We Going?*,
the Classical head of Aphrodite, the sculpture of King Menkaura (Mycerinus)
and queen from ancient Egypt, and the Japanese handscroll *Night Attack
on the Sanjō Palace*—all set a standard for appreciation, discernment, and
value. These iconic works both inspire community pride and encourage the
ambitions of collectors.

In a museum collection, iconic works serve to galvanize or punctuate a
narrative. They have the potential to take something in a new direction or
reinforce a specific idea. Matisse said that the greater the work of art, the
more stories it can tell. And so it is that iconic works of art can find their
place in many contexts, in each case encouraging exploration and discovery.

*Night Attack on the Sanjō
Palace* (detail), Japanese, third
quarter of the 13th century

Seen in the galleries of the Museum, collections presented the values of other cultures believed to be essential to any comprehensive education. The founders wished that the century-old concept of the Grand Tour could be translated into museum display, and achieved under one roof through a strategic assembly of cultural objects. They imagined that the MFA could be the beacon of this aspiration.

The great organizing principle of a museum, in both collecting and display, is narrative. The ordering of things creates a story-telling thread that encourages a way of thinking. Traditionally, and certainly in the early years of the Museum, this narrative has largely been that of a conventional, received art history. One style led to another, one civilization gave way to another, one set of values was passed to another, and the progression of values was encapsulated in art. The idea of progression and distinction in museum display has traditionally come from the conviction that the work of one artist or movement was connected to another by direct influence, the way Jackson Pollock said he had to work around the example of Picasso, or the way in which the values of a dominant culture or epoch replaced another—think of how Meiji art in Japan incorporated Western cultural values and challenged the character of art of the preceding Edo period, leading to changes in style and subject matter. In this view of artistic evolution, museums paralleled teaching in the humanities, suggesting the ways in which groups of objects could be gathered to tell the story of stylistic developments that marked cultural differences.

For much of the Museum's history, the display of objects in museums has followed categories of collecting and learning. Departments have geographic titles such as European or American, or media-based designations such as prints and drawings, and displays in the galleries have followed these divisions. And yet, as advances in technology and ease of travel link the world in new ways—making distances seem shorter and access greater—categories of learning and display have begun to change. There is much more connection between geographies, disciplines, areas of inquiry, and media than there has ever been before. Connections are celebrated, influences understood differently, and the relationship of art to the particulars of place and community the subject of more reflection and consideration.

In this moment, as we get to know more about works of art and as the world seems to get more familiar (or at least more accessible), we realize the stories we tell need expanding, and that our collections need to be questioned and built upon in order to recognize the many ways artists create art within global cultures. It is a generally shared belief that collections must be built to expand understanding of discrete sites of production and the

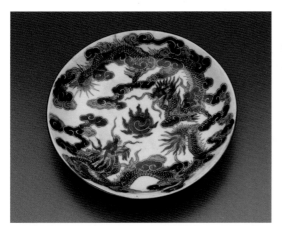

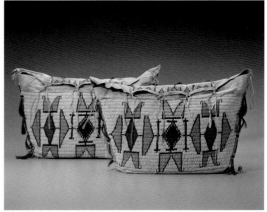

connections between them—more Vietnamese ceramics, but positioned in
the context of other Asian cultures; more African textiles, but understood in
relation to global belief systems; more Native American beadwork, but seen
in relation to landscape ideas in the Americas more broadly. If collections
represent the ideas of living cultures, it is critical that we think about how
to breathe new life into both the gathering and display of objects.

From its founding, the MFA has wanted to embrace the world. Long-
serving trustee Martin Brimmer noted that while great collections of art
"were formerly the private property of sovereigns . . . , the museums of today
open their doors to all of the world." In our generation, we understand and
accept that to be comprehensive is to be always a work in progress; comprehensiveness must be connected to the possibilities of new knowledge. Think
of our older ideas of the encyclopedia, a set of books on a shelf updated
once in a generation. Today, online encyclopedias are evolving constantly
and quickly, often with content generated by the audiences and users themselves. For all of the dangers of crowd-sourced knowledge, it would be hard
to argue the results are not in some manner authoritative or comprehensive.
We have to believe in the self-aware, self-editing process to achieve rigor-
ous standards, and in doing so, we will accept that the information shared
becomes the baseline of a new "encyclopedia."

Encyclopedic collections present challenges and opportunities. First and
foremost, they possess an ability to foster cross-cultural conversation, to
show that cultures exist in relation to one another, and to trace the movement of ideas and populations. Collections in encyclopedic museums offer
the possibility to engage with communities of origin, whether in ancestral
homelands or in the diasporas, and to say something clearly and in celebration: we can have many homes, and the objects that remind us of where

Left

Dish, Vietnamese
(Le-Trinh period), 1740–67

Right

Possible Bags, Native American
(Lakota [Sioux]), about 1890

we have been also assert the wonder of where we are. Objects can trace patterns of migration and bridge geographies.

And so the purpose of the collection in historic institutions such as the Museum of Fine Arts, Boston, changes somewhat over time, from seeing cultures "over there" to acclaiming their relevance "here." Collections can lead to self-awareness and empowerment in diasporic communities as we join in reflecting on history, legacy, and the role of founding values in communities. A museum need not replace its history but build upon it. It is perhaps a simple truth to note that collections grow in specificity to their communities and to the understanding of history in a given moment. It's true that each moment is reborn, but all moments are a continuum with what came before.

Many have joined together to contribute to the building of a collection for Boston and the world. Individual works have been donated, funds for iconic purchases contributed, whole collections from many corners of the world given. In all cases, acquisitions came to support an idea, to assert a different way of looking, or to embrace new traditions or art forms.

Over 150 years, supporters of the collections at the MFA have done so out of an admirable spirit of generosity and belief in the power of the Museum to engage deeply with its communities, here and elsewhere. Acquisitions have been made to encourage us to reach further. As we respond to the ideas of our time and challenge ourselves to think about how collections represent communities as much as they belong to them, we pause to acknowledge the generosity of collectors who share their works of art with us. They do so with a trust in our commitment to building audience and engagement through the presentation of the collections in our care. This volume is dedicated to all of them.

The William I. Koch Gallery

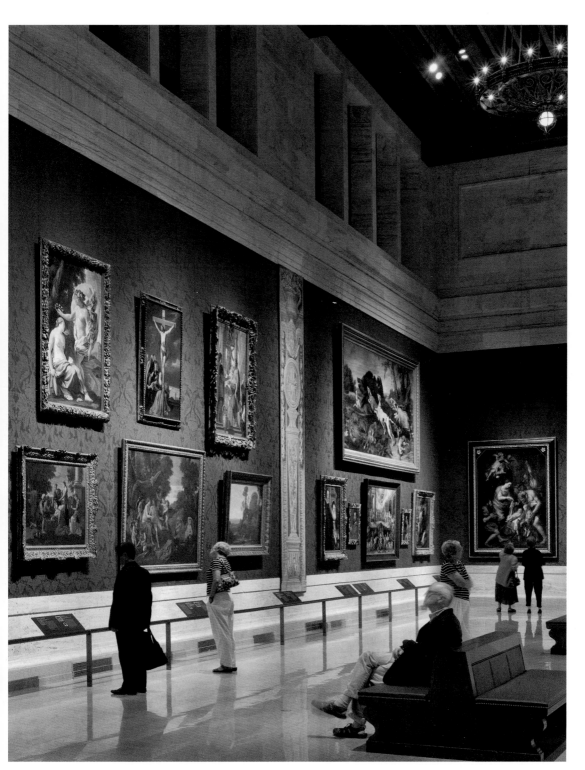

A Brief History of the MFA

Maureen Melton, *Susan Morse Hilles Director of Libraries and Archives and Museum Historian*

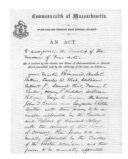

The Act of Incorporation for the Museum

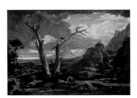

Washington Allston, *Elijah in the Desert*, 1818, Gift of Mrs. Samuel and Miss Alice Hooper, 70.1

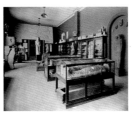

Egyptian gallery

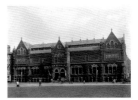

The MFA in Copley Square

February 4, 1870

The Commonwealth of Massachusetts approves the Act of Incorporation, which creates the founding Board of Trustees for the Museum of Fine Arts, Boston. Elected trustees include twelve leaders from Boston's educational, cultural, and business communities. Fourteen appointed and ex officio trustees also are welcomed from local institutions, including the Boston Athenaeum, Harvard College, and the Massachusetts Institute of Technology.

November 1870

The first work of art acquired by the Museum is *Elijah in the Desert* by Washington Allston, one of Boston's most admired local artists. The painting is donated by Mrs. Samuel Hooper and her daughter Alice. In a letter to the MFA trustees, Alice writes, "We thought we couldn't better testify our interest in this new art movement at home than by adding a really fine Allston to our public collection."

1872

Although construction had not yet begun on the planned building, the MFA gratefully receives donor C. Granville Way's gift of nearly 4,800 Egyptian antiquities collected in the 1820s and '30s by Robert Hay, a Scottish nobleman. Mainly objects of daily life and funerary items, the collection includes several mummies in their painted coffins that prove so popular with the public that trustees are encouraged to continue making acquisitions of Egyptian art.

July 4, 1876

The first home for the MFA opens to the public on the United States' centennial. Located in Copley Square, the red brick building with terra-cotta ornamentation offers two floors of exhibition galleries. Designed by local architects John Sturgis and Charles Brigham in the Gothic Revival style, this is the initial section of a more extensive plan for the building, which will expand in phases as additional gallery space is needed.

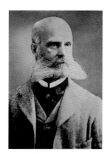

Dr. William Sturgis Bigelow

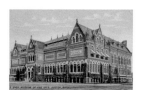

Postcard view of the Museum facade

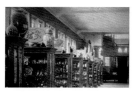

Japanese ceramics gallery

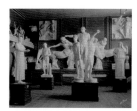

Cast gallery

1882

Inspired by intrepid Bostonians traveling to Japan in the late 1870s, Dr. William Sturgis Bigelow embarks on what his family believed would be an extended vacation there. However, Bigelow becomes so enthralled with the country that he remains for more than seven years. The wealthy physician travels broadly and collects art with exuberance. Bigelow eventually gives most of his collection to the Museum, becoming its most prolific patron by donating more than 50,000 works of art.

1890

Through the generosity of many donors, the MFA's art collection continues to expand rapidly throughout its first two decades of operation. In order to provide exhibition space for the flourishing collection, two major building expansions are required. In 1879, a new wing opens along the east side of the property. Just eleven years later, an even larger expansion is opened, offering many additional galleries for the Japanese collections, which had grown exponentially through loans and acquisitions.

1892

The Morse Collection of more than 5,000 Japanese ceramics is acquired by the MFA. Edward Sylvester Morse first travels to Japan in 1877 to teach zoology at Tokyo Imperial University while studying Japanese culture and collecting art. In addition to his work as a popular lecturer, Morse serves for more than thirty years as both the Keeper of Japanese Pottery at the MFA and as Director of the Peabody Academy of Science (later Peabody Museum) in Salem, Massachusetts.

1896

When the Museum first opened its doors in 1876, the collection included just over 5,000 works of art. Twenty years later, the collection has grown to more than 100,000 objects. With the classes and studios of the School of the Museum of Fine Arts located in the building's basement and attic, every work of art owned by or on loan to the MFA is on view. Thus, exhibition galleries once believed to be spacious have become alarmingly overcrowded.

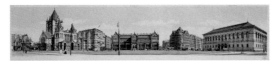

Panorama of Copley Square depicting Trinity Church (left), the MFA (center), and the Boston Public Library (right)

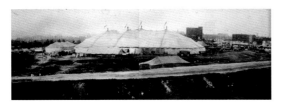

Circus tent at the proposed Huntington Avenue site, about 1895

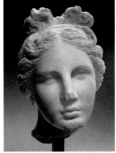

Aphrodite, Greek, about 330–300 B.C., Francis Bartlett Donation of 1900, 03.743

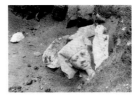

Unearthing a sculpture of King Menkaura (Mycerinus) at Giza, Egypt, 1910

1898

Although the MFA was one of the first buildings constructed in Copley Square, the neighborhood subsequently became home to many other important institutions, including Trinity Church and the Boston Public Library. By 1898, when the continuing growth of the art collection makes another expansion necessary, there is no land adjacent to the Museum available. The trustees realize with reluctance that the MFA will have to move to a new neighborhood.

1899

In searching for a new location, the Museum's trustees face a number of challenges. They want a site large enough for present and future building needs, but find no land in downtown Boston or the Back Bay that meets their requirements. As a result, they look west—just over a mile from Copley Square. There they purchase twelve acres in the Fenway, on a site frequently used for circus and rodeo shows.

1900

Boston attorney Francis Bartlett donates $100,000 for the purchase of Greek and Roman antiquities, many of which remain highlights of the Museum's collection today. Just twelve years later, Bartlett's generosity once again astonishes the trustees when he gifts an entire six-story commercial building in downtown Chicago to the Museum. The building is valued at $1.35 million, equivalent to more than $35 million today, making Bartlett the Museum's single most generous financial contributor by 1912.

1905

Dr. George Reisner organizes and directs the joint Harvard University–Boston Museum of Fine Arts Expedition at the Giza pyramids and twenty-two other sites in Egypt and Sudan until his death in 1942. Through this work, which continues until 1947, the MFA acquires more than 50,000 antiquities. As a result, the MFA is home to the finest collection of Old Kingdom art outside Cairo, a number of masterpieces from the Middle and New Kingdoms, and the most important collection of Nubian art outside Khartoum.

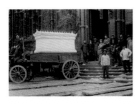

The move from Copley Square
to Huntington Avenue

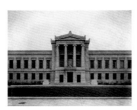

Museum facade on Huntington
Avenue, 1909

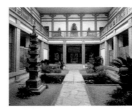

The Japanese garden courtyard

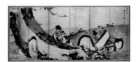

Soga Shōhaku, *The Four Sages
of Mount Shang*, around 1768,
Fenollosa-Weld Collection,
11.4514

1909

The MFA staff packs up
and moves, by horse and
cart, more than 110,000
rare and valuable works
of art from the Museum's
original building in Copley
Square to its new home
in the Fenway. In spite of
the challenge of transport-
ing fragile works of art
more than a mile down
an uneven road using two
very basic wooden carts,
the crew accomplishes the
feat without breaking or
damaging a single object.

November 1909

Designed by architect Guy
Lowell in the Classical
Revival style, the first
section of the new MFA
opens in the Fenway. At
more than 240,000 square
feet, it is nearly four times
larger than the original
building. Lowell's design
offers many double-height
galleries on the main
floor for the display of the
finest of each curatorial
department's holdings.
Stairways in each area
lead downstairs to the
more expansive study
collections held on the
ground floor.

1910

For many, a highlight of
the new building is the
enchanting two-level Jap-
anese garden courtyard.
Home to sculpture, stone
lanterns, and greenery, the
courtyard also includes
lotus pools stocked with
carp. The court is a serene
space for visitors to rest
and relax. However, as
the Asian art collection
continues to grow over the
decades, the need for more
exhibition space leads to
the replacement of the
garden with new galleries
that open in 1981.

1911

More than 1,000 works of
art acquired in Japan by
MFA curator Ernest Fenol-
losa are purchased by his
friend Dr. Charles God-
dard Weld and bequeathed
to the Museum in both
their names. The collection
is world renowned for ink
paintings dating to the
fifteenth century by artists
associated with Zen mon-
asteries; comprehensive
holdings of Kano-school
and *ukiyo-e* painting;
narrative handscrolls; and
folding screens, including
*The Four Sages of Mount
Shang*.

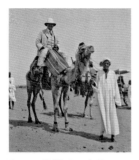
Denman Waldo Ross in Egypt

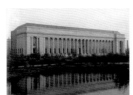
Evans Wing facade from the Fenway, about 1915

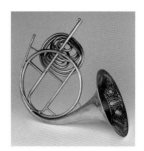
Charles-Joseph Sax, Omnitonic Horn, Leslie Lindsey Mason Collection, 17.2004

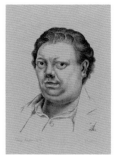
Diego Rivera, *Self-Portrait*, 1930, Gift of W. G. Russell Allen, 49.202

1913

Denman Waldo Ross, shown here in Egypt in 1913, is one of the most important donors in MFA history. An incurable traveler and passionate collector, Ross makes his first donation in 1878. Continuing his global explorations and art acquisitions until his death in 1935, Ross explains that he sought objects that are "an expression of life." He gives more than 11,000 objects, which enhance each of the MFA's curatorial departments, particularly the European, Chinese, Japanese, Islamic, and textile collections.

February 1915

The second section of architect Guy Lowell's master plan for the MFA opens along the Fenway. The Robert Dawson Evans Memorial Wing increases the size of the building by more than 40 percent, its galleries offering grand new exhibition spaces for paintings. Mrs. Evans funds the entire $1 million cost of the project— equivalent to more than $25 million today. Following her death in 1917, the Museum also receives her splendid art collection and a large financial endowment.

1915

Leslie Lindsey Mason is a Boston socialite who has the misfortune of booking her honeymoon aboard RMS *Lusitania* on its ill-fated final voyage. When a German U-boat torpedoes the ship, both Mason and her husband perish. In memory of their daughter, Mason's parents donate 560 musical instruments they have purchased from English collector Francis W. Galpin. The collection forms the core of the MFA's Musical Instruments Department, which now numbers more than 1,200 objects.

1923

MFA trustee W. G. Russell Allen makes the first of what would total more than 5,000 gifts of prints, drawings, and works on paper to the MFA. Encouraged by his parents to admire and acquire original works of art, Allen makes it his life's work. He is described as one of the most well-informed and passionate collectors of his time. Allen is a generous donor to many other museums, and a founder of the Boston Museum of Modern Art (later the Institute of Contemporary Art).

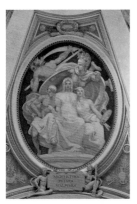

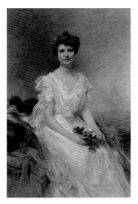

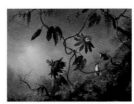

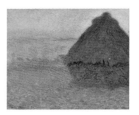

John Singer Sargent, *Architecture, Painting and Sculpture Protected by Athena from the Ravages of Time*, Francis Bartlett Donation of 1912 and Picture Fund, 21.10513

Théobald Chartran, *Harriet White Bradbury*, Bequest of George Robert White, 30.496

Martin Johnson Heade, *Passion Flowers and Hummingbirds*, about 1870–83, Gift of Maxim Karolik for the M. and M. Karolik Collection of American Paintings, 1815–1865, 47.1138

Claude Monet, *Grainstack (Sunset)*, 1891, Juliana Cheney Edwards Collection, 25.112

1925

In 1921, celebrated artist John Singer Sargent created an ambitious mural, sculpture, and ornamentation program for the MFA's rotunda. He then begins a similar project for the adjoining colonnade. In April 1925, after sending the last shipment of his work to Boston, Sargent dies unexpectedly in London. The colonnade installation, completed later that year, is unveiled in November 1925 along with a memorial exhibition to the artist.

1932

In the depths of the Great Depression, the Museum receives the heartening news of a remarkable gift from Mrs. Harriet White Bradbury. Through her family's success in pharmaceuticals and Boston real estate, Mrs. Bradbury has impressive financial resources and is a longtime donor to the Museum. Her magnanimous bequest of more than $4.4 million remains the largest financial gift in MFA history, equivalent to more than $80 million today.

1938

Maxim and Martha Codman Karolik donate the first of three major art collections: more than 350 fine examples of eighteenth-century American decorative arts and paintings. In 1947, they give their collection of 233 mid-nineteenth-century American paintings. After his wife's death in 1948, Mr. Karolik continues collecting and later donates more than 3,000 American watercolors and drawings in his wife's memory. Along with other generous gifts, especially American folk art, the couple's donations total more than 4,000 objects.

1939

Over the course of several years, the Museum receives a stellar collection of more than one hundred European and American paintings and choice decorative arts from the family of Jacob and Juliana Cheney Edwards. The collection features works by prominent Impressionist and Post-Impressionist painters, including Degas, Pissarro, Corot, Cézanne, and Sisley. Their gift includes six paintings by Renoir and ten by Monet, the largest donation of Monet's work to enter the MFA's collection.

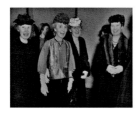

Elizabeth Day McCormick (center foreground)

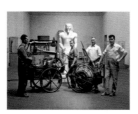

Wartime preparations

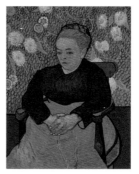

Vincent van Gogh, *Lullaby: Madame Augustine Roulin Rocking a Cradle (La Berceuse)*, 1889, Bequest of John T. Spaulding, 48.548

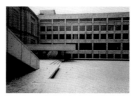

George Robert White Wing

1943

The very fashionable Elizabeth Day McCormick of Chicago (center) donates the first of more than 6,000 gifts of art. Her collection of European needlework, costumes, and accessories dating from the sixteenth to the nineteenth centuries is a great prize for the MFA's Textile and Fashion Arts Department. Museum director George Edgell enthuses about the "extraordinary" gift as he describes the "wealth and variety of the material, the richness and beauty of its individual pieces."

1944

During World War II, MFA trustees and staff are deeply concerned about the care and protection of the Museum's collection. Blackout shades are installed in all windows to mask light in case of a nighttime air raid, and many of the Museum's most valuable and fragile objects are moved to fortified storage areas for safekeeping. This rare photograph documents a training exercise in one of the Museum's Egyptian galleries, focusing on evacuation procedures and emergency response.

1948

In 1921, Boston collector John Spaulding, along with his brother William, donated an exquisite collection of more than 6,000 Japanese prints to the MFA. Spaulding then turned his eye toward acquiring American and European paintings and works on paper. Following his death in 1948, the Museum receives Spaulding's second collection, which features work by Homer, Hopper, Chardin, Gauguin, Renoir, Sisley, Degas, and van Gogh, including the vibrant portrait of Madame Augustine Roulin.

June 1970

As part of the 100th anniversary celebration, the George Robert White Wing opens on the west side of the MFA. The first wing of the Museum designed in the Modernist architectural style, the 45,000-square-foot expansion provides increased space for staff functions such as the research library and conservation laboratories. It also provides more exhibition spaces, improved educational venues, and additional visitor amenities, including a new restaurant and gift shop.

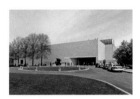

The West Wing

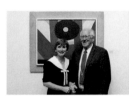

William H. and Saundra Lane

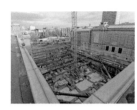

Building the New MFA

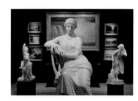

The Art of the Americas wing

1981

Designed by renowned architect I. M. Pei, the West Wing opens in July. The 80,000-square-foot wing offers new education and meeting spaces and an expansive special exhibitions gallery. The major architectural feature is the dramatic 200-foot-long skylight stretching above the second floor of the wing. Other popular amenities include modernized dining facilities, a large retail venue, and a spacious auditorium.

1990

The MFA acquires the Lane Collection of ninety highly prized American paintings and works on paper, donated by Massachusetts industrialist William H. Lane and his wife, Saundra. The gift features work by many leading mid-twentieth-century artists, including Georgia O'Keeffe, Stuart Davis, Arthur Dove, Marsden Hartley, and Charles Sheeler. The Lane Collection transforms the MFA's paintings department into one of the nation's most important centers for the study of American Modernism.

November 2005

After the most successful fundraising effort to date by any New England arts institution and several years of extensive master planning and design, work begins on the New MFA construction project. The focus of the comprehensive expansion and renovation—designed by Foster + Partners (London)—is to create new and improved spaces for the Museum's encyclopedic collections, especially the Art of the Americas, as well as new facilities for special exhibitions, educational programs, and visitor amenities.

November 2010

The New MFA project enriches ways that visitors encounter the Museum and increases space for its encyclopedic collections, special exhibitions, and educational programs. Highlights include the Shapiro Family Courtyard, a light-filled, grand public space offering art, dining, and special event facilities, and the Art of the Americas Wing, which dramatically enhances the ability to exhibit and interpret the collection of art from North, Central, and South America in fifty-three new galleries.

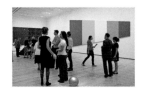

The Linde Family Wing for
Contemporary Art

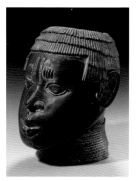

Commemorative head of a
defeated neighboring leader,
Benin Kingdom, Nigeria, late
fifteenth–early sixteenth
century, Robert Owen Lehman
Collection, 2012.250

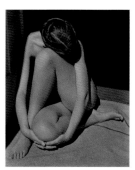

Edward Weston, *Nude*, 1936, The
Lane Collection, 2017.2286

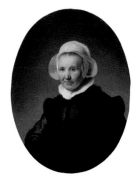

Rembrandt Harmensz. van Rijn,
Portrait of Aeltje Uylenburgh,
1632, Rose-Marie and Eijk van
Otterloo Collection

September 2011

The Linde Family Wing for
Contemporary Art opens
with seven new galleries
dedicated to contempo-
rary art exhibitions. The
wing offers innovative
opportunities for interac-
tion between the MFA's
encyclopedic collection
and its contemporary
holdings. It is also a lively
community and social
space, presenting contem-
porary culture in all its
forms through art, music,
performances, readings,
lectures, courses, and artist demonstrations.

2012

The Museum receives
the promised gift of the
Robert Owen Lehman
Collection. These thirty-
four rare West African
works of art compose the
single greatest private
holding of objects from
the Benin kingdom, dating
from the late fifteenth
century to the nineteenth
century. The gift, which
includes twenty-eight
bronzes and six ivories,
transforms the MFA's
collection and advances
scholarship about one
of the richest periods of
African art.

2017

Saundra B. Lane begins
donating a second major
collection to the MFA
that includes more than
6,000 photographs, 100
works on paper, and 26
paintings. One of the
finest private holdings
of twentieth-century
American art in the world,
it offers an unparalleled
collection of photography,
including Charles Sheel-
er's entire photographic
estate of nearly 2,500
works, an equal number of
images by Edward Weston,
and 500 photographs
by Ansel Adams. The
collection also features
paintings and works on
paper by major American
Modernists.

2017

The MFA announces that
Rose-Marie and Eijk van
Otterloo and Susan and
Matthew Weatherbie have
made a commitment to
donate their exceptional
collections of seventeenth-
century Dutch and Flemish
art. Including 113 works
by 76 artists, it will be the
largest gift of European
paintings in Museum
history. The gift also will
include a major research
library and funding to
establish a Center for
Netherlandish Art at the
MFA, the first of its kind
in the United States.

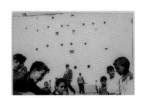
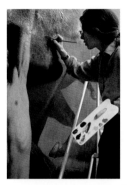
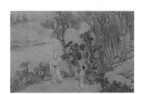
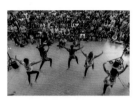

Henri Cartier-Bresson, *Madrid, Spain*, 1933, The Howard Greenberg Collection-Museum purchase with funds donated by the Phillip Leonian and Elizabeth Rosenbaum Leonian Charitable Trust, 2018.3229

Conservation of Henri Regnault, *Automedon with the Horses of Achilles*, 1868, Museum purchase with funds donated by contribution, 90.152

Wang Hui and Jiao Bingzhen, *Portrait of An Qi in His Garden* (detail), 1698. Gift of the Wan-go H. C. Weng Collection and family in memory of Weng Tonghe

Part of the MFA's annual Juneteenth celebrations

September 2018

The acquisition of the Howard Greenberg Collection of Photographs is announced. The collection includes 446 photographs by nearly 200 artists, including rare prints of modernist masterpieces and mid-20th-century classics. It traces the evolution of photography as an art form and explores social history and the human experience. Work by more than 80 notable photographers not previously represented will substantially enrich the MFA's photographic holdings.

2018

Work begins on a new state-of-the-art Conservation Center to open for the MFA's 150th anniversary in 2020. With 22,000 square feet of space and six laboratories, the Center will feature advanced technology and enhanced opportunities for interdisciplinary collaboration and training. The Center also will have a learning space for dynamic public programs and educational initiatives through which visitors of all ages will be welcomed to engage with art, science, world cultures, and history in new ways.

December 2018

The MFA receives the largest and most significant gift of Chinese paintings and calligraphy in its history, the 183 objects of the Wan-go H. C. Weng Collection. Particularly rich in works from the Ming and Qing eras, the collection has long been considered one of the finest private holdings of Chinese art in the United States and was passed down through six generations of Weng's family before being donated to the Museum.

February 4, 2020

The celebration of the MFA's 150th anniversary begins. In its strategic plan shared in 2017, the Museum outlined five pillars guiding its commitment to responding to new ideas, linking cultures, and cultivating a range of voices: Collaborate Generously, Invite Boldly, Welcome Warmly, Engage Deeply, and Collect Purposefully. By expanding partnerships and becoming a center for convening, the MFA has charted its path as an institution that is of the moment and of the community.

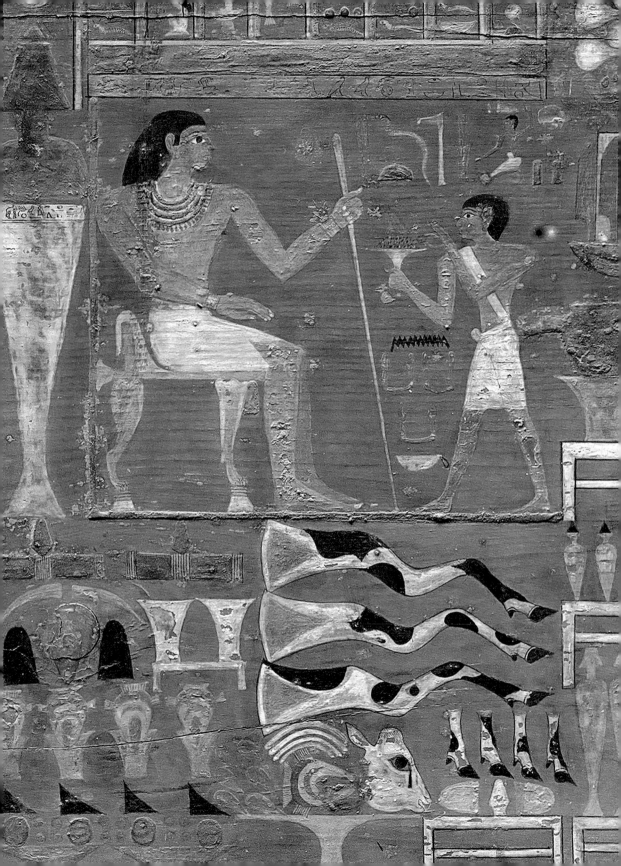

King Menkaura (Mycerinus) and queen

Egypt (Giza, Valley Temple of Menkaura)
Old Kingdom, Dynasty 4, reign of Menkaura,
2490–2472 B.C.

The Valley Temple at Giza, just outside Cairo, was
part of the pyramid complex of King Menkaura
(Mycerinus), which also included one of the three
great pyramids. It was excavated by George Andrew
Reisner and the Harvard University–Boston Museum
of Fine Arts Expedition between 1908 and 1910, and
as Reisner noted in his journal, it was here that the
extraordinary statue of Menkaura and his queen was
unearthed on January 18, 1910: "In the evening, just
before work stopped, a small boy . . . appeared suddenly at my side and said 'come.' . . . the female head
of a statue (¾ life size) of bluish slate had just come
into view in the sand . . . immediately afterward a
block of dirt fell away and showed a male head on the
right—a pair statue of a king and queen. A photograph was taken in failing light and an armed guard
of 20 men put on for the night."

This serene and idealized royal image is one of the
finest pieces of Egyptian sculpture known. Made of
stone, its surface is subtly modeled and gives a very
real sense of bodily forms and structure. Menkaura
assumes the classic pose for men in Egyptian art,
striding forward, his left leg advanced, arms rigid by
his sides. He wears the royal headcloth (*nemes*), kilt,
and false beard. The queen also steps forward, clasp-
ing Menkaura in a traditional gesture of intimacy
and respect.

Working with ancient texts and archaeological
evidence, scholars have constructed a chronology
from about 3100 B.C. to the country's conquest by
Alexander the Great in 332 B.C. Egyptian history is
subdivided into Kingdoms (times of strong central
government and political stability) and Intermediate Periods (times when central authority collapsed).
These divisions are further broken down into thirty
dynasties, each comprising a series of reigning pharaohs. Menkaura reigned between 2490 and 2472 B.C.,
in Dynasty 4 of the Old Kingdom.

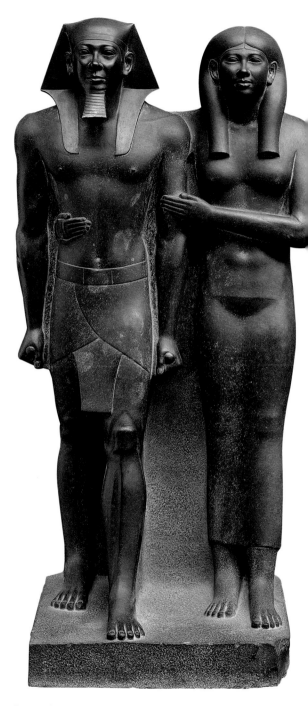

Greywacke
H. 56 in. (142.2 cm)
Harvard University–Boston Museum of Fine Arts Expedition
11.1738

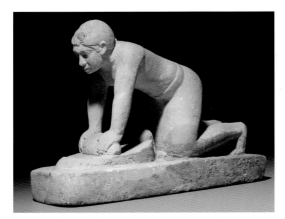

Woman grinding grain
Egypt (Giza, tomb G 2185)
Old Kingdom, Dynasty 5, 2500–2350 B.C.

Statuettes of people engaged in such domestic tasks as baking, weaving, and brewing were occasionally placed in tombs in the belief that they would magically become real to provide for the *ka* (that part of the human spirit that needed to be fed and sheltered) and to ensure the well-being of the deceased in the afterlife. This kneeling woman grinding grain for bread wears a kilt tied up at the side and a cloth to cover her hair. Flour spills over the front of the grindstone, while behind the stone is a part-empty sack of grain. Carved from limestone, this figure would originally have been covered with a fine layer of plaster and then painted.

Limestone
L. 12¼ in. (30.9 cm)
Harvard University–Boston Museum of Fine Arts Expedition
12.1486

Ptahkhenuwy and his wife
Egypt (Giza, tomb G 2004)
Old Kingdom, Dynasty 5, 2465–2323 B.C.

Although most Egyptian sculptures were originally painted, the color rarely survives. However, this statue is exceptionally well preserved. Ptahkhenuwy and his wife, wearing wigs and beaded collars, are painted in colors standard in Egyptian art: red for the skin of men and yellow for that of women. They stand in a pose very similar to that of King Menkaura (Mycerinus) and his queen, but they are not royal: the inscription on the statue's base identifies Ptahkhenuwy as "supervisor of palace retainers"; his spouse (whose name is indecipherable) is termed "his beloved wife." This statue was found in a *serdab*, a hidden chamber within the tomb that had a window through which the figures could "see" into the adjacent chapel, where gifts of food and drink were left for them.

Painted limestone
H. 27⅝ in. (70.1 cm)
Harvard University–
Boston Museum
of Fine Arts
Expedition
06.1876

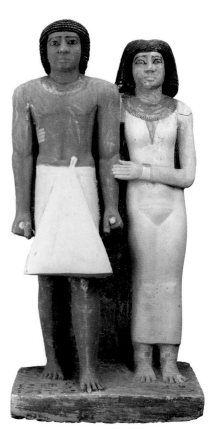

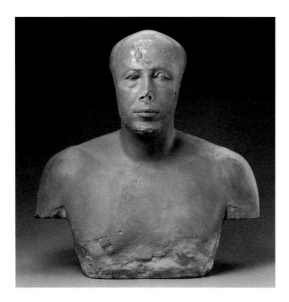

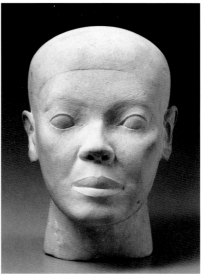

Bust of Prince Ankhhaf
Egypt (Giza, tomb G 7510)
Old Kingdom, Dynasty 4, reign of Khafra (Chephren),
2520–2494 B.C.

This portrait bust is one of the most remarkable creations in all Egyptian art. It is a true likeness, more naturalistic than the simplified and summarizing "reserve heads." Here the sculptor has captured the irregularities of Ankhhaf's skull, the lines beside his nose, the soft bags under his eyes, creating an indelible and very specific impression of maturity and intelligence. These telling details are modeled in a coat of plaster that covers the limestone core.

Ankhhaf was among the most important men of his time, serving as vizier, or senior administrative official, under King Khafra. The bust was found in Ankhhaf's tomb chapel, but its function is unknown. Although it was never part of a larger statue, it may have stood on a separately carved base that included arms stretched forward to receive offerings.

Limestone and plaster
H. 19⅞ in. (50.6 cm)
Harvard University–Boston Museum of Fine Arts Expedition
27.442

"Reserve head"
Egypt (Giza, tomb G 4440)
Old Kingdom, early Dynasty 4, 2551–2494 B.C.

The purpose of the "reserve heads" that were placed in Egyptian tombs remains a mystery, although many scholars believe they were regarded as potential substitutes for the mummy. If the mummy or its head (essential for continued existence in the afterlife) was damaged, the spirit of the deceased could inhabit the "reserve head" and live on. Most of the thirty surviving "reserve heads" were discovered at Giza in the vast cemetery used for courtiers and high officials of the Fourth Dynasty. Six of these sculptures are in the Museum, and no two are alike. They are modeled in broad, simplified forms, but in each case the sculptor has captured the individual's essential, identifying features. Such naturalism is rare in Egyptian art, where figures tend to be generalized and the subjects identified by inscriptions.

Limestone
H. 11¾ in. (30 cm)
Harvard University–Boston Museum of Fine Arts Expedition
14.719

Triad of King Menkaura (Mycerinus) with the goddess Hathor and the deified Hare nome

Egypt (Giza, Valley Temple of Menkaura)
Old Kingdom, Dynasty 4, reign of Menkaura, 2490–2472 B.C.

Found in one of the temples dedicated to the cult of Menkaura (Mycerinus), this magnificent sculpture of gray stone demonstrates the close relationship that the Egyptians perceived between their gods and their kings, whom they also believed to be divine. The central figure is the cow goddess Hathor, identified by the horns surrounding a sun disk on her head. Expressing her devotion to the pharaoh (on her left, wearing the crown of Upper Egypt), Hathor circles his waist with one hand and lightly touches his arm with the other. The third figure personifies a nome, or province, and her symbol, the hare, rises above her head. In her left hand she carries the *ankh*, symbol of life, as a gift to the king. On the base of the sculpture, an inscription reads: "The Horus (Ka-khet) King of Upper and Lower Egypt, Menkaura, beloved of Hathor, Mistress of the Sycamore. Recitation: I have given you all good things, all offerings, and all provisions in Upper Egypt, forever."

Greywacke
H. 33¼ in. (84.5 cm)
Harvard University–Boston Museum of Fine Arts Expedition   09.200

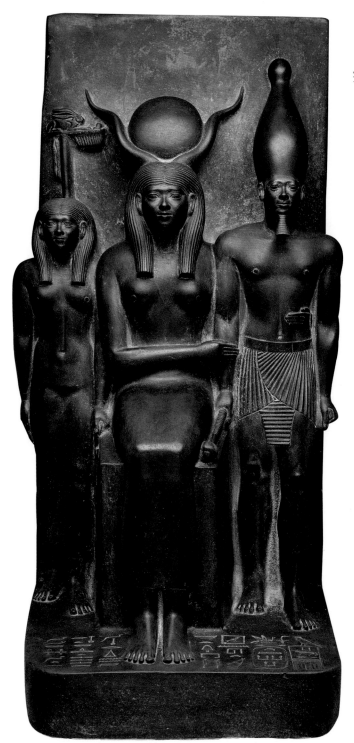

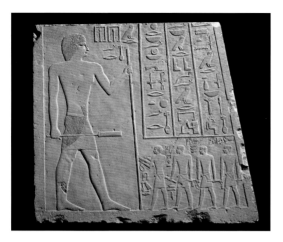

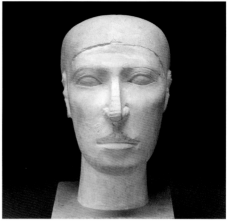

Relief of Nofer
Egypt (Giza, tomb G 2110)
Old Kingdom, early Dynasty 4, 2551–2494 B.C.

The stone walls of Egyptian tombs were often decorated with carvings that provide much fascinating
information about the life of the deceased and about
Egyptian society in general. This relief was placed just
inside the entrance to the tomb chapel of Nofer, a government official who was buried near the great royal
pyramids at Giza. Nofer is depicted on a scale befitting his importance; his distinctive aquiline nose and
firmly set lips are also evident in the "reserve head"
that was found in his tomb. To the right of Nofer, three
columns of hieroglyphs list his administrative duties
and titles, which included overseer of the treasury.
Below the hieroglyphic inscription is a procession of
four scribes, the first one taking dictation. Civil ser-
vants, like Nofer, and scribes, who recorded the details
of governmental affairs, were crucial to the complex,
centralized administration of the Egyptian state.

Limestone
37⅜ x 43⅛ in. (95 x 109.5 cm)
Harvard University–Boston Museum of Fine Arts Expedition
07.1002

"Reserve head" of Nofer
Egypt (Giza, tomb G 2110)
Old Kingdom, early Dynasty 4,
2551–2494 B.C.

Limestone
H. 10⅝ in. (27.1 cm)
Harvard University–Boston Museum of Fine
Arts Expedition   06.1886

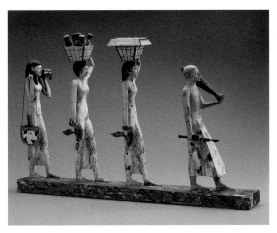

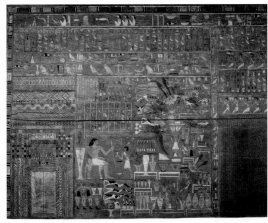

Procession of offering bearers
Egypt (Deir el-Bersha, tomb of
Djehutynakht)
Middle Kingdom, late Dynasty 11 or early Dynasty 12,
2010–1961 B.C.

In antiquity, Djehutynakht's tomb was plundered by
thieves searching for jewelry and precious materials.
When Museum archaeologists opened the tomb in
1915, they found complete chaos—the coffins disas-
sembled, the mummies torn apart, and more than one
hundred wooden models violently thrown aside and
shattered. These models, like the coffin paintings and
texts, were meant to ensure that the deceased would
enjoy for eternity the comforts of his earthly life. Most
such models are crudely made, but this is one of the
finest wood carvings from any period of Egyptian
history. It represents a procession, led by a priest carrying an incense burner and a ritual vase. Behind him,
two women bring ducks and baskets of provisions,
and a third carries a small chest and a mirror in a
patterned case. In this small sculpture, ancient Egypt
comes vividly to life.

Painted wood
L. 26⅛ in. (66.4 cm)
Harvard University–Boston Museum of Fine Arts Expedition
21.326

**Interior face of the outer coffin of Djehutynakht
(detail)**
Egypt (Deir el-Bersha, tomb of Djehutynakht)
Middle Kingdom, late Dynasty 11 or early Dynasty 12,
2010–1961 B.C.

Four thousand years ago, a provincial ruler named
Djehutynakht was buried in a tomb cut into dry limestone cliffs on the east bank of the Nile. His mummified body was placed within two nested coffins made
of thick, cedar boards covered on both sides with
paintings and inscriptions that would through magic
provide for his needs and protection in the afterlife.
Exquisitely adorned with vibrant color and a wealth
of detail, the interior of the outer coffin is perhaps the
finest surviving example of Middle Kingdom painting.
It depicts Djehutynakht seated before an attendant
who brings a dish of incense. Neat rows of offerings,
including the legs of spotted cows, are arranged below.
Behind Djehutynakht is a representation of the "false
door" through which his spirit could leave the coffin
and come into the tomb chapel to receive the food and
drink left there for him. The eyes on the door were
painted so that the mummy, laid on its side to face
them, could look out of the coffin.

Painted cedar
45¼ x 103½ in. (115 x 263 cm)
Harvard University–Boston Museum of Fine Arts Expedition
20.1822

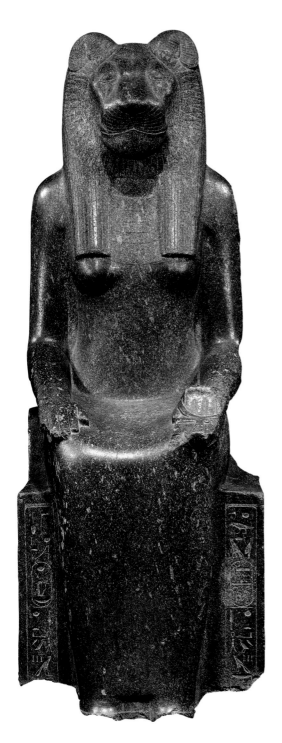

Seated Sekhmet
Egypt (Thebes, Karnak, temple of Mut)
New Kingdom, Dynasty 18, reign of Amenhotep III,
1390–1352 B.C.

Ancient Egyptians identified the lion-headed goddess
Sekhmet (her name means "The Powerful One") with
tempestuous weather, scorching heat, pestilence, and
war. Priests constantly strove to calm her destructive
and unpredictable nature with ceremonies and offerings. Sekhmet was believed to be especially threatening at the time of New Year (mid-July), because if she
was not pacified, the Nile might not rise, the new year
could not begin, and the cycle of life would cease. This
image of the goddess, brought to Boston from Egypt
in 1835, is probably one of 730 erected by King Amenhotep III in his temple at Thebes.

Granodiorite
H. 49¾ in. (126.6 cm)
Gift of John A. Lowell and Miss Lowell   75.7

Statue of Lady Sennuwy
Made in Egypt, found in Sudan
(Kerma, royal tumulus K III)
Middle Kingdom, Dynasty 12,
reign of Senwosret I, 1971–1926 B.C.

This serene image of Sennuwy, the wife of a provincial governor, is a masterpiece of Egyptian sculpture.
Worked in hard, black granodiorite, the rounded forms
of Sennuwy's body are beautifully proportioned, and
the smooth planes of her face are strikingly framed by
the ribbed patterning of her heavy wig. Sennuwy and
her husband were buried at Asyut, in central Egypt, in
an elaborate tomb for which this funerary statue was
probably made. However, the statue was found far to
the south of Egypt, in the burial of a Nubian ruler of
Kerma. Apparently, the statue was removed from the
tomb in Egypt and taken to Nubia several hundred
years after Sennuwy's death.

Granodiorite
H. 67¾ in. (172 cm)
Harvard University–Boston Museum of Fine Arts Expedition
14.720

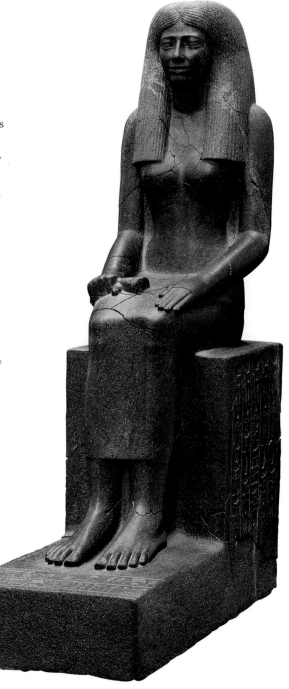

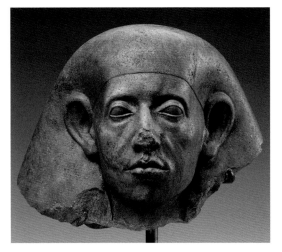

and Horace L. Mayer Funds, Norma Jean and Stanford Calderwood Discretionary Fund, Norma Jean Calderwood Acquisition Fund, Marilyn M. Simpson Fund, Otis Norcross Fund, Helen and Alice Colburn Fund, William E. Nickerson Fund, Egyptian Curator's Fund, Frederick Brown Fund, Elizabeth Marie Paramino Fund in memory of John F. Paramino, Boston Sculptor, Morris and Louise Rosenthal Fund, Arthur Tracy Cabot Fund, Walter and Celia Gilbert Acquisition Fund, Marshall H. Gould Fund, Arthur Mason Knapp Fund, John Wheelock Elliot and John Morse Elliot Fund, de Bragança Egyptian Purchase Fund, Brian J. Brille Acquisition Fund, Barbara W. and Joanne A. Herman Fund, MFA Senior Associates and MFA Associates Fund for Egyptian Acquisitions, and by exchange from an anonymous gift   2003.244

Head of a nobleman (The Josephson Head)
Egyptian
Middle Kingdom, late Dynasty 12, 1878–1841 B.C.

This head—once part of a complete body—is a supreme example of the animated, distinctively realistic images that appeared for a brief period in the Middle Kingdom and were never surpassed in Egyptian art. In striking contrast to the idealization and abstract generalization of most Egyptian images, this expressive, emotional face, beneath a smooth wig, is sensitively modeled and arrestingly individualized. The red stone—which echoes the color traditionally used for male skin in painted representations—is fine, polished quartzite, expensive and extremely difficult to work. Egyptians referred to quartzite as "a noble stone" associated with the sun. This portrait bears a strong resemblance to known images of Senwosret III. The extraordinary workmanship and the use of quartzite suggest that the head was made in a royal workshop by a master sculptor. The sitter was almost certainly a high official, perhaps a vizier, whose importance was surpassed only by that of the king.

Quartzite
7¼ x 9½ x 8¼ in. (18.5 x 24 x 21 cm)
Partial gift of Magda Saleh and Jack A. Josephson and Museum purchase with funds donated by the Florence E.

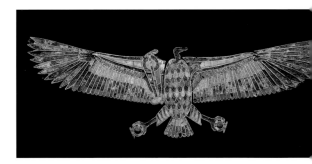

Pectoral
Egyptian
Second Intermediate Period, about 1783–1550 B.C.

Avid for the great wealth buried with the pharaohs, tomb robbers systematically and thoroughly plundered the royal tombs of Egypt—often, very soon after they were closed. Thus, few pieces of ancient jewelry have survived into modern times; this pectoral (chest ornament) is not only extremely rare but a splendid, skillfully crafted work of art. Composed of more than four hundred pieces of inlaid glass and carnelian (a reddish stone), the pectoral was probably made for a royal burial and attached to a gilded mummy case. It represents a vulture grasping two coils of rope, symbols of the universal power of the king. To the left of the bird's body is the stylized representation of a cobra, rearing up as if to strike.

Together, the vulture and the cobra signify the union of Upper and Lower Egypt and were standard symbolic attributes of the pharaoh.

Gold and silver with inlays of carnelian and glass
W. 14⅜ in. (36.5 cm)
Egyptian Special Purchase Fund, William Francis Warden Fund, Florence E. and Horace L. Mayer Fund   1981.159

Sarcophagus of Queen Hatshepsut, recut for her father, Thutmose I
Egypt (Thebes, Valley of the Kings, tomb 20)
New Kingdom, Dynasty 18, reign of Hatshepsut, 1473–1458 B.C.

The powerful Hatshepsut, who ruled for more than twenty years, was one of very few women in Egyptian history to become "king," and ultimately pharaoh. She even had herself represented in sculpture with a male torso. This sarcophagus, originally designed for Hatshepsut, was reinscribed for her father, Thutmose I, with the interior enlarged to hold his mummy and coffin. (Hatshepsut then ordered a matching sarcophagus, inscribed for herself as "king.") Made of a very hard stone, the sarcophagus is a fascinating historical document as well as an object of high artistic quality.

Painted quartzite
32¼ x 34¼ x 88⅝ in. (82 x 87 x 225 cm)
Gift of Theodore M. Davis   04.278.1–2

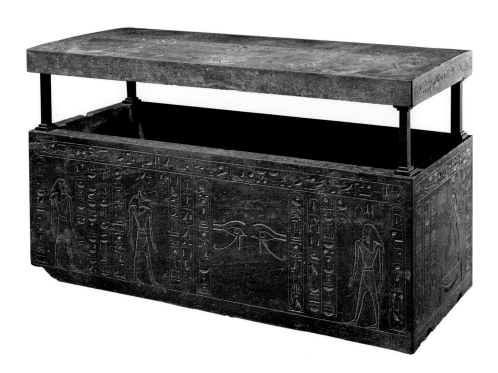

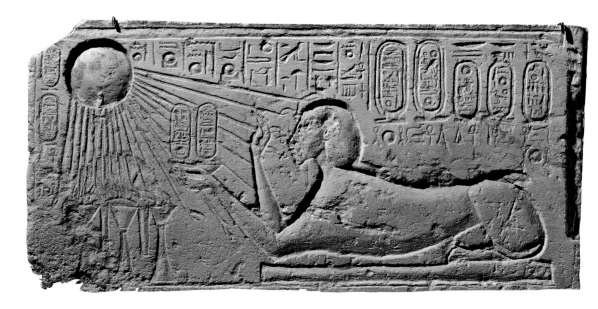

Relief of Akhenaten as a sphinx
Egyptian (probably from el-Amarna)
New Kingdom, Dynasty 18, reign of Akhenaten,
1349–1336 B.C.

A true individualist among the pharaohs, for seventeen years Akhenaten established his own, essentially
monotheistic religion, something previously unknown
in the ancient world. He rejected not only the supreme
state god, Amen, but the whole, age-old pantheon of
Egyptian gods—ordering their images to be smashed,
their temples closed, and even suppressing the plural
form of the word for god. Akhenaten's one god was a
manifestation of the sun called the Aten ("Disk"), and
in Middle Egypt, he built a new capital named Akhetaten, the "Horizon of the Aten" (modern el-Amarna).
This relief, probably from a palace wall at Akhetaten, depicts the king as a sphinx lying before a table
of offerings and presenting to the Aten oval tablets
inscribed with the god's names. Overhead, the disk
of the Aten sends down its life-giving rays. The Great
Hymn to the Aten, inscribed on the wall of a tomb at
Akhetaten, sings praises to the god-king:

Earth brightens when you dawn in lightland,
When you shine as Aten of daytime;
As you dispel the dark,
As you cast your rays,
The Two Lands are in festivity.
Awake they stand on their feet,
You have roused them;
Bodies cleansed, clothed,
Their arms adore your appearance.

After Akhenaten's death, one of his successors,
Tutankhamen, returned the royal residence to
Memphis and reinstated the old religion. The richly
decorated temples, palaces, public buildings, and
homes of Akhetaten were razed, and the city returned
to the desert.

Limestone
20⅛ x 41½ x 2 in. (51 x 105.5 x 5.2 cm)
Egyptian Curator's Fund   64.1944

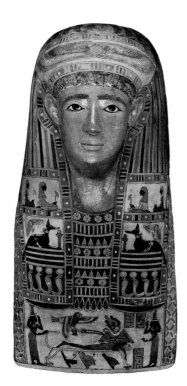

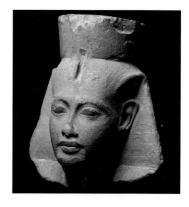

Mummy mask

Egyptian

Roman Imperial period, first half
of 1st century A.D.

To help preserve the features of the
mummified head and upper body
of the deceased, ancient Egyptians
often covered these parts with a
separate wooden mask. Long after
the Romans conquered Egypt in
the first century A.D., traditional
Egyptian religious beliefs and
funerary rituals persisted. This
mask, from the Roman period, is
constructed of cartonnage—a
material, similar to papier-mâché,
made of layers of linen coated with
plaster. Its rich gilding signifies
the status of its owner and also
evokes the golden flesh of the gods
with whom the deceased hoped
to be united. The mask is painted
with mourning and protective
figures. Across the bottom, the
god Osiris, reclining on a funerary
bier above the crowns of Egypt, is
shown being brought back to life
by the goddess Isis in the form of
a bird holding a feather and the
shen-ring of eternity.

Painted and gilded cartonnage,
inlaid glass
H. 22½ in. (57.2 cm)
Gift of Lucien Viola, Horace L. and
Florence E. Mayer Fund,
Helen and Alice Colburn Fund,
Marilyn M. Simpson Fund, William
Francis Warden Fund, and William
Stevenson Smith Fund   1993.555.1

King Tutankhamen

Egyptian

New Kingdom, Dynasty 18, reign of
Tutankhamen, 1336–1327 B.C.

Tutankhamen, possibly the son
of Akhenaten, reigned only from
his ninth to his nineteenth year,
but the discovery in 1922 of his
largely undisturbed tomb caused
a sensation throughout the world.
Although hastily assembled following the unexpected death of the
young king, the vast array of sumptuous gold and jeweled objects that
accompanied Tutankhamen's burial
gave archaeologists a realiza-
tion of just how magnificent must
have been the funerary treasures
of the royal tombs that had been
plundered. This sandstone head,
although not inscribed with his
name, almost certainly represents
Tutankhamen, its sensuous features strikingly similar to those
on the famous gold mummy mask
from his tomb.

Sandstone
H. 11¾ in. (29.6 cm)
Gift of Miss Mary S. Ames   11.1533

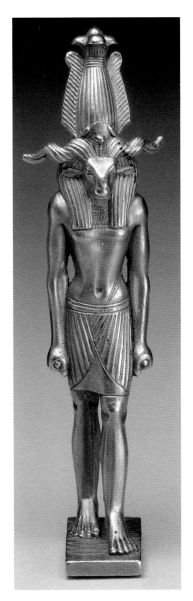

Amulet of Harsaphes
Egypt (Herakleopolis)
Third Intermediate Period,
Dynasty 23, 740–725 B.C.

This tiny amulet of solid cast gold represents the fertility god Harsaphes, depicted as a man with the head of a long-horned ram. He wears a royal kilt, and on his head is the Atef crown that associates him with the powerful Osiris, god of the Underworld. In hieroglyphs on the underside of the base, the statuette is inscribed with the name of Neferkara Peftjauawybast, ruler of the city of Herakleopolis (present-day Ihnasya, Egypt). Neferkara is recorded as a subject prince on the victory stela of the Nubian king Piankhy (Piye) who, "raging like a panther," conquered Egypt "like a cloudburst" about 724 B.C. With its delicate sculpting of muscles and bone and its fine, linear patterning of kilt, horns, and crown, this image of Harsaphes is a superb example of the gold-smith's art.

Gold
H. 2⅜ in. (6 cm)
Egypt Exploration Fund by subscription
06.2408

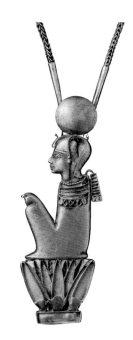

Pendant on a chain
Egyptian
Third Intermediate Period,
Dynasty 21–24,
1070–712 B.C.

An Egyptian creation story tells of the emergence of the sun god — the first living being — from a lotus flower growing in the receding waters of the primeval ocean called Nun. This pendant illus-trates that story and shows the newborn sun god in the form of the pharaoh as a child. It is made of hammered sheet gold, carefully worked on both sides, and still retains its chain of interlocking gold loops. The front was origi-nally inlaid with colored glass.

Gold with glass inlays
H. 2¾ in. (7.2 cm)
Gift of Mrs. Horace L. Mayer   68.836

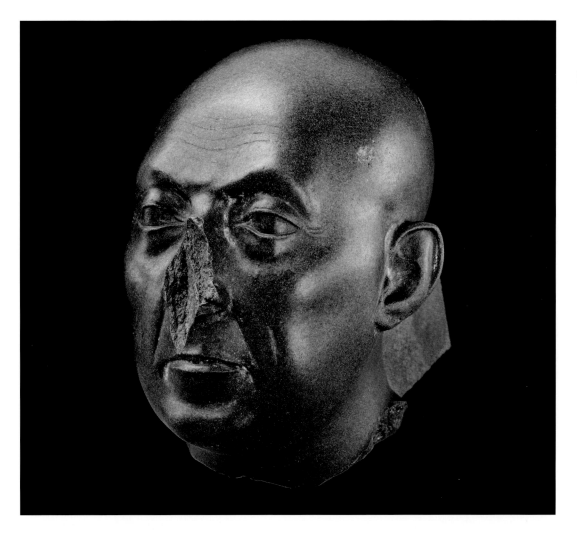

Head of a priest (The Boston Green Head)
Egyptian
Late Period, Dynasty 30, 380–332 B.C.

Only four inches high, the so-called Boston Green Head is admired throughout the world as one of the finest of all portrait sculptures from ancient Egypt. It is a masterpiece of naturalism—rare in Egyptian art, which tends to idealize—and is stamped with a remarkable humanity. Note the wrinkled forehead, the deep lines around nose and mouth, the crow's-feet, and such individualizing details as the mole on the left cheekbone. The subject is probably a priest, identified by his shaven head. On the back of the head is an inscription with the name of the Memphite funerary deity Ptah-Sokar, suggesting that the statue (of which this head is a fragment) was originally placed in a temple dedicated to that god. This agrees with the alleged findspot of the head: Saqqara, the cemetery of Memphis.

Greywacke
H. 4⅛ in. (10.5 cm)
Henry Lillie Pierce Fund   04.1749

Tomb group of Nesmutaatneru
Egypt (Thebes, Deir el-Bahari)
Late Period, Dynasty 25, about 760–660 B.C.

Nesmutaatneru, the wife of a high-ranking Theban priest, died sometime around 700 B.C., and her tomb remained undisturbed for over 2,500 years until it was excavated in 1894. Her mummy was contained within three wooden coffins, all decorated with inscriptions and depictions of the gods and goddesses who guaranteed protection in the afterlife. The vaulted lid and four corner posts of the outermost, rectangular coffin are meant to imitate the tomb of Osiris, god of the Underworld. This first coffin held the smaller one shaped roughly like a human body and painted with a face and wig. Within this lay a third coffin in the shape of the mummy itself, every inch covered with inscriptions and devotional images, including one of Nesmutaatneru worshipping Osiris as he lay on his funeral bed.

This elaborate housing was designed to protect the mummy—the preserved body of the deceased—because the ancient Egyptians believed that in the afterlife the spirit, or *ba*, continued to use the body as a home, and that the dead had the same physical needs as the living. To ensure the integrity of the body, they employed the process of mummification—removing the internal organs of the deceased (which were preserved and stored separately), dehydrating the corpse with salts, and wrapping it in linen cloth. These procedures were accompanied by elaborate rituals and took nearly three months. Central as mummification was to the afterlife, it was only one way in which care was taken to provide for the next world. Indeed, the majority of the objects in the Museum's Egyptian collection were buried in tombs for the comfort of the deceased. Many others were ritual objects used by the living on behalf of the dead.

Wood, plaster, linen, pigment
L. of outer coffin (95.1407d): 80¼ in. (204 cm)
L. of middle coffin (95.1407c): 73¼ in. (186 cm)
L. of inner coffin (95.1407b): 66½ in. (169 cm)
L. of mummy (95.1407a): 59½ in. (151 cm)
Egypt Exploration Fund by subscription 95.1407a–d

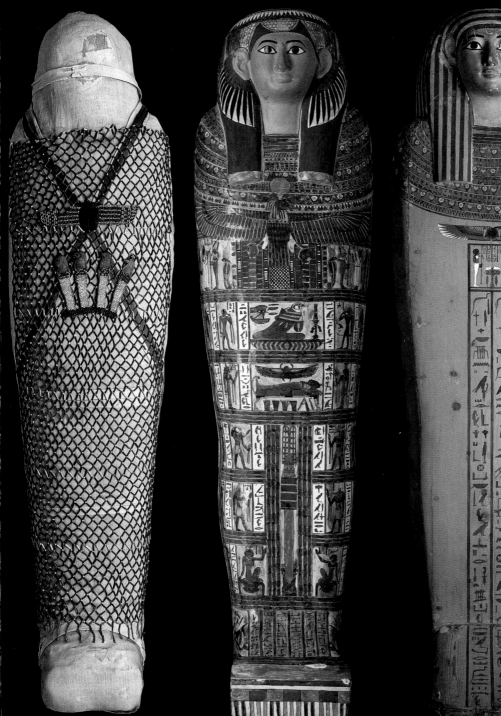

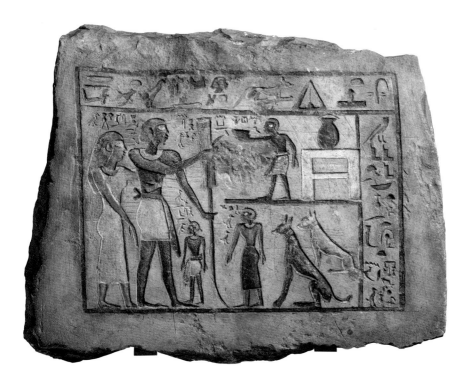

Stele of the Nubian soldier Nenu
Egyptian (said to be from el-Rizeiqat)
First Intermediate Period to Middle Kingdom,
2100–2040 B.C.

Ancient Nubia—a region encompassing modern-day southern Egypt and northern Sudan—provided a major trade route over which gold, ivory, ebony, incense, and spices traveled between central Africa and the lands around the Mediterranean. Nubia's history was closely intertwined with that of its neighbor, Egypt: social, political, religious, and artistic ideas moved back and forth as each country conquered or was conquered by the other. The ancient Egyptians called Nubia Ta-Sety ("Land of the Bow"), and Egyptian kings often hired the renowned archers of Nubia for their armies. Many of these mercenary soldiers settled in Egypt, married Egyptian women, and were buried in the Egyptian manner, but they still proudly maintained their Nubian identity. This limestone grave marker depicts a Nubian soldier named Nenu holding his bow and arrows; beside him is his wife, wearing the close-fitting linen dress typical of Egyptian women. Nenu has a short, curly, Nubian hairstyle and close-cropped beard and wears a kilt tied with a characteristically Nubian leather sash. In the upper right, an Egyptian servant presents a bowl of beer. Dogs are often included on the stelai of Nubian soldiers, suggesting the great affection they had for these pets.

Painted limestone
14⅝ x 17¾ in. (37 x 45 cm)
Emily Esther Sears Fund   03.1848

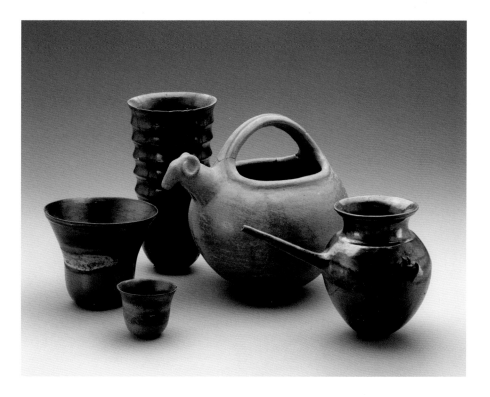

Beakers
Nubian
Sudan (Kerma)
Classic Kerma period, 1700–1550 B.C.

Despite close ties, both Egypt and Nubia retained their unique characteristics, and with intensified archaeological exploration of Nubia over the past decades, scholars have recognized its importance as a distinct culture. This recognition of culture has greatly enhanced our understanding of ancient Africa as a complex community of nations. Nubian ceramics are among the earliest and most sophisticated of the ancient world. About 1700 B.C., as Egypt declined, the great Nubian kingdom of Kush rose to power, its capital built on a fertile bend of the Nile where the modern town of Kerma now stands. A hallmark of the Kerma period is its extraordinarily fine black-topped red-polished pottery, which came in a variety of elegant, inventive shapes. Remarkably thin and delicate, this pottery was not thrown on a wheel but made entirely by hand. Much of it was produced to be included in burials along with furniture, household equipment, dress, and jewelry. The unusual shape of the tall ribbed, or rilled, beaker here suggests the nested stacks of individual cups that were often placed in Kerma tombs so that the thirst of the dead might be satisfied in the afterlife.

Pottery
H. of rilled beaker: 8⅞ in. (22.5 cm)
Harvard University–Boston Museum of Fine Arts Expedition
13.4080, 13.4075, 20.2006, 20.1714, 13.4102

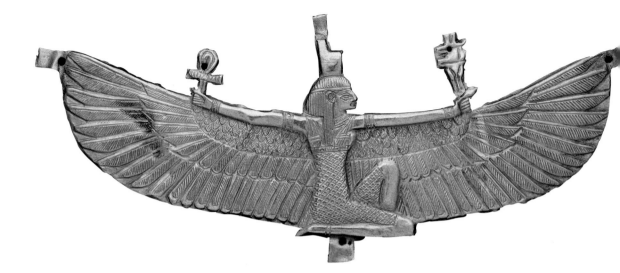

Winged Isis pectoral

Nubian

Sudan (Nuri, pyramid of King Amaninatakelebte)

Napatan period, reign of Amaninatakelebte,
538–519 B.C.

This gold pectoral, overlooked by the thieves who plundered the royal tombs at Nuri, represents the winged goddess Isis, holding an *ankh* (symbol of life) in her right hand and what may represent the hieroglyph for a sail (symbol of the breath of life) in her left. Twenty Nubian kings and fifty-four queens were buried at Nuri between the mid-seventh and the late fourth centuries B.C. The mummified bodies were placed within nested sets of gilded wooden coffins inlaid with colored stones. The mummies wore gold amulets, gold finger and toe caps, and probably gold face masks. This pendant would have been sewn onto a bead net draped over a king's mummy. Cut into the bedrock beneath the pyramids, the royal tombs were excavated by the Museum expedition between 1917 and 1920.

Gold
W. 6⅝ in. (16.7 cm)
Harvard University–Boston Museum of Fine Arts Expedition
20.276

opposite, left

Miniature dagger

Nubian

Sudan (Kerma, cemetery M, grave 48)

Classic Kerma period, 1700–1550 B.C.

In 1913 George Andrew Reisner and the Harvard University–Boston Museum of Fine Arts Expedition began a twenty-year excavation of major Nubian sites in the northern Sudan, among them the walled city and cemetery of ancient Kerma, capital of the kingdom of Kush. Sudanese authorities allowed the expedition to keep many of the objects found, and the Museum of Fine Arts now houses the finest and most extensive collection of Nubian art outside Sudan. Although many objects discovered in Kerma burials were either influenced by Egyptian art or were Egyptian in origin (see the statue of Sennuwy, page 37), exquisitely crafted miniature daggers like this one, found in the grave of a young boy, are entirely Nubian.

Gold, bronze, and ivory
H. 6¾ in. (17 cm)
Harvard University–Boston Museum of Fine Arts Expedition
21.11796b

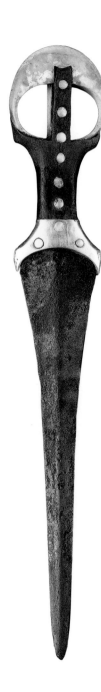

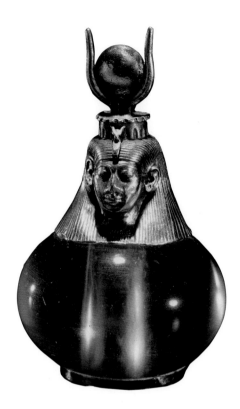

Crystal pendant with head of Hathor
Made in Egypt, found in Sudan (el-Kurru)
Napatan period, reign of Piankhy (Piye), 743–712 B.C.

Surmounted by a gold head of the goddess Hathor, this rock-crystal pendant served as a protective amulet. Worn by the living and buried with
the dead, amulets were believed to have special powers, embodied both
in their sacred imagery and in the precious materials of which they were
made. This example has a gold cylinder enclosed within the crystal globe.
Comparable cylinders have been found containing sheets of papyrus or
metal inscribed with magical texts; however, X-rays have shown that
this one is empty. The pendant was found in the tomb of a queen of the
Nubian king Piankhy (Piye), ruler of both Nubia and Egypt. The head of
Hathor is Egyptian in style, and the pendant was probably part of the
tribute paid to King Piankhy by Egyptian princes.

Rock crystal and gold
H. 2⅛ in. (5.3 cm)
Harvard University–Boston Museum of Fine Arts Expedition   21.321

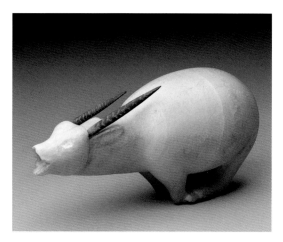

Vessel in the shape of a bound oryx

Nubian

Sudan (Meroe, tomb W 609)

Napatan period, early 7th century B.C.

In a grave excavated at Meroe, a hundred miles from the modern city of Khartoum, the body of a young woman was found surrounded by jewelry, amulets, mirrors, pottery, bronze vessels, and three travertine jars in the form of bound oryxes. At once lifelike and ingeniously functional, these elegant jars were containers for expensive perfume and ointments, which could be poured out through the open mouth. The bound legs made a practical handle. The wooden horns are modern reproductions of the original stone ones.

Travertine (Egyptian alabaster)
L. 6¾ in. (17.2 cm)
Harvard University–Boston Museum of Fine Arts Expedition
24.879

Leg from a funerary bed

Nubian

Sudan (el-Kurru)

Napatan period, reign of Shebitka, 698–690 B.C.

In traditional Nubian burials, the unmummified body of the deceased was laid out on a wooden bed. Later, in the period when Nubian kings ruled Egypt, mummification in the Egyptian fashion was introduced although the wooden funerary beds were retained. This bronze leg from such a wooden bed (long since decayed) incorporates the figure of a goose. In funerary texts from Old Kingdom Egypt, the deceased expresses his desire to rise to heaven as a goose, and, from the time of the New Kingdom, the goose was one of many forms taken by Amen, the principal Egyptian god.

Bronze
H. 22⅛ in. (56.1 cm)
Harvard University–Boston Museum of Fine Arts Expedition
21.2815

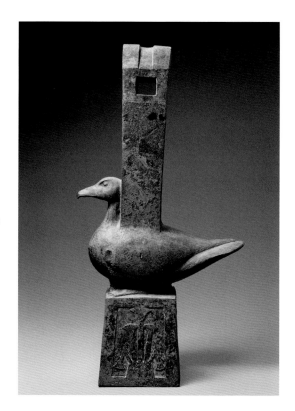

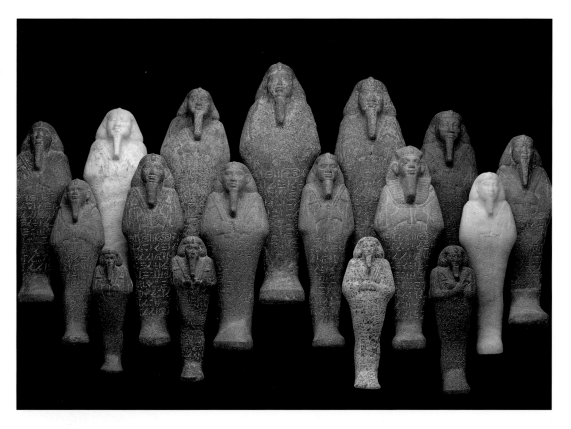

***Shawabty* figures of King Taharqa**
Nubian
Sudan (Nuri, pyramid of Taharqa)
Napatan period, reign of Taharqa, 690–664 B.C.

Various
H. 7⅛–20 in. (20–51 cm)
Harvard University–Boston Museum of Fine Arts Expedition

About 740 B.C. the Nubian king Piankhy (Piye) invaded Egypt and established his family as Egypt's Twenty-fifth Dynasty. Many Egyptian practices were adopted in Nubia during this period, including the construction of pyramids for royal tombs that contained *shawabty* figures intended to perform manual labor for the deceased in the afterlife. These *shawabty*s are some of more than one thousand that were discovered standing in neat rows in the burial chamber of King Taharqa's pyramid tomb at Nuri. Taharqa, a son and third successor of King Piankhy, was the greatest of the Nubian pharaohs. His empire stretched from Palestine to the confluence of the Blue and White Niles. In 667 B.C., Nubia lost control of Egypt to the Assyrians.

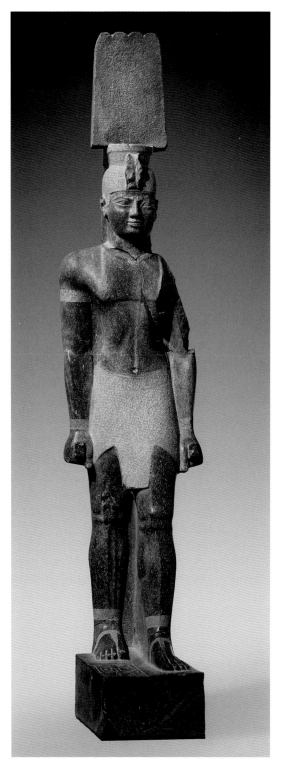

King Aspelta
Nubian
Sudan (Gebel Barkal)
Napatan period, reign of Aspelta, 593–568 B.C.

This monumental striding statue of King Aspelta, wearing the royal Nubian headdress, originally stood in the Great Temple of Amen at Gebel Barkal, the foremost religious center of Nubia. Eleven feet tall and weighing eight tons, the colossal image is smoothly polished except for the surfaces representing dress and jewelry, which were left rough to hold a thin layer of gold leaf. In 1916 this statue, which had probably been broken in 598 B.C. by members of an invading Egyptian army, was discovered in pieces by Museum archaeologists in a pit outside the temple entrance. The statue was reassembled at the Museum in 1924.

Granite gneiss
H. 130¾ in. (332 cm)
Harvard University–Boston Museum of Fine Arts Expedition
23.730

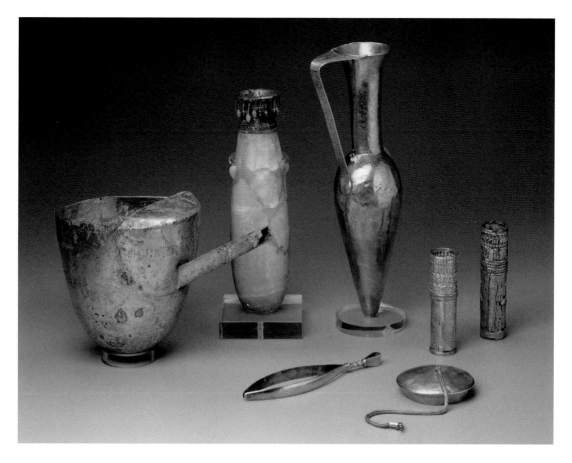

Tomb treasure of King Aspelta
Nubian
Sudan (Nuri, pyramid of Aspelta)
Napatan period, reign of Aspelta, 593–568 B.C.

Silver, gold, travertine (Egyptian alabaster), carnelian, Egyptian blue, megnotite, and amazonite
H. of gold vase: 12⅜ in. (31.5 cm)
Harvard University–Boston Museum of Fine Arts Expedition 24.901, 20.1070, 20.341, 21.339a–b, 21.340, 20.342, 20.334

The splendid pyramid tomb of King Aspelta (probably the great-grandson of King Taharqa) was the least plundered of all the royal burials at Nuri. Within it, Museum archaeologists discovered a wide array of precious grave goods buried in soil littered with gold beads and pieces of gold foil (in which the objects may originally have been wrapped). Included in the treasure were the objects illustrated here, among them a graceful gold vase and an alabaster perfume or ointment jar from whose gold cap beads of semiprecious stones hang on woven gold-wire chains.

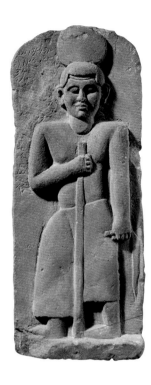

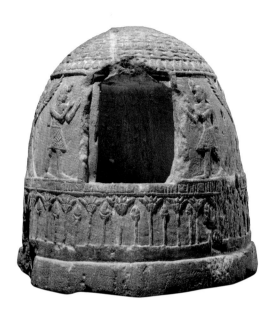

Funerary stele

Nubian

Meroitic period, 2nd–3rd centuries A.D.

This fine stele, or grave marker, represents a high-ranking Meroitic official with his characteristic long skirt, fly whisk, and staff. The cut in his forehead represents a decorative scar that some Sudanese still wear today to identify their community affiliation, and the sun disk above his head indicates that he has died and become divine. To the left of the figure, a Meroitic inscription probably gives his name and title. However, scholars are still unable to decipher this ancient language (composed of an alphabet of twenty-three letters), which appeared in the second century B.C.

Sandstone
H. 21⅝ in. (55 cm)
Gift of Horace L. and Florence E. Mayer, C. Granville Way, Denman Ross, the Hon. Mrs. Fredrick Guest, Bequest from Charles H. Parker, and Anonymous Gift, by exchange
1992.257

Shrine

Nubian

Sudan (Gebel Barkal, Great Temple of Amen)

Meroitic period, A.D. 100–200

This sandstone shrine, found in the Great Temple of Amen at Gebel Barkal, originally housed a statue of the god Amen hidden behind a sealed doorway. Once thought to imitate the form of a traditional African house, the shrine actually is a model of Gebel Barkal itself, the three-hundred-foot sacred "Pure Mountain" behind whose cliff Amen was believed to dwell. On either side of the opening of the shrine are carved images of a Nubian king and a winged goddess, standing above a stylized papyrus swamp. Nubians believed that Gebel Barkal was the "primeval hill" of Egyptian mythology, where the creator god first gave himself form and, amid the primordial swamp, caused the sun to rise on the first day of time.

Stuccoed and painted sandstone
H. 24⅝ in. (62.5 cm)
Harvard University–Boston Museum of Fine Arts Expedition
21.3234

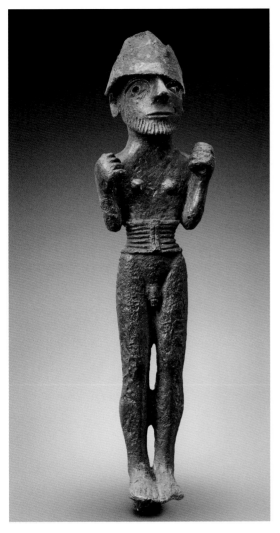
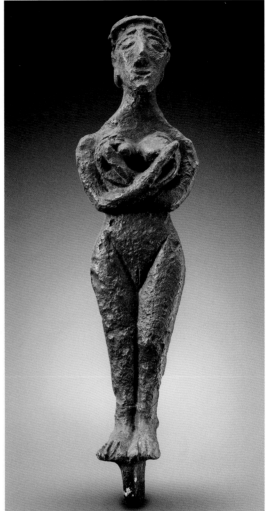

Male and female figurines

Syria (Tell Judaidah)

Early Bronze Age, 3200–2800 B.C.

Among the oldest surviving metal sculptures from the ancient Near East, these figurines were excavated at an Early Bronze Age site in northern Syria, along with four similar figures that all appeared to have been wrapped in cloth before burial. Cast in an unusual bronze alloy, these lively figures are nude; the woman (who once had silver jewels and curls) holds her breasts, and the man, who wears only a wide belt and a silver helmet, originally grasped small bronze weapons. Such figures may have been intended to magically enhance fertility and virility.

Low-tin bronze with silver
H. of male figure: 7 in. (17.8 cm)
H. of female figure: 7½ in. (19 cm)
Gift of the Marriner Memorial Syrian Expedition
49.118, 49.119

Mountain goat
Elamite
Proto-Elamite period, 3500–2700 B.C.

The artist who made this exquisite miniature mountain goat created an image of great dignity and naturalism, even incising its rear leg and tufted tail on the bottom of the sculpture. A fragmentary loop on the animal's back suggests that it may have been worn as an amulet. The sculpture dates from the brilliant Proto-Elamite period that saw the dawn of literacy in Iranian civilization.

Silver and sheet gold
L. 2¾ in. (7 cm)
John H. and Ernestine A. Payne Fund   59.14

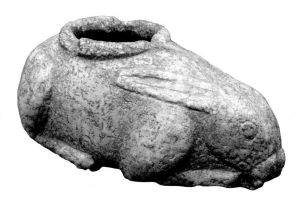

Vessel in the form of a hare
Syrian
Neolithic period, 6400–5900 B.C.

Carved about eight thousand years ago, this amazingly well-preserved vessel in the form of a hare is among the oldest works of art on view in the Museum. Simply shaped and economically detailed, the hollow vessel nevertheless vividly captures the essential hare—its round-eyed face resting on its paws and its long ears laid tightly against the body. An almost identical vessel was discovered in the 1970s at the Neolithic village site of Bouqras, on the Euphrates River in northern Syria.

Gypsum
L. 7¼ in. (18.5 cm)
Egyptian Curator's Fund and Partial Gift of
Emmanuel Tiliakos   1995.739

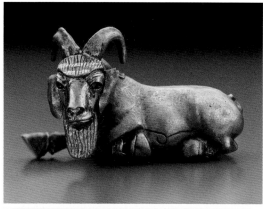

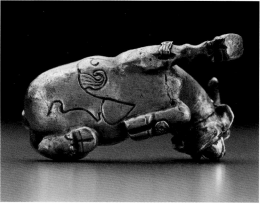

Drinking vessel

Hittite

Hittite New Kingdom, reign of Tudhaliya III,
14th century B.C.

This is one of few surviving objects in precious metal
made by the ancient Hittites, whose kingdom lay in
north-central Anatolia (part of present-day Turkey).
The strikingly lifelike and detailed cup was made
from a single sheet of silver to which a handle (now
lost) was attached. The frieze around the rim shows
a Hittite king pouring out a libation; to the left of his
head are the hieroglyphs of "Tudhaliya, Great King."
The king, followed by a procession of priests and
musicians, performs an offering ceremony to the
storm god, Tarhuna, who appears before him leading a bull. Stylistic evidence indicates that this cup,
most likely employed in the service of Tarhuna, was
made for the third of three known Hittite kings named
Tudhaliya. The fist shape evokes a Hittite hieroglyph
meaning strength, and hands clenched into fists and
held before the chest is a reverential gesture often
seen in Hittite art.

Silver
3⅞ x 6⅛ in. (10 x 15.5 cm)
Gift of Landon T. and Lavinia Clay in honor of
Malcolm Rogers   2004.2230

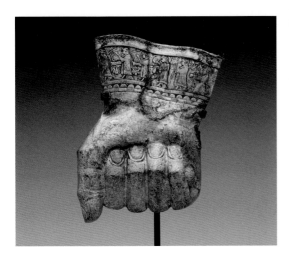

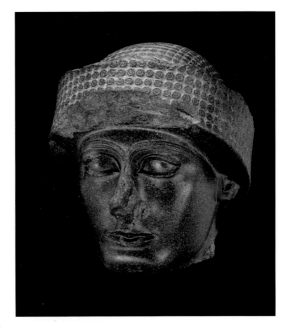

Head of Gudea

Sumerian

Neo-Sumerian period, reign of Gudea, 2144–2124 B.C.

During the turbulent era following the collapse of the
Akkadian empire, Gudea governed the small state of
Lagash (modern Tello) in southern Iraq. Ironically,
most major known pieces of late-Sumerian art represent this minor ruler, who filled the temples of his
local gods with statues of himself. These images are
mostly carved from diorite—a hard, black stone that
Gudea claimed to have brought by sea from "Magan,"
a distant land now believed to be somewhere on the
Arabian coast. Like the majority of surviving images
of Gudea, this one was vandalized in antiquity, the
head lopped from the body and the nose broken. Nevertheless, it remains a superb work of art, the remarkable surfaces of smooth, polished stone emphasizing
dramatically large eyes beneath sweeping eyebrows
and a wool crown formed of tight, stylized curls.

Diorite
H. 9⅛ in. (23 cm)
Francis Bartlett Donation of 1912   26.289

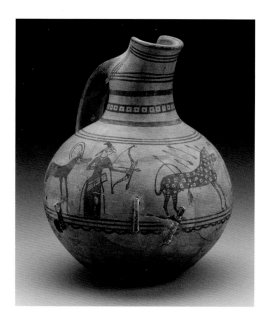

opposite, top

Lion

Iraq (Babylon, Processional Way)

Neo-Babylonian period, reign of Nebuchadnezzar II, 604–561 B.C.

In 1899 German archaeologists excavating the ancient site of Babylon found hundreds of thousands of glazed brick fragments—all that was left of the massive Ishtar Gate and the Processional Way that once led to the Great Temple of Marduk, chief deity of the city. The lion was sacred to the goddess Ishtar, and on both sides of the Processional Way, the walls were adorned with multicolored tiles depicting some 120 life-sized lions striding toward the temple in what must have been one of the most spectacular ensembles in antiquity.

Glazed bricks
41¾ x 91 in. (106 x 232 cm)
Maria Antoinette Evans Fund   31.898

Pitcher

Phrygian

Late Phrygian period, 699–600 B.C.

Most ceramics from the ancient kingdom of Phrygia in Anatolia (present-day Turkey) were painted with geometric designs. This highly unusual pitcher, however, was decorated with figures, probably reflecting the influence of Greek art. Many scholars consider it the most important surviving late-Phrygian ceramic. It seems to have been equally valued in antiquity, when it was carefully repaired with lead clamps (visible here). The decoration shows a huntress shooting at a leopard; an ibex stands behind her. The huntress is Kubaba or Cybele (known as Artemis to the Greeks), the powerful Anatolian mother goddess and mistress of the animals. This vessel may have been used in rituals at one of the goddess's shrines.

Painted pottery
H. 11¾ in. (30 cm)
Edward J. and Mary S. Holmes Fund   1971.297

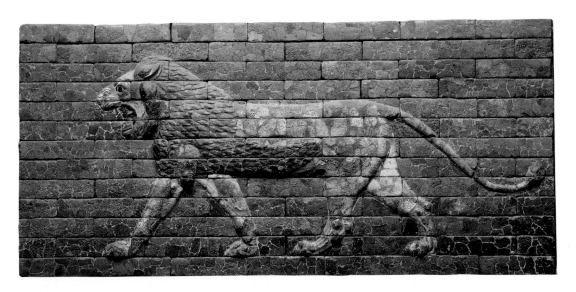

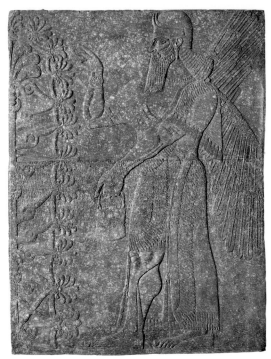

left

Protective spirit

Assyrian

Iraq (Nimrud, Northwest Palace)

Neo-Assyrian period, reign of Ashurnasirpal II,
883–859 B.C.

In the belief that they were constantly threatened by
a host of malignant supernatural forces, the Assyrians surrounded themselves with images of protective
deities, often represented as mighty, winged men. In
the palace of Ashurnasirpal II at Calah (present-day
Nimrud), huge carved reliefs such as this one covered
the walls of throne rooms, banquet halls, bedrooms,
and even lavatories. The deity depicted in this sculpture pollinates a sacred tree with a cone and situla,
or pail. Across the middle of this and every similar relief—all of which were once painted—is the
"standard inscription" of Ashurnasirpal II, in which
he describes himself as "the strong man who treads
on the necks of his foes . . . who shatters the alliance
of the rebels; the king who with the help of the great
gods . . . has mastered all the mountain regions and has
received their tribute."

Gypsum
87¼ x 69⅜ in. (221.7 x 176.3 cm)
Charles Amos Cummings Fund   35.731

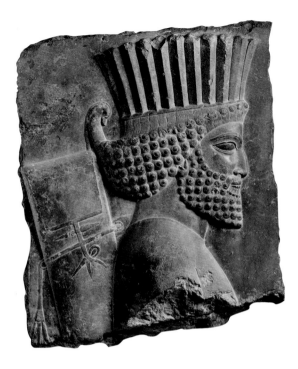

A Persian guard

Persian

Iran (Persepolis, Palace of Xerxes)

Achaemenid period, reign of Xerxes, 486–464 B.C.

This noble figure was a member of the elite guard of the Persian kings called the "Ten Thousand Immortals" because if one fell in battle another would immediately step forward to take his place. The Greek historian Herodotus described the Ten Thousand Immortals in his chronicle of the wars between the Persians and the Greeks, written about the time this relief was carved:

> *Of all the troops, these were adorned with the greatest magnificence, and they were likewise the most valiant. Besides their arms, they glittered all over with gold, vast quantities of which they wore about their persons. They were followed by litters, carrying their concubines, and a numerous train of attendants handsomely dressed. Camels and pack animals carried their provisions apart from those of the other soldiers.*

The fragment shown here was once part of a long frieze, portraying a single file of the Immortals, that decorated the palace of Xerxes at Persepolis, a royal residence of the Achaemenid Persian kings. With a quiver and bow case over his shoulder, the soldier wears a high, fluted helmet, and his beard and hair are rendered in rows of tight, spiraling curls. Traces of pigment on similar reliefs suggest that the figure was once painted in shades of yellow, blue, and purple.

Limestone
20⅞ x 18¼ in. (53 x 46.5 cm)
Archibald Cary Coolidge Fund   40.170

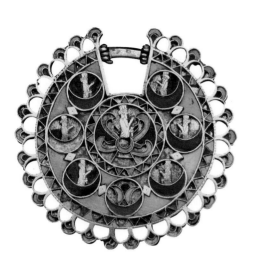

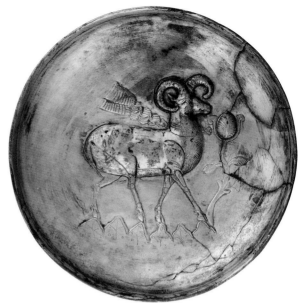

Earring

Persian

Achaemenid period, 525–330 B.C.

This sumptuous gold earring is decorated on both
sides with a dense web of inlaid semiprecious stones
(originally 460 individual pieces) that create a brilliant and complex composition. Around a central
roundel featuring a bearded regal figure, seven
smaller roundels contain six male figures and a lotus
blossom. The design closely parallels one carved over
the royal tombs at Persepolis, and it probably represents simultaneously the king revered by the six Great
Houses of the empire, the land of Persia (present-day
Iran) surrounded by the six world regions, and the
god Ahuramazda surrounded by the six Bounteous
Immortals. The lotus blossom may identify the king
as the sun, as it does in Egypt, or it may symbolize a
seventh world region, the ocean.

Gold with inlays of turquoise, carnelian, and lapis lazuli
Diam. 2 in. (5 cm)
Edward J. and Mary S. Holmes Fund   1971.256

Plate

Persian

Sasanian period, A.D. 400–699

The nimble mountain sheep on this silver bowl picks
his way daintily across flower-covered peaks to sniff
a magical blossom. A symbol of royalty, and more
specifically of Ardashir, founder of the Sasanian
dynasty—the last to rule Persia (present-day Iran)
before the empire fell to the Arabs in the mid-seventh
century—the sheep wears a studded bell collar with
the fluttering ribbons often depicted streaming from
the king's crown and royal vestments. On this exquisite plate, the blossom and the animal's body, head,
and horns were made separately, attached to the surface, and then gilded.

Silver with mercury-gilded details
Diam. 8¼ in. (21.2 cm)
John H. and Ernestine A. Payne Fund   1971.52

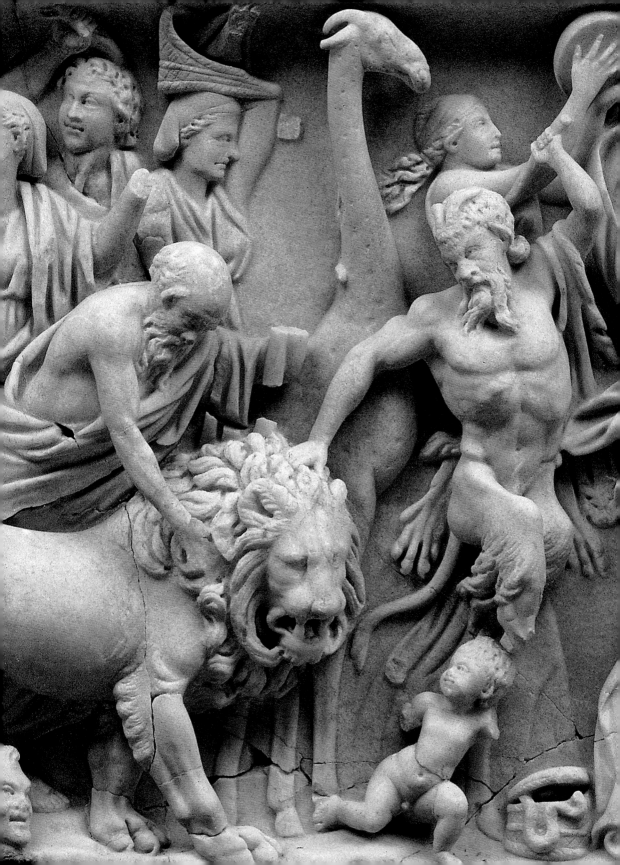

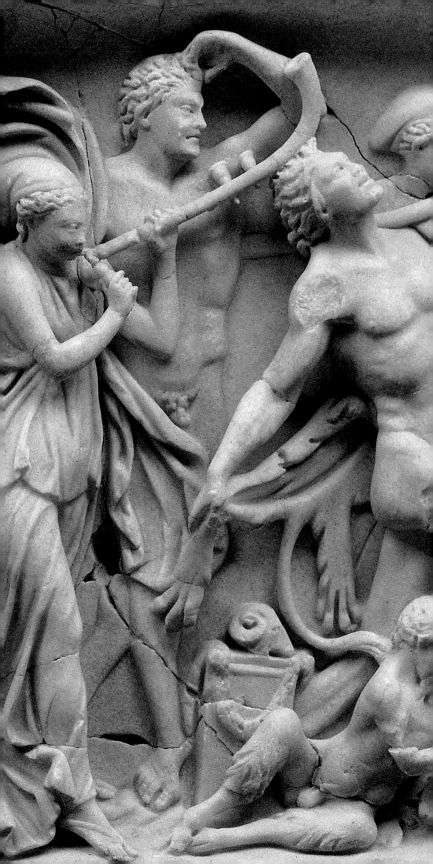

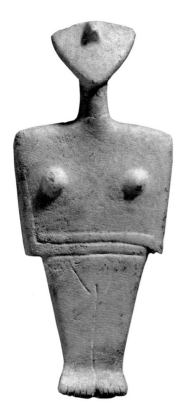

Female figurine

Cycladic

Early Cycladic period, about 2300–2000 B.C.

The first of the remarkable Bronze Age civilizations that flourished in what is now Greece and the Aegean developed on the islands called the Cyclades. Skilled artisans created fine vessels and sculptures from white marble that was cut, incised, and probably smoothed with emery (a hard, abrasive mineral). The most characteristic Cycladic sculptures are stylized human figures whose abstracted forms and timeless serenity are particularly attractive to the modern eye. Most of the figures represent women and were found in tombs; this one belongs stylistically with those from Chalandriani on the island of Syros. Were they intended as images of a deity? Portraits of the deceased? Fertility symbols? Although their meaning remains a mystery, Cycladic figurines stand as the earliest examples of the classical world's extraordinary tradition of shaping stone into works of art.

Marble
H. 7¾ in. (20 cm)
Gift of Mr. and Mrs. J. J. Klejman   61.1089

Votive double ax

Minoan

Late Minoan period, about 1550–1500 B.C.

Only three inches high, this delicate and exquisitely worked miniature ax is said to have been found in the sacred cave of Arkalokhori on Crete. The cave was first discovered in 1912 by local residents who collected and sold for scrap metal the many pounds of ancient bronze weapons they found there. Alerted to the find, archaeologists excavated hundreds of bronze, gold, and silver weapons from the site. This ax, made of thin sheet gold mounted on a hollow gold shaft, seems to have been a religious offering, although its precise significance is unknown. On the left blade is a rare inscription in the early, still-undeciphered script called Linear A.

Gold
H. 3½ in. (9 cm)
Theodora Wilbour Fund in memory of Zoë Wilbour   58.1009

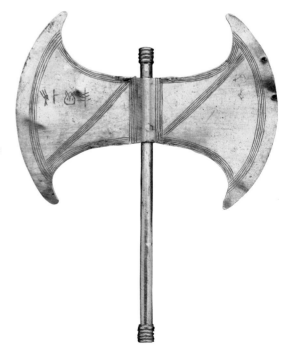

Vessel for mixing wine and water (*krater*)
Cypriote
Late Cypriote period, 1350–1250 B.C.

Large ceramic vases painted with scenes of aristocratic pursuits testified to their owner's wealth and
status and were often placed in tombs. This vase is
decorated with horse-drawn chariots and an unusual
representation of an athletic contest: the two men
standing in front of the horse are belt-wrestling,
trying to pull each other off balance while bound
together at the waist. The abstract and exaggerated
painting style is typical of the art associated with
Mycenae, the brilliant Bronze Age civilization of
Greece whose influence spread throughout the Aegean
and into the eastern Mediterranean.

Ceramic
H. 17¼ in. (43.6 cm)
Henry Lillie Pierce Fund   01.8044

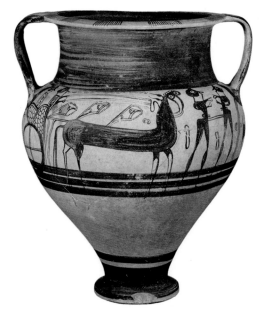

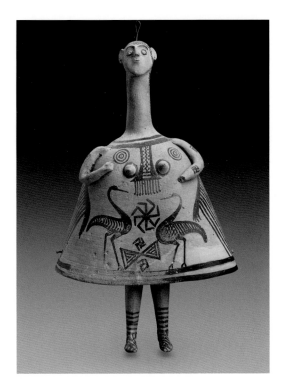

Figurine
Greek
Geometric period, 720–690 B.C.

This is one of a small group of similar objects that
most likely came from Boiotia on mainland Greece.
The context in which they were found is unknown,
and their original purpose and use remain a mystery.
However, it has been suggested that this doll-like
figure may have served as an offering to a deity and
been hung from a tree at one of the outdoor sanctuaries typical of this early period. Because the legs were
made separately and attached beneath the skirt, the
figure might have appeared to "dance" in the wind and
ring like a chime.

Ceramic
H. 11¾ in. (30 cm)
Henry Lillie Pierce Fund   98.891

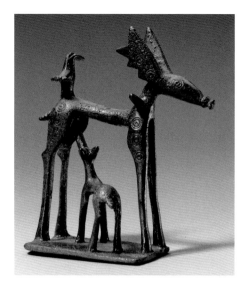

Deer nursing her fawn
Greek
Geometric period, 8th century B.C.

Fragile legs braced, this slender doe stands nursing her fawn. A bird perches on her rump, and her body is decorated with concentric circles. Her antlers are those of a male deer, and, although inaccurate, these give added weight to the upper portion of the sculpture and enhance its distinctive silhouette. This tiny and appealing cast-bronze figure is among the most accomplished early Greek sculptures both in design and technique. Like the ceramic "doll" (page 65), it was probably made as an offering to a deity and placed in an outdoor sanctuary in Boiotia — perhaps by a hunter hoping that the deer on whom his livelihood depended would thrive and multiply.

Bronze
H. 2⅞ in. (7.2 cm)
Henry Lillie Pierce Fund   98.650

Apollo
Greek
Late Geometric period, about 700–675 B.C.

This powerfully expressive figure comes from an important transitional moment in the development of Western art. The simplified, elongated forms and emphatic symmetry (the torso is even bisected with an incised line) typify the conventions for depicting the human figure in this period. However, the artist reached beyond this tradition toward a greater naturalism, and the figure projects a striking new sense of mass and volume, particularly in the heavy coils of hair and the rounded curves of shoulders, thighs, and chest. It almost certainly portrays Apollo and possibly once held a silver bow in the left hand. On the thighs, a metrical inscription in ancient Boiotian script states that the statuette was dedicated to Phoibos (Apollo) by a man named Mantiklos: "Mantiklos donated me as a tithe to the far-shooter, the bearer of the Silver Bow. You, Phoibos, give something pleasing in return."

Bronze
H. 8 in. (20.3 cm)
Francis Bartlett Donation of 1900   03.997

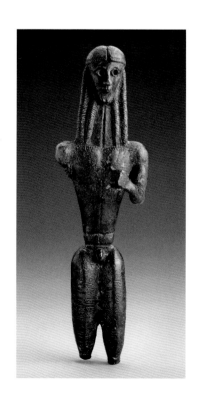

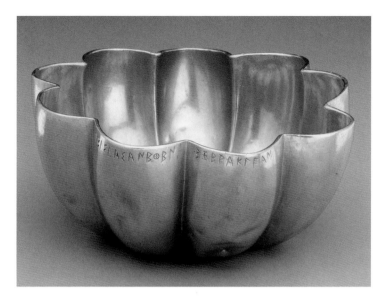

Libation bowl

Greek

Late Orientalizing or Archaic period, about 625–600 B.C.

This hammered bowl—marks of the hammer are still visible on the surface—is a unique example of the work of early Greek goldsmiths. Under the rim an inscription in the Corinthian alphabet reads: "The sons of Kypselos dedicated [this bowl] from Heraclea." In the late seventh century, Kypselos was the ruler of Corinth, the richest city on the Greek mainland. Reportedly found at Olympia, the bowl was probably offered as a thanksgiving after a successful battle at Heraclea. Only the extremely wealthy could make such a lavish offering, and the bowl is evidence both of the opulent lifestyle of early Greek rulers and of the skill of its maker—although the gift was valued at the time only for its quantity of precious metal. Unusually, the inscription does not name the god to whom the bowl was dedicated, but very likely it was Zeus.

Gold
Diam. 5⅞ in. (15 cm)
Francis Bartlett Donation of 1912   21.1843

Oil flask (*aryballos*)

East Greek

Archaic period, 6th century B.C.

Less than two inches high and made of faience (a synthetic substance related to glass), this vessel was intended to contain perfume or precious oil. It represents an African man, and—probably because it is a representation of a "foreigner"—exhibits an attention to realistic detail that is striking among Greek images of this period, which were usually idealized. The naturalistic representation suggests that the artist worked from the direct observation of a live model. Ancient Greeks took great interest in representing the different cultures and peoples they encountered through travel, warfare, and commerce.

Glazed ceramic (faience)
H. 1¾ in. (4.6 cm)
Francis Bartlett Donation of 1900
03.835

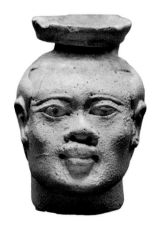

Two-handled jar (*amphora*)

Greek

Archaic period, about 540–530 B.C.

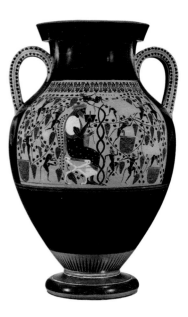

Dionysos was the Greek god of wine and its attendant pleasures—intoxication, physical delight, and the banishment of care. In the sixth century B.C. the cult of Dionysos became extremely popular at all levels of society, and in Athenian art representations of this god outnumber those of any other. Dionysos was, of course, a natural subject for the decoration of vessels used in the production, storage, and drinking of wine. On this black-figure storage jar—made in Athens, and painted by an artist whose style resembles that of the master Exekias—the god sits on a folding stool sipping wine from a *kantharos*. In the huge, laden grapevine, diminutive satyrs appear to be diligently harvesting the fruit (closer inspection reveals that they are all at play). The satyr above Dionysos's head, lolling back with his arm hooked around a vine, leisurely examines the ornamental border. The scene is idyllic, humorous, and masterfully organized. The ivy that trails over Dionysos's shoulder is echoed on the handles of the vase, and the whole image is energized by the rhythm of the vine that twists across the surface.

Ceramic

H. 20¼ in. (51.4 cm)

Henry Lillie Pierce Residuary Fund and Francis Bartlett Donation of 1900   63.952

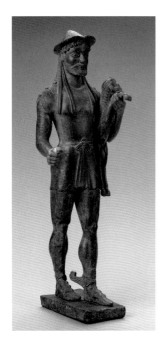

Hermes Kriophoros

Greek

Late Archaic period, about 500–490 B.C.

Greek artists often portrayed the messenger god Hermes in the guise of Kriophoros, the "ram-bearer." According to one legend, to ward off plague, Hermes carried a ram around the walls of Tanagra, a city north of Athens. Stories such as this one likely helped fuel a belief that the god would provide protection from harm if plied with gifts and prayers, and this bronze statuette may have been offered as a votive at one of his sanctuaries. The distinctive costume helps identify him: winged sandals allude to his swiftness in relaying information, while his broad-brimmed *petasos*, associated with travel and rural life, denotes Hermes's role as divine patron of shepherds. Notice his stance, with one straight leg thrust in front of the other. While not entirely naturalistic, it lends the sculpture a lively sense of motion—fitting for a god constantly on the move.

Bronze

H. 9⅞ in. (25 cm)

Henry Lillie Pierce Fund   99.489

Upper part of a grave stele
Greek
Archaic period, about 530 B.C.

The sphinx, like the lion, was favored as a guardian figure and often placed on grave monuments to protect the deceased from malevolent forces in this world and the next. This sphinx, crouching on a capital that originally surmounted a tall shaft, is all taut curves; her wings and haunches are lifted, her body ready to spring. The sculpture is expertly carved of warm, golden marble and traces remain of its original painted decoration—the hair was black, for example, and the wing feathers alternately green, black, red, and blue. Grave monuments of this quality and complexity could only have been afforded by the rich, and sometime after the mid-sixth century B.C., laws against ostentatious display put an end to their production. Almost every surviving example was deliberately broken in antiquity, possibly during a period of civil unrest; the Museum's sculpture is in unusually good condition.

Marble
H. 55¾ in. (141.7 cm)
1931 and 1939 Purchase Funds   40.576

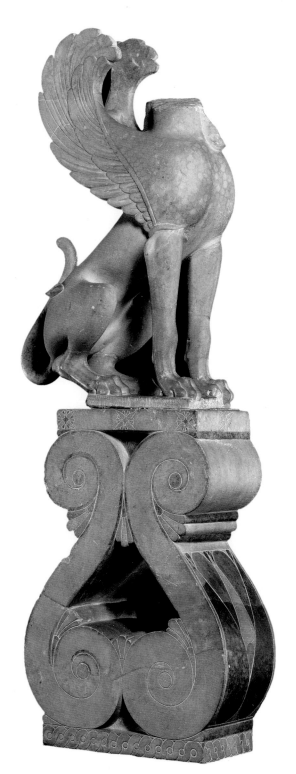

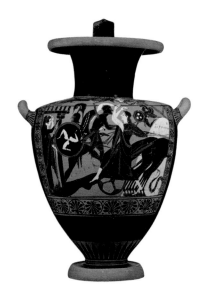

Water jar (*hydria*)
Greek
Archaic period, about 520–510 B.C.
Attributed to the **Antiope Group**

The Trojan War was a favorite subject among Greek vase painters. This Athenian *hydria* depicts the harrowing story of the Greek hero Achilles, whose best friend Patroklos was killed in battle by the Trojan prince Hector. Distraught and thirsting for revenge, Achilles killed Hector and defiled the body by dragging it behind his chariot. The painter has abridged the story, compressing two locations and the events of three days into a single image. Achilles (holding a round shield) mounts the chariot to which Hector's body is bound. Hector's grieving parents stand in a portico at left. At the far right, beyond the horses, is Patroklos's tomb. The winged female figure is Iris, sent by the gods to urge Hector's father to offer ransom for his son's body and so end its brutal violation. The whole composition — packed with detail and the vigorous movement of overlapping forms — is anchored in the center by the stern, anonymous figure of the charioteer.

Ceramic
H. 19¾ in. (50 cm)
William Francis Warden Fund   63.473

Bowl for mixing wine and water (*krater*)
Greek
Early Classical period, about 460 B.C.
The **Dokimasia Painter**

On his return from the Trojan War, Agamemnon, commander of the victorious Greek army, was murdered by his wife, Clytemnestra, and her lover, Aegisthus. On this Athenian *krater*, Aegisthus, grasping Agamemnon's head, has plunged his sword into his victim's body and prepares to strike again. Clytemnestra, bearing an ax, is close behind. The sense of urgency and drama is conveyed in the swing of draperies and the bold gestures that resonate against the empty spaces of the background. The figure of Agamemnon is extraordinary, naked and helpless in a snare made of sheer and costly fabric. In Aeschylus's play *Agamemnon* (first presented in 458 B.C., soon after this vase was painted), Clytemnestra describes this moment:

> He had no way to flee or fight his destiny —
> our never-ending, all embracing net, I cast it
> wide for the royal haul, I coil him round and round
> in the wealth, the robes of doom. . . .

Ceramic
H. 20⅛ in. (51 cm)
William Francis Warden Fund   63.1246

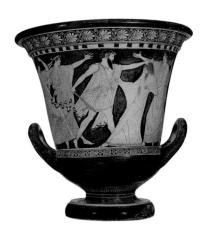

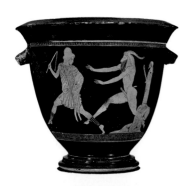

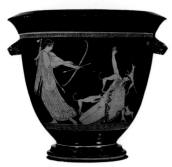

Bowl for mixing wine and water (*krater*)
Greek
Early Classical period, about 470 B.C.
The **Pan Painter**

This *krater* is among the greatest of all Athenian painted vessels. One side of the *krater* shows one of the first representations in Greek art of Pan, the goat god. Across the vessel's broad surface, Pan pursues a frightened young shepherd; the god's impressive erection is echoed in the herm, a kind of pillar with the head of the god Hermes that marked the intersections of roads.

The image on the other side of the *krater,* although inherently more brutal, is as lyrical as the depiction of Pan and the shepherd is explosively energetic. It shows the death of Aktaion at the hands of Artemis, goddess of the hunt. Aktaion had angered Artemis, and she caused his own hounds to turn on him and tear him to pieces. As Artemis leans back to draw the arrow she will not need, Aktaion falls before the onslaught of the dogs.

Ceramic
H. 14⅝ in. (37 cm)
James Fund and Museum purchase with funds donated by subscription   10.185

Covered drinking cup (*kylix*)
Greek
Classical period, about 460–450 B.C.
Possibly by the **Carlsruhe Painter**

Both the form and decoration of this Athenian cup are extremely unusual. The cover, seen here from above, was not designed to open. The cup was filled through a hollow in its stemmed base, and libations were poured out through the opening in the cover. Most Greek vessels were painted either in the black-figure or red-figure technique. This cup, however, is decorated with the white-ground technique, in which a layer of white slip (a thin mixture of fine clay and water) was applied to all or part of a vessel. The figures were drawn in outline on the unfired clay and painted with a range of delicate colors. Because many of these colors were subject to deterioration, white-ground vessels were primarily reserved for ritual or funerary use. This one depicts the god Apollo opening

his cloak to reveal himself (both actually and meta-phorically) to one of the nine Muses, goddesses of the arts, whom he led and inspired.

Ceramic
Diam. 6½ in. (16.6 cm)
Henry Lillie Pierce Fund   00.356

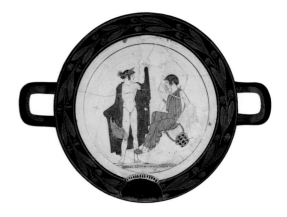

Three-sided relief
Greek
Classical period, about 450–440 B.C.

This monumental sculpture forms the front of a three-sided marble structure that probably served as a windbreak to protect sacrifices being burned on an altar. It depicts Eros, god of love, weighing two small spirits on a balance (the lost arm of which was secured in the three rectangular holes). On the right is Demeter, goddess of agriculture, and on the left is Aphrodite, goddess of love, fertility, and fate.

The sculpture is closely related to the so-called Ludovisi relief, found in Rome in 1887, and it has been challenged as a forgery inspired by the Ludovisi sculpture. However, recent scientific examination has shown that both reliefs are made of the same rather rare marble, and that the Boston relief shows evidence of ancient weathering. It is possible that both sculptures were brought to Rome years after they were carved and placed in a sanctuary.

Marble
32⅜ x 63⅜ in. (82 x 161 cm)
Henry Lillie Pierce Fund   08.205

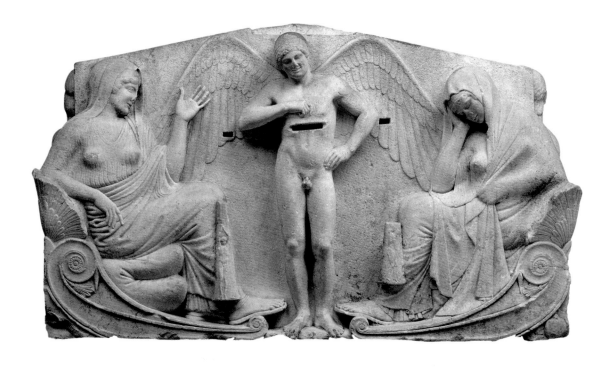

Two-handled jar (*amphora*)
Greek
Archaic period, about 525–520 B.C.
The **Andokides Painter** and the **Lysippides Painter**

Both sides of this Athenian vase depict the legendary strong man Herakles driving a bull. In design the
scenes are almost identical, but in other ways they
are completely different. Their differences illustrate
the two main styles of Greek vase painting known,
appropriately enough, as black-figure and red-figure.
Black-figure vases were made by painting a design
on an unfired pot with slip (a thin, paint-like mixture
of clay and water). The artist then scratched in the
details of the design, such as the ribs on the bull's
flank, revealing the main body of the vase underneath.
Although they were the same color when wet, the slip
and the clay of the vase took on different colors (red
and black) when baked in the kiln. Red-figure vases
were made in exactly the opposite way. The artists
painted the whole vase with slip except for the design,
which was left unpainted. Details such as Herakles's
lion skin were then drawn with slip.

This vase was painted by two different artists in
two different styles. By law, potters and painters all
worked in the same part of Athens, creating ample
opportunity for artistic exchange. "Bilingual" vases
such as this one, featuring both red- and black-figure
paintings, date from about the time of the introduction of the red-figure technique. They were most likely
made to show the strengths of each style, the old and
the new, perhaps as an advertisement to potential
customers.

Ceramic
H. 20⅞ in. (53.2 cm)
Henry Lillie Pierce Fund   99.538

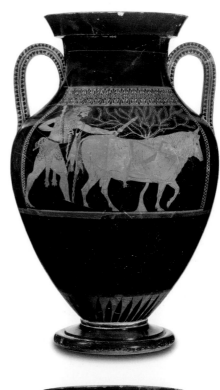

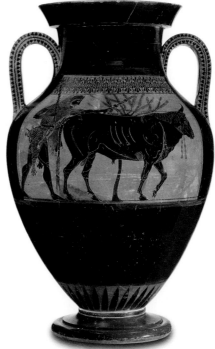

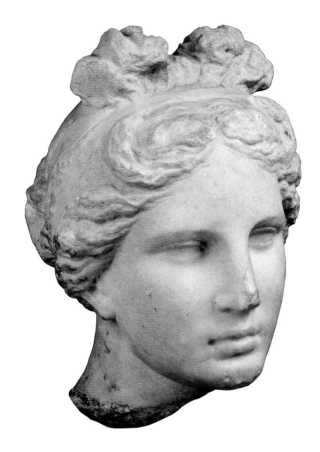

Earring

Greek

Late Classical or Early Hellenistic period, about 350–325 B.C.

Two inches high, this earring was perhaps created to adorn the statue of a deity. It represents Nike, goddess of victory, a symbol of success in war and other contests. She is depicted driving a chariot, her face focused and determined, her wings sweeping behind her. She holds her horses on a tight rein, and they rear sharply, muscles tensed. Every detail of Nike's costume and the harness of her horses is minutely rendered—hundreds of tiny pieces of gold soldered together with marvelous precision to create a harmonious whole.

Gold
H. 2 in. (5 cm)
Henry Lillie Pierce Fund   98.788

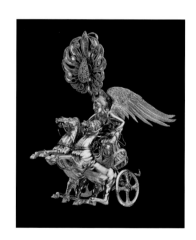

Aphrodite

Greek

Late Classical or Early Hellenistic period, about 330–300 B.C.

This sensuous and beautiful head is one of the finest surviving Greek sculptures of the late Classical period. It represents Aphrodite, goddess of love, and was originally set into a full-length statue. The sculpture's idealized grace, subtle modeling, and contrasting textures of skin and hair recall the workmanship and revolutionary style of Praxiteles, among the most celebrated of all classical sculptors. Greek sculptures of this period and quality are very rare, and most are known today primarily through later Roman copies.

Marble
H. 11¼ in. (28.8 cm)
Francis Bartlett Donation of 1900   03.743

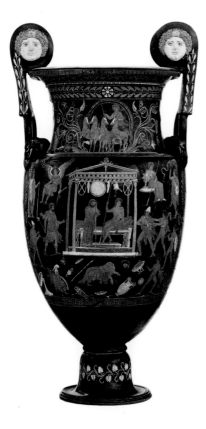

Oil bottle (*lekythos*)
Greek
Late Classical period, mid-4th century B.C.

The body of this Athenian vessel depicts the birth of the goddess Aphrodite from the sea. Framed by the scallop shell in which, according to legend, she sailed to the island of Cyprus, she is accompanied by two erotes, their wings lifted to catch the ocean breezes. At once delicate and extravagant, this vessel—appropriately decorated with the goddess of love and beauty—probably held precious perfumes or oils.

Ceramic
H. 7½ in. (19 cm)
Museum purchase with funds donated by Mrs. Samuel Torrey Morse   00.629

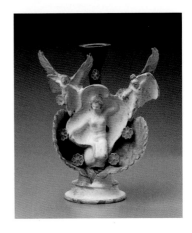

Vessel for mixing wine and water (*krater*)
Greek, South Italian
Late Classical period, about 340 B.C.

The Greek colonists who settled on the coast of Italy maintained close contact with their homeland, and South Italian vases derive from Greek models. Indeed, early examples were often made by immigrant Greek craftsmen. This sumptuously ornamented *krater* is among the finest (and largest) South Italian vases from the area of Apulia and is painted with a complex, multifigured composition that emphasizes dramatic expression and gesture. The subject is an event of the Trojan War. The Greek hero Achilles, seated within a pavilion, has just beheaded Thersites, the Greek soldier whom Homer called "the most obnoxious rogue who ever went to Troy." All around, mortals and deities are identified by neat inscriptions. The large size of this *krater* suggests that it was probably made for burial in the tomb of an important person rather than for actual use.

Ceramic
H. 49⅛ in. (124.6 cm)
Francis Bartlett Donation of 1900   03.804

Cinerary urn

Etruscan

Hellenistic period, late 3rd century B.C.

This urn contained the ashes of Fastia Velsi, wife of Larza Velu; her name is inscribed on the rim of the cover, and her idealized portrait reclines on top. On the front of the urn is an image of Scylla, a marine monster with the body of a woman and fishtails for legs. It was probably placed there to protect Fastia Velsi's remains, as many Etruscans believed the journey to the Underworld included a perilous sea voyage. The urn is said to have been found in Chiusi, in a chamber tomb with those of four other upper-class women of the Velsi family, surrounded by gaming pieces, mirrors, jewelry, and other luxury goods for use in the afterlife. The urn originally was painted, and the many traces of pigment are a rare survival.

Limestone (possibly travertine)
41 x 29½ in. (104 x 75 cm)
Francis Bartlett Donation of 1912   13.2860a

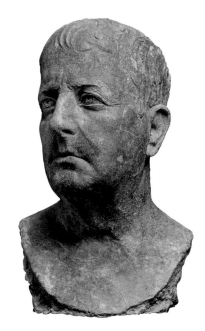

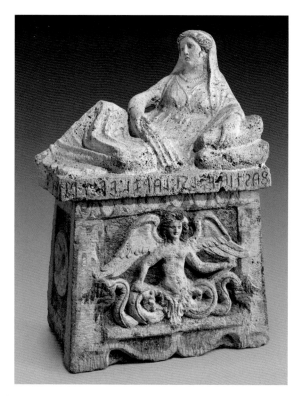

Portrait of a man

Roman

Republican period, about 50 B.C.

The striking naturalism that emerged in Roman portrait sculpture of the late Republican period is unparalleled in the ancient world. Nevertheless, it does reflect the influence of other civilizations, particularly that of the Etruscans, whose impact on Roman culture ranged from funerary customs to architecture and city planning. Such portraits as this one expressed the Roman conviction that a person's individuality was seen solely in the face. Possibly a preparatory study for a sculpture in bronze or marble, this terra-cotta bust unflinchingly records signs of aging that would have been appreciated as marks of experience and wisdom. Interestingly, only mature individuals seem to have been considered subjects worthy of major portraiture in this period.

Terra-cotta
H. 14⅛ in. (35.7 cm)
Museum purchase with funds donated by contribution
01.8008

Sarcophagus lid

Etruscan

Late Classical or Hellenistic period, late 4th or early
3rd century B.C.

This stone sarcophagus lid, found in the cemetery of
Vulci, is carved with the image of a married couple
whose affectionate embrace conveys the continuation
of their love for all eternity. Only the woman's name,
Ramtha Visnai, is inscribed on the sarcophagus, and
she may have been buried alone in it. However, it is
possible that the body of her husband was interred
later and his name added in paint that has since worn
away. This type of sarcophagus lid, which originally
would have been painted, is uniquely Etruscan, and
very few examples survive. Two are in the Museum
collection; the other was apparently made for this
couple's son, Larth Tetnies, and his wife.

Volcanic tuff
82¾ x 28¾ x 34⅝ in. (210 x 73 x 88 cm)
Museum purchase with funds by exchange from a
Gift of Mr. and Mrs. Cornelius C. Vermeule III   1975.799

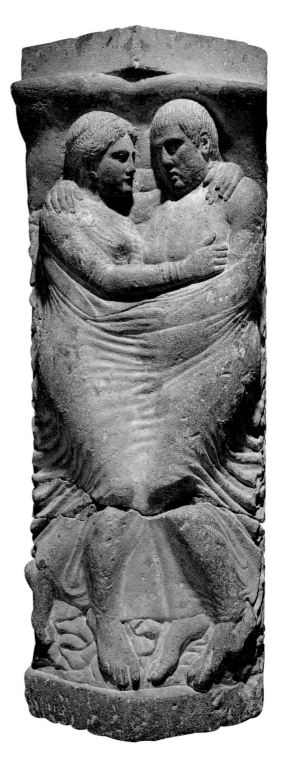

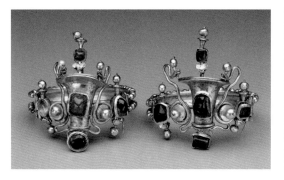

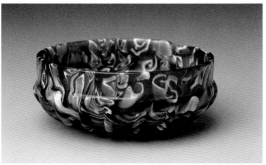

Bracelets
Greek or Roman
Late Hellenistic or early Imperial period, about
40–20 B.C.

Although it is not known where these opulent bracelets were made, they may be from Egypt; similar
examples are painted on representations of the
deceased on mummy shrouds of Egypt's early Roman
period. The gold bands are studded with two rows
of pearls and hinged to a central projecting ornament surrounded with emeralds and coiling snakes
crowned with pearls. In the classical imagination,
snakes were beneficent creatures associated with
Asklepios, god of health, and with the revels of
Bacchus (Dionysos), god of wine and nature. In Egypt,
the snake was an emblem of the creator god, Atum,
and the green color of emeralds was associated with
Osiris, god of the Underworld, and with the concept
of rebirth.

Gold, emeralds, and pearls (modern)
H. 2¾ in. (6.4 cm)
Classical Department Exchange Fund   1981.287–288

Bowl
Roman
Late Republican or Imperial period, late 1st century
B.C. or early 1st century A.D.

Roman glass was widely produced and universally
admired in ancient times. Many richly colored glass
objects were made in the city of Alexandria, in Egypt,
which was a major center for the production of luxury
goods during the Roman Empire. This bowl was
made by assembling slices or spirals of multicolored
glass canes into molds that were then placed into a
furnace for slow fusing. After the discovery of the
technique of glassblowing in the mid-first century
B.C., glass became readily available and affordable.
Nevertheless, objects made by such complex and
labor-intensive techniques continued to be highly
prized. Very little ancient glass has survived unaffected by the moisture and acids of the soil in which
it was buried.

Mosaic glass
H. 1¾ in. (4.4 cm)
Henry Lillie Pierce Fund   99.442

Juno

Roman

Late 1st century B.C.–early 1st century A.D. (body) and 2nd century A.D. (head)

At thirteen feet tall and more than six tons, this commanding statue is the largest Classical sculpture in the United States. The diadem and facial features identify her as the Roman goddess Juno, protector and special counselor of the state, and wife of Jupiter, king of the gods. Made in Rome, Juno would have originally stood within a large architectural complex. The body, which once belonged to a muse, was carved more than a century earlier than the head, which was added sometime later.

Although the date of Juno's discovery is unknown, by 1633 she was listed in the posthumous inventory of Cardinal Ludovico Ludovisi's vast art collection in Rome. After that collection's dispersal in the late nineteenth century, the sculpture was shipped across the Atlantic, arriving at a private estate in Brookline, Massachusetts, in 1904. It stood there, just a few miles from the MFA, for more than a century before coming to the Museum in 2012.

Marble
H. 160½ in. (407.7 cm)
Museum purchase with funds donated anonymously   2011.75

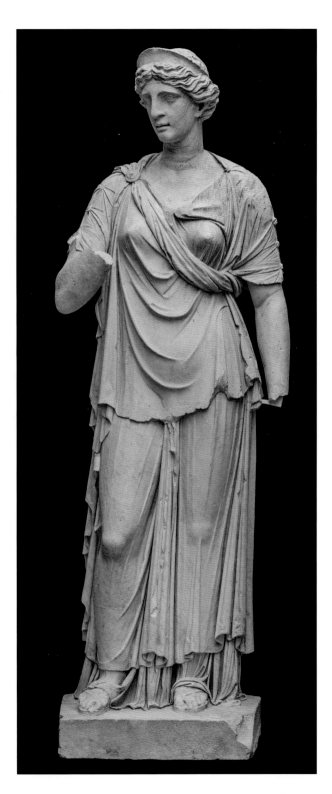

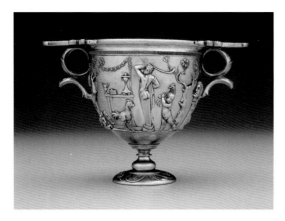

Two-handled cup (*skyphos*)
Roman
Early Imperial period, A.D. 1–30

This silver wine cup was probably made during one of the most extravagant periods of Roman history—the reigns of the emperors Augustus and Tiberius. Such superbly made and expensive objects were avidly collected, and this taste for luxury could be carried to excess; the historian Pliny noted that the Roman governor of Lower Germany carried "12,000 pounds weight of silver plate with him when on service with an army confronted by tribes of the greatest ferocity."

The cup is decorated with scenes showing the preparations for a sacrifice in honor of Bacchus (Dionysos), god of wine, fertility, and good times. The plain background sets off the poses of the figures, and the outdoor setting is filled with sacrificial equipment—a portable altar and offering table, an incense burner, cups for wine—all rendered with precision and delicate detail. Two thousand years after its creation, the cup is in remarkable condition.

Silver with traces of gold leaf
H. 4⅜ in. (11.1 cm)
William Francis Warden Fund, Frank B. Bemis Fund,
John H. and Ernestine Payne Fund and William E. Nickerson
Fund   1997.83

The playwright Menander
Roman
Imperial period, late 1st century B.C. or
early 1st century A.D.

The Roman conquest of Greek colonies in southern Italy and ultimately of Greece itself led to a passionate appreciation and emulation of Greek culture, of which this bust is evidence. It represents the playwright Menander and was probably modeled after a statue that stood in or near a theater in Athens. The Greek sculptures that Roman armies brought back to Rome were set up in public places throughout the city, and wealthy Romans commissioned local artists to make the copies and adaptations to which we owe much of our knowledge of lost Greek masterworks.

This idealized image of a somber, handsome man takes the form of a herm—a roadside marker often found in the Greek countryside—and has holes in the sides of the shoulders for wooden inserts designed to be hung with garlands.

Marble
H. 20¼ in. (51.5 cm)
Catharine Page Perkins Fund   97.288

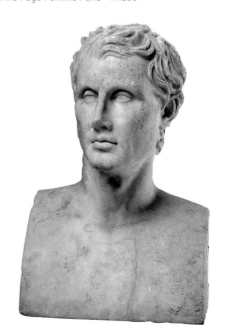

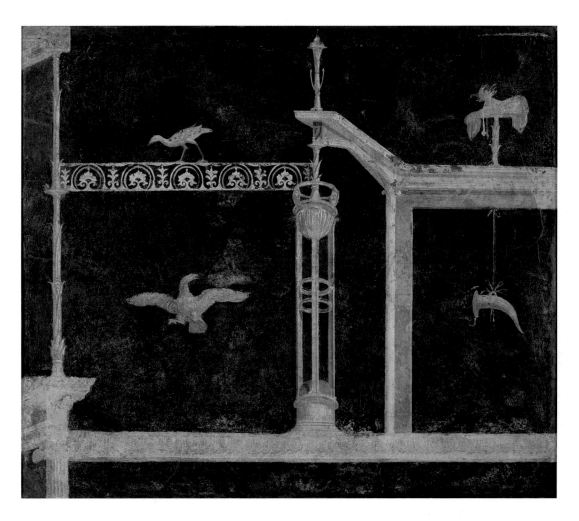

Wall painting

Roman

Imperial period, about A.D. 14–62

This is one of an extraordinary group of Roman wall paintings in the Museum's collection that was excavated in the early twentieth century from the Contrada Bottaro Villa, near Pompeii. The villa and the paintings on its walls were superbly preserved when buried in molten lava by the eruption of Mount Vesuvius in A.D. 79. Known as the Third Style of Campanian wall painting, the decoration of this image incorporates delicate and fanciful architectural elements and floral and figural details, all silhouetted against an expanse of color that respects and emphasizes the flat, solid surface of the wall. In Herculaneum and Pompeii, where middle-class Romans had second homes, almost every room in every house was painted. In no other society was so much effort bestowed on decorating ordinary living spaces, and such painting attracted the most talented artists of the period.

Fresco

38¼ x 46 in. (97 x 117 cm)

Richard Norton Memorial Fund   25.45

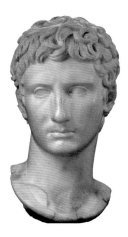

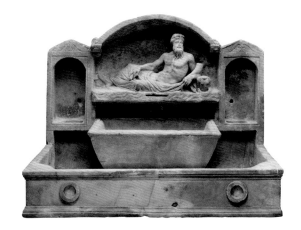

The emperor Augustus
Roman
Imperial period, 1st or 2nd century A.D.

Augustus (63 B.C.–A.D. 14), the designated heir of his great-uncle Julius Caesar, was Rome's first emperor and began a long imperial tradition of commissioning art as a form of political propaganda. In the previous, late Republican period, young people were seldom considered deserving of political or artistic consideration. Therefore, when Augustus became emperor at the age of thirty-two, artists looked for inspiration to fifth-century Greece, a time when youthful beauty was much admired. Until his death at seventy-six, Augustus was always represented as a handsome young man with a full head of thick curls. As imperial icons, these idealized portraits continued to be made long after the emperor's death. This superb example, which was probably inserted into a full-length statue, may have been created for a private villa near Rome.

Marble
H. 17 in. (43.3 cm)
Henry Lillie Pierce Fund   99.344

Fountain basin
Roman
Imperial period, about A.D. 98–138

This unique and complex fountain, which reflects ancient Roman fascination with Egypt, probably came from the courtyard of a private villa near Rome. It is highly unusual among surviving objects of its type in that it creates an architectural setting for water, a sophisticated arrangement of boxes within boxes, each a different shape. Water splashed into the basins from the niches in the back, flowing out through holes in the front. The delicately modeled figure is Nilus, god of the Nile, identified by the sphinx on which he leans. He holds a cornucopia in one hand and may have held a sheaf of grain in the other—both symbolic of the agricultural prosperity that the Nile brings to Egypt. The side niches once contained statuettes of water nymphs, perhaps representing the daughters of Nilus.

Marble
26 x 34⅝ x 29⅛ in. (66 x 88 x 74 cm)
Museum purchase with funds by exchange from a Gift of Mr. and Mrs. Henry P. Kidder, a Gift of Thomas Gold Appleton, a Gift of Edward Jackson Holmes, a Gift of Mrs. Francis C. Lowell, Otis Norcross Fund, and a Gift of Edward Perry Warren   2002.21

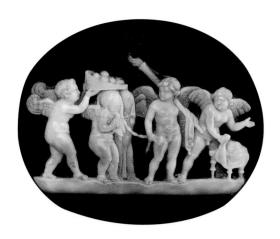

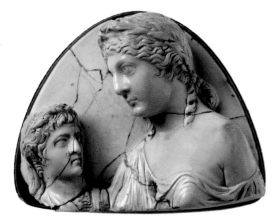

Cameo

Roman

Late Republican or early Imperial period,
mid- to late 1st century B.C.

Signed by **Tryphon**

The carving of tiny images on precious stones was
a Greek art form that was later enthusiastically
adopted by the Romans. In the first century, the
Roman scholar Pliny wrote in his *Natural History*:
"Very many people find that a single gemstone alone
is enough to provide them with a supreme and perfect
aesthetic experience of the wonders of Nature." This
cameo—a stone carved in relief on one layer against
the background of a lower, contrasting layer—depicts
the marriage of Cupid and Psyche. Venus, goddess
of love and beauty, was so jealous of the beautiful
Psyche that she sent Cupid to make Psyche fall in love
with some insignificant man. Predictably, Cupid fell
in love with Psyche himself, and after many tribula-
tions the enamored couple was brought to heaven
and married. This cameo, which bears a signature
("Tryphon made it"), once belonged to the celebrated
Flemish artist Peter Paul Rubens, a self-proclaimed
"lover of antiquities."

Onyx
1½ x 1¾ in. (3.7 x 4.5 cm)
Henry Lillie Pierce Fund   99.101

Cameo

Roman

Imperial period, A.D. 14–37

In Roman times, high officials and members of the
imperial family often commissioned carved gem-
stones as private or official gifts. To promote imperial
power and political ideology, images of the emperor
Augustus and his family were disseminated throughout the vast Roman Empire. Coins placed such images
in the hands of Roman citizens of every class, but
precious cameos were special gifts. This exquisite
example, made of turquoise, depicts Augustus's
widow, Livia, holding a bust of her deceased husband.
Although created late in her life, the cameo shows the
empress as a lovely young woman; indeed, she is represented as Venus—an acknowledgment of the fact
that, in his will, Augustus declared his wife a member
of the family of Julius Caesar, whose patron goddess
was Venus.

Turquoise
1¼ x 1½ in. (3.1 x 3.8 cm)
Henry Lillie Pierce Fund   99.109

Portrait of a man

Roman

Imperial period, about A.D. 200–230

This remarkable head once belonged to a painted, life-sized statue made of costly bronze. The portrait is a private one, very different from the idealized images created for public display, with politics and propaganda in mind (see page 82). Portraits such as this one were not serially produced; the sculptor studied the sitter in person and worked directly on a wax cast of his clay model. Here, the tool marks are still evident, giving the work a fresh immediacy — the wrinkled brow, sunken eyes, and creased forehead of an individual. The realistic style of portraiture was popular in the Roman Republic (see page 76) — this work reflects its revival three hundred years later. This sculpture may have been reused on a triumphal arch erected on a bridge over Rome's Tiber River. It is believed to have been recovered from the river in the late nineteenth century.

Bronze
H. 12¼ in. (31 cm)
Catharine Page Perkins Fund   96.703

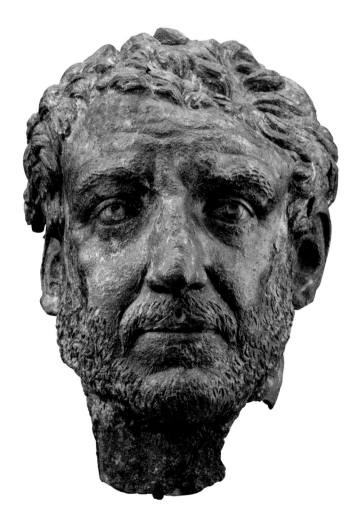

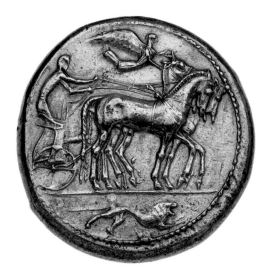
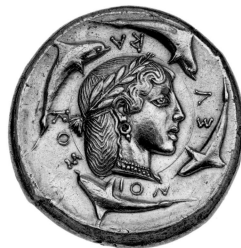

Ten drachma coin

Greek, mint of Syracuse (Sicily)

Early Classical period, about 465 B.C.

Silver

Diam. 1⅜ in. (3.5 cm)

Theodora Wilbour Fund in memory of Zoë Wilbour 35.21

Denarius commemorating the assassination of Julius Caesar

Roman, northern Greek mint

Late Republican period, 43–42 B.C.

Silver

Diam. ¾ in. (2 cm)

Theodora Wilbour Fund in memory of Zoë Wilbour 2002.129

Coins throughout their history have always been more than money: if these little pieces of metal were simply currency, they could be blank (or nearly so). However, coins are ambassadors, and the symbols they bear matter. Greek city-states began issuing coins decorated with local gods and symbols as early as the seventh century B.C. The Syracusan ten-drachma piece illustrates a format still seen on most modern coins: a head on one side (the nymph Arethusa, associated with a famous spring in Syracuse) with a more complicated scene on the other (Nike, goddess of victory, crowning the horses of a victorious racing team).

About the time of Alexander the Great (356–323 B.C.), kings and emperors began celebrating their reigns by issuing coins bearing their own images. The Romans took up the habit with enthusiasm. This silver coin (_denarius_) commemorates the Ides of March, the day in 44 B.C. on which Julius Caesar was assassinated by a group of senators led by Brutus, whose portrait appears on the obverse of the coin. On the reverse is a _pileus_ (a felt cap symbolizing the liberty that Caesar's murder was designed to obtain), flanked by two daggers and the inscription EID.MAR (Ides of March). Perhaps inspired by Shakespeare's play _Julius Caesar_, March 15 remains an unlucky day in the popular imagination.

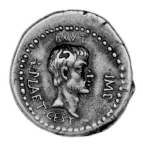
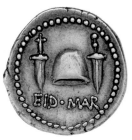

Athena Parthenos
Roman
Imperial period, 2nd or 3rd century A.D.

A monumental figure of Athena Parthenos, the masterpiece of the sculptor Phidias, was the principal image
in the Parthenon, the temple dedicated to Athena that
still crowns the Acropolis in Athens. Made between
447 and 438 B.C., Phidias's statue of the goddess of
wisdom was sheathed in ivory and gold and stood
almost forty feet high. It was gone from the Acropolis by about A.D. 450 (possibly destroyed by fire), but
before that time numerous copies had been made for
export throughout the Mediterranean world.

   This small replica is one of the most accurate
known, preserving details—found in no other copy—
that match a description of the original written about
A.D. 150 by the Greek traveler and writer Pausanias.
Athena's aegis—a breastplate emblematic of majesty—is adorned with twining snakes and an image
of one of the Gorgons, fearsome sisters of Greek
mythology whose glance had the power to turn people
to stone.

Marble
H. 60⅝ in. (154 cm)
Classical Department Exchange Fund   1980.196

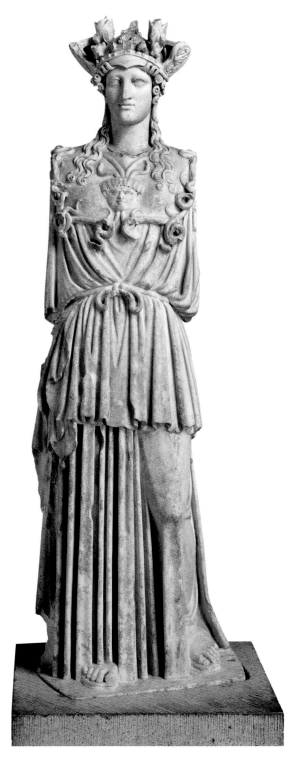

Homer

Roman

Late Republican or Imperial
period, late 1st century B.C. or
1st century A.D.

Although the ancient Greeks
believed that the great epics the
Iliad and the *Odyssey* were the
work of the poet Homer, reliable
information about the poet's life
was as elusive then as it is today.
This sculpture, therefore, is not
a real portrait but a conceptual
image of creative genius: the
unruly hair and knitted brow
suggest intensity and passion;
the worn, furrowed face reflects
experience; the eyes, sightless in
accordance with ancient tradition,
reflect the belief that Homer and
other great bards saw beyond this
world and into the future.

   Probably once set into a seated
statue, this head is the best of
many Roman copies of a lost Greek
sculpture from the Hellenistic
period, a time in which art was
characterized by an interest in
expressiveness, naturalistic detail,
and technical virtuosity.

Marble
H. 16⅛ in. (41 cm)
Henry Lillie Pierce Fund   04.13

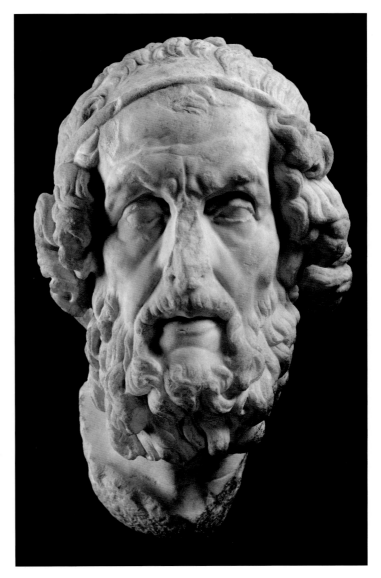

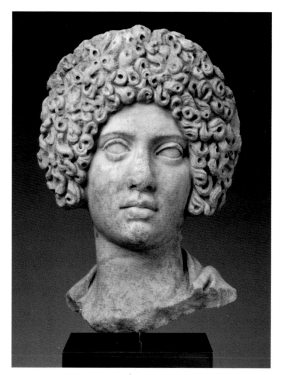

Portrait of a woman
Roman
Imperial period, A.D. 100–125

This unknown woman's full lips and sweet expression suggest portraiture, but the sculpture is really about the extravagant hairstyle, made up of tight curls twisted into a great crest. Behind this "facade" the hair is wound into a wide, flat bun. Such a coiffure may have been inspired by the masks worn by actors although, in a more subdued form, it had been made popular decades earlier by women of the imperial family. With great skill, the artist used a drill to create the strong contrasts of light and shadow that give substance and vitality to the marble curls.

Marble
H. 13¾ in. (35 cm)
Gift of Samuel and Edward Merrin and Museum purchase with funds by exchange from the Benjamin and Lucy Rowland Collection and a Gift of Barbara Deering Danielson, and the William Francis Warden Fund   1992.575

Funerary relief
Roman
Imperial period, about A.D. 150–200

The Syrian city of Palmyra was a major commercial hub for the merchants that traded between the Persian Gulf and the Mediterranean. There the cultures of east and west met and fused, creating an artistic style unique in the Roman world. This Palmyrene funerary monument is inscribed in Greek: "Aththaia, daughter of Malchos, Happy One, Farewell." Adorned for eternity, Aththaia wears jewelry that reflects the taste and craftsmanship of the Greek, Roman, and Near Eastern cultures that shaped her city—elaborate pendant earrings, a large circular pin, two signet rings on her left hand, a betrothal or wedding ring on her right, bracelets made of twisted gold or silver, and two necklaces. All this jewelry has been rendered with such precision that this relief and others like it are invaluable resources for charting the fluctuations of fashion among the prosperous residents of ancient Palmyra.

Limestone
21⅝ x 16½ in. (55 x 42 cm)
Museum purchase with funds donated by Edward Perry Warren in memory of his sister   22.659

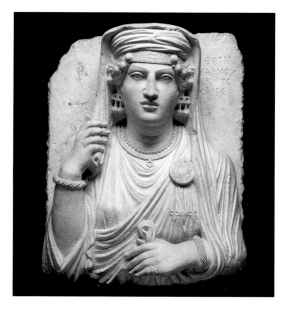

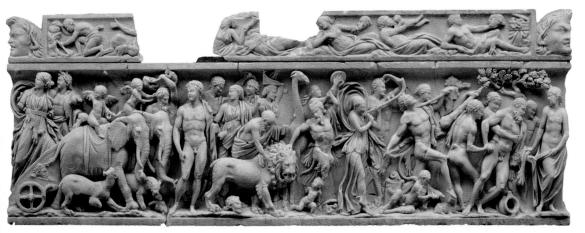

Sarcophagus

Roman

Imperial period, about A.D. 215–25

The scene that sweeps along the side of this sarcophagus depicts the triumphant return of the god Bacchus
(Dionysos) from India, where he had been spreading
his cult of joyous physical abandon. On the left edge,
Bacchus steps into a chariot drawn by two Indian
elephants. Before him, his merrymaking attendants
(many part-human, part-beast) celebrate with wine,
dance, and music. At the far right is Hercules, who
has lost a drinking contest to Bacchus and staggers
toward a coyly welcoming maenad, one of Bacchus's
lustful female followers. Almost every inch of the
relief is covered with figures of astonishing variety
and vitality, carved in such high relief that some are
almost free of the block.

Marble
30½ x 81⅞ in. (77.5 x 208 cm)
William Francis Warden Fund   1972.650

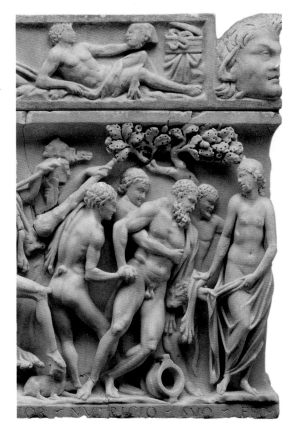

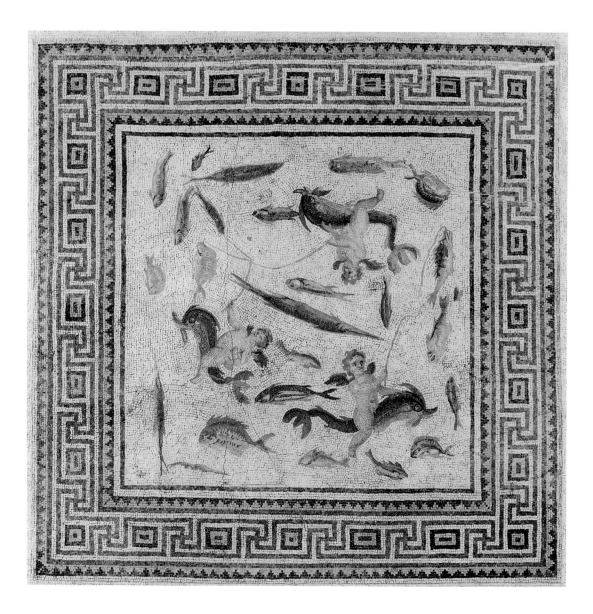

Mosaic
Roman
Imperial period, A.D. 200–30

About nine feet square, this mosaic was excavated in the 1930s in Seleucia Pieria, the port of Antioch (present-day Antakya, Turkey). It once paved the court-yard of an early-third-century Roman house where diners reclined on couches and enjoyed spectacular views of the Mediterranean Sea and the mountains of Syria. At one end of the courtyard, a fountain provided the refreshing sound of water. The preeminent picto-rial medium of the time, mosaics are made of tesserae, small cubes of stone or glass, skillfully set into lime mortar to create painterly effects of shading and mod-eling. In this mosaic, cupids riding on dolphins fish in the sea, with twenty-five varieties of saltwater fish (expensive, and symbols of status) are recognizably depicted. Evocative of its now-lost domestic setting, this mosaic is particularly valuable for its documented architectural and archaeological setting. Beginning in 2004, the Museum spent two years cleaning, stabiliz-ing, and restoring the mosaic for display.

Stone and glass tesserae
114¾ x 113 in. (291.5 x 287 cm)
Museum purchase and conservation with funds donated by

George D. and Margo Behrakis, The Getty Foundation, Jane's Trust, John F. Cogan, Jr. and Mary L. Cornille, Daphne and George Hatsopoulos, the Estate of Dr. Harold Amos, Peter and Widgie Aldrich, Mrs. I. W. Colburn, Mary B. Comstock, The Hellenic Women's Club, Inc., an anonymous donor, Katherine R. Kirk, Peter Vlachos, Mrs. James Evans Ladd, Irene and Grier Merwin, Suzanne R. Dworsky, Mr. and Mrs. Robert K. Faulkner, Francis J. Jackson and Nancy M. McMahon, Meg Holmes Robbins, Otis Norcross Fund, Helen and Alice Colburn Fund, Arthur Tracy Cabot Fund, Charles Amos Cummings Fund, and by exchange from the John Wheelock Elliot Fund, Henry Lillie Pierce Fund, Benjamin Pierce Cheney Donation, Bequest of Benjamin Rowland, Jr., Gift of a "class of young ladies," Museum purchase by contribution, Gift of Barbara Deering Danielson, General Funds, William Sturgis Bigelow Collection, Gift of Mr. and Mrs. G. W. Wales, Gift of Paul E. Manheim, Bequest of Mrs. May Sheppard Jordan, Gift of Mr. and Mrs. William de Forest Thomson, Francis Bartlett Donation, Gift of James Howe Proctor, Gift of Benjamin W. Crowninshield, Gift of the Estate of Dana Estes, Gift of Thomas Gold Appleton, Gift of Edward Perry Warren, Gift of an anonymous donor, Gift of Francis Amory, Gift of J. J. Dixwell, Gift of Edward Austin, Gift of Edward Robinson, Gift of Horace L. Mayer, Everett Fund, Gift of the Misses Norton, Gift of the Misses Amy and Clara Curtis, Gift of Charles C. Perkins, Gift of Mrs. Walter Scott Fitz, Gift of Harold Murdock in memory of his brother, Rear-Admiral J. B. Murdock, Gift of the Estate of Alfred Greenough, and Gift of Edward Southworth Hawes   2002.128.1

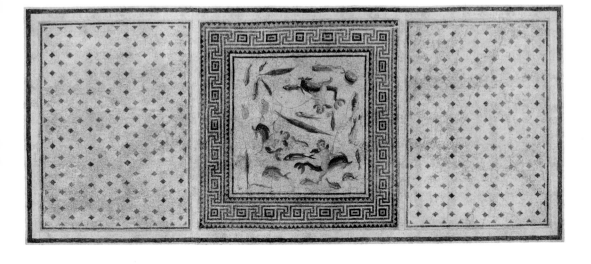

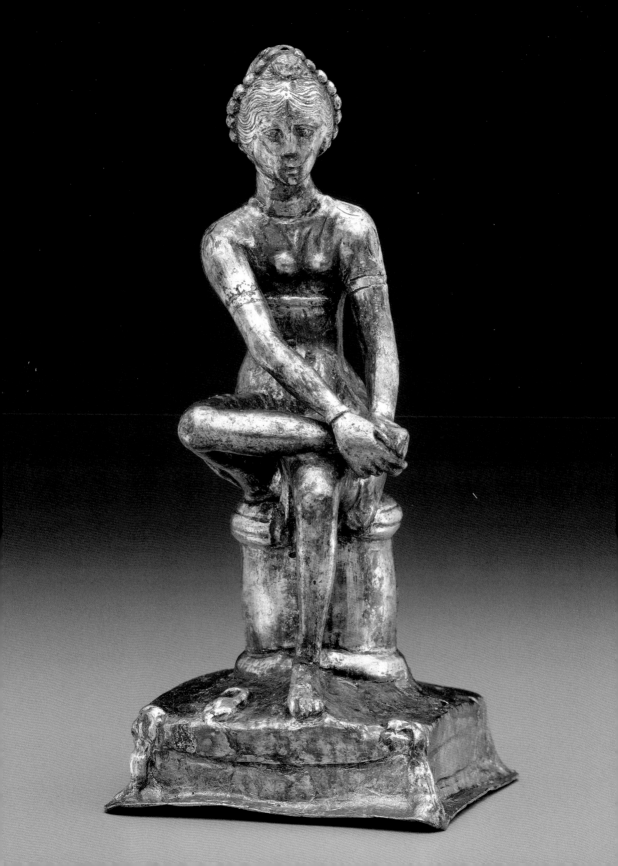

opposite

Seated dancer

Roman

Late Imperial period, late 4th century A.D.

A dancer sits on a stool, massaging her tired foot and perhaps preparing to put on the slipper that rests on the sculpture's rectangular base. Images of seated figures adjusting a sandal or slipper had a long history in ancient Greek sculpture. The artist who created this figurine hundreds of years later, in the late Roman Imperial period, clearly was still attracted by classical ideals of grace and beauty. The sculpture is exquisitely worked, cast in silver with lion-headed supports at the corners of the base and details of hair, costume, and jewelry picked out in gold.

Silver with gold details
H. 4¾ in. (12 cm)
Frederick Brown Fund   69.72

Neck ornament

Found in Egypt

Late Antique period, 4th century A.D.

This tapestry-woven neck ornament with a jeweled neck band and end panels decorated with mythological figures on a purple ground illustrates the richness of clothing decoration. Originally part of a linen tunic, the ornament is woven in fine wool, linen, and gold-wrapped silk yarns. The tapestry weaver enhanced the richness of the design by using gold-wrapped thread as well as vividly dyed wool yarns. The purple wool of the ground could be Tyrian purple, the finest and most expensive dye of antiquity, which was extracted from a species of eastern Mediterranean mollusk and was originally made famous by the Phoenicians of Tyre, in present-day Lebanon. The figural motifs are woven in an illusionistic style widespread in figural representations of the third and fourth centuries.

Linen, wool, silk, and gold-wrapped yarns; tapestry weave
22⅜ x 6¼ in. (56.9 x 15.8 cm)
Charles Potter Kling Fund   46.401

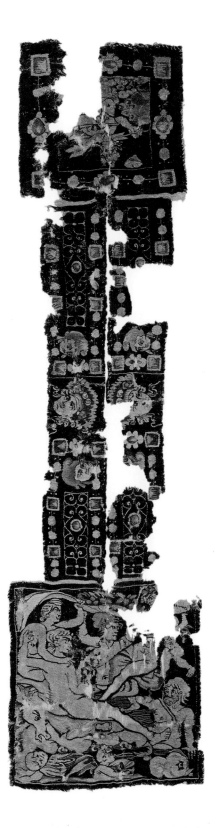

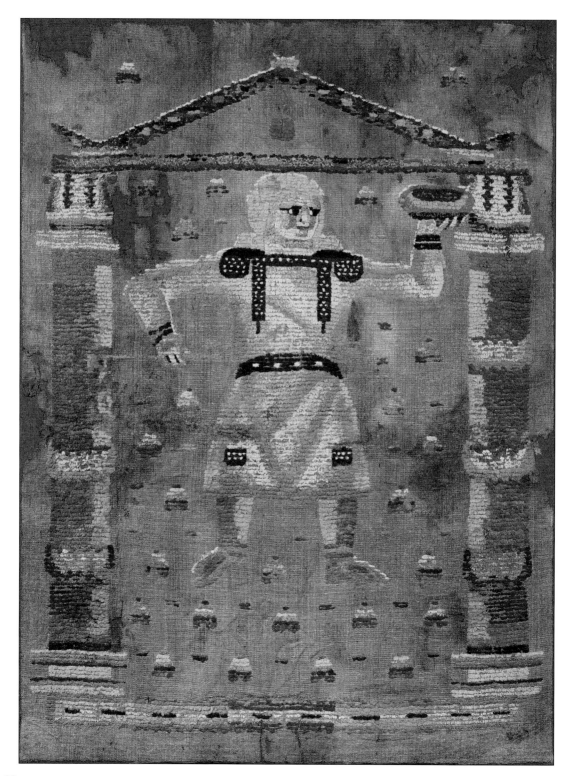

opposite

Fragment of a curtain
Roman
Late Roman period, 4th–6th century A.D.

Ancient Egyptian culture changed course dramatically when Alexander the Great conquered the
country in 332 B.C. and founded the city of Alexandria—a magnet for thousands of Greek immigrants.
Three hundred years later, in 31 B.C., Egypt became
a Roman province and, along with the rest of the
Roman Empire, eventually adopted Christianity as
its official religion. Gradually a new and original
civilization known as Coptic (a word derived from the
Greek for "Egyptian") developed in Egypt, incorpo-
rating Greek, Roman, and Christian influences. This
curtain fragment (like the neck ornament on page 93)
is a highlight of one of the most extensive American
collections (some twelve hundred pieces) of Eastern
Mediterranean weavings from the Early Christian
period. Woven in loops of warm, rich colors, it features a man—perhaps a temple acolyte—holding a
staff and raising a libation bowl. Roses are scattered
on the ground around him.

Linen plain weave with weft wool pile loops
38⅜ x 51½ in. (97.5 x 131 cm)
Charles Potter Kling Fund   49.313

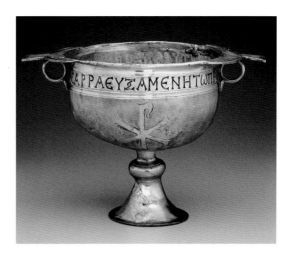

Chalice
Byzantine
Early Byzantine period, 6th century A.D.

The chalice was among the most precious objects
employed in the liturgy of the Byzantine Orthodox
Christian church, all of which had a symbolic meaning as well as a practical function. The chalice was,
symbolically, the bowl that collected the blood of the
crucified Christ and also the cup used in the church
for Holy Communion. The hammered bowl of this
chalice is inscribed, in Greek, "Having vowed, Sarah
offered [this chalice] to the First Martyr," who was
Saint Stephen. The chalice was probably Sarah's gift
to her church in Syria. On each side of the body of the
bowl is a *chrismon* (monogram of Christ), a Chi-Rho
formed from the first two letters of Christ's name in
Greek. The small alpha and omega, first and last letters of the Greek alphabet, refer to Jesus's statement
in the New Testament: "I am alpha and omega, the
beginning and the end."

Silver and niello with gilding
7 x 10½ in. (18 x 26.6 cm)
Edward J. and Mary S. Holmes Fund   1971.633

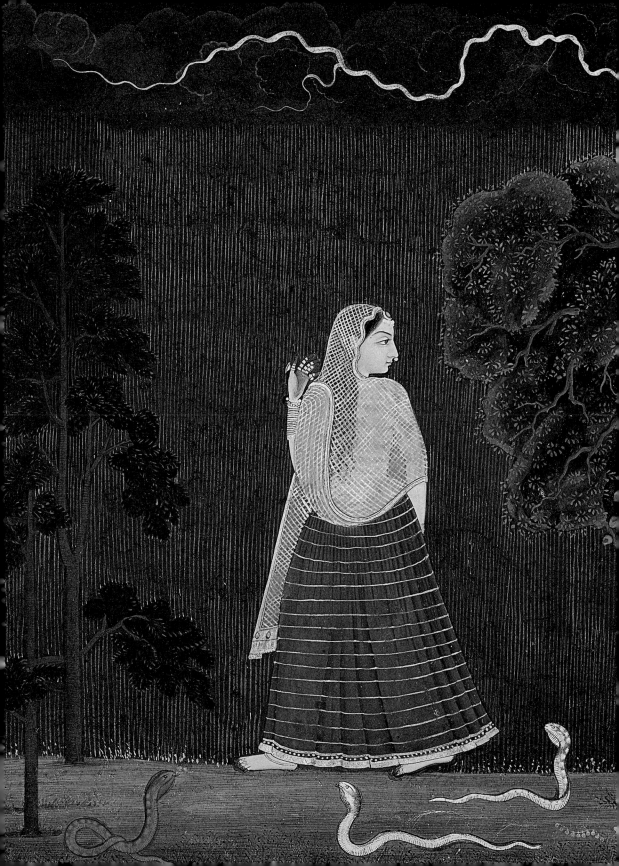

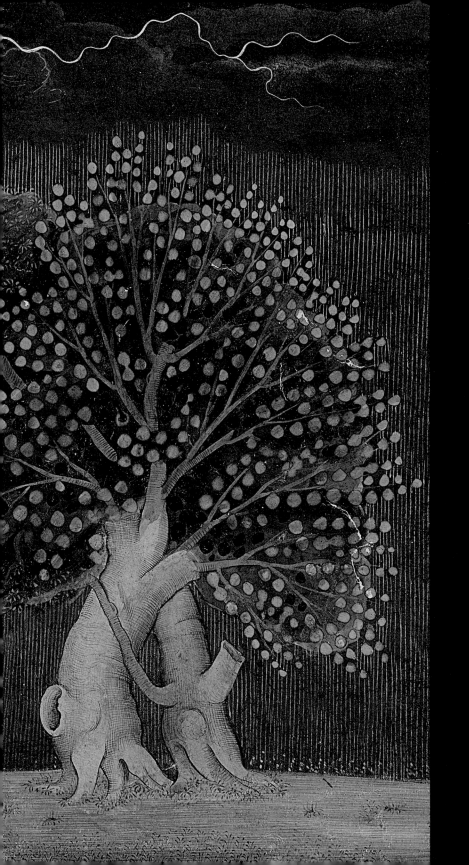

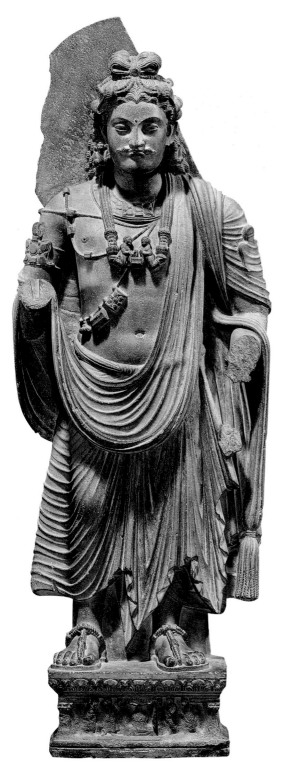

Bodhisattva Maitreya
Northwestern Pakistan (Gandhara),
3rd century A.D.

Bodhisattvas are enlightened beings who postpone their own entry into nirvana and remain on earth to assist other beings in their quest for salvation. This is an extremely important concept in Buddhism, a religion that stresses altruism and compassion. Reflecting the origins of the historic Buddha, who was born a prince, bodhisattvas wear elaborate jewelry and layers of rich garments. Details of this sculpture, such as the stiff folds and ridges of the heavy drapery, reflect the Gandharan region's contacts with the contemporary Greco-Roman world and Gandharan artists' knowledge of Western sculptural traditions.

Gray schist
H. 43⅛ in. (109.5 cm)
Helen and Alice Colburn Fund   37.99

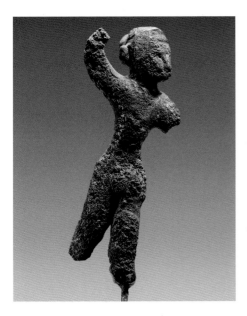

Male spear thrower or dancer
Pakistan (Sindh, Chanhudaro)
Indus Valley civilization, 2600–1900 B.C.

The pose of this tiny, fragmentary figure suggests that he is either dancing or throwing a
spear. Many similar male figurines with their
hair tied back in buns have been found at Indus
Valley sites in present-day Pakistan, but their
function and meaning are unknown. The met-
alworking techniques of this early civilization,
however, were remarkably sophisticated, and
this sculpture was probably cast using the
lost-wax process. In this process, a wax model
is encased in clay that is heated until the wax
melts; the wax is then poured out and replaced
with molten bronze or copper. When cool, the
clay casing is broken away from the metal cast,
which is then smoothed and finished.

Copper
H. 1⅝ in. (4.1 cm)
Joint Expedition of the American School of Indic
and Iranian Studies and the Museum of Fine Arts,
1935–1936 Season   36.2236

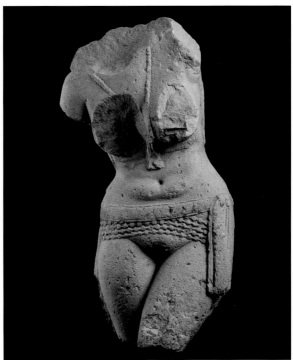

Torso of a fertility goddess (*yakshi*)
Central India (Sanchi, from a gateway of the Great Stupa),
25 B.C.–A.D. 25

Prior to the development of Buddhism in India, *yakshi*s were
honored as semidivine nature spirits believed to bring good
luck, wealth, and other blessings such as the birth of children.
Incorporated into the early imagery of Buddhism, *yakshi*s and
their male counterparts, *yaksha*s, were placed at the entrances
to religious monuments to provide protection and welcome the
faithful. This sensuous sculpture comes from a gateway at one
of the oldest and most important Buddhist monuments in India,
the Great Stupa at Sanchi. Like figures still found on gateways
at the site, this *yakshi* stood beneath a tree, her left arm raised
to hold a branch. Since it was believed that the touch of a beautiful woman would cause a tree's sap to run, making that tree
flower and bear fruit, such figures were powerful symbols of
fertility and abundance.

Sandstone
H. 28⅜ in. (72 cm)
Denman Waldo Ross Collection   29.999

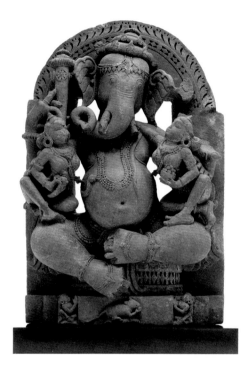

Ganesha with His Consorts
Northern India (Madhya Pradesh or Rajasthan),
early 11th century

Ganesha is a Hindu god represented with the body
of a boy and the head of an elephant. Elephants are
symbols of royalty and very auspicious animals in
Indian culture, and part of Ganesha's function is
to help clear obstacles from the worshiper's path
to enlightenment. Sculptures of Ganesha, like this
one, are often placed on the exterior wall of temples
so that they are the first images encountered by
the reverent visitor, who circles the temple before
entering. In this lively sculpture, Ganesha is shown
with his consorts, Siddhi (Success) and Riddhi
(Prosperity). Below him is a rat, his traditional means
of transportation.

Sandstone
H. 41⅜ in. (105.2 cm)
John H. and Ernestine A. Payne Fund, Helen S. Coolidge
Fund, Asiatic Curator's Fund, John Ware Willard Fund, and
Marshall H. Gould Fund   1989.312

Lovers (*mithuna*)
Eastern India (Orissa),
13th century

This exquisitely carved ivory sculpture may have been
designed to ornament a piece of furniture—perhaps
the throne of a king or a deity. The sensual interplay of
intricate jewelry and softly rounded flesh reflects the
eastern Indian origin of the sculpture. Such images
of lovers (*mithuna*) are often found in Indian art as
part of the decoration on both Buddhist and Hindu
monuments; they symbolize the union between the
male and female principles—the equal yet opposing
forces of nature. With the sense they convey of fertile
energy and infectious optimism, they are also prized
as good luck charms. Stylistically, this object is very
close to the erotic stone sculptures on the sun temple
at Konarak in Orissa, built in the thirteenth century.

Ivory
H. 6¼ in. (15.9 cm)
Keith McLeod Fund   1987.622

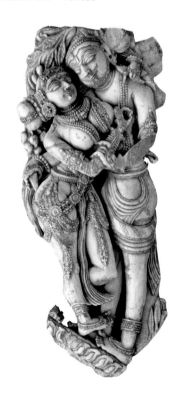

Shiva
Southern India (Tamilnadu region), late 10th century

Hindu gods are often depicted in human form but with superhuman attributes such as multiple heads and eyes that symbolize enhanced knowledge and vision. This figure's many heads are associated with Brahma, the god of creation, but the third eye in the forehead and the tall, matted hair indicate that he is, in fact, Shiva—the god of destruction who also embodies the life force. With five faces (a fifth, looking upward, is implied), this image represents the god as supremely powerful and would probably have been placed in a niche on the outside of a temple wall. Hindu temple sculptures function both as representations and physical embodiments of the gods; they are there to be seen by and also to see the worshipers.

Green schist
H. 63¾ in. (162 cm)
Gift of Mrs. John D. Rockefeller, Jr.
42.120

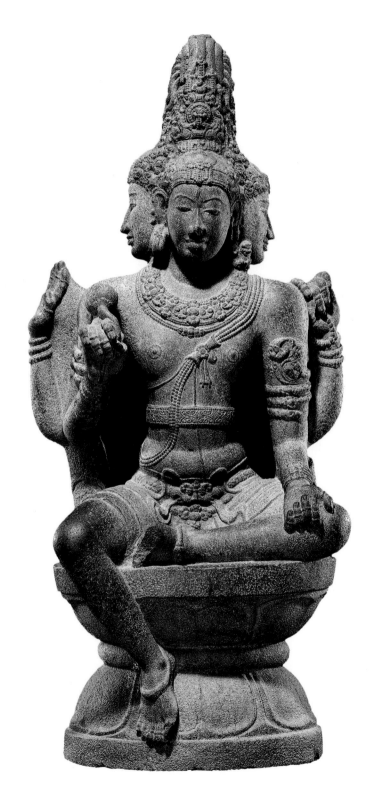

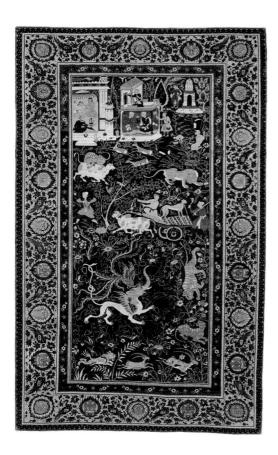

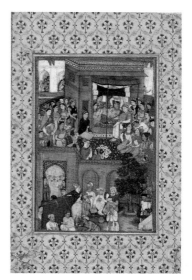

Pictorial carpet
Northern India (Lahore), about 1590–1600

This carpet brilliantly translates into knotted pile the lively painting style of the court of the Mughal emperor Akbar, where it was probably made. The wealth of imagery includes scenes of palace life, hunting, and fabulous beasts in combat, and a border filled with glowering monster masks. The celebrated nineteenth-century American architect Henry Hobson Richardson selected this carpet for the house of an important client, Boston businessman Frederick L. Ames.

Cotton warp and weft, wool knotted pile
95⅝ x 60⅝ in. (243 x 154 cm)
Gift of Mrs. Frederick L. Ames, in the name of
Frederick L. Ames   93.1480

Attributed to Bishandas
Indian, active about 1590–1650
Birth of a Prince, about 1620

Seventeenth-century Mughal painting is one of the great glories of Indian art. This vivid, meticulously executed image of courtly life is probably a page from a manuscript illustrating the life of the Mughal emperor Jahangir, son of the great emperor Akbar, and may depict his birth. The infant's jewel-encrusted crib is placed near the bed of his mother, who is surrounded by female attendants, musicians, eunuchs, and Akbar's other wives. Male attendants bring platters of presents, the court astrologers (at bottom center) forecast the child's future, and the entrance to the harem (at left) is garlanded with flowers in honor of the festive occasion. The painting is attributed to Bishandas, one of the most celebrated Mughal painters, whom Jahangir called "unequaled in his age for making likenesses."

Opaque watercolor on paper
10⅜ x 6½ in. (26.4 x 16.4 cm)
Francis Bartlett Donation of 1912 and Picture Fund   14.657

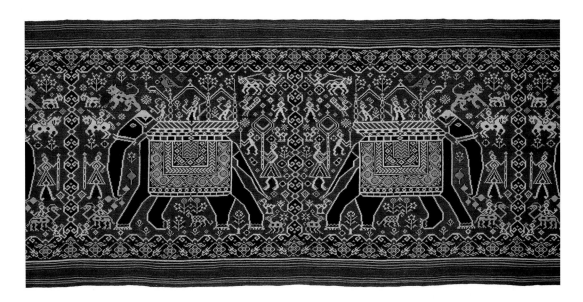

Ceremonial hanging (*patola*)
Western India (Gujarat), late 18th or
early 19th century

Ikat is a Malay-Indonesian word for an intricate clothmaking process in which threads are patterned by repeated binding and dyeing before they are placed on the loom and woven. *Patola*—Indian silk textiles richly patterned in the exacting double-ikat technique—were prized as heirlooms and luxury trade goods. Valued also for their spiritual potency, fragments of *patola* were even powdered and mixed with medicines. Many of these textiles were made for the Indonesian export market and have survived in excellent condition because their use was reserved for religious and ritual functions. Their superb quality and vibrant color inspired the Indonesian name *patola*, which means "gifts from the sky." This example was probably given to an Indonesian ruler by officials of the Dutch East India Company as a mark of special esteem.

Silk; double ikat (resist-dyed warp and weft yarns)
43 x 191 in. (109.2 x 485 cm)
Marshall H. Gould Fund   1985.709

Maharao Kishor Singh of Kota Worshiping Brijrajji
India (Rajasthan, Kota), about 1830

The rulers of Kota, in Rajasthan, put special emphasis on the worship of icons. The small metal icon called Brijrajji (a form of the god Krishna) was housed in the palace compound at Kota, where it played a major role in numerous elaborate rituals. This painting commemorates a specific *puja* (the act of showing reverence through prayers, songs, and rituals) in which the icon was placed on a couch in an elaborate shrine made of silver panels. The *maharao* ("great king") stands at left; he has shaved his head and put on simple clothing to demonstrate his humility. By keeping a revered and powerful icon in the palace and by treating it as the true ruler of Kota, the *maharao*s sought to protect their state as well as to exhibit their own humility before the divine.

Opaque watercolor, silver, and gold on paper
10¾ x 8½ in. (27.1 x 21.5 cm)
Gift of John Goelet   66.159

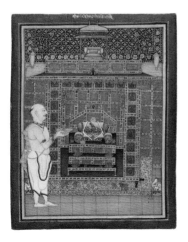

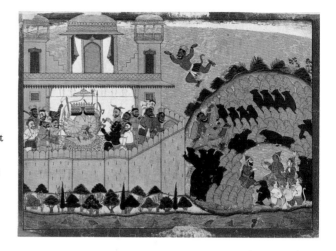

Attributed to **Manaku**
Indian, about 1700–1760
Rama and His Armies Encamped; One Spy Returns to Ravana
Northern India (Punjab Hills, probably Guler), about 1725

Remarkable for its vivacious draftsmanship and flat expanses of intense color, this page is from an oversized manuscript of the *Ramayana*, the Indian epic that recounts the life of the warrior-king Rama. A reincarnation of the god Vishnu, Rama descends to earth to vanquish Ravana, the multiheaded, multiarmed king of the demons, and restore the balance of the universe. Having been roughed up and warned of impending conflict by Rama's army, a demon returns to report to Ravana. Throughout the series, demons appear as a diverse group of misshapen characters, many of them more humorous than frightening. Ravana's palace is usually described as outrageously opulent and stands in stark contrast to the forested areas inhabited by Rama and his woodland allies.

Opaque watercolor and gold on paper
24¼ x 33 in. (61.5 x 83.6 cm)
Ross-Coomaraswamy Collection   17.2746

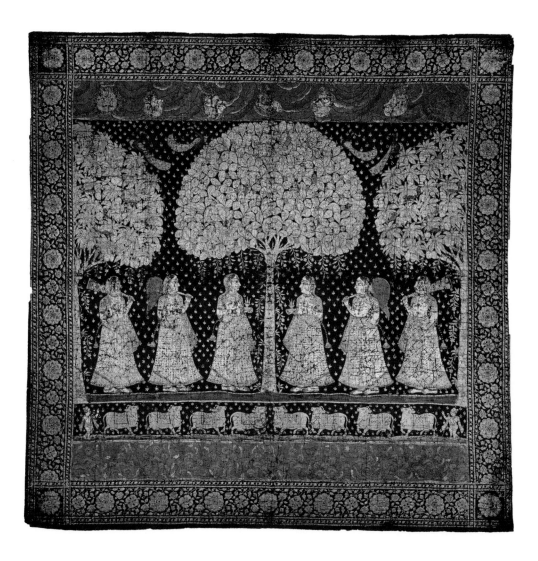

Temple hanging (*pechhavai*)
Central India (Telangana), 19th century

A *pechhavai* ("that which hangs at the back") is a
painted wall hanging created as a backdrop for sacred
icons in temple shrines. These shrines are usually
dedicated to Krishna, the Hindu god who embodies
love and the divine joy that destroys pain and sin.
Krishna grew up in a family of cow herders, and this
pechhavai shows six *gopi*s (cow-herding girls devoted
to Krishna) carrying flywhisks and dishes of offerings.
At the sides are mango trees, heavy with fruit, and

the background is filled with a shower of blossoms,
perhaps signifying nourishing rain. Below the *gopi*s
is a row of cows above a lotus pond, and six Hindu
deities appear in a band of clouds at the top. Like so
many works of art in museums, we must imagine this
rich vision of fruition in its original context—behind
an altar bearing images and offerings of sweets
and spices.

Opaque watercolor, gold, and silver on painted cotton
plain weave
96 x 100 in. (244 x 254 cm)
Gift of John Goelet   67.837

Lute (*tambura*)
Northern India, 19th century

An essential component of classical Indian music, the *tambura* provides a drone accompaniment to the human voice or solo instruments such as the sitar. The strings are plucked slowly in repeated sequence, and a prolonged buzzing tone is achieved by tying silk thread around the strings where they make contact with a wide bridge. In this splendid example, the bridge is ivory and the instrument, undoubtedly created for a wealthy patron, is finely decorated with ivory inlay.

Tun wood, calabash gourd, ivory, black mastic
H. 53⅛ in. (135 cm)
Mary L. Smith Fund   1992.259

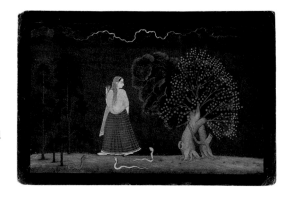

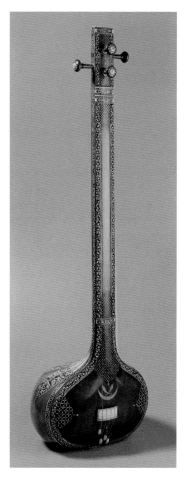

Heroine Rushing to Her Lover (*Abhisarika nayika*)
Northern India (Punjab Hills, Kangra), late 18th century

Paintings from the state of Kangra are celebrated for their delicacy of detail, juxtapositions of brilliant and muted colors, and evocation of complex emotions. The word *nayika* in the title refers to the female personification of the notion of human love. Here, the heroine ignores the perils of the night—darkness, lightning, beating rain, snakes—as she hurries to meet her lover. The storm symbolizes her passion, and the trees represent intertwined lovers. Paintings of such secular subjects were popular among painters at the Hindu Rajput courts of Rajasthan and the Punjab Hills, which prospered in close proximity to the Muslim Mughal courts of northern India.

Opaque watercolor and gold on paper
6⅜ x 9⅞ in. (16.2 x 25 cm)
Ross-Coomaraswamy Collection   17.2612

Dancing celestial figure (*apsaras*)
Cambodia, late 11th century

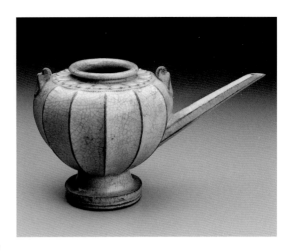

Sprightly female *apsaras*es appear on temples
throughout southern Asia. Heavenly beings, they are
usually shown dancing or playing musical instruments as they entertain and pay homage to the gods.
In this example, the elegant figure is framed by a
flamelike arch and dances on a lotus flower whose
branch sprouts two additional buds. The sculpture
was originally part of an incense burner or a hanging
lamp whose flickering light would have enhanced its
sense of graceful movement. This is one of the most
exquisitely worked and best preserved of the very few
fragments of such fragile bronzes that have survived
from Cambodia.

Bronze
H. 15½ in. (39.3 cm)
Denman Waldo Ross Collection   22.686

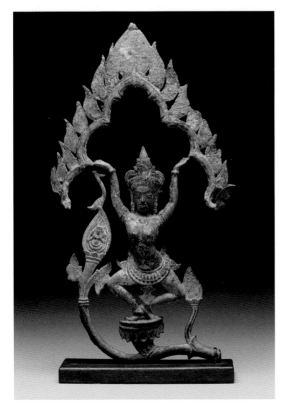

Ewer
Vietnam, 11th–12th century

Ceramics from Vietnam often reflect that region's
role as a bridge between eastern and southern Asia.
This ewer was probably made for royal patrons or
temple officials in Thang Long (present-day Hanoi).
The vessel's rolled lip and collar of modeled lotus
petals are typical of Vietnamese ceramics, but the
creamy, crackled glaze recalls Chinese wares. The
ewer's dramatic silhouette may have been inspired
by metal vessels that originated in India but were
used in Buddhist and Hindu rituals throughout
southern Asia.

Stoneware with white slip and light green glaze, carved lotus
petals, molded and applied handles
H. 4⅞ in. (12.5 cm)
Anonymous gift   1991.969

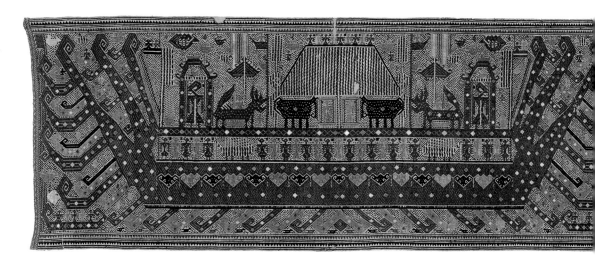

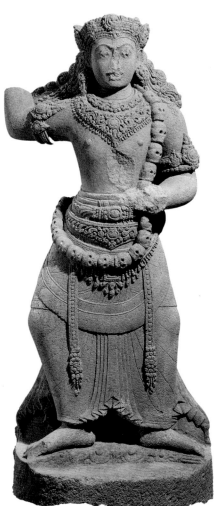

Bhairava or *Mahakala*
Indonesia (eastern Java), 14th century

Striking a pose from traditional Javanese dance, this
large, stone sculpture may represent either Bhairava
(a Hindu deity) or Mahakala (a Buddhist deity); Hin-
duism and Buddhism coexisted in Javanese culture
and often shared imagery. Wearing royal attire—an
ornate crown, belts, necklaces, earrings, and arm-
bands—this figure may have been intended as an
idealized portrait, combining the representation of
a deceased royal personage with that of a deity. The
rope of skulls indicates that this is a wrathful deity,
representing the power to overcome fears and frightening only to those who are not part of the faith.

Volcanic stone (andesite)
H. 78 in. (198 cm)
Frederick L. Jack Fund   1972.951

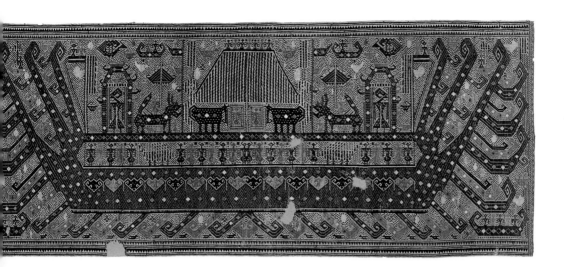

above

Ceremonial hanging (*palepai*)

Indonesia (Sumatra, southern Lampong region), 1825–75

Depictions of ships have appeared on Southeast Asian artifacts for millennia; long associated with funeral rites, ship imagery in the culture of Sumatra stands not only for death but also for the transition from one social or spiritual state to another. Owned and displayed only by the aristocracy, large *palepai* or "ship cloths" of Sumatra, like this one, were hung as backdrops for the important ceremonies of initiation into adulthood, marriage, and the attainment of rank. The fabulous sailing vessels depicted on *palepai* have elaborately curled bows and sterns, multiple decks with royal pavilions and banners, and cargos that include elephants—creatures associated with royal power.

Cotton; discontinuous supplementary patterning wefts on plain-weave ground
29 x 150½ in. (74 x 382 cm)
The William E. Nickerson Fund No. 2   1980.172

Lid of a ritual vessel

Indonesia (eastern Java), 13th century

No ordinary box top, this lid of a ritual vessel is densely covered with swirling waves, lotus flowers, and delicate spangles. Lotus flowers are considered sacred in much of Asia. The beauty of the flowers, which thrive in the water of muddy ponds, has long been associated with the ideal of attaining purity of body and mind while living in a world of earthly suffering. Lotuses are found at the center and at the base of the wired spangles, which themselves suggest flowers emerging from the pond. Made of very thin, beaten gold, the spangles would have shimmered as the lid was moved. The flowers, water creatures, and snakes that also decorate it are auspicious symbols that appear frequently in the religious and courtly arts of Southeast Asia.

Gold
H. 5 in. (12.7 cm)
Keith McLeod Fund   1982.141

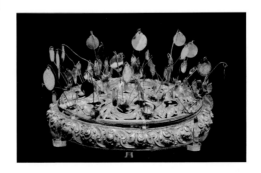

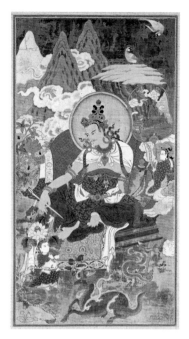

The Fifth King of Shambhala
Tibet or China, second half of the 17th century

This painting is one of a set portraying the pious kings of Shambhala, a mythical region in Central Asia. These kings were believed to have transmitted from one generation to the next an esoteric spiritual system that is an essential part of Lamaism, the Tibetan form of Buddhism. Although the brilliant colors of this painting are characteristically Tibetan, the work may have been created in neighboring China—the scrolling clouds are Chinese in style and the oversized fan held by the attendant at right is decorated with a Chinese landscape that echoes the painting's mountainous setting.

Opaque watercolor on cotton
17 x 13⅞ in. (43.2 x 35.2 cm)
Denman Waldo Ross Collection   06.324

Avalokiteshvara
Tibet, about 12th–13th century

Avalokiteshvara is the most compassionate and beloved of all Buddhist bodhisattvas—spiritually enlightened beings who postpone their entry into nirvana to help others in their quest for salvation. This Tibetan image, with its open stance and lively, fluid pose, is unusually approachable and graceful. Cast in one piece—an amazing feat considering the very large size—the figure holds a lotus flower, symbol of spiritual purity, and extends the other hand in the *mudra* (gesture) of wish granting. He wears elaborate jewelry, reflecting the historical Buddha's origins as a prince; a remarkable, sinuous garland frames his body. After extensive examination, Museum conservators and curators concluded that the sculpture was made in western Tibet, although most sculptures from that area have more static poses and more surface decoration. This Avalokiteshvara may have been made during the late period, when artists had more access to Western influence.

Bronze
H. 36¾ in. (93.5 cm)
Keith McLeod Fund   2003.339

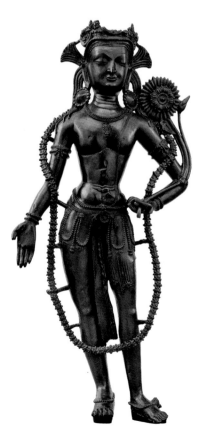

Buddha of Eternal Life and Eight Bodhisattvas
Tibet, 13th century

Seated on an elaborate peacock throne with typically Nepalese architectural elements, the Buddha of Eternal Life is encircled by elephants, snakes, lions, flying goats, boys, and—at the peak of the throne—the bird deity Garuda. Around the Buddha are eight bodhisattvas, enlightened beings who remain on earth to assist others to achieve salvation. Other Buddhist deities are ranged across the top and bottom of the painting. Known as *thangka*s, painted textiles such as this were displayed in Buddhist temples throughout the Himalayan region. This extraordinary example, probably painted by a Nepalese artist working in an important Tibetan monastery, belonged to a set of five; each depicted one of the Five Transcendental Buddhas, representations of the qualities of the Buddha that constitute a central tenet of tantric Buddhism.

Opaque watercolor on cotton
16¼ x 13 in. (41.3 x 33 cm)
Gift of John Goelet   67.818

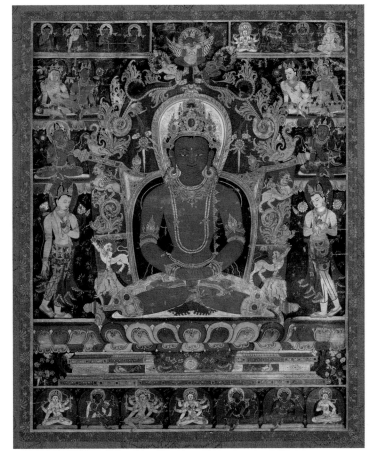

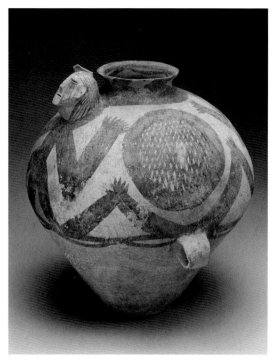

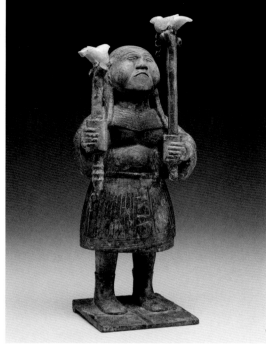

Granary jar
China
Neolithic period, Machang type,
late 3rd millennium B.C.

Human images seldom appear on ancient Chinese
ceramics, and this vessel is extremely unusual in that
its decoration includes a three-dimensional human
head with a painted body below. The tattooed face and
elaborate hairstyle make us wonder what sort of special role the figure depicted might have played in this
prehistoric society—perhaps a shaman or official
who communicated with the spirit world? Made to
hold grain, the jar may have been buried in the tomb
of a chieftain or a high priest. Its painted decoration
represents one of the earliest surviving examples of
the Chinese tradition of brush painting.

Earthenware with painted and applied decoration over slip
H. 15½ in. (39.5 cm)
E. Rhodes and Leona B. Carpenter Foundation Grant and
Edwin E. Jack Fund   1988.29

Standing youth
China
Bronze: Eastern Zhou dynasty, Warring States
period, early 4th century B.C.
Jade: Shang dynasty, 1600–1045 B.C.

The Eastern Zhou dynasty was marked by a new
interest in more accurate and specific portrayals of
the human figure. This young man's facial features,
braided hair, jewelry, dagger, and boots suggest that
he represents a member of a nomadic group that
inhabited China's northern border regions until the
first century B.C. The jade birds, roughly a millennium
older than the bronze figure, were attached to the
sticks by a crafty art dealer in the 1930s. Originally,
the sticks supported reservoirs for lamp oil, and this
figure would have been placed in a tomb to provide
eternal light in the afterlife.

Cast bronze with applied jade
H. 11¾ in. (30 cm)
Maria Antoinette Evans Fund   31.976

Ritual vessel with cover (*you*)
China
Western Zhou dynasty, 11th–10th century B.C.

Throughout the Bronze Age in China (about 2000–
221 B.C.), bronze vessels were prized symbols of
power, authority, and wealth. Each of the more than
fifty different types of bronze ritual vessels had a
specialized function; this *you* was a ceremonial con-
tainer for wine. Stylized horned creatures (possibly
water buffaloes) dominate the design, and the eight-
character inscription on the interior of the body and
on the lid indicates the vessel's use in the practice of
ancestor worship. It reads: "Dui Cheng had this ritual
vessel made for his accomplished late father Ding."

Chinese bronzes of this early period were created
by a process quite different from lost-wax casting (see
page 99). Sectional clay molds, carved on the inside
with designs, were placed around a solid clay core,
and molten bronze was poured into the space between
them. After the bronze cooled, the mold sections and
core were removed, revealing the completed vessel.

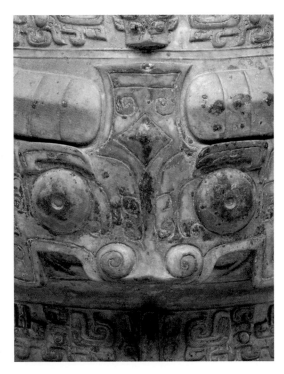

Cast bronze
H. 9⅞ in. (25 cm)
Anna Mitchell Richards Fund   34.63a–b

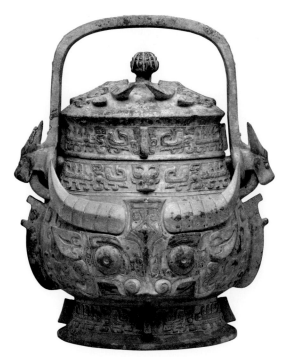

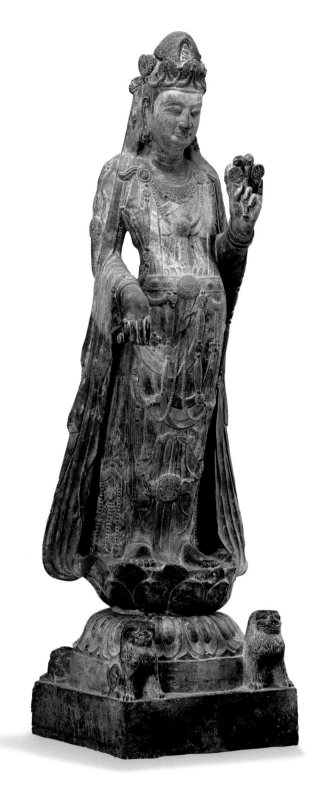

Guanyin
China
Northern Zhou or Sui dynasty, about A.D. 580

Guanyin, the Bodhisattva of Compassion and the divine figure that responds most directly to human prayers, became the most beloved Buddhist deity after the religion reached China from India in the first century A.D. Guanyin stands on a lotus throne and holds a cluster of lotus pods. This plant, which rises from the mud to release a white flower, is a Buddhist symbol of spiritual purity. Surviving traces of paint and gilding indicate that this monumental sculpture was once richly decorated. The figure's lithe, elongated body and flowing garments are characteristic of sculpture in the Xi'an area during the last decades of the sixth century.

Limestone with traces of paint and gold
H. 98 in. (249 cm)
Francis Bartlett Donation of 1912
15.254

Altarpiece
China
Sui dynasty, A.D. 593

At the center of this serenely beautiful altarpiece sits the Amitabha
Buddha, whose good favor ensured
rebirth after death into a Western Paradise "full of sweet smells,
clouds of music, showers of jewels,
and every other beauty and joy."
The altarpiece was commissioned
by eight women of the Pure Land
Buddhist faith to guarantee their
own rebirths and those of their
children and ancestors. Before the
Buddha, surrounded by his attendants, is an incense burner flanked
by lions and images of the Guardian Kings. The altarpiece was
discovered in a pit in the late nineteenth century. The incense burner,
lions, and Guardian Kings, not part
of the altarpiece at the time of purchase in 1922, were finally reunited
with the altar twenty-five years
after it came to the Museum.

Cast bronze
H. 30⅛ in. (76.5 cm)
Gift of Mrs. W. Scott Fitz and
Edward Jackson Holmes   22.407
Museum purchase with funds donated
by Edward Jackson Holmes in memory
of his mother, Mrs. W. Scott Fitz
47.1407–1412

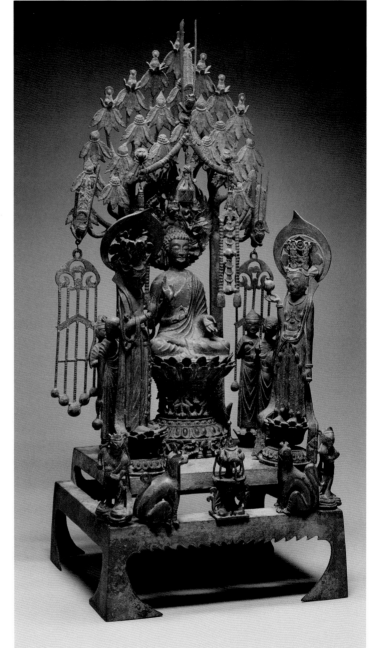

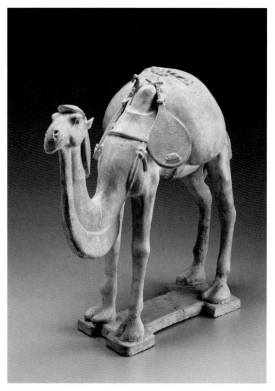

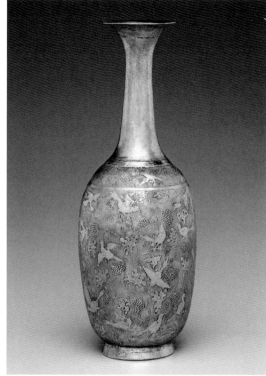

Bactrian camel

China

Sui–early Tang dynasty, late 6th–7th century A.D.

The Bactrian camel is a shaggier, two-humped relative of the more familiar dromedary camel. Native to central Asia, it long has served as a pack animal on the trade routes of the Silk Road. This charming figure's saddlebags are held in place between the two humps by straps passing under the tail, base of neck, and belly. On either side of the front of the bags are *pipa* (lutelike musical instruments; see page 124) and in back are flasks.

Earthenware with ivory-white glaze and applied motif
13¹¹/₁₆ x 16¾ in. (34.7 x 42.5 cm)
Bequest of Charles Bain Hoyt—Charles Bain Hoyt Collection
50.897

Bottle

China

Tang dynasty, about 8th century A.D.

This is a rare survival—an eighth-century example of a kind of bottle produced in ceramic and metal beginning in the sixth century. It reflects a technique common in the Tang dynasty of fashioning objects from sheets of silver. Four hammered sheets were soldered together to make this bottle, with bands of gilding both concealing the soldering and emphasizing the form. The decoration is exceptionally fine, with a vine bearing grapes winding around the body and a phoenix surrounded by a variety of gilded birds. A network of tiny, hammered circles forms an exquisite background to the design.

Hammered silver with chased and parcel-gilt design
7⅞ x 2⅞ in. (20 x 7.3 cm)
William Francis Warden Fund   47.1436

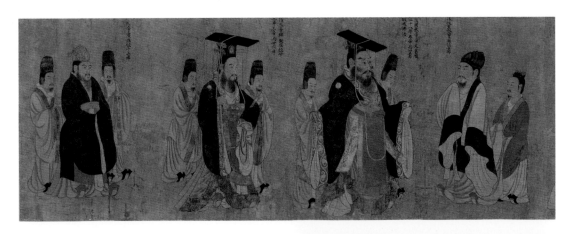

Attributed to Yan Liben

Chinese, about 600–673 A.D.

The Thirteen Emperors (detail)

Tang dynasty, second half of the 7th century A.D.

(with later additions)

This is the oldest Chinese handscroll in an American collection. Although Tang-dynasty figure painting was a high point of Chinese art, few nonreligious images remain; this is the only surviving example of its subject. The scroll depicts thirteen emperors who reigned from the second century B.C. to the seventh century A.D. Each individually characterized figure is identified by an inscription and accompanied by attendants. From the twelfth century, the scroll has been attributed to Yan Liben, a court artist and prime minister who was the most celebrated painter of the period. His painting demonstrates a profound sense of volume, grandeur, and movement, with exquisite drawing, forceful brushstrokes, and strong, simple coloring. The scroll was most likely painted for didactic purposes, with the historical rulers serving as moral and political examples to the nobility.

Handscroll; ink and color on silk

20³/₁₆ x 209¹/₁₆ in. (51.3 x 531 cm)

Denman Waldo Ross Collection   31.643

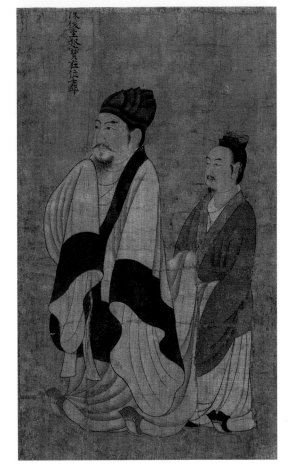

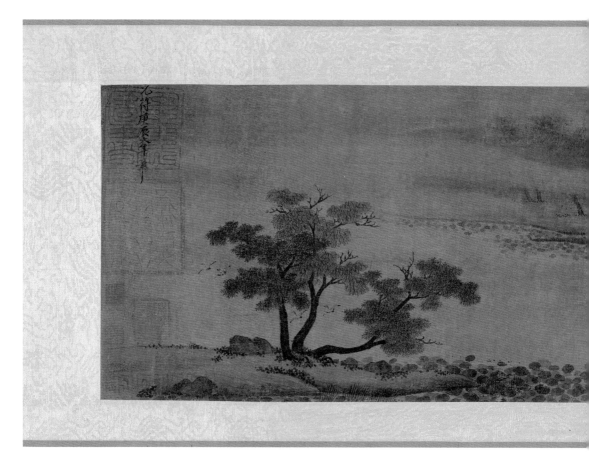

Zhao Lingrang
Chinese, active late 11th–early 12th century
Summer Mist along the Lakeshore (detail)
Northern Song dynasty, 1100

A handscroll (this one is more than five feet long) was slowly unrolled so that the viewer studied and appreciated only one part at a time, like the details you see here. Striking for its elegant brushwork and naturalistic effects, this handscroll depicts a lakeshore during summer, with bands of mist winding among the trees. Unlike traditional compositions—which captured the grandeur of nature through scale and dazzling detail— Zhao's paintings are quiet, lyrical, and more intimate in their observation of nature. Nonetheless, small, low-perspective compositions such as this one later became a highly popular painting style. Signed, dated, and including two seals by his hand, this is one of few paintings known to be by Zhao Lingrang.

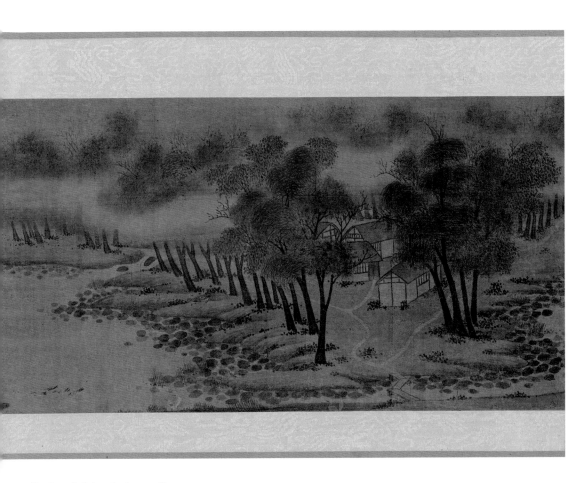

Handscroll; ink and color on silk
7½ x 63½ in. (19.1 x 161.3 cm)
Keith McLeod Fund   57.724

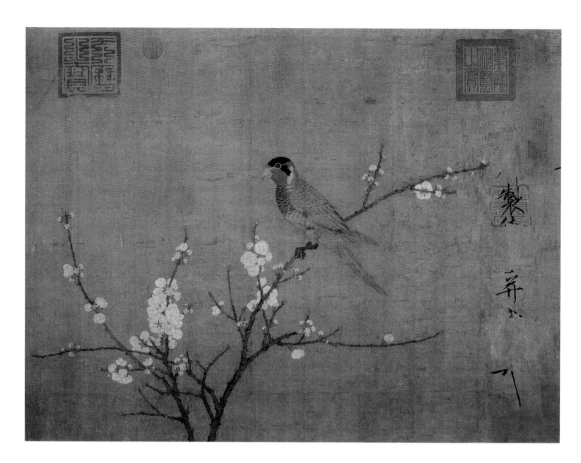

Emperor Huizong
Chinese, 1082–1135
The Five-Colored Parakeet (detail)
Northern Song dynasty, about 1110

This handscroll by Emperor Huizong (reigned 1101–1125) may have originally been part of a large album that he compiled to record rare birds and flowers, exquisite objects, and important events. In the poem inscribed on it, the emperor describes the exotic parakeet that perched one spring day on an apricot branch in the imperial garden. He depicted each feather of the bird and every petal of the apricot blossoms in the meticulous style of academic court painting he established. Huizong's paintings were often copied by court painters; this is one of few surviving works in which the distinctive style of the calligraphy and painting makes it likely to have come from the emperor's own hand.

Handscroll; ink and color on silk
21 x 49¼ in. (53.3 x 125.1 cm)
Maria Antoinette Evans Fund   33.364

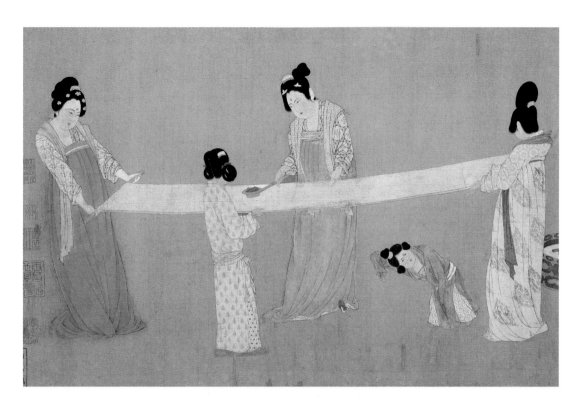

Attributed to Emperor Huizong
Chinese, 1082–1135
Court Ladies Preparing Newly Woven Silk
Northern Song dynasty, early 12th century

This celebrated handscroll—one of the great masterpieces of Chinese painting—depicts three scenes of elegant court ladies beating, sewing, and ironing new silk. The engagement of these aristocratic women in domestic labor may reflect a traditional, springtime event in which the empress led her attendants through the ancient ritual of producing silk. In the detail above, the women stretch a long piece of newly woven silk near a charcoal fire kindled to heat the iron.

Handscroll; ink, color, and gold on silk
14⅝ x 57¼ in. (37 x 145.3 cm)
Special Chinese and Japanese Fund   12.886

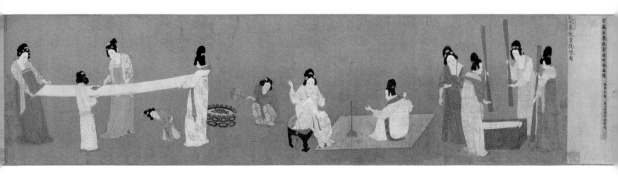

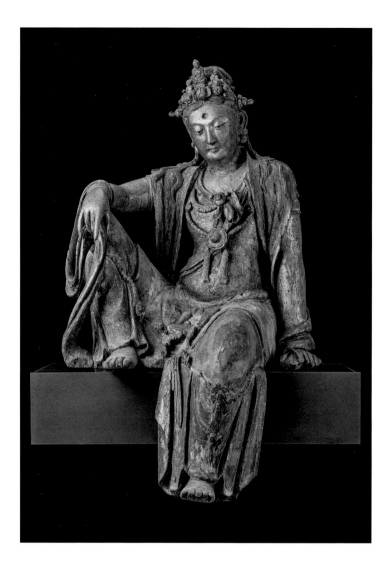

Guanyin, Bodhisattva of Compassion
China
Late Northern Song or Jin dynasty, early 12th century

In Buddhism, bodhisattvas are enlightened beings who have chosen to remain in the human realm to help others in their efforts toward nirvana. Guanyin, bodhisattva of compassion, was the subject of wide devotion in twelfth-century China, when artists carved this magnificent statue from several blocks of *Paulownia* wood joined together. With his benevolent, downcast gaze, Guanyin sits in the pose of "royal ease," wearing richly polychromed garments, heavy jewelry, and a crown with beads, lotus buds, and a small figure of the Amitabha Buddha, his spiritual teacher.

For centuries, the sculpture resided in a temple in Jishan county, in northern China's Shanxi province, where it received prayers and offerings from devotees eager to gain religious merit or achieve worldly goals. One donor, probably in the fifteenth or sixteenth century, gave money to paint the figure's face and torso gold, in accordance with the aesthetic fashion of the time.

Wood (*Paulownia tomentosa*) with polychrome, gilding, and glass beads
H. 55½ in. (141 cm)
Hervey Edward Wetzel Fund   20.590

Zhou Jichang

Chinese, active late 12th century

*Luohan Manifesting Himself as
an Eleven-Headed Guanyin*

Southern Song dynasty, about
A.D. 1178

In Buddhism, *luohan*s are disciples of the Buddha who have
achieved enlightenment and
gained release from their earthly
existence. In this enigmatic
painting, an enthroned *luohan*
seems to be either putting on a
mask or pulling aside his skin to
reveal the features of the eleven-
headed Guanyin, Bodhisattva
of Compassion. This painting is
unique in its inclusion of portraiture in a religious composition—figures representing the
artist Zhou Jichang and his colleague Lin Tinggui stand rapt in
discussion over a sketch in the
foreground. Behind them stands
the monk Yishao, from the Hui'an
Monastery, who raised funds to
commission an ambitious set of
one hundred *luohan* paintings, of
which this is one. The MFA has ten
from the set, sold in the late 19th
century by a Japanese temple.

Hanging scroll mounted on panel;
ink and colors on silk
43⅞ x 20⅞ in. (111.5 x 53.1 cm)
Gift of Denman Waldo Ross   06.289

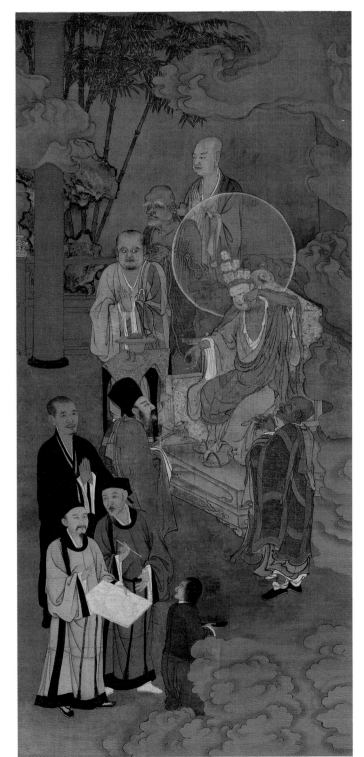

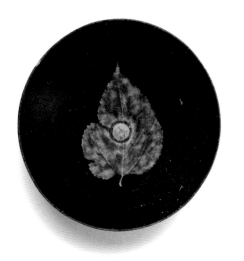

Lute (*pipa*)
China
Qing dynasty, 1891

Probably originating in Central Asia, the four-stringed *pipa* was a favorite instrument at Chinese court banquets since the Tang dynasty (A.D. 618–906). The *pipa* was originally played with a pick, but in later periods performers plucked the strings with their fingernails. Carved at the head of this *pipa* is a stylized phoenix, a mythological bird with such a discerning ear that it is attracted only by the most accomplished musicians.

Teak, wutong wood, ivory
H. 41 in. (104 cm)
Leslie Lindsey Mason Collection
17.2049

Tea bowl
China
Southern Song dynasty, 12th–13th century

Elegantly simple ceramic tea bowls such as this one are unique to the kilns of Jizhou in the southern Chinese province of Jiangxi. To create them, potters placed a leaf in the tea bowl before applying the glaze. The leaf itself was consumed in the heat of firing, leaving behind a delicate, yellow-ochre pattern of the leaf's structure. When the bowl is filled with green tea, the leaf design seems to float within the liquid.

Jizhou ware; stoneware
Diam. 5⅞ in. (14.9 cm)
Charles Bain Hoyt Collection   50.2014

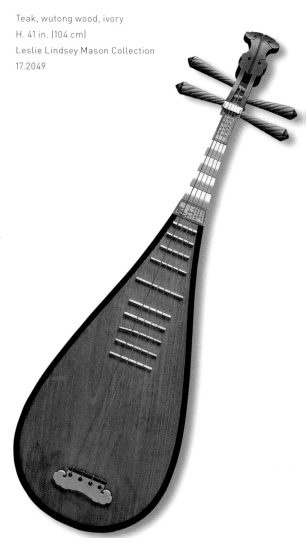

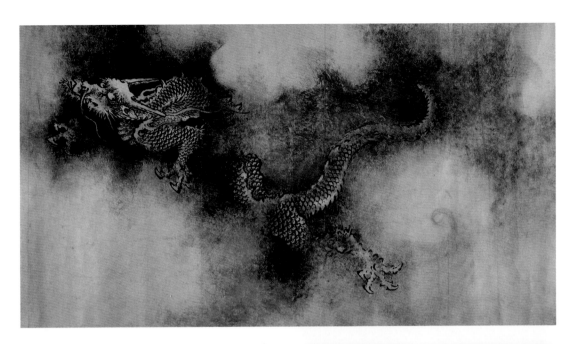

Chen Rong
Chinese, first half of the 13th century
Nine Dragons (detail)
Southern Song dynasty, 1244

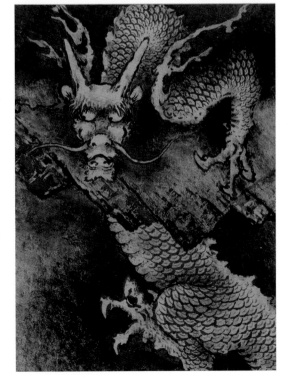

Arguably the greatest of all Chinese dragon paintings,
this handscroll—almost thirty-six feet long in its
entirety—is the work of Chen Rong, an impoverished
painter, poet, and scholar from south China's Fujian
province. He treats the dragon as a manifestation of
the principles of Daoism, a Chinese philosophy that
explores the relationship of people and the natural
world. The dragons in his painting, hidden and then
revealed amid mist, waves, and clouds, may symbolize
the Great Dao itself—a mysterious, natural force.

Handscroll; ink with touches of red on paper
Entire scroll: 18¼ x 377⅜ in. (46.2 x 958.4 cm)
Francis Gardner Curtis Fund   17.1697

Jar
China
Yuan dynasty, 14th century

Few ceramic wares have been as widely admired as the porcelain commonly known as Chinese blue-and-white. It was traded throughout the Near and Far East and to Europe, where it was imitated widely. This jar is an early example of Jingdezhen porcelain, decorated in underglaze cobalt blue, from the Yuan period (1279–1368). It is decorated with a scene from *Yuchi Gong Defeats Shan Xiongxin with His Iron Whip*, a historical event frequently reenacted in the popular theater of the Yuan period. The jar's robust form, the brilliance of the cobalt blue, and the vigorous brushwork all contribute to its exuberance and vitality.

Jingdezhen ware; porcelain with underglaze blue decoration
H. 11 in. (27.8 cm)
Bequest of Charles Bain Hoyt—Charles Bain Hoyt Collection   50.1339

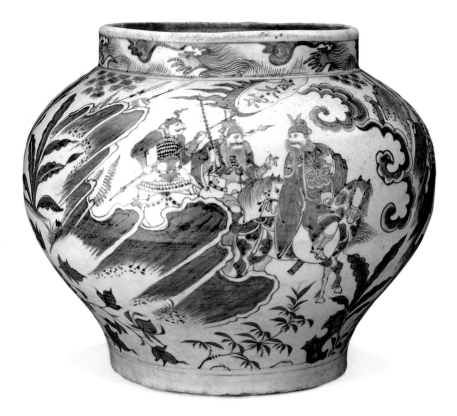

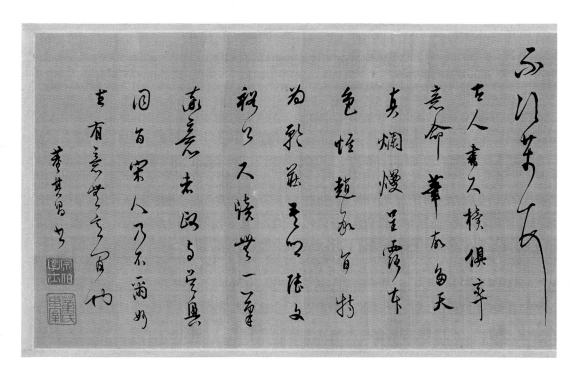

Kesi **tapestry of calligraphy (detail)**

China

Qing dynasty, Qianlong period, 1736–96

Calligraphy by **Dong Qichang** (1555–1636), copying letters from the **Four Masters of the Northern Song** (960–1126)

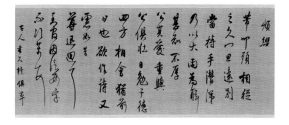

Although it closely resembles calligraphy rendered with ink and brush on paper, this work is a textile in which the weaver skillfully captured the fluid motions and marks of an ink-laden brush. The "calligraphy" is that of Dong Qichang, who was paying homage to the calligraphy of four masters of the Song dynasty. Thus, woven into this eighteenth-century *kesi* are many centuries of admiration for particular examples of calligraphy—considered the most pure and lofty of the arts. The tapestry appears to have been woven in one segment (more than nine feet long), then adhered to paper and mounted as a handscroll. A work of this astonishing virtuosity and quality undoubtedly was made in the imperial workshops of the Qing palace, where Dong Qichang's original scroll, now lost, was kept.

Kesi tapestry weave; silk yarns
11⅝ x 114 in. (29.5 x 289.5 cm)
Charles Bain Hoyt Fund   2005.193

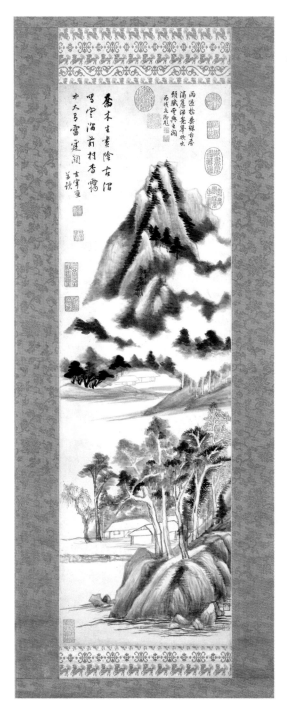

Dong Qichang
Chinese, 1555–1636
Stately Trees Offering Midday Shade
Ming dynasty, about 1616–20

Dong Qichang was a highly influential figure, both
for his own paintings and for his theories about the
history of Chinese painting, which he divided into
two dominant strains: the Northern School, professional painters who painted commissions for money,
and the Southern School, scholar-artists who painted
to express their erudition and creativity. In his own
work, Dong focused on the materials of the Chinese
scholar—ink, brush, and paper—painting multiple
layers of ink on nonabsorbent paper so that other
scholar-artists might appreciate each brushstroke.
Although this work reflects some inspiration from
the natural world, it is equally inspired by earlier
paintings. The many red seals are from the hand of
an eighteenth-century Qianlong emperor, who owned
and clearly treasured this important work.

Hanging scroll; ink on paper
35¾ x 11¼ in. (90.8 x 28.8 cm)
Frederick L. Jack Fund   55.86

Wang Yuanqi
Chinese, 1642–1715
Southern Hills after Spring Rain
Qing dynasty, late 17th–early 18th
century

The legendary Southern Mountain, or *nanshan*, has long been a symbol of longevity. In his inscription on this scroll, the painter and scholar Wang Yuanqi dedicates *Southern Hills after Spring Rain* to his friend and fellow official at the court of China's Kangxi emperor, Shi Kui (1661–1713), in celebration of Shi's mother's sixtieth birthday. Wang, the youngest of a lineage of painters and one of the Qing dynasty's most important artists, was himself fifty-seven when he completed the painting. With bold strokes of ink, he brings life to the imagined landscape's rocky slopes. Certain elements betray his admiration for the Yuan-dynasty master Huang Gongwang (1269–1354); Wang skillfully adapts the older artist's signature "moss-dot strokes" and, in the mountaintops, "alum-head strokes" with distinctive flair.

Hanging scroll; ink and color on paper
49 x 24⅞ in. (124.5 x 63.2 cm)
Gift of the Wan-go H. C. Weng
Collection and the Weng family, in
memory of Virginia Dzung Weng
2013.4155

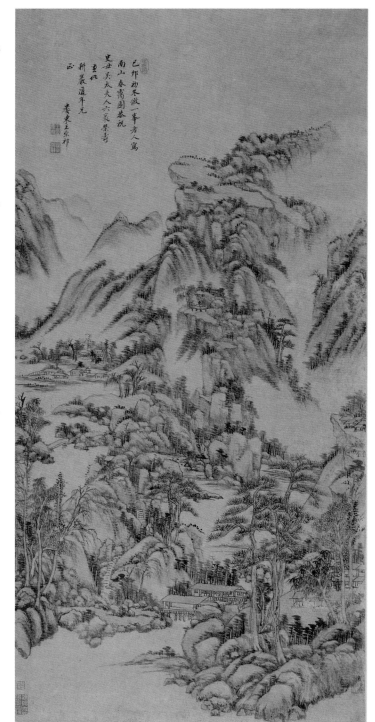

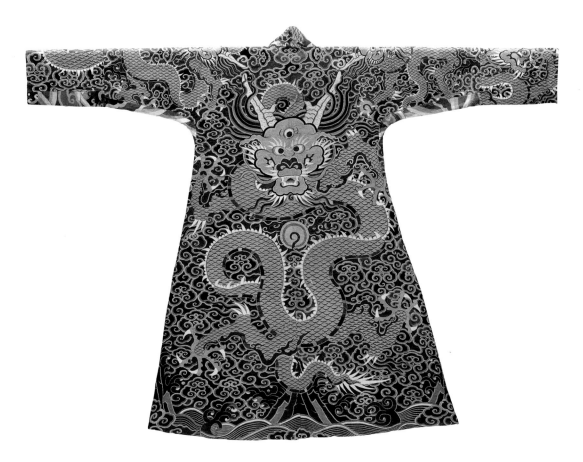

Man's robe (*chuba*) of Chinese fabric
Tibet, 19th century
Fabric: China, late Ming or early Qing dynasty,
17th century

The luxurious fabric of this Tibetan robe is Chinese
in origin and may have arrived in Tibet as a diplomatic gift. Created with the labor-intensive tapestry-
weaving technique known as *kesi*, the textile includes
silk threads wrapped in gold and peacock feathers.
Symbols of power, dragons also represented the
emperor in China, meaning their use as ornamentation on robes was restricted to members of the
imperial household and court in Beijing. The bold and
dominating appearance of the dragons on the front

and back of this robe is seventeenth century in style,
but the inclusion of late Qing fabrics in the robe's
lining indicates that the *chuba* was not assembled in
Tibet until at least the nineteenth century.

Silk and silk threads wrapped with metal and peacock
feathers; slit tapestry
H. 57¾ in. (146.7 cm)
Museum purchase with funds donated anonymously
2001.145

Broken Bamboo Slips and Damaged Sheets
China
Qing dynasty, about 1880

Only recently have scholars begun to piece together the
history of *bapo* ("eight brokens"), a revolutionary genre of
painting whose name refers to the auspiciousness of both
the number eight and things that are broken or incomplete.
The MFA possesses the largest and most important collection
of these works anywhere. *Bapo* emerged in mid-nineteenth-
century China, forged by artists whose works were a radical
departure from classical landscape and figure paintings.
Broken Bamboo Slips and Damaged Sheets, like most *bapo*
works, depicts decaying fragments spread seemingly haphaz-
ardly across its surface. Painted with painstaking, illusionistic realism, many of those items hold great cultural and
historical meaning and would have been instantly recognizable to the work's intended audience—a sophisticated,
aspiring urban middle class. That audience would have also
appreciated the poetic tradition of "longing for the past"
that these paintings embody. Embedded in this composition is a sheet of fine stationery inscribed with a famous
ancient poem. Recalling the transiency of life, it reads in part:
"Facing my wine, I sing a song. How long is a person's life?"

Hanging scroll; ink, color, and gold on paper
61 x 15½ in. (154.9 x 39.4 cm)
Anonymous gift in memory of William W. Mellins   2017.10

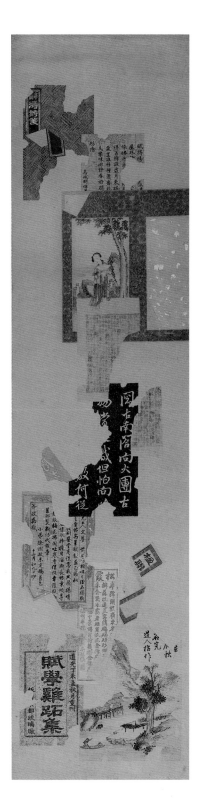

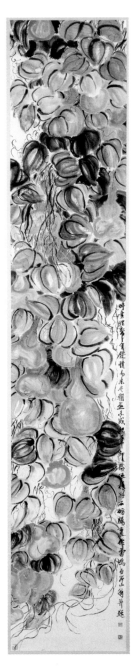
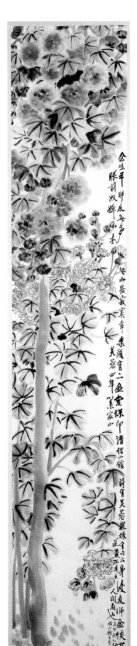
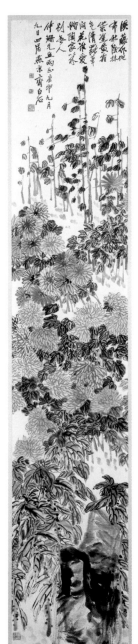
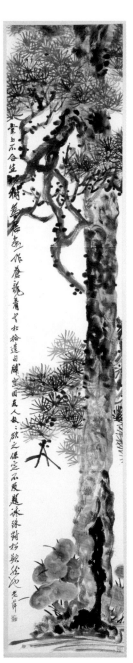

opposite

Qi Baishi

Chinese, 1863–1957

***Gourds, Hibiscus, Chrysanthemums, and Pine Tree*, 1920**

Admired by individuals as different as Picasso and Chairman Mao (who came from the artist's home county), Qi Baishi was born a farmer, trained as a carpenter, and learned to paint from manuals and from studying the work of old masters. Unlike many of his contemporaries, he knew little of Western art and trained himself in traditional themes and techniques. Eventually, he developed his own style, which favored rustic elegance, directness, and lack of artifice. Created at the very beginning of his artistic breakthrough, these works were painted for Cao Kun, who later became the third president of the Republic of China.

Hanging scroll; ink and color on paper
111¼ x 21¼ in. (282.5 x 54 cm)
Gift of Madame Fan Tchun-pi and her sons in memory of Dr. Tsen Tson Ming
1980.99–102

Medicine Buddha
Korea
Unified Silla dynasty, 8th century A.D.

The Chinese monks who first brought Buddhism to Korea provided medical care as well, and the Buddha of Medicine has always been popular there. Known as *Yaksa yeorae*, he is identified by the medicine jar in his hand. This small figure of the deity may originally have been placed in a household shrine or it may have been displayed with similar statues at a temple. It is closely related to a group of more than fifty gilt bronzes once placed on the branches of an ancient elm tree in a temple in the Diamond Mountains of North Korea. A masterpiece of Korean Buddhist sculpture, it reflects the influence of Tang-dynasty China, although the rather heavy proportions, large head and hands, and octagonal base are all typically Korean.

Gilt bronze
H. 14⅛ in. (36 cm)
Gift of Edward Jackson Holmes in memory of his mother,
Mrs. W. Scott Fitz   32.436

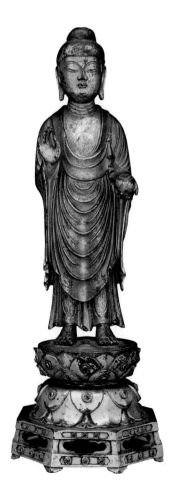

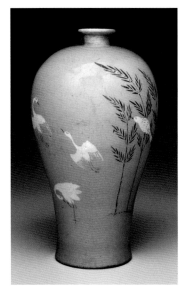

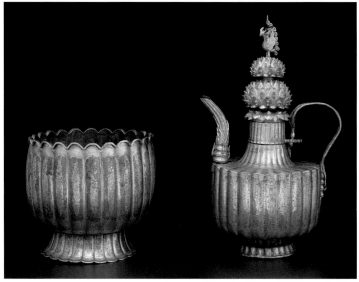

Plum bottle (*maebyeong*)
Korea
Goryeo dynasty, early 13th century

Ewer and basin
Korea
Goryeo dynasty, 12th century

Korea is well known in the West for its fine ceramics, particularly those with the subtle, grayish-green glaze known as celadon. This vase, with its sensuous shape and delicate design of cranes and another bird in bamboo branches, is an early example of inlaid celadon, a technique perfected in the course of the twelfth century. Not many other *maebyeong* of this same design are known.

Although similar in form and decoration to ceramic examples, this sumptuous ewer and basin are made of silver partially covered with gold. Commissioned by a wealthy patron, they were used to serve wine or other liquids in a domestic setting; the ewer was placed inside the basin where hot water kept its contents at the desired temperature. Bamboo inspired the basic shape of both pieces as well as the handle and spout of the ewer. The cover to the ewer consists of three stylized lotuses surmounted by a phoenix—both auspicious symbols in Buddhist art.

Glazed stoneware with inlaid decoration
H. 12¼ in. (31.1 cm)
Bequest of Charles Bain Hoyt—
Charles Bain Hoyt Collection   50.989

Parcel gilt silver with engraved decoration
Ewer: H. 13½ in. (34.3 cm)
Basin: H. 6⅝ in. (16.8 cm)
George Nixon Black Fund   35.646.1a-d, 35.646.2

Perfect Enlightenment Sutra
Illumination
Korea
Goryeo dynasty, 14th century

In the center of this scroll, the
Vairocana Buddha (the central member of the Five Buddhas) sits on a
lotus throne with his hands raised in
the gesture of exposition. Below him
are bodhisattvas and other members of the Buddhist pantheon, their
names in gold on red cartouches. The
Vairocana Buddha is teaching the
Sutra of Perfect Enlightenment, one
of the discourses of the Buddha that
compose the basic text of Buddhist
scripture. His followers take turns
asking questions about some aspect
of his teaching, and his responses
constitute the substance of the sutra.
The bodhisattva who kneels in the
lower center—the focal point of the
composition—effectively draws the
viewer into the scene. Rich in color
and gold, this monumental work creates the abstract beauty of the celestial sphere and may have been used as
part of a ritual observance. Reflecting the influence of Chinese painting
on that of Korea, the work was long
thought to be Chinese.

Hanging scroll mounted as a panel;
color and gold on silk
65⅛ x 33⅝ in. (165.5 x 85.5 cm)
William Sturgis Bigelow Collection
11.6142

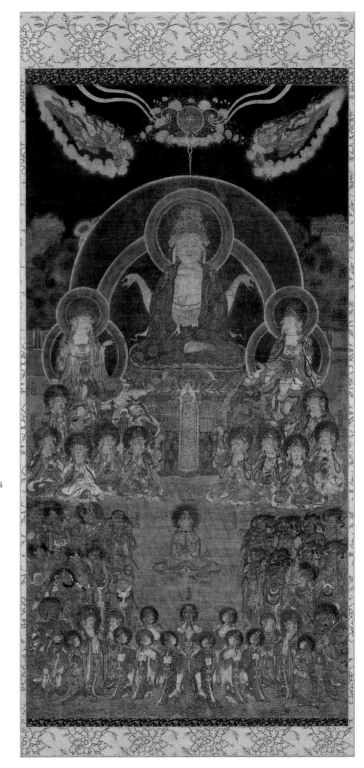

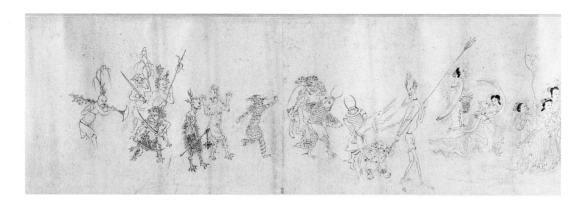

Shitao
Chinese, 1642–1707
Conversion of Hariti to Buddhism (detail)
Qing dynasty, 1683

Terrorized by the ogress Hariti, who stole and devoured children, the populace appealed to the Buddha to stop her. The Buddha—giving Hariti a taste of her own medicine—stole her youngest child and hid him under a large bowl used for receiving alms. Desperate with grief and anxiety, Hariti employed all her powers to recover her son, summoning flying demon-warriors to attack the Buddha and engaging other ogres to try to raise the bowl. But the demon's weapons broke in mid-air, and the bowl could not be moved. At last, recognizing the power and supremacy of the Buddha, Hariti converted to Buddhism and became the protector of mothers and newborns. The artist of this whimsical and fantastic work was a Buddhist priest, arguably the most influential painter and theoretician in the history of later Chinese painting.

Handscroll; ink on paper
10¾ x 139⅛ in. (27.2 x 353.3 cm)
Marshall H. Gould Fund   56.1151

below
Mirror
Japan
Kofun period, 5th century A.D.

Historically, mirrors have had special significance in Japan where, particularly in this early period, they were thought to possess magical properties and were associated with the power of the sun goddess. Mirrors with highly decorated backs, such as this one, were often buried with important officials as emblems of their authority. Here, in the broad band of decoration inside the raised rim, are symbols of the four points of the compass: the Tortoise and the Snake for the North, the Red Bird for the South, the Green Dragon for the East, and the White Tiger for the West.

Bronze
Diam. 9¼ in. (23.5 cm)
Museum purchase with funds donated by contribution   08.160

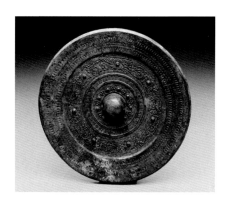

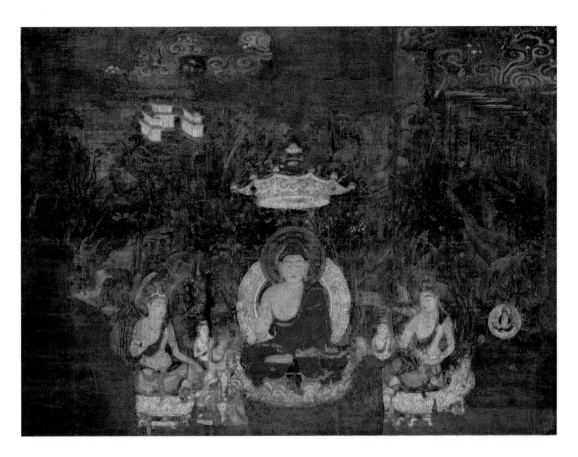

Shaka, the Historical Buddha, Preaching on Vulture Peak

Japan

Nara period, 8th century A.D.

One of few surviving examples of eighth-century Japanese painting, this panel depicts the Historical Buddha surrounded by his disciples and bodhisattvas. He is preaching the *Lotus Sutra*, a highly influential text that promises salvation to both men and women. The painting has suffered greatly over time and was repaired as early as the twelfth century. Despite surface abrasion and other losses, craggy mountain peaks and deep ravines can be discerned in the background and swirling clouds representing mystical energy at the top. This painting was once installed in the Hokkedō (Lotus Hall) at the celebrated temple Tōdai-ji in Nara. In 1884, at a time when many Buddhist temples were selling their treasures because of financial hardship, it was acquired by Bostonian William Sturgis Bigelow.

Panel; ink, color, and gold on ramie
42⅛ x 56½ in. (107.1 x 143.5 cm)
William Sturgis Bigelow Collection   11.6120

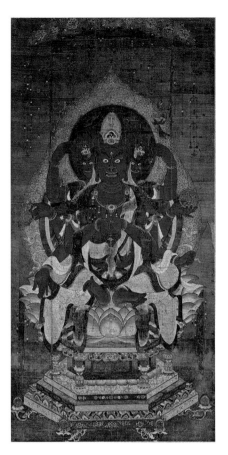

Batō Kannon, the Horse-Headed Bodhisattva of Compassion
Japan
Heian period, 12th century

Years of training were required to master the complicated tenets and rituals of the sect known as Esoteric Buddhism, and art was an important means of communicating the complexities of its theology and pantheon of deities. During the Heian period, the Esoteric Buddhist deity Batō Kannon, identified by the horse's head in his crown, was believed to look after those individuals reborn as animals. He was also revered as the protector of horses, cattle, and warriors. This painting was executed in the sumptuous style—featuring the lavish use of gold and silver (here darkened with age)— that dominated Japanese art during the twelfth century. Batō sits under a floral canopy festooned with strands of jewels. With some of his hands, the bodhisattva performs the ritual gestures, or *mudra*s, essential to Esoteric Buddhist practice; in others he holds symbolic objects.

Panel; ink, color, gold, and silver on silk
65⅜ x 32½ in. (166.1 x 82.7 cm)
Fenollosa-Weld Collection   11.4035

Minister Kibi's Trip to China (detail)
Japan
Heian period, late 12th century

This celebrated handscroll depicts the legends that grew up around Kibi no Makibi, a Japanese courtier who served as ambassador to the imperial court of China in A.D. 753. In scene after scene, the scroll illustrates and describes Kibi's progress as he matches wits with Chinese bureaucrats determined to belittle his (and, by extension, Japan's) scholarly accomplishments. Locked into a haunted tower, Kibi impresses the resident ghost—that of the previous Japanese ambassador, Abe no Nakamaro—with his integrity and upright demeanor. Assisted by Abe, Kibi outwits the Chinese using magic, artifice, and his native cunning. Remarkable for its vigorous, often humorous,

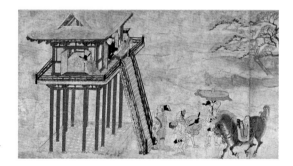

narrative style and its elegant calligraphy, this scroll was originally over eighty feet long; it has been divided into four sections to facilitate handling and ensure its preservation.

Set of four handscrolls; ink, color, and gold on paper
Entire scroll: 12⅝ x 961½ in. (32.2 x 2442 cm)
William Sturgis Bigelow Collection, by exchange   32.131

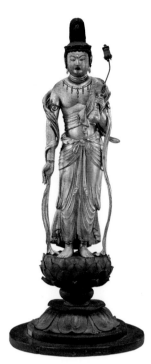

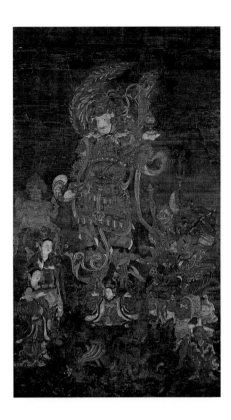

Kaikei

Japanese, active 1189–1223

Miroku, the Bodhisattva of the Future

Kamakura period, 1189

At the end of the twelfth century in Japan, the military class ascended to power in a series of bloody civil wars. During the rebuilding of temples destroyed in the conflict, the Kei school—of which Kaikei was a founder—produced most of the major sculptural commissions, creating a new, naturalistic style that dominated Japanese sculpture for over five hundred years. In this extraordinary carved and gilded image (Kaikei's earliest dated work), emerging naturalism is evident in the proportions of the body, the fall of the drapery, and the use of inlaid crystal for the eyes. The figure represents Miroku, the Bodhisattva of the Future, who will become the next Buddha. A scroll found inside the sculpture explains that it was made in 1189 for the repose of Kaikei's deceased parents and teacher.

Japanese cypress with gold and inlaid crystal;
split-and-joined construction
H. 42 in. (106.6 cm)
Special Chinese and Japanese Fund   20.723.1–3

*Bishamonten, the Guardian of the North,
with His Retinue*

Japan

Kamakura period, late 12th–early 13th century

Possibly because he is guardian of the North, the traditional source of malevolent forces, Bishamonten is the only one of the four celestial guardians of the cardinal directions who is worshiped as an independent Buddhist deity. In this highly dramatic painting, tall flames rise behind the head of Bishamonten, who wears armor embellished with the heads of demons and wields a silver-edged sword. The painting is remarkable for its vivid details and for the range of supernatural beings who surround the deity, including (to his right) his voluptuous consort Kichijō-ten, the Goddess of Good Fortune.

Panel; ink, color, gold, and silver on silk
46⅞ x 26⅞ in. (119.1 x 68.1 cm)
Special Chinese and Japanese Fund   05.202

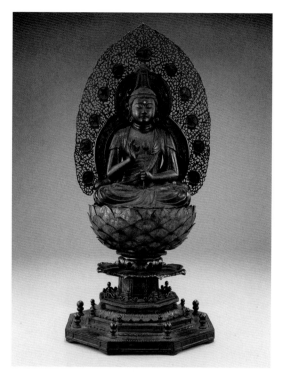

opposite, top

Takeshiba Toshiteru and others
Japanese, dates unknown
Set of matched mountings for a long and a short sword (*daishō*) with design of autumn plants and insects
Edo period, mid-19th century

Amid the incessant civil wars that erupted in Japan during the fifteenth and sixteenth centuries, middle-ranking and senior samurai began to carry two swords: the *katana* and the shorter *wakizashi*, a combination known as "large and small" (*daishō*). During the Edo period, the mountings for these *daishō* sets grew increasingly elaborate, employing fragile materials such as lacquer, silk, gold, and soft copper alloys. This example features a unified design of autumn grasses and insects, supposedly based on a painting by Kano Tan'yū. The metal fittings include the pommel (*kashira*) and collar (*fuchi*) covering each end of the hilt, which were made as a matching set; the *menuki*, a pair of fittings underneath the hilt's silk wrapping, intended to improve the grip; the hand guard (*tsuba*) at the beginning of the polished, sharp part of the blade; the handle of a small knife (*kozuka*) carried in the scabbard; and a skewerlike implement, the *kōgai* (not visible here), carried in the opposite side of the scabbard.

Scabbards: gold-lacquered wood; hilts: wood covered in ray skin wrapped with silk bands; metal fittings: gold, silver, and copper alloys; tying cords: silk
L. 28⅛ and 39 in. (71.4 and 99.2 cm)
William Sturgis Bigelow Collection   11.11291b–i, 11.11292b–i

Saichi
Japanese, dates unknown
Shō Kannon, the Bodhisattva of Compassion
Kamakura period, 1269

The white lotus symbolized purity throughout Asia because it perches above the water on its long stem as if growing miraculously out of the mud. Here the Bodhisattva of Compassion is shown holding a lotus bud and seated on a lotus blossom throne that indicates his divinity. His distinctive halo is decorated with floral designs and eleven disks on which appear Sanskrit letters representing his name and that of the Cosmic Buddha. Cast in separable parts, this intricate sculpture is one of the finest surviving examples of thirteenth-century Japanese bronze work. It was originally enshrined in the main hall of Kongōrin-ji, a Buddhist temple east of Kyoto.

Gilt bronze; cast from piece molds
H. 19¾ in. (50.3 cm)
William Sturgis Bigelow Collection   11.11447

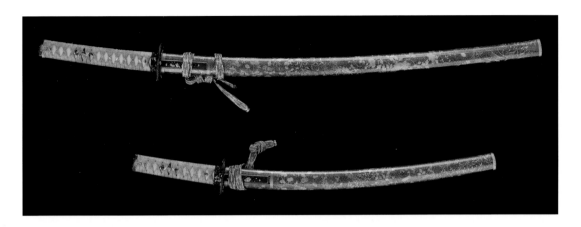

Night Attack on the Sanjō Palace (detail)
Japan
Kamakura period, third quarter of the 13th century

The bloody civil war between the Taira and Minamoto clans in the twelfth century was a perennial source of inspiration for later artists. The earliest surviving images are three scrolls and some isolated fragments known as *The Illustrated Handscrolls of the Events of the Heiji Era*. First in the series, this scroll powerfully re-creates Minamoto's attack of 1159 on the Sanjō Palace, from which the influential retired emperor Go-Shirakawa was abducted. The brilliant flames of the burning palace dominate the composition, swirling above crowds of combatants who are rendered in minute and brutal detail. Several artists were probably involved in the production of these paintings, but none of their names is known.

Handscroll; ink and color on paper
Entire scroll: 16¼ x 275½ in. (41.3 x 699.7 cm)
Fenollosa-Weld Collection 11.4000

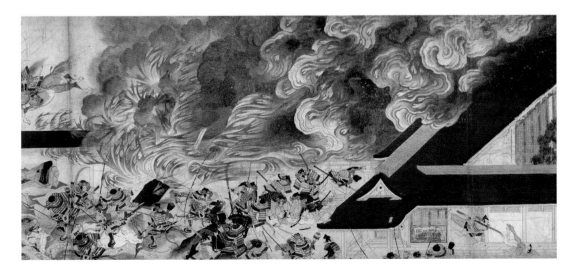

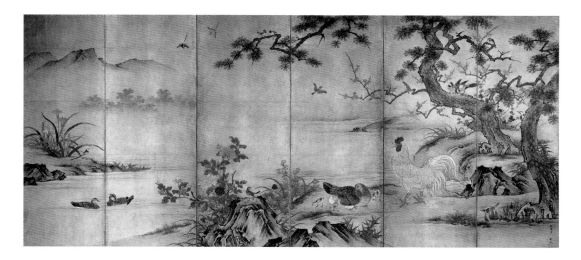

Kano Shōei
Japanese, 1519–1592
Fowl in Spring and Summer Landscape
Muromachi period, 16th century

The delightful painted decoration of this folding
screen places meticulously rendered birds and flowers within a soft, evocative landscape. The signature in the lower right corner is that of Kano Tan'yū,
who attributed this work to his great-grandfather,
Kano Shōei, son of Kano Motonobu—one of the
early leaders of the highly influential Kano school.
In this screen, Shōei achieved a synthesis of *kanga*
(the subtle, monochrome ink painting of China) and
yamato-e (the traditional bright and decorative painting of Japan). It is a style well suited to large-scale
compositions such as screens and sliding doors and
was popular into the modern period.

Six-panel folding screen; ink and light color on paper
59⅝ x 146½ in. (151.5 x 372 cm)
Fenollosa-Weld Collection   11.4347

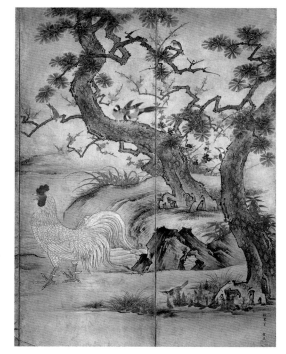

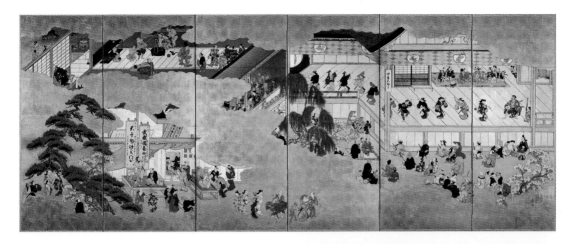

Hishikawa Moronobu

Japanese, died 1694

Scenes from the Nakamura Kabuki Theater and
the Yoshiwara Pleasure Quarter

Edo period, about 1684–1704

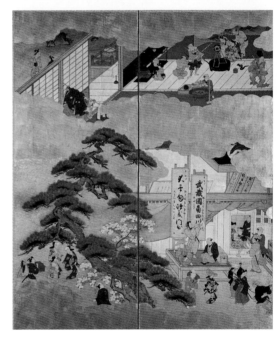

This screen is a vivid, early example of *ukiyo-e*,
"images of the floating world." As a subject for art, the
pleasures of the entertainment world became highly
popular in the seventeenth century when members of
the prosperous middle class increasingly frequented
kabuki theaters as well as the brothels and teahouses
of "pleasure quarters" such as the Yoshiwara in Edo
(present-day Tokyo). This screen shows three areas
of the Nakamura-za, a famous kabuki theater. In the
lower left, men and women of varied occupations and
social levels walk along the street in front of the theater. Depicted above is a backstage area where actors
and musicians prepare for a performance. The right
half of the screen shows the stage and the area for
the audience. On stage, costumed figures dance to the
lively rhythms of the *shamisen* and drums.

One of a pair of six-panel folding screens; ink and color on
gold-leafed paper
55 x 137⅞ in. (139.8 x 355.2 cm)
Gift of Oliver Peabody   79.468

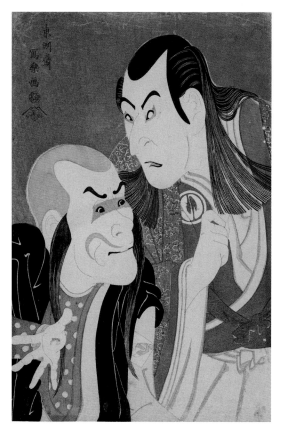

Tōshūsai Sharaku

Japanese, active 1794–1795

Actors Sawamura Yodogorō II as Kawatsura Hōgen and Bandō Zenji as Oninosadobō

Edo period, 1794

Published by **Tsutaya Jūzaburō (Kōshodō)**

The enigmatic Tōshūsai Sharaku, known only by his pen name (meaning "Pleasure in Drawing"), is today the most highly admired of all Japanese print artists. Active for less than a year, from 1794 to the beginning of 1795, he designed about 150 known prints, almost all depicting Kabuki actors. This double portrait juxtaposes good and evil characters from the same play, *The Thousand Cherry Trees of Yoshitsune.* The extreme, deliberately exaggerated, caricature-like style of his actor portraits generates an emotional intensity that still resonates with viewers more than two centuries later.

Color woodblock print
15 ⅛ x 9 ⅞ in. (38.3 x 25.2 cm)
William Sturgis Bigelow Collection   11.14676

opposite, bottom

Clothing tray (*midarebako*) with decoration of shells, autumn grasses, and crests

Japan

Momoyama period, late 16th–early 17th century

In lacquerwork, the resin or sap of a lacquer tree is colored with pigments and applied over a wooden understructure in many thin layers—sometimes more than forty. The result of this painstaking process is a smooth, strong, and lustrous surface that was often inlaid with designs in precious metals. This shallow tray made to hold clothing combines bold designs

and naturalistic detail. The tray is a particularly fine, large-scale example of Kōdai-ji ware, the most popular type of lacquerwork of the Momoyama period. The crests of paulownia flowers and chrysanthemums found throughout the tray's decoration associate it with the patronage of the clan of Toyotomi Hideyoshi, one of the three great warlords of Japan during this period.

Lacquered wood with gold and silver overlays
22 ¼ x 21 x 3 in. (56.6 x 53.3 x 7.7 cm)
Keith McLeod Fund   1998.58

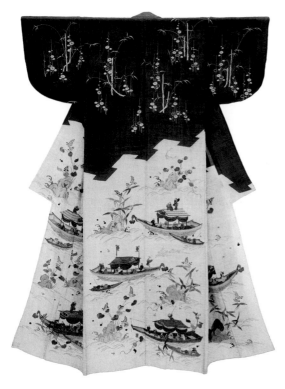

Summer robe (*katabira*)
Japan
Edo period, 18th century

Unlined robes made from hemp or ramie (an Asian plant fiber) were worn during the summer by upper-class Japanese women. The designs of these luxurious garments often include water motifs appropriate for times of oppressive heat, and the lower section of this robe shows aristocrats enjoying themselves on pleasure boats. The robe was decorated using a technique in which the artist outlined each part of the design with rice paste to prevent bleeding of the dyes. The dyes were applied with a brush and the rice paste washed away when the colors were set. The plum blossoms and bamboo in the upper section of this *katabira* were made by this same method and further embellished with embroidery in colored threads and gold paper.

Ramie; plain weave with resist and stencil dyeing, hand-painting, silk and gilt paper, and embroidery
H. 64 in. (162.4 cm)
William Sturgis Bigelow Collection   21.1134

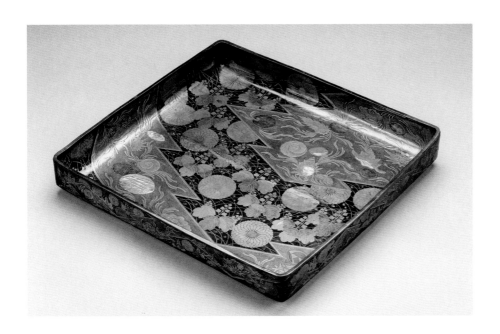

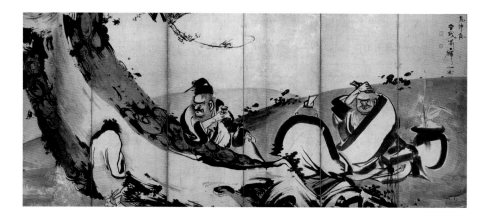

Soga Shōhaku
Japanese, 1730–1781
The Four Sages of Mount Shang
Edo period, about 1768

Shōhaku's career coincided with a remarkable period of artistic innovation in Japanese art, when eccentricity and originality of vision enhanced rather than hindered a painter's reputation. An individualist in both his life and his art, Shōhaku worked almost exclusively in monochrome ink, painting in a spontaneous, expressionistic style. The energy and dexterity of his swift, broad brushwork are nowhere more fully realized than in this late work, one of a pair of screens illustrating a popular subject from Chinese legend. The Four Sages were elderly paragons of virtue who retreated to Mount Shang during the political unrest of the third century B.C., remaining there until they felt that moral rectitude had returned to the world of human affairs.

One of a pair of six-panel folding screens; ink and gold on paper
60⅞ x 142¼ in. (154.5 x 361.4 cm)
Fenollosa-Weld Collection   11.4514

Itō Jakuchū
Japanese, 1716–1800
White Cockatoo on a Pine Branch
Edo period, late 18th century

Like his contemporary Shōhaku, Jakuchū was one of the celebrated "eccentric" painters of the Edo period whose success reflects the diminishing dominance of official styles of art at this time. Of humble origins and primarily self-taught, Jakuchū began by copying Chinese paintings preserved in the temples of Kyoto but soon found his inspiration in *shaseiga*, or painting from nature. It is said that the artist raised birds himself in order to study more closely their appearance and behavior and to sketch them from life.

Hanging scroll; ink and color
15¾ x 21⅞ in. (40.1 x 55.6 cm)
Bequest of Charles Bain Hoyt—Charles Bain Hoyt Collection
50.1493

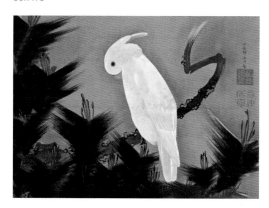

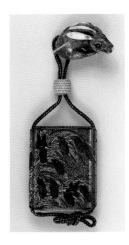

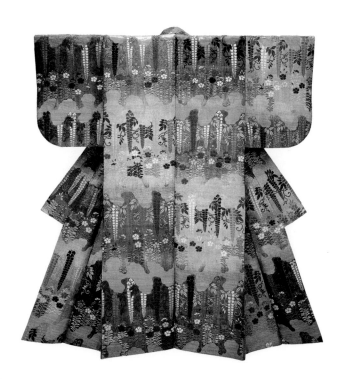

Attributed to Garaku Risuke
Japanese, dates unknown
**Toggle (*netsuke*) in the form of a hare
scratching its chin with its right hind leg**
Edo period, early–mid-18th century

Netsuke are toggles used to secure items such
as *inrō* (medicine cases) suspended on cords
from the wearer's sash. The earliest examples
were probably simple ivory rings, but at some
point in the seventeenth century, these were
replaced first by imported Chinese carvings
and then by figurative pieces produced in
workshops in Kyoto and Osaka. Although the
ivory hare illustrated here is unsigned, its
powerfully carved, deeply stained fur, large
inlaid horn eyes, and compact form all suggest
the work of Garaku Risuke, who worked in
Osaka. In the later eighteenth century, *netsuke*
production spread to other urban centers,
including both Edo and Nagoya, and wood
became increasingly popular as a less expensive alternative to ivory.

Carved and stained ivory with eyes inlaid in
dark horn
1⅛ x 1⅞ x 1 in. (2.7 x 4.8 x 2.5 cm)
Gift of Major Henry Lee Higginson 18.221b

Robe for the Nō theater (*karaori*)
Japan
Edo period, late 18th–early 19th century

Silk robes woven with sumptuous floral motifs are worn by
actors in the highly stylized performances of the Nō theater,
which integrate speech, music, dancing, and mime. Perform-
ing on a spare stage with minimal props, the actors (who are
all men) depend upon their robes and wooden masks to com-
municate their characters to the audience. The red color of
this robe indicates that the character portrayed was a young
woman. Although seen from a considerable distance by the
audience (which in the Edo period was often members of the
military elite), *karaori* are extremely elegant and sophisticated in materials, design, and craft.

Silk; twill weave with pattern-dyed warps and silk and gilt paper
supplementary pattern wefts
H. 60¼ in. (153 cm)
William Sturgis Bigelow Collection   15.1148

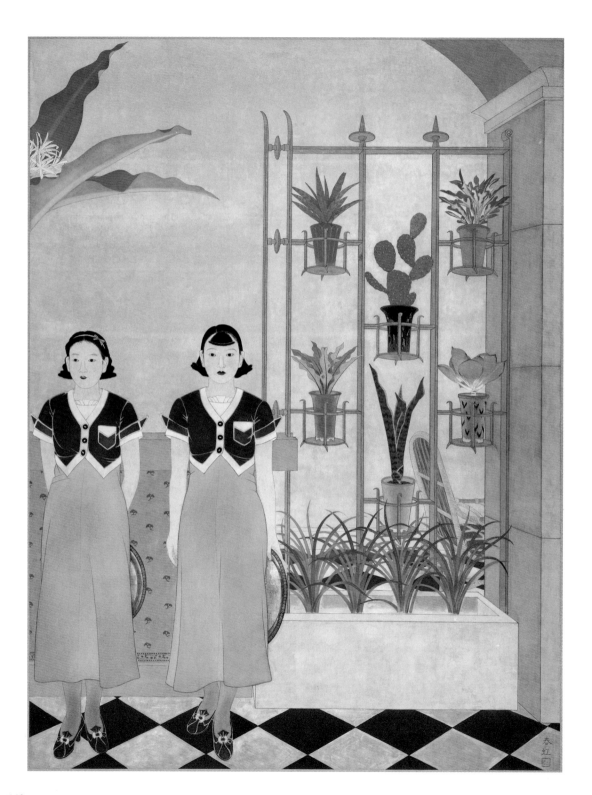

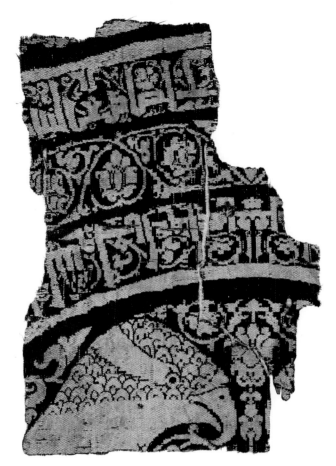

opposite

Saeki Shunkō

Japanese, 1909–1942

Tearoom

Shōwa era, 1936

With the government's campaign to modernize Japan in the second half of the nineteenth century, Japanese artists debated the very form that their paintings should take. Some championed Western-style works (*yōga*), executed in European oil paints, while others advocated Japanese-style compositions (*nihonga*), with their mineral pigments and classic formats. Still others, including Saeki Shunkō, explored the possibilities offered by synthesizing the two. Here, using traditional Japanese materials, Shunkō presents the interior of a Western-style tearoom—a popular subject among painters in the 1920s and '30s in a rapidly changing Tokyo. Shunkō, who had a successful career in textile design before turning to painting, portrays two "modern girls" (*moga*), devotees of European and American fashions, in richly colored garb. They stand on a tiled floor before a display of carefully and vibrantly rendered plants— including an imported cactus.

Panel; ink, color, and silver on paper
104 x 78 in. (264.2 x 198.1 cm)
Charles H. Bayley Picture and Painting
Fund and Museum purchase with funds
donated anonymously   2007.815

Silk fragment

Iran, 11th or 12th century

Reportedly found near the city of Tabriz, in northwestern Iran, this textile fragment once featured pairs of beautifully rendered falcons encircled by vine scrolls and Arabic inscriptions wishing the owner "lasting glory, all-embracing bounty, felicity, good fortune, and abundant ease." Islam's proscription against the depiction of living things usually did not apply to textiles, and roundels enclosing human or animal figures were common designs. Within Islamic cultures, silk weaving was a major art form, and lavishly patterned silks were symbols of authority, rank, and prestige. This small fragment masterfully illustrates the refinement and technical sophistication of Islamic silk weaving and textile design.

Silk, double cloth
7⅞ x 5½ in. (20 x 14 cm)
Denman Waldo Ross Collection   04.1621

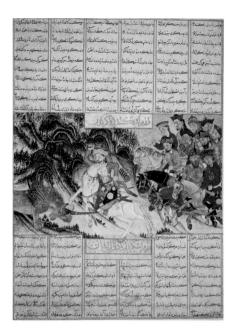

Alexander Fights the Monster of Habash
Page from a manuscript of the *Shahnama*
Iran (Tabriz)
Mongol period, before 1335

The *Shahnama* (Book of Kings) is the national epic of
Persia (today's Iran) and the most frequently illustrated manuscript in Islamic art. A blend of myth and
history numbering nearly sixty thousand rhymed cou-
plets, the *Shahnama* was written by the poet Firdawsi
over a period of thirty years at the turn of the elev-
enth century. This page shows a historical figure,
Alexander the Great, slaying a fantastic, mythological
beast. The mountains in the background, rendered in
a distinctly Chinese manner, are typical of Eastern
stylistic elements often found in fourteenth-century
Persian manuscript painting. This superb page was
part of a royal commission known as the "Great Mongol Shahnama"—one of the earliest surviving illustrated versions of the epic poem.

Opaque watercolor, gold, and ink on paper
23¼ x 15⅝ in. (59 x 39.6 cm)
Denman Waldo Ross Collection   30.105

Wasma'a Chorbachi
American (Iraqi, born in Egypt), born 1943
The Profession of Faith (Al Shahada), 1994

Ceramic artist Wasma'a Chorbachi incorporates
Arabic inscriptions into many of her works, drawing upon a centuries-old tradition of ornamenting
vessels with sacred phrases or secular blessings. The
Islamic profession of faith, *shahada*, appears twice
on this plate, rotated 180 degrees around a point—an
effect known among calligraphers as a "two-sided
structure." Rather than painting them in slip or glaze,
Chorbachi impressed the words into the clay before
firing, using a carved wooden block from the seventeenth century, made for patterning Indian textiles.
The letters appear as depressions in the white-glazed
porcelain, and the words—"There is no God but God
and Muhammad is the messenger of God"—seem to
emerge from within the clay itself. Ripples at the edge
suggest their movement outward, into the world.

Porcelain with matte glaze
2¾ x 16¾ in. (7 x 42.7 cm)
Asiatic Deaccession Fund   2002.107

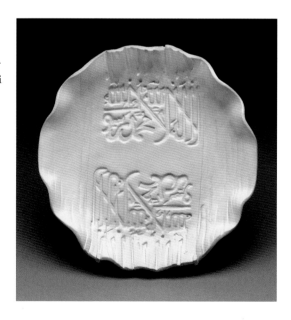

Design for a water clock
Egypt (probably Cairo)
Mamluk period, 1354

Written in 1206 by the engineer Ibn
al-Razzaz al-Jazari, *The Book of
Knowledge of Mechanical Devices*
detailed the construction of elaborate mechanical devices ranging
from clocks and locks to auto-
mated vessels for washing hands.
This design for a clock is from a
manuscript of al-Jazari's text created in 1354 for an official serving
the Mamluk sultan of Egypt. Run
by water, the clock is operated
with a complex system of reservoirs, floats, and pulleys. Every
hour of the day, a figure emerges
from one of the twelve doorways
in the arcade below the signs of
the zodiac, and the two falcons on
the sides come out and drop balls
from their beaks. Hourly during
the night, one of the twelve circles
in the lower arch lights up. At the
sixth, ninth, and twelfth hours, the
musicians play their instruments.

Opaque watercolor, gold, and ink
on paper
15½ x 10⅞ in. (39.5 x 27.5 cm)
Francis Bartlett Donation of 1912 and
Picture Fund 14.533

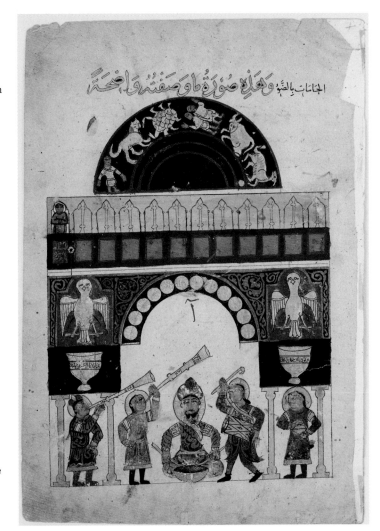

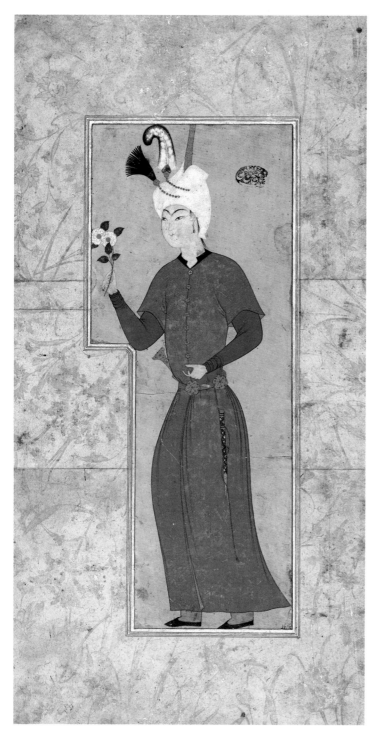

A Young Prince Holding Flowers

Iran

Safavid, 16th century

From his round face shown in conventional three-quarter view to his tiny feet in profile, this elegant youth resembles many others depicted in sixteenth-century Persian painting. If this "portrait" once represented a specific individual, the young man's identity is now unknown. His turban, however, establishes that he is a nobleman at the court of Shah Tahmasp I (ruled 1524–1576), whose followers wore a felt cap (*taj*) with a tall projection around which a length of silk or cotton was wrapped in a graceful, tapering shape. A nobleman could embellish his turban with jewelry and feathers.

Opaque watercolor on paper
19 x 12⅜ in. (48.2 x 31.4 cm)
Francis Bartlett Donation of 1912 and Picture Fund   14.590

Woman's coat (*munisak*)
Uzbekistan (Bukhara region), 1850–1900

The laborious process of ikat—the repeated tying and dyeing of the threads of a cloth before weaving—has long been practiced in many parts of the world. The ikat textiles created in Central Asia during the nineteenth century, however, are unrivaled in their vibrant colors and explosive patterns. In such isolated desert cities as Bukhara and Samarkand (in today's Uzbekistan), sumptuous ikat wall hangings and robes brought vibrant color to life in a stark, barren landscape. Both men and women wore ikat clothing; the *munisak*, a woman's coat characterized by extra fullness at the hips, was the most costly item of a bride's dowry.

Silk; cut-velvet, resist-dyed (ikat) pile warp
H. 46½ in. (118 cm)
Gift in memory of Jay Abrams   58.342

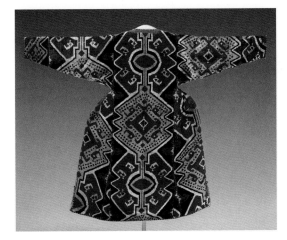

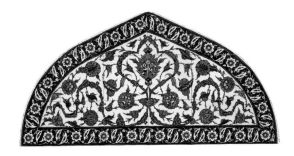

Tile panel
Turkey (Iznik)
Ottoman period, about 1573

Present-day Turkey was once the core of the Ottoman Empire, which dominated large areas of the Middle East, North Africa, and southern Europe in the sixteenth century. The city of Iznik in northwestern Turkey was a center for the production of ceramic tiles used to decorate many buildings, including mosques and palaces. This panel was probably placed above a window or doorway in the palace complex at Istanbul of Piyale Pasha, grand admiral of the Ottoman fleet. Iznik ceramic artists frequently adopted designs from illuminated manuscripts and textiles. Here, the artist employed a vocabulary of Chinese-inspired plant forms known as the *saz* (enchanted forest) style, as well as Chinese cloud bands rendered in a distinctly Turkish iron-oxide red.

Composite body (quartz, clay, and glass frit) with colors
painted on white slip under clear glaze
W. 57⅛ in. (145.1 cm)
Bequest of Mrs. Martin Brimmer   06.2437

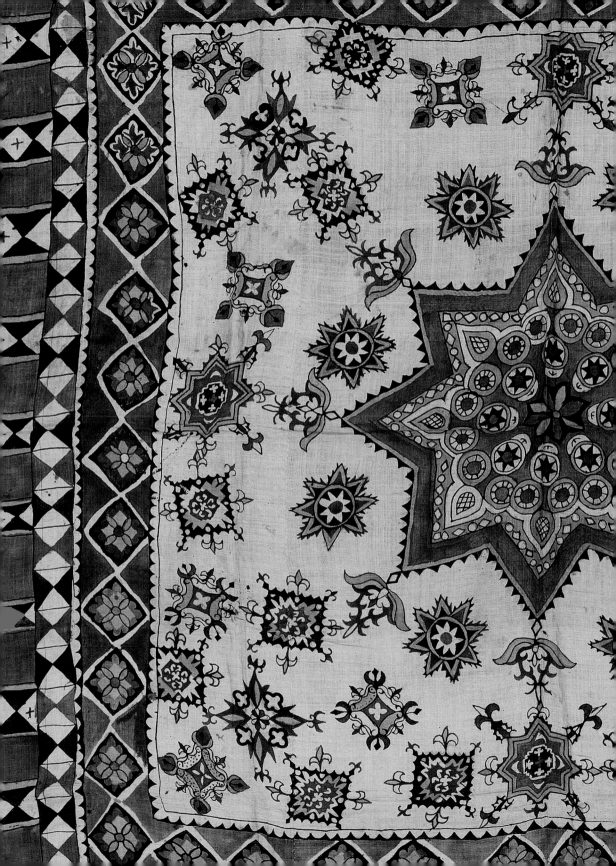

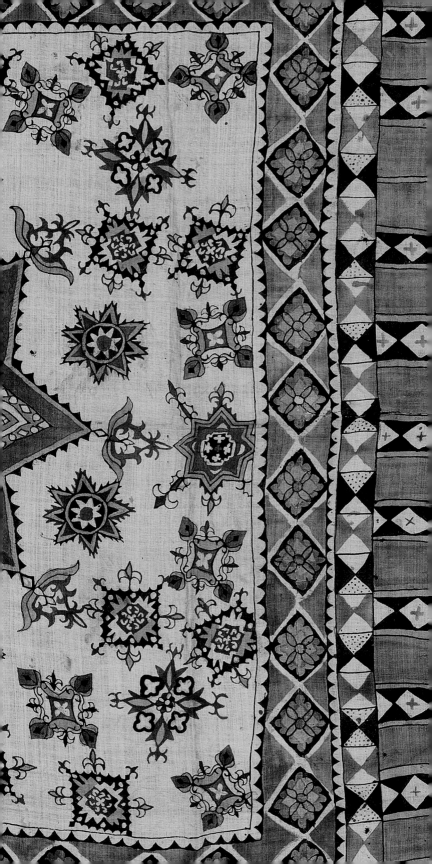

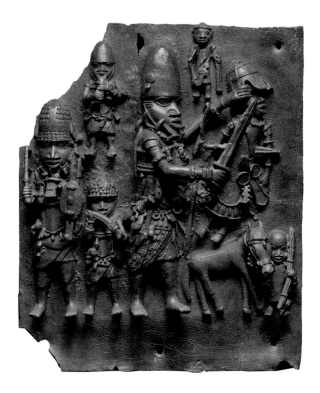

Relief plaque of a battle scene
Benin kingdom
Edo state, Nigeria, about 1530–70

Created using the lost-wax technique of casting, this magnificent plaque
once hung among more than 850 others in the audience hall of the palace of the *oba* (or king) of Benin. It is one of only six "battle plaques," so
called for their imagery. Here, a victorious Benin warrior takes a parting
thrust at his slain enemy, whose facial markings have been associated
with kingdoms north of Benin City, in present-day Nigeria. (Northern
kingdoms had horses, which Benin had difficulty keeping due to endemic
sleeping sickness.) The scene may refer to historical events: perhaps the
wars of expansion under Oba Orhogbua (r. 1550s–70s), or the earlier war
against the neighboring Idah kingdom under Oba Esigie (r. 1517–50s).
Note the masterful details throughout, which the sculptor achieved not
by chiseling into the final cast metal but by forming them in the wax
model before casting.

Copper alloy
18½ x 15¾ in. (47 x 40 cm)
Robert Owen Lehman Collection

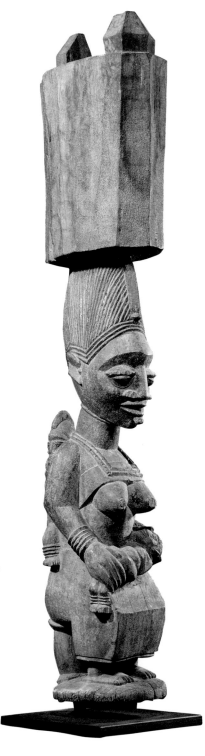

opposite, right

Agbonbiofe

Nigerian (Yoruba), active by 1900,
died 1945

Palace pillar

Efon-Alaye, Ekiti state, Nigeria,
about 1912–16

This massive architectural sculpture presents a regal woman of power and compassion, her status affirmed by her necklace, lip ornament, and towering coiffure. She supports two infants, symbols of royal continuity, one on her lap, another strapped to her back. After a fire in 1912, Agbonbiofe, master of the Adeshina family of sculptors and beadworkers, carved about twenty-five new pillars for an inner courtyard of the palace in Efon-Alaye, in present-day southwestern Nigeria. One of only seven surviving examples, this post once supported a beam and rested on a carved figure, now lost.

Wood and pigments
H. 58 in. (147.3 cm)
Gift of William E. and Bertha L. Teel
1994.425

Master of Oroma Etiti Anam

Nigerian (Igbo)

Altar to the hand (*ikenga*)

Oroma Etiti Anam, Anamba West,
Nigeria, about 1910

An *ikenga*, or altar to the hand, celebrates an Igbo man's accomplishments thus far in life. It serves as both a monument to what its owner has achieved through the work of his own hands, and a location that facilitates prayer and sacrifice to ensure his future success. The elements of this *ikenga* speak of aggression. The figure sits with spine straight, head held erect, his mouth stretched into a grimace. Above, a whirling superstructure of snakes, rams' heads, bats, and a leopard allude to qualities of stealth, perseverance, and stubbornness. This daring composition was devised by an experienced artist working in the village of Oroma Etiti Anam. The sculpture's size suggests it was commissioned by a highly successful man; the diagonal lines on the figure's forehead are a mark of leadership in the *ozo* organization, a group of spiritual leaders. While more modest *ikenga* might stay in the homes of their owners, a masterfully carved sculpture like this one may have been kept in a community shrine.

Wood, pigment
H. 43 in. (109.2 cm)
Gift of William E. and Bertha L. Teel
1994.421

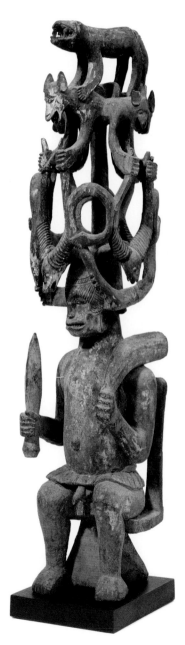

Mounted ruler (so-called Horseman)
Benin kingdom
Edo state, Nigeria, 16th century

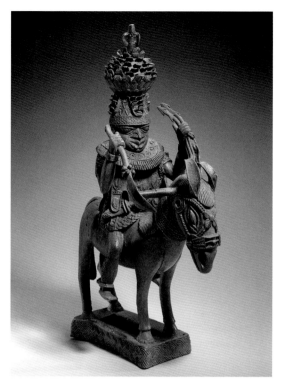

A finely dressed warrior heads into battle atop a horse—a rare luxury in the Benin kingdom. A band of coral beads rests on the warrior's forehead, while rings of feathers encircle the basketry projection at the top of his head, a regional symbol of high rank. His broad, elegant fringed collar and tunic with cowrie shell appliqués also assert the man's authority. Although some scholars once identified this figure as a king of Benin, others convincingly argue that he is a foreigner—possibly the king of the Idah, a neighboring state that attacked Benin in the early 1500s. The sculpture would have been placed on a commemorative altar for a deceased king, likely alluding to Benin's decisive victory in this critical battle.

The sculpture's deep brown patina obscures the fact that the horse and figure (and base) are cast from different materials: bronze and nearly pure copper, respectively. Copper is particularly difficult to cast since, in liquid form, it curdles when exposed to air. When originally installed, this sculpture would have gleamed yellow and red.

Copper alloy
H. 18 in. (45.7 cm)
Robert Owen Lehman Collection

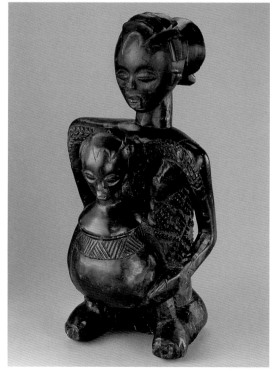

opposite, bottom

Possibly by Kitwa Biseke
Congolese (Luba Kingdom), active
1910–1935
Bowl bearer (*mboko*)
Mwanza, near Luba Kingdom,
Democratic Republic of the Congo,
1910–30s

This sculpture is a luxuriously
embellished vessel that most
likely held a simple gourd filled
with white chalk. It may have been
owned by a high-ranking official,
who would have expected his guests
to daub themselves with chalk as a
sign of respect before greeting him;
or by a royal diviner, who would
rub chalk onto visitors himself
as a mark of healing. The sharp
angles of the woman's shoulders,
her abstract, shortened legs, and
the crests of her hair are typical of
sculpture from the Mwanza region,
at the heart of the Luba Kingdom.

Made early in the twentieth
century, this *mboko* represents
the work of a master artist at a
time of intense social change.
Through taxation, occupation, and
forced labor, the Belgian colonial
government eroded local political structures, causing declining
patronage for royal arts. At the
same time, Protestant missionaries in this region sought to convert
local leaders while also purchas-
ing artworks as souvenirs.

Wood
H. 18½ in. (47 cm)
Gift of William E. and Bertha L. Teel
1996.386

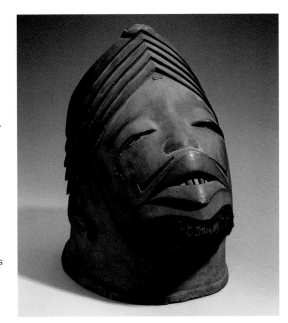

Mask (*lipiko*)
Mueda Plateau, Mozambique, 1930s

The 1930s witnessed significant political change in the Mueda Plateau in
northern Mozambique, as Portuguese colonial forces began dominating
the area. Thousands of young Makonde men and women fled north into
Tanzania, returning home to visit with new ideas and imported luxuries.
In response, the style of the Makonde *lipiko* changed—accommodat-
ing a more mobile generation's aesthetic preferences and embracing the
increasingly cosmopolitan faces of daily life. This mask depicts a Sikh
trader from abroad. Dancing with quick steps in the center of town, a
male performer would have supported the mask on the top of his head,
his eyes peering out from the parted lips. Only his feet and hands would
have been visible to the crowd, the rest of him concealed by a fabric ruff
and tight costume.

In performance, the *lipiko*—the word refers to both mask and masked
performer—is considered at once an ancestral spirit, a man, and a character in the dance's narrative. The dance is both a celebration and an
opportunity for public examination of important topics, including politics, satires on village scandals, or mimicry of daily events.

Wood, paint, hair
H. 13 in. (33 cm)
Gift of Peter von Burchard in memory of Gisela and Joachim von Burchard
2014.1968

Carved stone (*atal* or *akwanshi*)
Cross River state, Nigeria, 18th–19th century

This stone sculpture is one of three hundred monoliths found in villages in northern Cross River state, Nigeria. The heavy basalt rock, smoothed into an ovoid shape by the current of a river a few miles away, has been carved into an expressive face, with wide eyes and brows raised in an expression of surprise. Below the chin, abstract patterns cover the area where a torso might be. During the British occupation of Nigeria, a British officer saw the sculptures on multiple sites and later published information about them in Europe. Many of the sculptures were overgrown with vines in the center of abandoned towns. Although the original artists' intentions are unclear, today the sculptures have found a new purpose: serving as memorials to previous generations during a celebration of bountiful harvests, the New Yam festival. Some families have moved the sculptures into the center of their villages, and women paint the surfaces for the festival to refresh the sculptures and honor the ancestors they may represent.

Basalt
H. 29 in. (73.7 cm)
Gift of William E. and Bertha L. Teel   1994.419

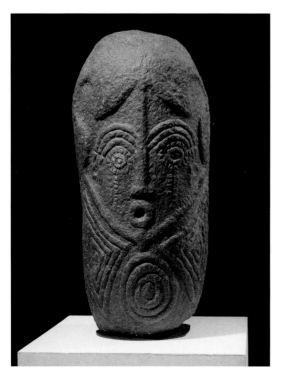

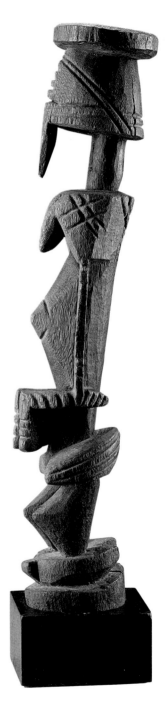

opposite, right

Figure

Bandiagara cliffs, Mali, late 19th–early 20th century

With its echoing interplay of curving and angular, vertical and horizontal elements, the slight body of this Dogon shrine figure dissolves into a cascade of perfect geometry. The artist has delicately carved diagonal lines into the shoulders, arms, and hips to accentuate their shape and volume. The double line on the head separates the face from the hair. The briefest suggestion of features on the face creates a moving profile with parted lips. The figure is also androgynous: the breasts are reminiscent of a woman who has nursed children, but a beard projects from the chin.

Dogon families keep shrines in the home of the oldest man in the family to honor their ancestors. Placed within the shrine, sculptures like this one are viewed as sites for the deceased's spirit to rest when it leaves the body after death. On this figure, the weathered stomach and upper thighs, and the remains of offerings on the back, suggest the sculpture aided prayerful worship for many years.

Wood
H. 20 in. (50.8 cm)
Gift of William E. and Bertha L. Teel
1991.1068

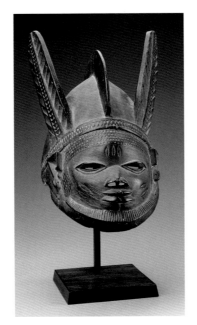

Master of Anago

Beninese (likely Yoruba), active 19th century

Gelede headdress

Near Anago, Benin, 19th century

The annual Yoruba gelede festival honors mothers, with dancing beginning in the late afternoon and continuing until the early hours of the morning. During the spectacle, masked dancers celebrate women's contributions to their families and communities, tease them about gossiping and nagging, and cajole them to use their powers to sow harmony rather than discord. This striking mask was carved by the Master of Anago; the rectilinear ears are particular signatures of his style. Two feathers rise from the top, their height balanced by the crest in the center of the hair. The eyes are narrow, almond-shaped slits to conceal the dancer and also to reflect a polite woman's reserved gaze. Clusters of parallel lines punctuate the smoothly finished surface—representations of incisions that were considered beauty marks in southwestern Yorubaland. The band of incised triangles on the forehead and temples is a decoration of the artist's invention. Most gelede masks are colorfully painted, and this one would have been too, but at some point its paint was removed. Today, only the form remains.

Wood, pigment
H. 16½ in. (41.9 cm)
Gift of William E. and Bertha L. Teel   1991.1081

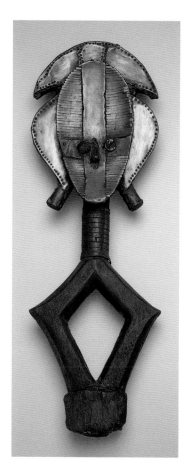

Master of the Sébé

Gabonese, active in the 18th century

Reliquary figure (*mbulu ngulu*)

Sébé River area, Gabon, 18th century

Made in Gabon, this reliquary guardian is one of only nine known figures by an unidentified sculptor referred to as the Master of the Sébé.
Imagine its concave face glimmering inside a dimly lit room. Delicate,
diminutive, it represents a younger woman. The smooth semicircles on
the top and sides of the head represent the figure's hair; the small spools
on either side, her earrings. Originally, the sculpture would have been
part of a group of three, with a senior woman and a man. Together, they
represented ideal ancestors whose relics were held in baskets below each
figure. Obamba communities, often mistakenly called Kota, moved every
few years, when the quality of the soil could no longer guarantee abundant crops. Reliquary baskets helped families maintain continuity with
their beloved deceased relatives when they moved to a new place.

    After the Obamba converted to Christianity around 1900, communities
abandoned the reliquary figures or destroyed them as proof of their new
faith—leaving opportunistic traders and colonial officials to market the
cast-off sculptures to collectors in Europe.

Wood, metal
H. 18½ in. (47 cm)
Gift of Geneviève McMillan in memory of Reba Stewart   2009.2696

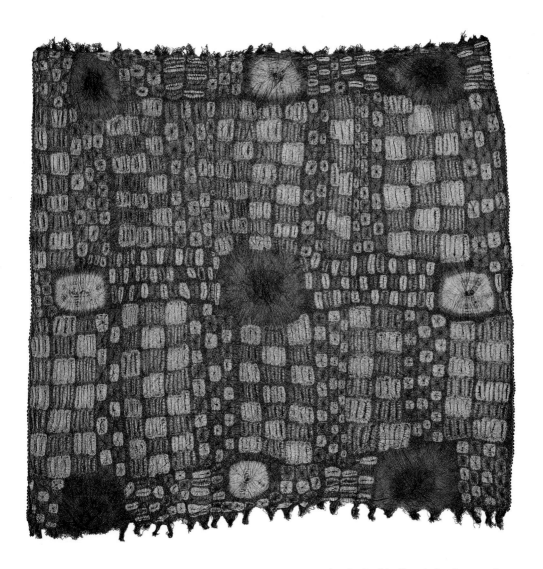

Man's wrapper

South-central Côte d'Ivoire, about 1900

With their dynamic compositions and almost sculptural tactility, the works of female Dida weavers of southern Côte d'Ivoire are unmistakable. The talented woman who made this wrapper did so using a multistage, labor-intensive process. First, she braided together individual threads of the raffia palm by hand, without the help of a loom, resulting in a fine, linen-like cloth. Next, she bound the fabric and utilized a tie-dye technique to produce the striking color patterns. The tie-dye bindings helped create the textural "map" of color across the surface, whose peaks and valleys translate even in a photograph. Due to the intensive, time-consuming labor involved, the man who owned this garment would have worn it only on very special occasions.

Raffia; plaited and tie-dyed
59½ x 59½ in. (151 x 151 cm)
Frederick Brown Fund, Textile Income Purchase Fund, The Elizabeth Day McCormick Collection, by exchange, and Alice J. Morse Fund   2000.575

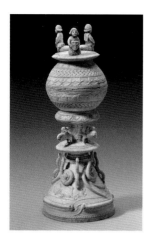

Saltcellar

Coast of Sierra Leone or Guinea, late 15th–early 16th century

During the fifteenth century, European traders began to ply the West African coast for new markets and, like many modern travelers, they brought home souvenirs of the places they visited. This ivory saltcellar is a particularly luxurious memento, made to hold an expensive commodity. It was likely commissioned by a wealthy Portuguese traveler from a Sapes (formerly called Sapi) artist, whose identity remains unknown. Certain motifs—the three kneeling Portuguese figures on the top, the hunting scene on the base, and initially the form of the saltcellar itself—would have been shown by the client to the artist on etchings or playing cards. Other elements likely represent a longer Sapi tradition (and reflect the artist's own taste), including the curling snakes, prominent birds, interlace pattern, and bands of small, inset spheres. More than fifty such saltcellars, or sections of them, survive, mostly in the curiosity cabinets of European royal households.

Ivory
10 x 4 in. (25.4 x 10.2 cm)
Robert Owen Lehman Collection

Master of the Flat Hands

Sierra Leonean (possibly Sherbro), active last half of the 19th century
Female figure
Possibly Bonthe Island, Sierra Leone, 1850–94

This is the earliest sculpture in any collection by the Master of the Flat Hands, an artist active on or near Bonthe Island in Sierra Leone in the late nineteenth century, and whose name remains unknown. ("Master of the Flat Hands" refers to a signature characteristic of the sculptor's works.) In this region of Sierra Leone, sculptures of women were used for four distinct purposes: as commemorations on a person's grave, like a tombstone; as sculptures kept and cared for inside the home to commemorate a twin who has died in infancy; as icons in a healing and leadership organization called Njayei; or as decorative objects in the home of a chief, announcing his support for a women's organization called Sande. However, judging by its unworn finish, this sculpture was probably purchased directly from the artist before it could be used locally for any particular purpose.

Wood
H. 30⅞ in. (78.5 cm)
Gift of Helen Howe Braider in memory of Fitzmaurice Manning   2017.854

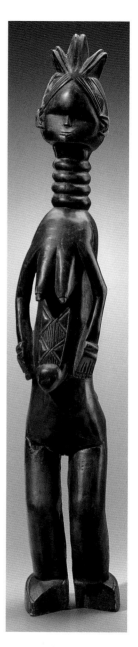

Feeding funnel (*korere*)
New Zealand, 19th–20th century

In the Maori art of tattooing, *tā moko*, designs are carved into the skin using chisel-like tools, creating grooves to be filled with dark pigment. Practitioners are accorded great respect, and their works—often adorning the face and lips—are considered marks of prestige for the bearer. For men of rank, it was forbidden (*tapu*) for cooked food to touch any part of the skin during the process, which could stretch on for days. Liquefied foods would be proffered by means of special funnels. This one is a masterpiece, surely made for a wealthy Maori man. Imagine gazing up from below as the deeply carved, whirling lines come into focus as abstract faces staring back. The sharp carving reflects a period after the adoption of imported iron tools in the nineteenth century, which made it easier to create the kinds of complex decorative patterns seen here. With its curling, ornamental detail, this particular funnel is the work of an artist of incredible skill.

Wood
H. 6½ in. (16.5 cm)
Gift of William E. and Bertha L. Teel   1991.1071

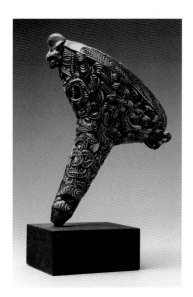

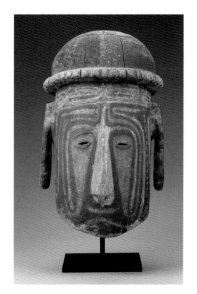

Helmet mask (*kakaparaga*)
Witu Islands, Papua New Guinea, late 19th century

Robust trade networks throughout New Guinea's Huon Gulf allowed Witu Islands traders to bring home not only goods, but new ideas—helping spur constant innovation in the arts. Most types of Witu Islands masks are made from delicate materials like cane fiber, feathers, and leaves. This colorful *kakaparaga* mask, with its flat, smooth surface and cylindrical shape, is one of the few carved from wood, a material choice likely inspired by masks by Kilenge artists on the island of New Britain, to the north. The curving ocher lines forming the face are highlighted against contrasting passages of bright turquoise, their looped patterns echoing the shape of the pendant ears. Only the name "death mask" was recorded when it was collected, between 1893 and 1895, and it remains unclear whether the mask was used in funerary celebrations or worn in memory of a deceased person. The mask is a rare monument to a turn-of-the-century artist's innovations in Witu Islands art.

Wood, pigment
H. 21 in. (53.3 cm)
Gift of William E. and Bertha L. Teel   1991.1075

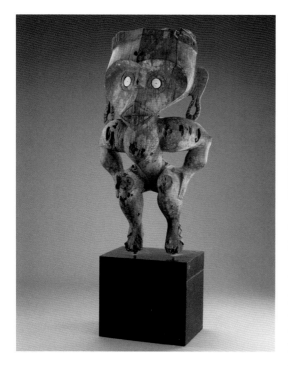

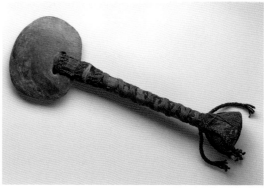

Ceremonial axe
New Caledonia, 19th century

This axe is not a functional tool, but an object of prestige. Such works were exchanged as gifts between elites—signaling both the wealth of the giver and the prominence of the recipient. This axe would have been owned by a chief and brought out only on special occasions, such as weddings, funerals, and community celebrations. The bottom is a rattle, shaken during a chief's oration to an assembly; the greenstone head was carefully worked from a much larger block and polished with wet sand to achieve its remarkably smooth finish. After the onset of the French occupation in New Caledonia, axes were also given as gifts to colonial officers on Bastille Day. The blue calico on the haft suggests that this particular axe was made during the colonial period, although the individual who owned it (and the person who gifted it) remains unknown.

Nephrite, wood, fiber, trade cloth, seeds
20½ x 7½ in. (52.1 x 19.1 cm)
Gift of Eric and Esther Fortess in memory of Leo and Lillian Fortess   2016.394

Funerary figure
East Kalimantan, Indonesia, mid-18th–19th century

The Dayak peoples live on the island of Borneo in villages of multifamily longhouses. Village entrances, houses, and tombs are guarded by *hampatong*, guarding against illness, misfortune from spirits, and enemy raiders. With its wide eyes, exposed teeth, and squat, powerful body, this figure was made by a sculptor from a subset of the Dayak, the Bahau peoples. The flat head and diminutive feet hint at the sculpture's original position, attached to the end of a coffin. Notice how the concave planes of the face emphasize the forcefully projecting curves of the chest and shoulders. It's made from hardy ironwood—a material that would have proven difficult to carve but would have endured the elements in eastern Borneo's dense rain forests.

Wood, shells
H. 35⅞ in. (91 cm)
Gift of William E. and Bertha L. Teel   1994.411

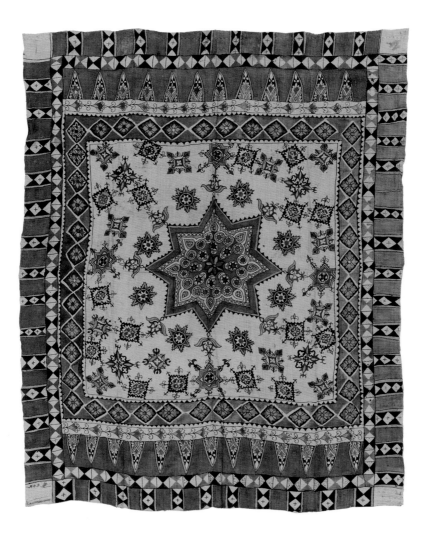

Bedcover

Lake Lanao region, Mindanao, Republic of the
Philippines, about 1900

An artist working in the Lake Lanao region of the
Philippines created this textile using a painstaking
process: weaving the cloth from banana palm fibers
and painting the cloth to create the patterns. The design
itself represents an interpretation of the patterns found
on Persian carpets, which have been traded interna-
tionally for centuries. Only six cloths like this one are
known in American museums, all of them collected
from the same region on the island of Mindanao.

Between 1899 and 1902, Philippine forces fought
American soldiers for their independence. U.S. troops
and officials occupied the country during the war
and its aftermath. Following the war and subsequent
occupation, many Americans returned home with art
they admired — including this textile, which was purchased by an army officer.

Leaf fiber (abaca), pigment; plain weave, hand-painted
and stamped
94 x 78 in. (238.8 x 198.1 cm)
Denman Waldo Ross Collection   03.714

Male figure

Lake Sentani, Papua province, Indonesia, early 20th century

In the Lake Sentani region of New Guinea, wealthy men's homes were built over the lake on piles sunk into the water and connected by elevated walkways. Sculptures decorating those houses and walkways were situated above eye level, punctuating visitors' views of the lake. With its curving shape and compact body, this figure is a symbol of a male ancestor and would have expressed a village chief's responsibility to link past generations and their living descendants. Chiefs' houses doubled as sacred spaces in which the living could honor and pray for blessings from the spirits of their ancestors. In the early twentieth century, Protestant missionaries burned these impressive buildings in an effort to convert the local population to Christianity and destroy all evidence of earlier religion. The sculptures, however, were sunk into Lake Sentani: some sources say that the missionaries cast them into the lake, while others suggest the inhabitants themselves submerged them in an effort to protect them. In 1929, the French traveler and art dealer Jacques Viot dredged up and subsequently sold some sixty submerged sculptures, including this one.

Wood
H. 26¾ in. (68 cm)
Bequest of William E. Teel   2014.328

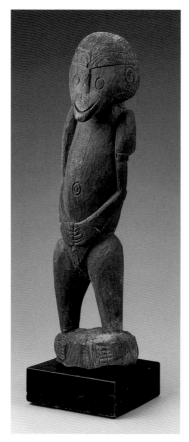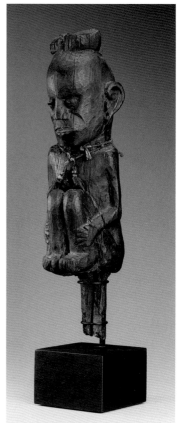

Figure (*gana gana*)

North Sumatra, Indonesia, 20th century

Gana gana are protective guardians, sculpted by priests to ward off illness and other evils. The scowling face on this figure was intended to scare spirits away; the six fingers on one hand are a symbol of supernatural powers. A cavity in the sculpture's chest would have held empowering substances. Its squatting posture, almost a fetal crouch, reflects the pose in which the deceased are buried in the region; it is also a posture of respectful waiting and listening. Since each *gana gana* is animated by a soul, the posture here may relate to the deceased whose soul resides within. This example was likely placed in the house of a well-to-do Batak family, and while such sculptures were given names, the name of this particular figure is unknown.

Wood, fiber, metal, and beads
H. 22 in. (56 cm)
Bequest of William E. Teel   2014.207

Helmet mask
Papuan Gulf, Papua New Guinea, 19th century

This large mask is deceptively light. The artist created it using a strong but remarkably lightweight cane infrastructure covered in bark cloth; its detailed surface designs were painted with blue and red pigments, now faded, and outlined with additional pieces of cane. Among the Elema, who live along the Papuan Gulf in southeast New Guinea, Eharo masks featured in the most secular of three masked rituals performed as part of a twenty-year initiation cycle. Called "things of gladness," such masks were worn over the head by men who danced in pairs in playful, lighthearted performances. This particular mask would have represented a specific spirit, though we do not know which one—the European colonial officer who collected it in the 1880s did not record that information. Prior to colonialism in the Pacific, Eharo masks were kept by the men who made and wore them. When they were no longer needed, they were discarded. Later, unneeded masks were often sold to travelers and government officials and have since entered museums.

Bark cloth, bamboo, raffia, reed, pigments
H. 31 in. (78.7 cm)
Gift of William E. and Bertha L. Teel
1996.400

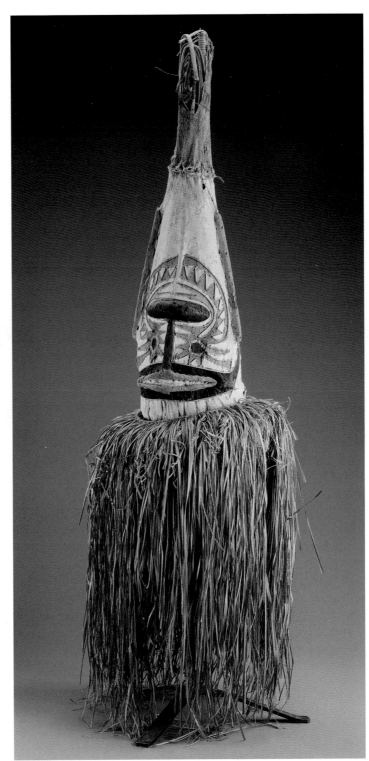

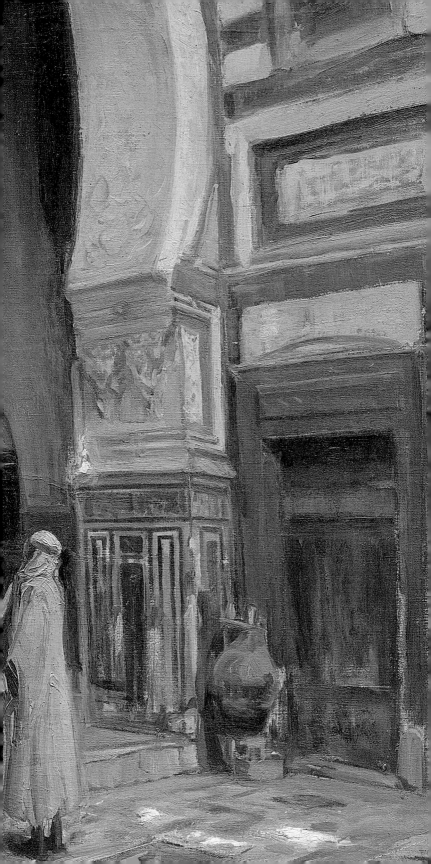

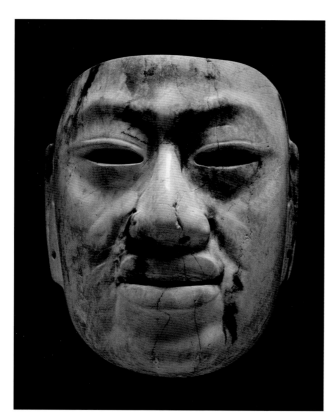

Portrait mask
Olmec culture
Mexico, 900–600 B.C.

Beginning three thousand years ago in what are today Mexico, Central America, and South America, great civilizations arose, prospered, declined, and were absorbed into succeeding cultures that built upon their achievements. The art, architecture, city planning, science, religion, social structure, and political organizations that existed before the Spanish invasions of the sixteenth century represent the accomplishments of societies that—along with Mesopotamia, Egypt and Nubia, India, and China—are among the cradles of civilization.

The Olmec, who lived along what is now the Gulf Coast of Mexico, were the first inhabitants of the Americas to develop a writing system, to create complex visual symbolism, and to use art as a means of embodying their beliefs. Olmec civilization influenced all subsequent societies in ancient Mesoamerica (present-day Mexico, Guatemala, Belize, Honduras, and El Salvador). Olmec artists excelled in working precious, green jadeite that they presumably acquired through trade with distant places. Jadeite is an extremely hard stone, and the Olmec, who had no metal tools, worked it with other stones and abrasives such as crushed garnet. This powerful Olmec mask may have been displayed as a symbol of authority, worn during ceremonies, or attached to the cloth-wrapped mummy bundle containing the body of a deceased lord.

Jadeite
H. 8½ in. (21.6 cm)
Gift of Landon T. Clay   1991.968

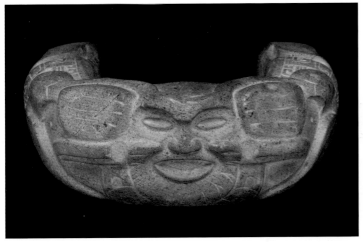

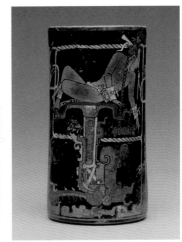

Ballgame yoke
Veracruz culture
Mexico, A.D. 450–700

Drinking vessel (cylinder vase)
Maya culture
Guatemala, A.D. 755–780

Throughout Mesoamerica, players of the ritual ballgame wore U-shaped yokes around their waists. The remains of the sole surviving examples are wood. Players used the yoke to hit a solid rubber ball, batting it between two teams or two players and never allowing it to touch the ground. This stone yoke was too heavy to be worn, and its carved image of a bearded person—perhaps the mythic hero Quetzalcóatl—suggests a ritual function. The yoke may have been a prized possession or a trophy that eventually was placed in a tomb as a funerary offering.

Carved stone
L. 16½ in. (42 cm)
Gift of Lavinia and Landon T. Clay   2003.855

The sophisticated civilization of the Maya reached its height in the Classic period (A.D. 250–900). During this time, artists—who were highly educated members of elite society—produced extraordinary painted ceramics that served ritual functions in life and were also buried in tombs of the honored dead. This vessel is one of the masterpieces of Maya art. The artist has exploited the watercolor-like potential of slip paint (clay diluted to a watery consistency and colored with mineral pigments) to create the subtle washes on the figures' bodies. The painting depicts the birth of a supernatural being whose supple body is framed by a stylized white umbilical cord.

Earthenware with red, white, gray, and black slip paint on cream slip ground
H. 8¾ in. (22.5 cm)
Gift of Landon T. Clay   1988.1168

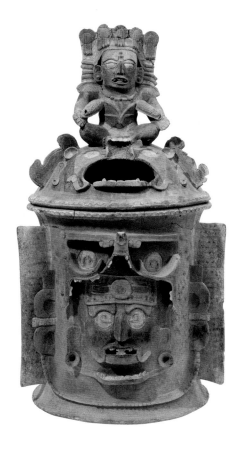

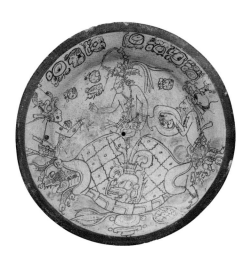

Burial urn
Maya culture
Guatemala, A.D. 650–850

The K'iché Maya people of highland Guatemala buried royal and noble individuals in large, ceramic urns such as this. The body of the deceased was tightly flexed and wrapped in cloth, placed in the urn with offerings of pottery and jadeite, and then buried inside pyramids or sacred caves. The lid of this urn is sculpted as the head of a supernatural being whose open mouth may have been used to make offerings to the deceased in the afterlife. The figure on top of the lid, holding two cobs of corn (maize), is the Maize god.

Earthenware with white, black, yellow, green, blue, and red slip paint
H. 52 in. (132.1 cm)
Gift of Landon T. Clay   1988.1290b

Codex-style plate
Maya culture
Guatemala, A.D. 680–750

The Maya believed that the first humans were formed from ground corn (maize), and they saw the reappearance of maize in the fields each spring as a metaphor for the resurrection of the human soul. This plate depicts the Maize god "growing" from the crack in a turtle shell, symbol of the earth. The Maize god (also known as First Father) is flanked by his sons, the Hero Twins, who defeated the Lords of the Underworld, rescued their father's bones, and thus created the path of resurrection from death. The style of painting on this plate, which was used to hold corn tamales, is similar to that found in a Maya codex, or book made of folded leaves of fig-bark paper. Thousands of these books were burned by the Spanish, who believed they contained "lies of the devil," and only four fragments are known to exist today. The scenes painted on codex-style vessels are therefore important evidence of the kinds of knowledge contained in the now-lost ancient books.

Earthenware with brown-black and red slip paint on cream slip ground
Diam. 12⅝ in. (32 cm)
Gift of Landon T. Clay   1993.565

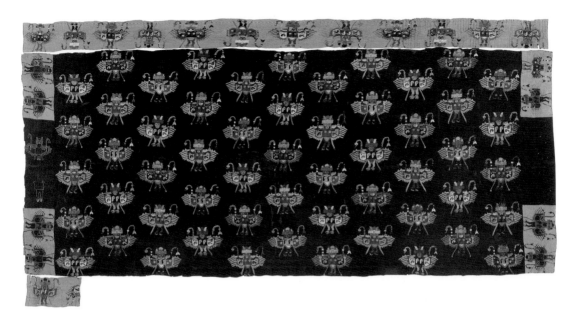

Mantle
Paracas culture
Peru, A.D. 50–100

In the ancient Andean world, textiles played a profound symbolic role in sacred and secular life. Andean
textiles are among the most complex ever made
(some of their techniques have never been replicated),
and the prestige of cloth was directly related to the
extraordinary energy that spinners, dyers, weavers,
and embroiderers expended to produce it.

When burials of the Paracas civilization were
uncovered in the early twentieth century, the bodies
were found wrapped in textiles that had been per-
fectly preserved in the desert sands of Peru's coastal
plain for almost 2,000 years. It has been estimated
that all the textiles in one large mummy bundle may
have taken between 11,000 and 29,000 hours to complete. The ritual figures embroidered on this mantle
wear elaborate headdresses, masks, embroidered
tunics, and feathered capes. They hold serpent-headed
staffs and decapitated heads that denote their power.

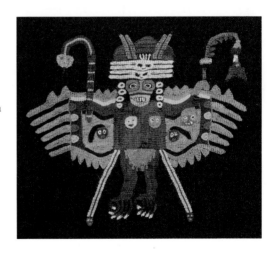

Camelid fiber; plain weave with stem-stitch embroidery
39¾ x 96⅛ in. (101 x 244.3 cm)
Denman Waldo Ross Collection   16.34a–c

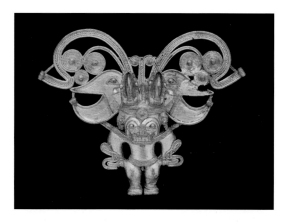

Shaman effigy pendant
Tairona culture
Colombia, A.D. 1000–1530
Gold alloy
H. 6⅜ in. (16 cm)
Gift of Landon T. Clay   2000.813

Funerary mask
Coclé style
Panama, A.D. 700–1520
Gold
W. 10⅜ in. (26.3 cm)
Gift of Landon T. Clay   1971.1127

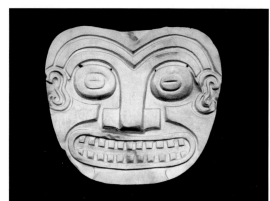

Called "sweat of the sun" by the Inca of Peru, gold was believed by many ancient American civilizations to embody the essence of the sun. Gold ornaments were used in religious ceremonies, buried with the dead, and worn as emblems of political power and social status. Skilled artisans showed a fine sensitivity to the inherent beauty of the metal and produced an amazing variety of forms that, like all ancient American art, embodied symbolic meanings and functions. Gold, mostly mined from riverbeds, was plentiful. Although goldsmiths worked only with stone and bronze tools, they developed most techniques known today, including cold-hammering, embossing, soldering, welding, casting, gilding, and fabricating alloys.

The Spanish who invaded Central and South America in the mid-sixteenth century were interested only in the monetary value of gold. They melted down thousands of objects, sending an estimated 18,000 pounds of American gold to Spain. The vast majority of precious metal objects known today survive because they were hidden in burials. The Spanish invaders believed that male figures of this sort, wearing masks and fantastic headdresses and grasping ritual objects, represented caciques, or chiefs.

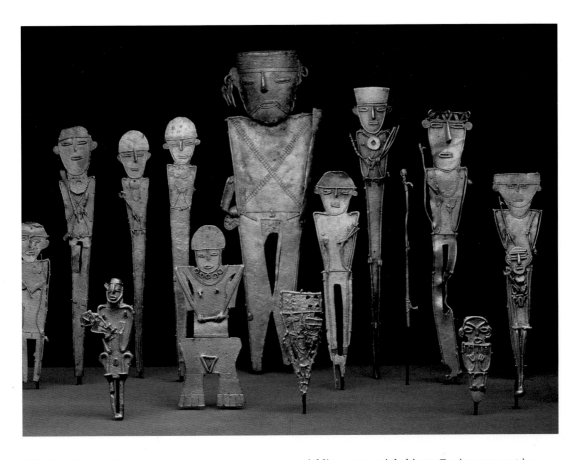

Offering figures (*tunjos*)

Muisca culture

Colombia, 1300–1550

In an isolated highland valley near modern-day Bogotá, Colombia, the Muisca people developed unique works of art in metal, including these distinctive offering figures, or *tunjos*. Many represent men with implements and headdresses indicating political, religious, or social affiliation. Others represent women, some holding children, some wielding ceremonial objects. *Tunjos* were cast in a single mold using only one flow of metal. In their search for gold, the Spanish invaded Muisca lands three times. Enslaved and with no resistance to European diseases, the Muisca were extinct by the seventeenth century.

Gold, copper, and tin alloy
Height of tallest figure: 8¼ in. (21 cm)
Gifts of Landon T. Clay

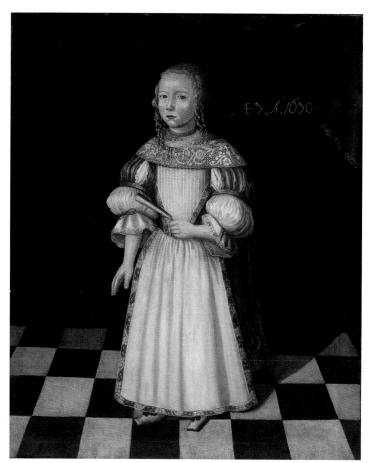

Freake-Gibbs painter
Margaret Gibbs, 1670

Robert Gibbs, the fourth son of
a knight, left England to seek his
fortune in the New World and
became a prosperous Boston
merchant. As a statement of his
own social and economic success,
Gibbs commissioned portraits of
his children—Margaret, Robert
(also in the Museum's collection),
and Henry (Sunrise Museum,
Charleston, West Virginia). Even
the elaborate lace and needlework
on Margaret's dress testify to her
father's status, because Massachusetts law forbade the wearing of
such finery unless the man of the
house "possessed either a liberal
education or an annual income
of £200." This charming image of
seven-year-old Margaret is one
of very few surviving portraits
from seventeenth-century New
England; its emphasis on detail
of costume and on line reflect a
style—fashionable at the court
of Queen Elizabeth—which was
still current in parts of England
in the 1660s.

Oil on canvas
40½ x 33⅛ in. (102.9 x 84.1 cm)
Bequest of Elsie Q. Giltinan   1995.800

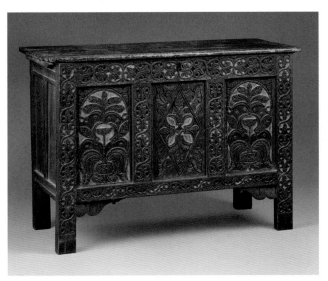

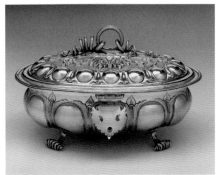

Sugar box
Massachusetts (Boston),
about 1680–85
John Coney, American, 1655/56–1722

Joined chest
Massachusetts (Ipswich), 1670–1700
Attributed to the shop of **Thomas Dennis,** American
(born in England), 1638–1706

This oak chest is a highlight of the Museum's extensive collection of seventeenth-century New England furniture. The chest is believed to be from the shop of Thomas Dennis, a furniture maker (or joiner) trained in England. Chests of this kind, which could be used for seating as well as storage, were the most common furniture form in the small houses of the period. The vigorous carving — with its abundance of stylized leaves and flowers contained within geometric fields — and the indication of an original, brightly painted surface testify to the love of pattern and color in the Puritan society of early New England.

Oak, white pine
30½ x 44⅜ x 19 in. (77.5 x 112.7 x 48.3 cm)
Gift of John Templeman Coolidge   29.1015

John Coney was the most versatile and productive American silversmith of his generation. Like many silversmiths, he was an active citizen, engraving paper money for the colony of Massachusetts and serving as constable and tithingman. This sugar box, which weighs almost two pounds, testifies to the preciousness of sugar and demonstrates Coney's remarkable skill in embossing, engraving, and casting. Such boxes were often given as wedding presents, and the cast handle of this one takes the form of a coiled snake — a traditional emblem warning against interfering in quarrels between husband and wife. The box was made for Mary Mason Norton, wife of the Reverend John Norton of Hingham, Massachusetts.

Silver
H. 4⅞ in. (12.2 cm)
Gift of Mrs. Joseph Richmond Churchill   13.421

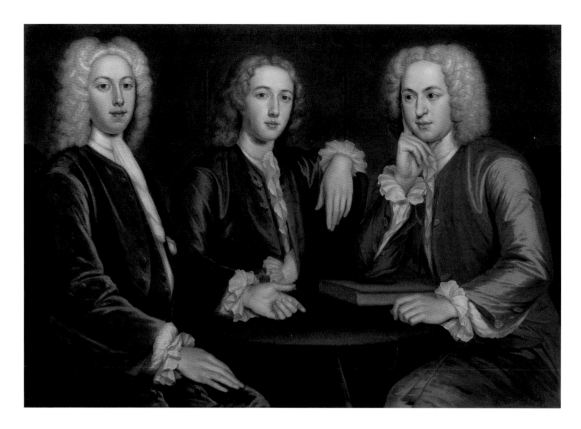

John Smibert
American (born in Scotland), 1688–1751
Daniel, Peter, and Andrew Oliver, 1732

In the eighteenth century, portraits were incontrovertible evidence of wealth and status. Arriving in Boston in 1729, London-trained Smibert was commissioned to paint almost 250 portraits during the seventeen years he lived there. His up-to-date style, ability to capture appearance and character, and deft modeling of three-dimensional form were much admired. This is one of eleven portraits Smibert painted for the affluent and accomplished Oliver family, among his most devoted patrons. Depicting the three sons of Daniel and Elizabeth Belcher Oliver (instead of the more usual single individual), the portrait tested Smibert's skills. He placed the three young men around a table—a common device for group portraits—and wove the figures together through the gestures of their hands. The challenge was increased by the fact that Daniel, on the left, had died in London five years before. Smibert based his likeness on a miniature that Daniel had had painted in London to send to his parents.

Oil on canvas
39 ¼ x 56 ⅞ in. (99.7 x 144.5 cm)
Emily L. Ainsley Fund   53.952

Chest-on-chest

Massachusetts (Boston), 1715–25

Until the discovery of this chest-on-chest in
the mid-1980s, little early-eighteenth-century
Boston furniture was known that was close to
contemporary, high-style English furniture.
Based on its stylistic features and construction, this chest was originally believed to be
English, but it is made of American woods
and was owned by the Warland family of
Cambridge, Massachusetts. In addition,
microanalysis of dirt particles undisturbed
by restoration or refinishing revealed pollen
from plants that grow in Massachusetts and
Rhode Island—a strong indication of the
chest's American origins. As such, this chest-
on-chest has provided exciting evidence that
English furniture designs reached Boston
very early, apparently brought by London-
trained craftsmen attracted by Boston's
thriving economy. A visitor, writing in 1725,
commented: "A Gentleman from London
would almost think himself at home at Boston
when he observes the numbers of people,
their Houses, their Furniture, their Tables,
their Dress and Conversation, which perhaps
is as splendid and showy as that of the most
considerable Tradesman in London."

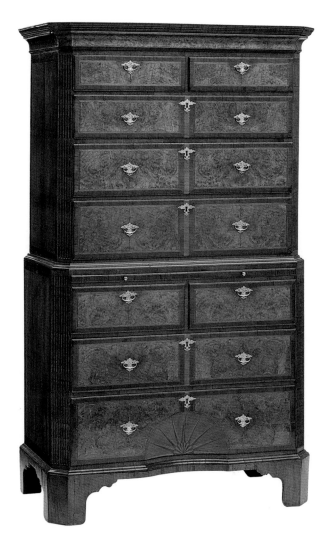

Black walnut, burl walnut veneer, eastern
white pine
70¾ x 42¼ x 21½ in. (179.7 x 107.3 x 53.8 cm)
Gift of a Friend of the Department of American
Decorative Arts and Sculpture and
Otis Norcross Fund   1986.240

Covered cup

Massachusetts (Boston), 1740–45

Jacob Hurd, American, 1702/3–1758

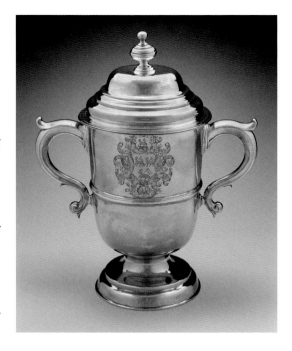

For the few colonial Americans who owned them, objects made of silver testified to wealth, social position, and discerning taste. They could also be (and often were) melted down and converted back to money in times of need. A Virginia gentleman wrote in 1688: "I esteem it as well politic as reputable, to furnish my self with an handsom Cupboard of plate which gives my self the present use & Credit, is a sure friend at a dead lift, without much loss, or is a certain portion for a Child after my decease." Jacob Hurd was among the most prolific of early American silversmiths, and this finely proportioned cup is evidence of his mastery of strong, sculptural form and elegant engraving. Such "grace cups" (traditionally passed around the table for a final toast after grace was said at the end of a meal) were favored in Boston as presentation pieces for ceremonial occasions. The cup bears the coat of arms of its first owner, John Rowe, a prosperous Boston merchant and shipowner.

Silver
H. 13½ in. (34.3 cm)
Helen and Alice Colburn Fund   36.415

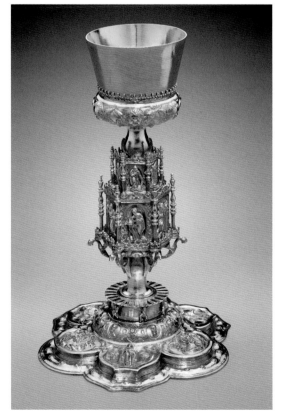

opposite, bottom

Chalice

Guatemala (Santiago de los Caballeros de
Guatemala), about 1560

Pedro Hernández Atenciano, Spanish (worked in
Guatemala and Peru), 1510–1584

The Spanish conquered Guatemala in the sixteenth
century. In 1543, they established their third colonial
capital at Santiago de los Caballeros de Guatemala
(present-day Antigua, Guatemala), in the country's
central highlands. It quickly became one of the richest
cities in Spanish America and served as the administrative center of the Real Audiencia of Guatemala,
which encompassed present-day Guatemala, Belize,
Costa Rica, Nicaragua, El Salvador, Honduras, and
parts of Mexico. Using precious metals mined in
Spain's colonial realms, the Spanish-trained silversmith Pedro Hernández Atenciano created this
remarkable gilded silver chalice and matching paten
for the celebration of the Catholic Mass (the cup holds
the wine, the paten the Eucharistic host). The chalice
includes small figures of Jesus's followers, the apostles, and their attributes, in two registers of niches;
cherubs' faces appear above, at the base of the cup.
The foot incorporates three additional figures, including Saint Dominic—patron of the Dominican religious
order. In all likelihood, the Dominicans commissioned this costly set for their local monastery, which
became one of the region's largest and wealthiest.

Silver gilt
H. of chalice: 11⅛ in. (28.3 cm)
Gift of Thomas, Jr., Kathleen, Daniel, Claire, Ann, and
Timothy Phillips in memory of Thomas and Clare Phillips
2011.2101.1-2

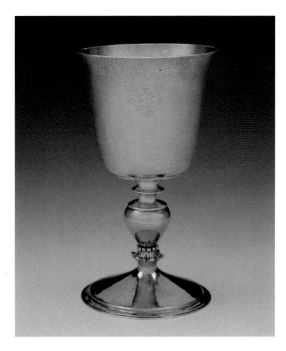

Wine cup

Massachusetts (Boston), about 1660–80

John Hull, American (born in England), 1624–1683,
and **Robert Sanderson, Sr.,** American (born in
England), about 1608–1693

As was often the case in early Puritan churches, this
simple, elegant wine cup is a domestic form that was
used as liturgical silver in communion services. It
was given to the First Church of Boston (now the First
and Second Church) and was owned continuously by
that church until acquired by the Museum. The cup
was made by the partnership of John Hull and Robert Sanderson, North America's first silversmiths. A
masterpiece of American silver, the wine cup is also a
major landmark in the evolution of the silversmith's
craft and is a significant document of American history and culture. Its importance is increased by its
impeccable provenance and outstanding condition.

Silver
H. 8 in. (20.3 cm)
Museum purchase with funds donated anonymously in honor
of Jonathan L. Fairbanks   1999.91

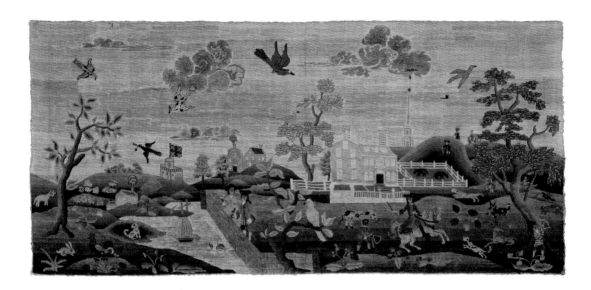

View of Boston Common

Massachusetts (Boston), about 1750

Hannah Otis, American, 1732–1801

Like many well-to-do girls of her time, Hannah Otis learned genteel skills at school, including drawing, letter writing, conversation, and fine needlework. Large embroidered pictures, like this "chimneypiece" for display above the fireplace, were often framed or mounted and kept as a reminder of a woman's girlhood. Most schoolgirl embroidery reproduced standard compositions derived from European prints, but Otis's needlework picture is unique. She depicted a scene she knew—Boston Common, with the beacon on Beacon Hill and the fashionable stone mansion built in 1737 by wealthy merchant Thomas Hancock.

Otis's brother James led radical colonial opposition to Britain, and her sister Mercy Otis Warren became the first historian of the American Revolution. Otis herself never married but lived with her widowed father in Barnstable, Massachusetts, and later kept a shop and ran a boardinghouse in Boston.

Silk, wool, metallic threads, and beads on linen canvas; predominantly tent stitch

24 ¼ x 52 ¾ in. (61.6 x 134 cm)

Gift of a Friend of the Department of American Decorative Arts and Sculpture, a Supporter of the Department of American Decorative Arts and Sculpture, Barbara L. and Theodore B. Alfond, and Samuel A. Otis; and William Francis Warden Fund, Harriet Otis Cruft Fund, Otis Norcross Fund, Susan Cornelia Warren Fund, Arthur Tracy Cabot Fund, Seth K. Sweetser Fund, Edwin E. Jack Fund, Helen B. Sweeney Fund, William E. Nickerson Fund, Arthur Mason Knapp Fund, Samuel Putnam Avery Fund, Benjamin Pierce Cheney Fund, and Mary L. Smith Fund   1996.26

Desk and bookcase
Mexico (Puebla), mid-18th century

This extraordinary desk is one
of the most remarkable pieces
of furniture made in viceregal
Mexico. The striking geometric
exterior features exquisite, inlaid
wood-and-bone Mudéjar designs,
reflecting the popular Hispano-
Moresque style from southern
Spain. Opening the doors reveals
dramatic chinoiserie-style painting in gold on a vermillion background. Inside, painted maps chart
views of an extensive Veracruz
hacienda, depicted in a manner
that recalls early colonial maps
drawn by indigenous artists. Once
owned by a wealthy Spaniard of
the Rivadeneira family, the estate
was the site of one of the earliest
free African settlements in Mexico.
The interior maps, with their small
figures, likely depict descendants
of enslaved Africans or free blacks.

Inlaid woods and incised and painted
bone, *maque* (lacquer), gold and polychrome paint, metal hardware
87 x 41 x 26½ in. (221 x 104.1 x 67.3 cm)
Henry H. and Zoe Oliver Sherman Fund
2015.3131

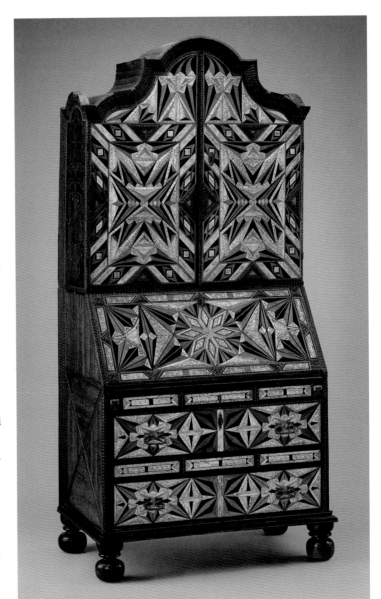

Writing cabinet (*escritorio*)
Mexico (Oaxaca), Villa Alta de
San Ildefonso, about 1671

This writing cabinet is among the
finest of its type. Inside and out,
nearly every surface is covered
with intricate marquetry panels
and incised designs. The outside
features a panoramic view of the
town Villa Alta de San Ildefonso
in southern Mexico, and the surrounding highlands of Oaxaca;
the inside boasts a dazzling mix
of imagery borrowed and adapted
from European prints. It was
probably commissioned around
1671 by Villa Alta's Spanish administrator Don Fernando Velasco y
Castilla. A seventeenth-century
visitor to Villa Alta reported that
such fine furniture was made
by indigenous craftsmen in the
nearby neighborhood of Analco,
shown on the side of the desk, and
"exported as far away as Italy,
both for the unusual nature of
the marquetry and for the beauty
and fragrance of the wood."

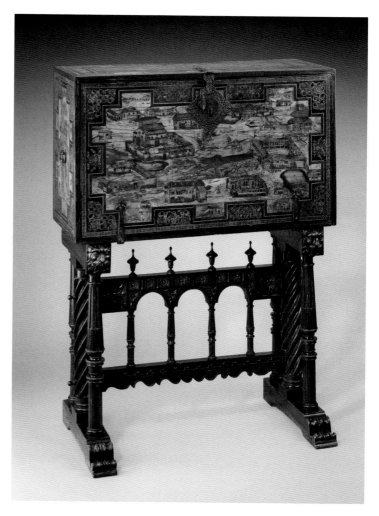

Linaloe, granadillo, Spanish cedar, with marquetry and *zulaque*-filled engraving
24¾ x 41⅜ x 17¾ in. (63.1 x 105 x 45.1 cm)

Museum purchase with funds donated anonymously, William Francis Warden
Fund, American Decorative Arts Deaccession Fund, Arthur Tracy Cabot Fund,
Edwin E. Jack Fund, and by exchange from a Gift of Harold Whitworth Pierce, Gift
of Miss Ellen Graves, Mr. Samuel Cabot and Mrs. Roger Ernst in memory of their
father and mother, Mr. and Mrs. Edmund P. Graves, Gift of Mary W. Bartol, John W.
Bartol, and Abigail W. Clark, William E. Nickerson Fund, Gift of Mrs. Henry Lyman,
Bequest of Barbara Boylston Bean, Charles Amos Cummings Fund, Gift of Mrs.
Charles L. Bybee, Bequest of Dudley Leavitt Pickman, Gift of Henry G. E. Payson,
and from funds donated by Mrs. Walter Hunnewell in memory of Walter Hunnewell
2010.370

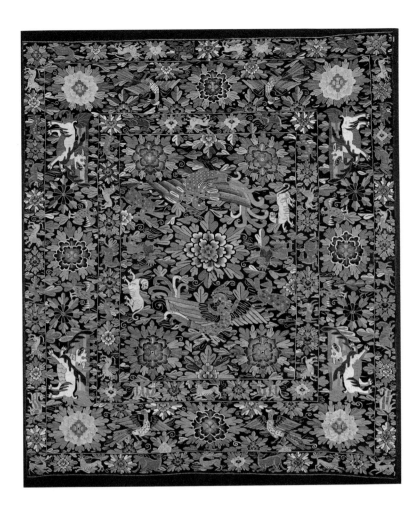

Cover with Chinese-influenced motifs
Peru, late 17th–early 18th century

Before the European conquest, Andean weavers in South America were among the most sophisticated in the world, creating complex textiles for clothing and burial shrouds. During the colonial period, the Spanish employed Andean weavers to create cloth for household use. This cover mixes Andean subjects (there are llamas in the narrow interior border) with images of peonies and mythical beasts derived from Chinese silks, which came to the Andes through yet another of Spain's colonies, the Philippines. The Museum's collections of colonial art frequently demonstrate the circuitous travel of people, goods, and artistic styles during the colonial period.

Cotton, wool, silk and linen; tapestry weave
93¾ x 81½ in. (238.1 x 207 cm)
Denman Waldo Ross Collection   11.1264

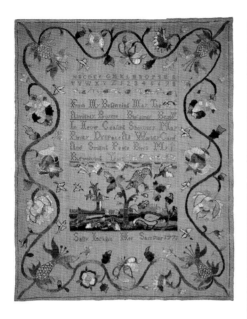

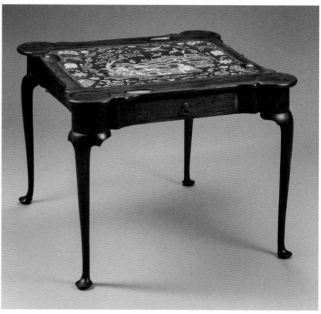

Sampler

Massachusetts (probably Boston), 1771

Sally Jackson, American, born 1760

Card table

Massachusetts (Boston), 1730–50

The Museum's collection of needlework executed by girls and women of colonial New England is among the finest in the world. Samplers were a schoolgirl's first needlework project, and Sally Jackson made this finely executed example—striking for its fresh and brilliant state of preservation—when she was only eleven. Her sampler, embroidered with silk in cross, split, French knot, satin, and stem stitches, includes an alphabet, a moral verse, and a pastoral scene, all within an elaborate floral border. The scene, with its running stag and parrot on a branch, relates closely to other embroidered textiles from eighteenth-century Boston.

Despite laws dating to the Puritan era that regulated such social vices as alcohol, tobacco, and card playing, the existence of this card table and a small group of related examples made between 1730 and 1750 proves that wealthy Bostonians of the time participated in these forbidden activities. This table and its mate were originally owned by Peter Faneuil, one of the city's most prominent merchants and the builder of Boston's Faneuil Hall. This piece's finely wrought needlework playing surface—no doubt the handiwork of a young woman—belies the small transgression that the table represents. The embroidered scene, derived from contemporary print sources, depicts a shepherdess resting on her elbow amid an abundance of flora and fauna. Thus, secular rebellion and the innocence of young womanhood collide in this single piece of furniture.

Linen plain weave, embroidered with silk
30 x 20 in. (76.2 x 50.8 cm)
Museum purchase with funds donated anonymously
and Frank B. Bemis Fund   2001.739

Mahogany, chestnut, eastern white pine; original needlework top
27 x 35⅝ x 35⅛ in. (68.6 x 90.5 x 89.2 cm)
Museum purchase with funds donated anonymously and
William E. Nickerson Fund   49.330

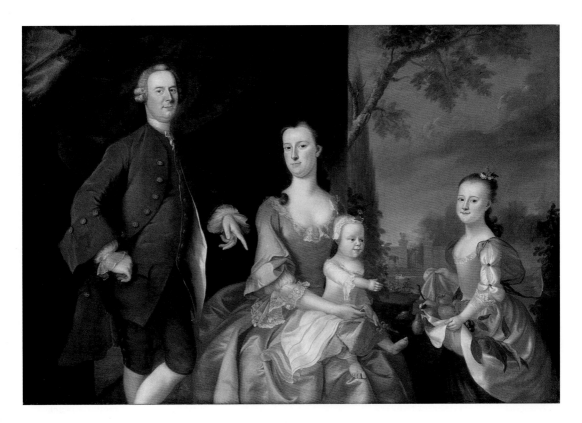

Joseph Blackburn

American (born in England), active in America
1753–1763

Isaac Winslow and His Family, 1755

Trained in England, Joseph Blackburn came to New
England from Bermuda in 1753. For the next ten years,
he was a highly successful painter of portraits that
reflected the decorative grace and silvery colors of
current London style. He particularly delighted his
female sitters by painting them with dainty heads
on long, slender necks and by rendering their elegant
dress and the textures of luxurious fabrics with

skill and precision. In this ambitious group portrait,
Blackburn posed the Winslows informally before an
imaginary garden setting far grander than any exist-
ing in Boston. Isaac Winslow, who made his fortune in
the shipping business, stands beside his wife, Lucy; in
her lap, baby Hannah holds a coral-and-bells teething
toy. Daughter Lucy holds fruit, possibly alluding to
the family's prosperity.

Oil on canvas
54½ x 79¼ in. (138.4 x 201.3 cm)
A. Shuman Collection   42.684

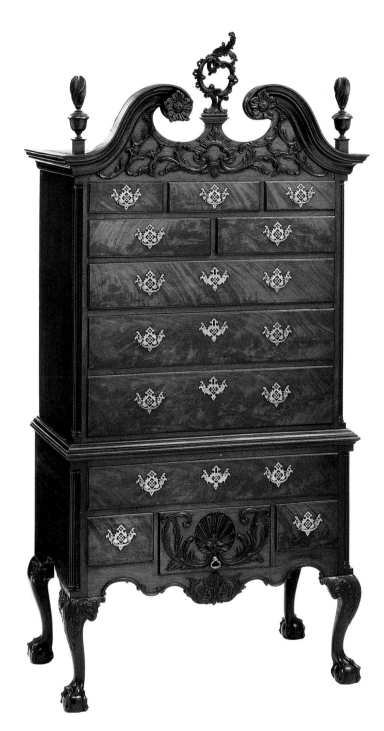

High chest of drawers
Pennsylvania (Philadelphia), about 1760–70

Handsome, monumental high chests proclaimed their owners' wealth and taste while providing ample storage at a time when closets were still uncommon. In the last quarter of the eighteenth century, long after the high chest had lost favor in England, the form reached its artistic peak in Philadelphia—the fastest growing city in America. Fine Philadelphia high chests, like this one, are well proportioned and richly ornamented. The wood is highly prized mahogany possibly imported from the Spanish territories of Cuba, Honduras, or Santo Domingo. On the drawer fronts, the warm color and lively patterns of mahogany crotch-grain veneer are enhanced by pierced brasses, placed to curve slightly inward, lightening the basic rectilinearity of the chest. The carved decoration, accentuated by the use of different-colored mahogany, reflects the fluid, graceful Rococo style that dominated European art in the mid-eighteenth century. More than seven feet above the ground, the flourish of an asymmetrical cartouche provides the crowning touch.

Mahogany, yellow-poplar, yellow pine
85¾ x 43 x 23 in. (217.9 x 109.2 x 58.4 cm)
The M. and M. Karolik Collection of
Eighteenth-Century American Arts
39.545

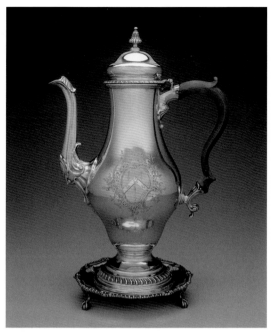

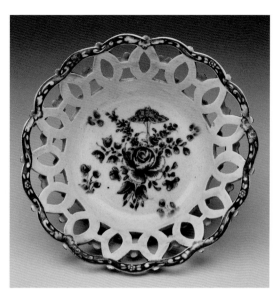

Fruit basket
Pennsylvania (Philadelphia), 1771–72
American China Manufactory

Coffeepot

Pennsylvania (Philadelphia), about 1770–80
Richard Humphreys, American (born in the British
West Indies), 1749–1832

Philadelphia was the American center of the Rococo
style, with its animated ornament of entwined scrolls,
shells, leaves, and other natural forms. The shape of
this coffeepot, with its stepped foot and domed cover,
expresses the Rococo love of curving movement, as
do the applied decoration and the delicate foliate
engraving. The Rococo style—also exemplified by the
high chest on the preceding page—was introduced
to America from England through imported objects,
immigrant craftsmen, and such books of design as
Thomas Chippendale's *The Gentleman and Cabinet-
Maker's Director* (1754). Made by one of Philadelphia's
foremost silversmiths, this coffeepot is unusual in
that it retains its original stand.

Silver with wooden handle
H. 13⅝ in. (34.4 cm)
Gift in memory of Dr. George Clymer by his wife, Mrs. Clymer
56.589

One of the first porcelain factories in the colonies was
established in Philadelphia in 1770 by Gousse Bonnin
and George Anthony Morris, who imported English
workers to produce domestic wares comparable to the
soft-paste porcelain (a bone china) made in English
factories. The Non-Importation Agreements of the late
1760s, which urged the boycott of imported British
goods and encouraged colonial industry, made this
seem a perfect moment for such a venture. However,
expenses were much higher than expected, and many
local merchants, ignoring the Non-Importation Agreements, continued to trade with England. Quantities
of inexpensive English and Chinese wares were available in America and, after only two years, Bonnin's
and Morris's factory closed. This open fretwork fruit
basket is a very rare survivor of what was known in
its day as "American China."

Soft-paste porcelain with underglaze blue decoration
Diam. 6⅞ in. (17.5 cm)
Frederick Brown Fund   1977.621

Cupboard

Massachusetts (probably Ipswich or Newbury),
1685–90

Oak, maple, white pine

58¾ x 48½ x 19⅜ in. (149.2 x 123.2 x 49.2 cm)

Gift of Maurice Geeraerts in memory of
Mr. and Mrs. William R. Robeson   51.53

opposite, left

Desk and bookcase

Rhode Island (Providence), about 1770–90

Mahogany, chestnut, pine, cherry

95¼ x 39⅞ x 23⅝ in. (241.9 x 101.3 x 60 cm)

The M. and M. Karolik Collection of Eighteenth-Century
American Arts   39.155

opposite, right

Chest-on-chest

Massachusetts (Salem), 1806–9

Design and carving attributed to
Samuel McIntire, American, 1757–1811

Mahogany, pine, ebony, satinwood

90⅜ x 46¾ in. (229.6 x 118.7 cm)

The M. and M. Karolik Collection of Eighteenth-Century
American Arts   41.580

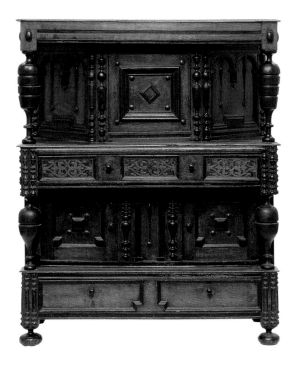

The Museum has one of the world's finest collections
of colonial New England furniture. In the seventeenth
and eighteenth centuries, such monumental chests as
those illustrated here were the supreme expression
of their makers' skill and their owners' affluence and
status. Exploring the elegant proportions, handsome
carving, rich surface ornamentation, and intricately
worked brass handles of these solid and imposing
pieces of furniture can offer the viewer visual delight.

A good example is this chest-on-chest (opposite
page, right)—among the greatest masterpieces of
Salem furniture. The chest's form is of the eighteenth
century, but its ornament reflects both the international taste for Neoclassicism and the new American
nation's search for cultural unity in symbols that
would be meaningful to all. The artistic vocabulary
of ancient Greece and Rome seemed tailor-made for
Americans who compared their infant democracy to
the revered societies of the ancient world. Thus, on
this chest, urns, garlands, and cornucopias over-
flowing with fruit speak optimistically of America's

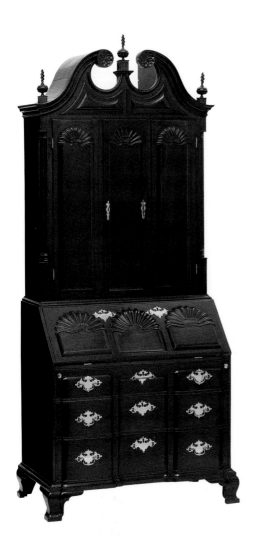

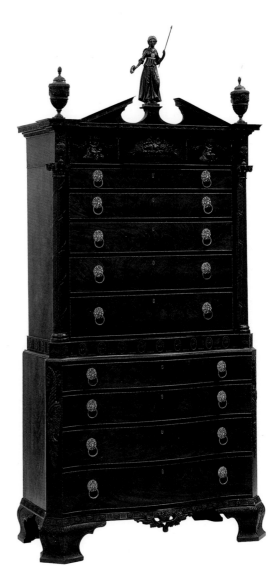

prosperity, and the crowning female figure bears
attributes symbolic of the new nation's ideals—truth,
virtue, and power. The chest was made for Elizabeth
Derby West (see page 206) the daughter of Salem merchant Elias Hasket Derby whose success embodied
the American dream. The chest was undoubtedly
among its owner's proudest possessions, but when
the collector Maxim Karolik rediscovered it in 1941,
its drawers were being used for ripening pears.

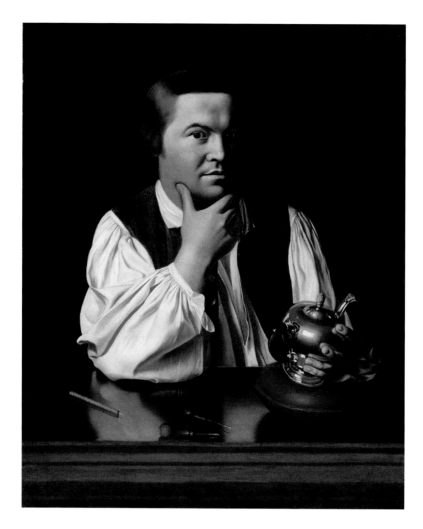

John Singleton Copley

American, 1738–1815

Paul Revere, 1768

This image of a craftsman at work, one of the most familiar and beloved icons of American art, is unusual in colonial portraiture. Paul Revere (1735–1818) was a distinguished Bostonian, active in public affairs, an impassioned patriot, and a prominent silversmith. The circumstances surrounding the commissioning of this portrait are unknown, but it was as a silversmith that Copley painted Revere—wigless and informally dressed in a white linen shirt and unbuttoned waistcoat. With his engraving tools spread before him, Revere seems to be contemplating the design he will engrave on a silver teapot. Teapots were among the most expensive items made by Revere; the inclusion of a teapot in his portrait may simply signify his craft, but the portrait was painted at the time of the much-resented Townshend Acts, which imposed heavy duties on imported tea. The teapot might thus be read as a provocative political statement.

Oil on canvas

35 ⅛ x 28 ½ in. (89.2 x 72.4 cm)

Gift of Joseph W. Revere, William B. Revere and Edward H. R. Revere   30.781

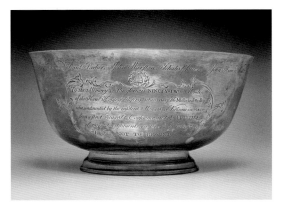

Sons of Liberty Bowl

Massachusetts (Boston), 1768

Paul Revere, American, 1735–1818

The Liberty Bowl is a powerful and eloquent symbol of America's struggle for independence. It was commissioned by fifteen members of the Sons of Liberty, a secret, revolutionary organization to which Paul Revere belonged. The bowl was intended to honor ninety-two members of the Massachusetts House of Representatives who had refused to rescind the circular letter sent throughout the colonies to protest against the Townshend Acts (1767), which taxed tea, paper, glass, and other commodities imported from England. The legislators' defiant act of conscience directly embodied growing colonial resentment of high-handed British policies, and "the glorious Ninety-two" soon became a catchphrase expressing revolutionary sentiment. The Liberty Bowl, the Declaration of Independence, and the Constitution have been called the nation's three most cherished historical treasures. The bowl was purchased in 1949, with funds that included 700 donations by Boston public school children and the general public.

Silver
Overall: 5½ x 11 in. (14 x 27.9 cm)
Gift by Subscription and Francis Bartlett Fund   49.45

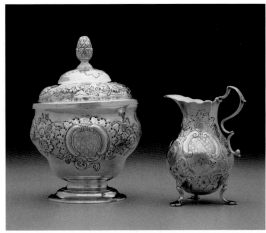

Sugar bowl and creampot

Massachusetts (Boston), 1761

Paul Revere, American, 1735–1818

This sugar bowl and creampot are highlights of the Museum's collection of almost 200 pieces of Paul Revere silver. The sheer variety of Revere's work is evident when we compare the intricate, curvilinear shapes and opulent decoration of these pieces with the simple elegance and rich, reflecting surface of the Sons of Liberty Bowl. The shape of the Liberty Bowl is influenced by imported Chinese porcelain bowls, while these objects are superb examples of the Rococo style that dominated American and European decorative arts at the time.

Silver
H. of sugar bowl: 6½ in. (16.5 cm)
H. of creampot: 4⅜ in. (11.1 cm)
Pauline Revere Thayer Collection   35.1781, 35.1782

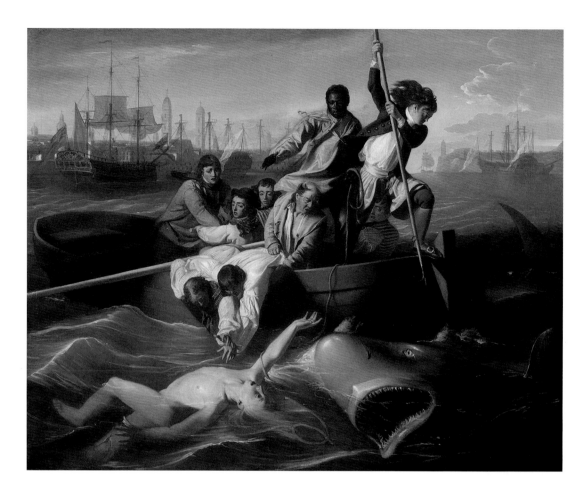

John Singleton Copley

American, 1738–1815

Watson and the Shark, 1778

"Was it not for preserving the resemblance of particular persons," Copley complained about colonial America, "painting would not be known in the place." He dreamed of working in England's more cosmopolitan artistic environment and of making "history paintings," those images of religious, mythological, or historical events that were traditionally considered the apex of artistic achievement. In 1774 Copley left America and began a forty-year career in London.

Watson and the Shark, his first large-scale history painting, depicts the heroic rescue of English merchant Brook Watson (1735–1807) who, as a young cabin boy, lost a leg to a shark while swimming in the harbor of Havana, Cuba. *Watson and the Shark* is an astonishing achievement for an artist who before this had mainly painted portraits.

Oil on canvas
72¼ x 90⅜ in. (183.5 x 229.6 cm)
Gift of Mrs. George von Lengerke Meyer   89.481

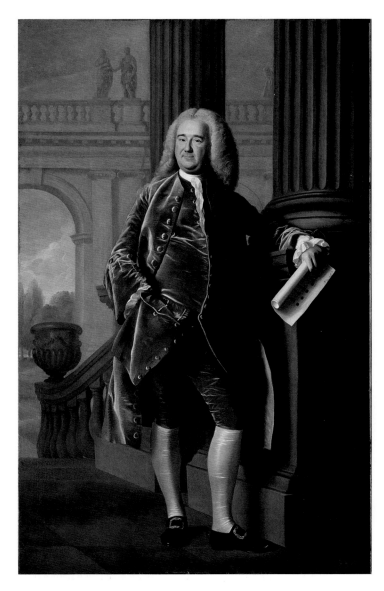

John Singleton Copley
American, 1738–1815
Nathaniel Sparhawk, 1764

This painting of wealthy merchant Nathaniel Sparhawk was Copley's first attempt at a life-size, full-length portrait—a format indicative of both grandeur and expense. He based the composition on traditional European images of heroes and rulers. Sparhawk was neither; a well-off merchant, he had gained social standing through his marriage to Elizabeth Pepperrell, a member of a politically prominent family. Copley shows Sparhawk at ease in an imaginary, grandiose setting, leaning against a fluted column, wearing an elegant velvet suit. On close examination of his waistcoat, shadowy indications of another set of buttons are visible, revealing that the artist reworked the painting to increase Sparhawk's girth. In Copley's day, excess weight was a sign of health and prosperity.

Oil on canvas
91 x 59 in. (231.1 x 149.9 cm)
Charles H. Bayley Picture and Painting
Fund   1983.595

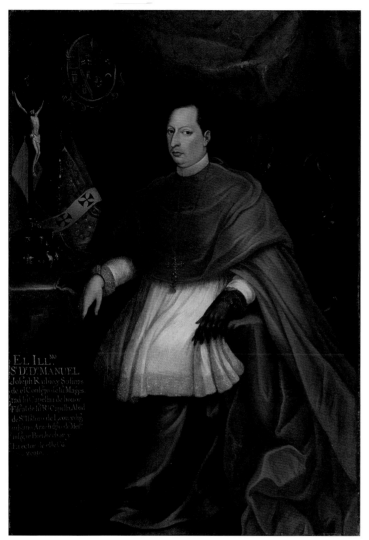

EL ILL.MO
S'D'D'MANUEL
Joſeph Rubio y Salinas
de el Conſejo de ſu Magºs
[...]ad ſu Capellan de honor
Fiſcal de la R¹ Capilla Abad
de S'Ildefonso de Leon y oy
[...]uſsimo Arzobiſpo de Mex[...]
[...]ſsºr Don benedicto XIV
[...] ector [...]ollet[...]o
yento.

Miguel Cabrera
Mexican, 1695–1768
Don Manuel José Rubio y Salinas, Archbishop of Mexico, 1754

Surrounded by reminders of his position and seated in a carved, throne-like chair, Archbishop Rubio y Salinas possesses an air of authority—one appropriate to the leader of Mexico's Roman Catholic Church. He wears a rich red cape and sumptuously jeweled pectoral cross; removing his glove, he reveals an episcopal ring on his right hand. Miguel Cabrera was official artist to the archbishop and made numerous portraits of him; this is the earliest known. The year in which this portrait was created proved to be momentous for both the sitter and the Mexican church: at the archbishop's urging, Pope Benedict XIV made the Virgin of Guadalupe the patroness of New Spain in 1754, reportedly inspired to do so by an image of the Virgin that Cabrera had made and sent to Rome. Under the archbishop's patronage, Mexican-born Cabrera would become New Spain's most famous painter of the eighteenth century.

Oil on canvas
71⅝ x 49⅛ in. (181.9 x 124.9 cm)
Charles H. Bayley Picture and Painting Fund   2008.1

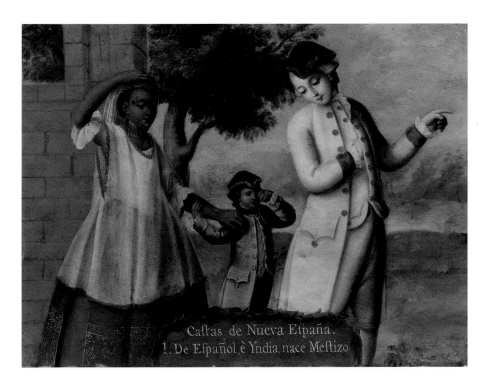

Caſtas de Nueva Eſpaña.
1. De Eſpañol è Yndia, nace Meſtizo

Ignacio de Castro

Mexican, active 1750–1800

Castas de Nueva España (Castes of New Spain): 1.
De Español e Yndia, nace Mestizo (From Spaniard
and Indian, a Mestizo is born), about 1775

The elites of viceregal Mexico developed a complex social hierarchy based on race. Called the *sistema de castas*, or the system of castes, it was intended both to categorize the colonial population and to provide a measure of social control. So-called *casta* paintings seek to visually represent the possible outcomes that might result from the union of men and women of different races. Most often, artists made them for European clientele in numbered sets of sixteen. The first painting in the series (as shown here) usually depicts the encounter between a Spaniard and an indigenous woman. Subsequent paintings categorize combinations of people with mixed Native, European, and African heritage, attempting to document and reflect the classification systems that emerged in the eighteenth century. Confused pseudoscientific labels for mixed-race individuals, such as "Return-Backwards," not only reflect the racism of the time, but also show the ultimate failure of imperial efforts to contain people in such artificial structures.

Oil on copper
13⅜ x 18⅛ in. (34 x 46 cm)
Charles H. Bayley Picture and Painting Fund, Grant Walker
Fund, and funds by exchange   2015.3132

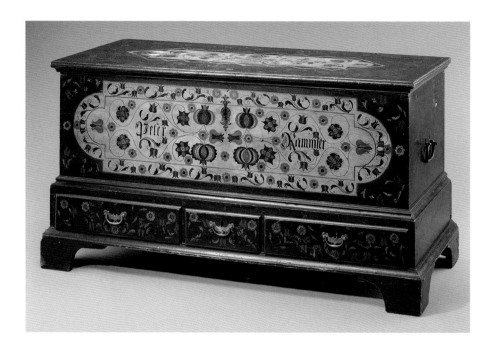

Chest with drawers

Pennsylvania (Berks or Lebanon County), about 1784–90

Germans were among the largest immigrant groups in eighteenth-century America, and they settled mostly in Pennsylvania. Often, they're called the Pennsylvania Dutch, a corruption of "Deutsch," or German. Well into the nineteenth century, these settlers favored a distinctive type of German-style painted furniture, including chests like this one, which would have been made to mark a major event in a person's life. This example was made for Peter Rammler (1770–1850) when he was a young man. Delicate and intricate, the beautiful painting on this chest is by an unidentified but highly regarded craftsman now called the "Embroidery Artist," after the similarity of his work to needlework designs of the day.

Painted pine, poplar, original brasses, iron handles and iron hinges
26¾ x 50 x 22½ in. (67.9 x 127 x 57.2 cm)
Gift of Barbara L. and Theodore B. Alfond in honor of Malcolm Rogers on the occasion of his twentieth year as Director of the MFA, Boston
2014.1477

Desk and bookcase
Massachusetts (Boston), 1770–85
George Bright, American,
1726–1805

Admired as "the neatest workman
in town," George Bright was among
Boston's most successful cabinetmakers in the years just before and
after the Revolution. The superb
craftsmanship that made Bright
famous is evident in this massive, handsomely proportioned
desk and bookcase. The front and
sides are bombé in form, from
the French *bomber,* "to bulge." In
America, the bombé form was a
specialty of Boston cabinetmakers, used on the most expensive
and fashionable furniture. This
desk and bookcase was made for
wealthy merchant Samuel Barrett
and is fitted with drawers, shelves,
pigeonholes, and several secret
compartments to hold his papers.
On the front of the doors are mirrors within curving gilded frames.

Mahogany, white pine, glass
99½ x 43 x 24 in. (252.7 x 109.2 x 61 cm)
Bequest of Miss Charlotte Hazen
56.1194

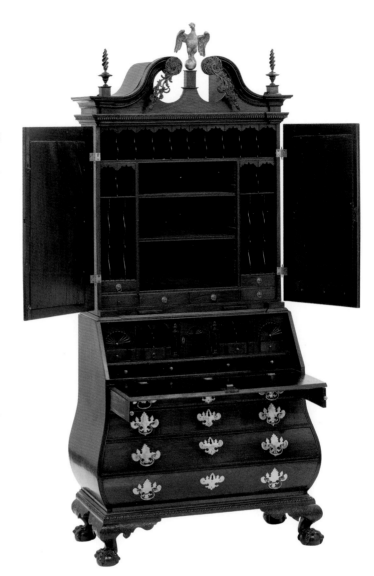

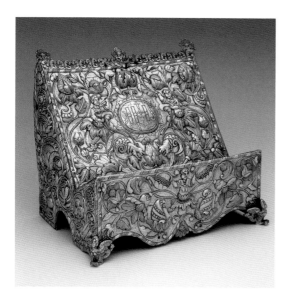

Missal stand (*atril*)
Bolivia (Moxos mission region), 1725–30

This early Baroque-style silver *atril*, or missal stand, was created of local silver for a Jesuit church in Bolivia in the early eighteenth century. Composed of a wooden frame and five sheets of elaborately shaped silver, the stand held the clergy's liturgical books during Mass. The iconography of the stand incorporates both Latin American and Spanish imagery, including local flora and fauna such as the vizcacha, a small rodent with large ears, and passionflowers, a native symbol of resurrection appropriated by the Catholic Church to symbolize the Passion of Christ. Each figure flanking the central monogram combines the ancient pagan *hombre verde*, or green man—a symbol of life, nature, and fertility—with the square-necked costume of archangels. The monogram, "IHS" with a cross and three nails, is the seal of the Jesuit order.

Silver, replaced wooden frame
11⅝ x 13⅝ x 10⅝ in. (29.5 x 34.8 x 27 cm)
Gift of Landon T. Clay   2001.843

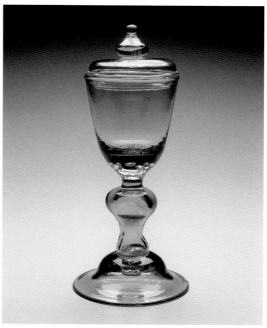

Covered goblet (pokal)
Maryland (New Bremen), about 1785–95
Probably made at the **New Bremen Glass Manufactory**

Although many glass factories were set up in the colonies, eighteenth-century American glass is very rare because few factories survived the competition from inexpensive, high-quality imported glass. In 1784 John Frederick Amelung (1741–1798) emigrated from Germany with sixty-eight skilled workers and established a factory at New Bremen, Maryland, that employed at its peak 500 people. This goblet bears no maker's mark, but its chemical composition matches that of objects known to be from Amelung's factory. Probably made for an Evangelical Lutheran church, the goblet's form seems appropriate for use in a church dedicated to "those who preach the Word [of God] in its simplicity and purity."

Glass
H. 12⅜ in. (31.4 cm)
Gift of The Seminarians and Mr. and Mrs. Daniel F. Morley
1994.82a–b

John Neagle

American, 1796–1865

Pat Lyon at the Forge, 1826–27

At the end of his career, the Philadelphia entrepreneur Patrick Lyon (1779–1829) commissioned John Neagle to portray him as the lowly blacksmith he once was rather than as the successful businessman he had become. The portrait also includes, in the upper left, a view of Philadelphia's Walnut Street jail, where the young Lyon, falsely accused of theft, had been briefly imprisoned. In celebrating Lyon's humble origins and the dignity of skilled physical labor, the painting captures the optimistic spirit of America at a time when conviction was widespread that individuals could rise to greatness from poverty and adversity. Lyon is depicted on a heroic scale, his powerful forearms bared, his virile figure dramatically set off by the flames and smoke of his forge. Neagle's reputation rests almost entirely on this monumental work, which was acclaimed at exhibitions in Philadelphia, New York, and Boston.

Oil on canvas

93¾ x 68 in. (238.1 x 172.7 cm)

Henry H. and Zoe Oliver Sherman Fund

1975.806

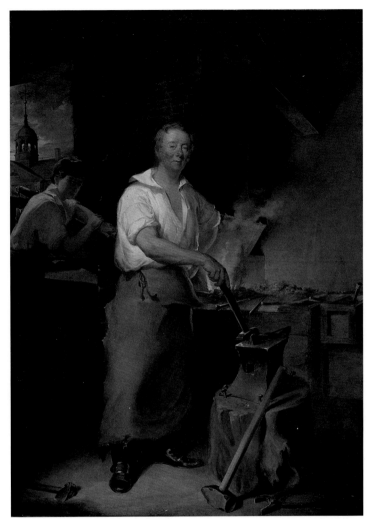

Gilbert Stuart
American, 1755–1828
Martha Washington, 1796
George Washington, 1796

This unfinished portrait of George Washington may well be the most
famous of all American paintings. As Washington (1732–1799) neared the
end of his second term as president, his wife, Martha (1731–1802), commissioned paintings of them both from the celebrated portraitist Gilbert
Stuart. The works were never delivered; instead, Stuart kept them in his
studio and used them as models for the many images of Washington he
created in later years. Stuart painted numerous portraits of Washington,

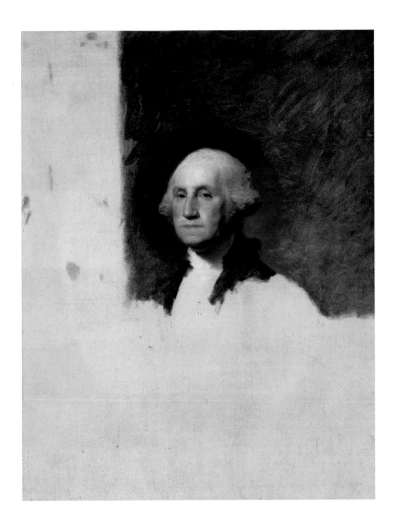

testifying to the new nation's hunger for visual symbols of its strength and pride. Aside from Stuart's own replicas, the painting was copied many times by other artists; a printed version appears in reverse on the dollar bill. "Every American considers it his sacred duty," a French visitor observed, "to have a likeness of Washington in his home, just as we have images of God's saints."

Oil on canvas
Each 47¾ x 37 in. (121.3 x 94 cm)
William Francis Warden Fund, John H. and Ernestine A. Payne Fund, Commonwealth Cultural Preservation Trust. Jointly owned by the Museum of Fine Arts, Boston, and the National Portrait Gallery, Washington D.C.   1980.1, 1980.2

Commode

Massachusetts (Boston), 1809
Made by **Thomas Seymour**, American
(born in England), 1771–1848,
probably assisted by **James Cogswell**,
American, 1780–1862
Painted by **John Ritto Penniman**,
American, 1782–1841
Probably carved by **Thomas Wightman**,
American, active 1802–1820

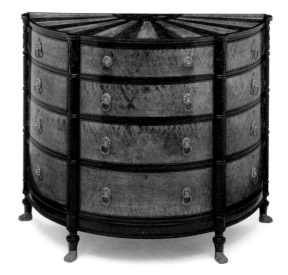

The museum owns three rooms reconstructed with woodwork from Oak Hill, a house built in 1800–1801 in South Danvers, Massachusetts. Filled with furnishings that belonged to the Derby-West families, the Oak Hill rooms provide a vivid picture of the taste and lifestyle of prosperous New Englanders at the turn of the nineteenth century.

The house, probably designed by Samuel McIntire (see page 192), was built for Captain Nathaniel West and his wife, Elizabeth, daughter of Salem millionaire merchant Elias Hasket Derby. Elizabeth Derby West spared no expense in decorating her house with fashionable objects of the highest quality. The design and ornament of this magnificent commode express the love of geometry and contrasting color fundamental to the Neoclassical style. The commode survives with rare documentation: the bill from Thomas Seymour, which reads: "Large Mahogany Commode, $80.00. Paid Mr. Penniman's bill for painting Shels on Top of Do [ditto] $10.00."

In the parlor are carved mahogany side chairs and superb upholstered armchairs and sofas that testify unequivocally to Mrs. West's insistence on the best. Since the original fabrics did not survive, the Museum, following a description in the Oak Hill inventory, re-covered the furniture in an "orange" silk damask. Both the block-printed wallpaper and the

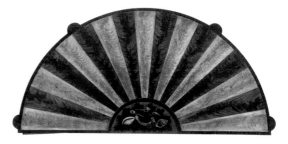

woven Brussels carpet re-create costly items that Mrs. West probably imported from abroad. A selection of engravings and a gilded looking glass with a broadly reflecting convex surface complete the decoration of a room where visitors enjoyed conversation, tea parties, and games of cards.

Mahogany; mahogany, birch, rosewood, and bird's-eye maple veneers; satinwood and rosewood banding; eastern white pine, maple, white ash, brass
41½ x 50 x 24½ in. (105.4 x 127 x 62.4 cm)
The M. and M. Karolik Collection of Eighteenth-Century American Arts   23.19

Desk and bookcase

Philadelphia (Pennsylvania),
about 1830
Anthony G. Quervelle, American
(born in France), 1789–1856

Born in France, Anthony Quervelle
trained as a cabinetmaker there,
probably in the imperial workshops of Napoleon. By 1817 he
was in America, where he quickly
became one of Philadelphia's leading craftsmen working in the late
Neoclassical style. Quervelle's
work combined French motifs
with the British forms that were
popular in his adopted city. In
this majestic desk and bookcase,
he combines the massive form
and richly grained woods derived
from British designs with tapered
columns, paw feet, and fan doors
that add a French flair. Reflecting popular taste, Quervelle also
incorporated Gothic arches on
the glass doors and pigeonholes
and pressed glass knobs on the
interior drawers.

Mahogany, bird's-eye maple, burl ash,
yellow-poplar, white pine, cedar, maple,
glass, pressed glass
102 ¼ x 49 ¼ x 24 in. (259.7 x 125.1 x 61 cm)
Henry H. and Zoe Oliver Sherman Fund
2004.562

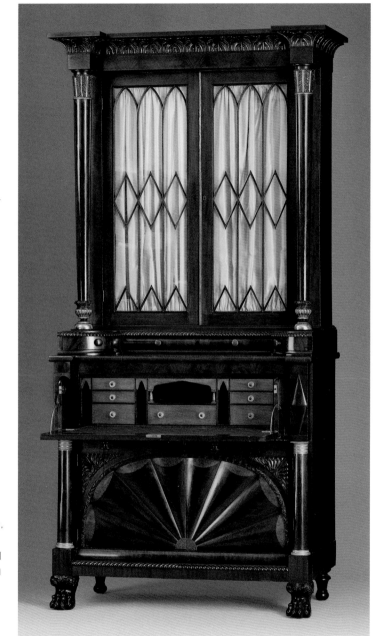

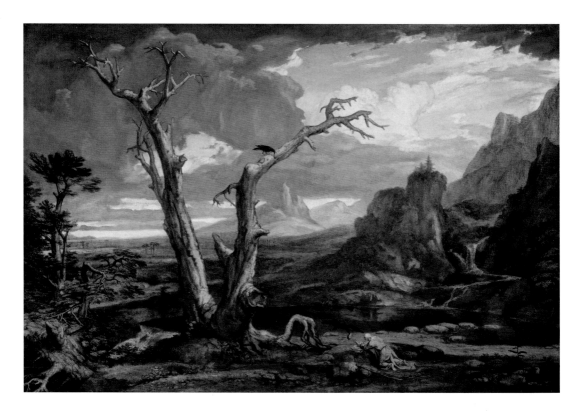

Washington Allston
American, 1779–1843
Elijah in the Desert, 1818

According to the Bible's first book of Kings, the Lord sent the prophet Elijah into the desert where "the ravens brought him bread and flesh in the morning and bread and flesh in the evening; and he drank of the brook." Allston conveyed the mood and meaning of this subject by the stark landscape, the turbulent clouds, and the dry texture of the paint. Elijah kneels in prayer, his figure echoed by the gnarled roots of a barren tree. Allston spent many years in Europe and viewed himself as a painter in the tradition of the old masters. His fellow Americans admired his learned biblical and literary subjects and romantic, imaginary landscapes. *Elijah in the Desert*, painted shortly before Allston returned to Boston from London, was the first work of art acquired by the Museum.

Oil on canvas
49¼ x 72¾ in. (125.1 x 184.8 cm)
Gift of Mrs. Samuel and Miss Alice Hooper   70.1

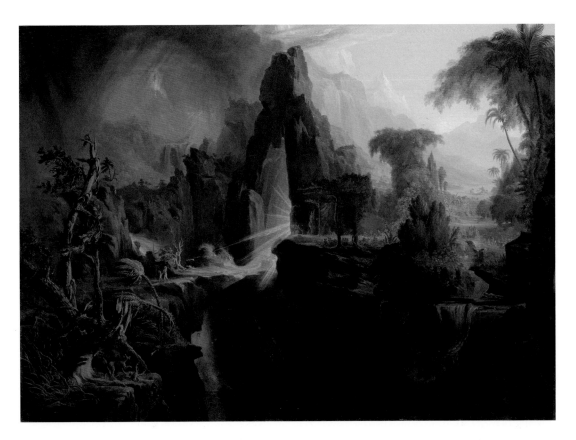

Thomas Cole

American (born in England), 1801–1848

Expulsion from the Garden of Eden, 1828

The pioneer of American landscape painting, Thomas Cole made his reputation with images of the wilderness of New York's Hudson River Valley. In this painting, which Cole called an attempt "at a higher type of landscape than I have hitherto tried," he combined landscape with the kind of religious theme accepted for centuries as the proper subject matter for "serious" artists. The story is that of Adam and Eve who, having angered God by eating the forbidden fruit that gave them knowledge of good and evil, were expelled from the Garden of Eden. Cole conveys their anguish, not through pose and expression (as was traditional) but through landscape, contrasting serene, light-filled Paradise with the harsh world outside. Dwarfed by the power of nature, the helpless figures seem propelled from the garden by a shaft of supernatural light.

Oil on canvas
39¾ x 54½ in. (101 x 138.4 cm)
Gift of Martha C. Karolik for the M. and M. Karolik Collection
of American Paintings, 1815–1865   47.1188

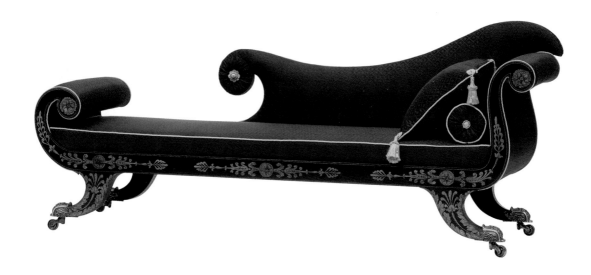

Grecian couch
Maryland (Baltimore), about 1820
Attributed to **Hugh Finlay**, American, 1781–1831

The new American nation, proudly associating itself with the ancient republics of Greece and Rome, turned to the classical world for everything from household furnishings and architecture to the names of its new towns. The "Grecian" couch—with one high, bolstered end—was among the most stylish furnishings of early-nineteenth-century parlors. Prosperous Baltimore favored painted furniture in the classical style. For more than forty years, Irish-trained brothers John and Hugh Finlay, working singly and together, provided Baltimore with the richest and most attractive examples. This couch, boldly sculptural in form, is enriched with superb painted ornament—classical anthemia, rosettes, and acanthus leaves. The freehand painting was not intended to imitate expensive materials but to be a vibrant art form in its own right. Fabrics rarely survive time and use, and the Museum reupholstered the couch in a crimson silk damask based on threads of the original material that survived under the nail heads.

Yellow-poplar, cherry, white pine, rosewood graining, and gilded painting; partial original foundation and new foundation materials, cover, and trim
35¾ x 91½ x 24¼ in. (90.8 x 232.4 x 61.6 cm)
Museum purchase with funds donated by Mr. and Mrs. Amos B. Hostetter, Jr., Anne and Joseph P. Pellegrino, Mr. and Mrs. Peter S. Lynch, Mr. William N. Banks, Jr., Eddy G. Nicholson, Mr. and Mrs. John Lastavica, Mr. and Mrs. Daniel F. Morley, and Mary S. and Edward J. Holmes Fund   1988.530

Girandole wall clock

Massachusetts (Concord), about 1816–21
Lemuel Curtis, American, 1790–1857

Made when clocks were still costly and prized possessions, the girandole is a design unique to America.
It was patented by Lemuel Curtis in 1816 and took its
name from the circular, convex looking glasses popular in the period. Such clocks, which were the work of
many skilled craftsmen, are characterized by the convex glass of their dial faces and pendulum chambers,
their gilded cases with eagle finials, and their reverse-
painted glass panels—here, depicting a medieval
wedding ceremony. Soon after this particular piece
was made, Curtis's business declined, undercut by the
mass production of thirty-hour shelf clocks. In 1832
he became a merchant and grocer, but was declared
bankrupt ten years later and died in poverty.

Carved, painted, and gilded wood; brass;
reverse-glass painting
46 x 13¾ x 5¾ in. (116.8 x 34.9 x 14.6 cm)
Gift of Mrs. Charles C. Cabot in memory of
Dr. and Mrs. Charles J. White   1991.241

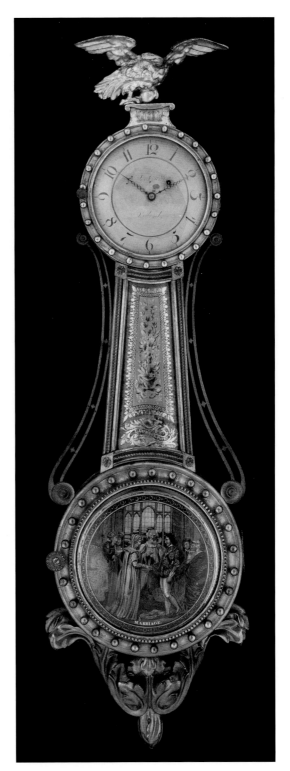

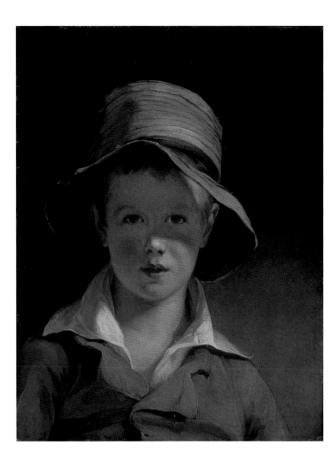

Thomas Sully
American (born in England), 1783–1872
The Torn Hat, 1820

In portraits of the seventeenth and eighteenth centuries, children were usually posed and dressed as miniature adults (see the portrait of Margaret Gibbs, page 178). But Philadelphia painter Thomas Sully discarded this convention in favor of more informal, naturalistic images, such as this one of his son Thomas. The curved brim of the boy's straw hat is torn, and this gives Sully the opportunity to display his skill at rendering the play of light and shadow on skin and fabric. The enthusiasm that greeted this unaffected image reflects the early nineteenth century's new appreciation of the appealing and distinctive nature of childhood.

Oil on panel
19⅛ x 14⅝ in. (48.6 x 37.2 cm)
Gift of Miss Belle Greene and Henry Copley Greene in memory of their mother,
Mary Abby Greene (Mrs. J. S. Copley Greene)   16.104

opposite
William Sidney Mount
American, 1807–1868
The Bone Player, 1856

The musician depicted here plays the bones, thin bars of ivory or bone that were clicked together to create complex and energetic rhythms. *The Bone Player* has the sensitivity and specificity of a portrait, but Mount created it to be reproduced as a color lithograph in Paris, where images of "exotic" figure types enjoyed widespread popularity.

Mount, who lived on rural Long Island, New York, was the first major American artist to devote his career to depictions of the work and play of ordinary people. He wrote in his diary: "Paint pictures that will take with the public. In other words, never paint for the few, but for the many. Some artists remain in the corner by not observing the above."

Oil on canvas
36⅛ x 29⅛ in. (91.8 x 74 cm)
Bequest of Martha C. Karolik for
the M. and M. Karolik Collection of
American Paintings, 1815–1865   48.461

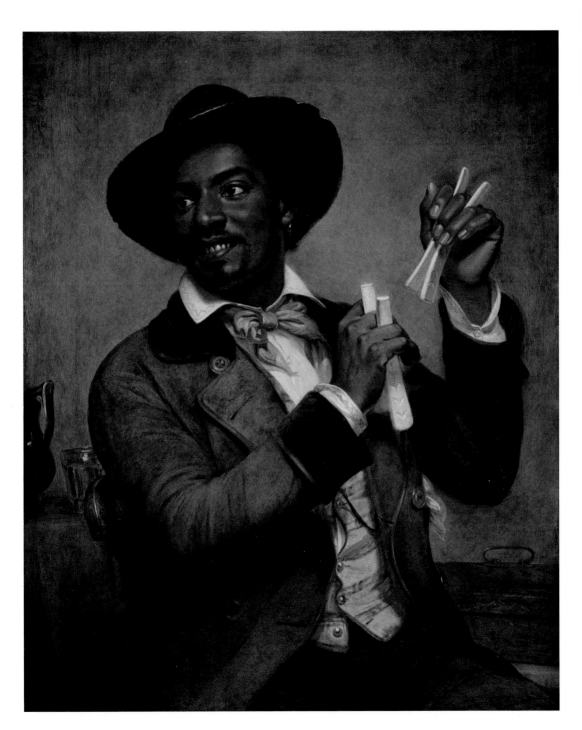

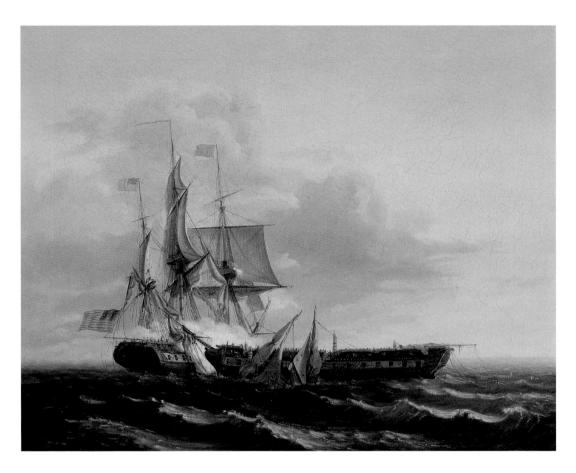

Thomas Birch
American (born in England), 1779–1851
***Engagement between the "Constitution" and the
"Guerrière,"*** 1813

During the War of 1812, the infant American navy—to everyone's surprise—regularly defeated the supposedly invincible British fleet. Birch, who emigrated from England to Philadelphia in 1794, made his reputation with depictions of these naval battles, which were both as accurate as he could make them (details were often derived from interviews with members of the ships' crews) and romantically thrilling. In this picture, Birch documented, with fine patriotic passion, the defeat of the British warship *Guerrière* (on the right) by the USS *Constitution*. As the damaged *Guerrière* is driven up against the *Constitution*, the British standard sinks into the sea, and American flags wave triumphantly against a sky pink with clouds and smoke. The *Constitution*, nicknamed "Old Ironsides" for the virtually impenetrable oak planking of its hull, now is docked at the Charlestown Navy Yard in Boston.

Oil on canvas
28 x 36¼ in. (71.1 x 92.1 cm)
Ernest Wadsworth Longfellow Fund and Emily L. Ainsley Fund   1978.159

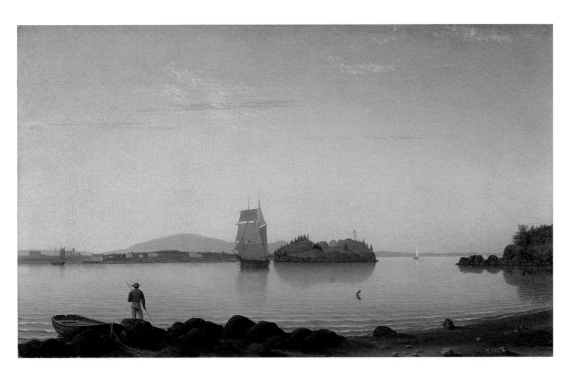

Fitz Henry Lane
American, 1804–1865
Owl's Head, Penobscot Bay, Maine, 1862

The son of a sailmaker in Gloucester, Massachusetts, Lane spent his life painting the coast of New England. Disabled as a result of a childhood illness, he moved about on land only with the aid of crutches. But he roamed widely by water. "The sea is his home," wrote a contemporary critic. "There he truly lives, and it is there, in that inexhaustible field, that his victories will be won." This is among the most spare and poetic of Lane's coastal views—small pictures whose horizontal shape emphasizes the line that separates land and sea from an expanse of clear, delicately tinted sky. Although Lane depicts a specific spot in Maine and a specific moment in time, this painting's true subject is light, and its evocative stillness renders it timeless. Like Martin Johnson Heade (see page 216), Lane was forgotten until his rediscovery by Maxim Karolik in the 1940s.

Oil on canvas
15¾ x 26⅛ in. (40 x 66.4 cm)
Bequest of Martha C. Karolik for the M. and M. Karolik Collection of American Paintings, 1815–1865   48.448

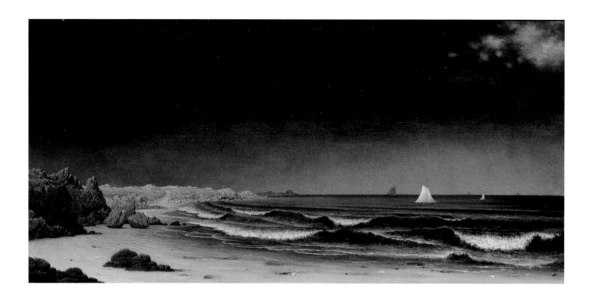

Martin Johnson Heade

American, 1819–1904

***Approaching Storm: Beach
near Newport,*** about 1861–62

Oil on canvas

28 x 58⅜ in. (71.1 x 148.3 cm)

Gift of Maxim Karolik for the M. and
M. Karolik Collection of American
Paintings, 1815–1865   45.889

"Who ever accused me of being a gentleman? I am
a tenor!" Trained as an opera singer in his native
St. Petersburg, Russia, Maxim Karolik (1893–1963) came
to the United States in the early 1920s and became
a champion of American art and a great benefactor
of the Museum. In 1927 he married Martha Codman
(1858–1948), who was descended from several prominent New Englanders and was herself a distinguished
collector of eighteenth-century American art. Together
they assembled three major collections for the Museum
of Fine Arts that transformed the institution's holdings
and rewrote the history of American art.

Martha Karolik was a more reserved figure than
her husband—it would have been difficult not
to be—but it was she who introduced him to the
Museum and her money that allowed them to gather
what Maxim called "the trilogy." The first collection
was dedicated to eighteenth-century furniture and
painting; the second to paintings of the half century
between 1815 and 1865; and the last to drawings,
watercolors, and folk art of the same period. It is for
their taste in paintings that the Karoliks are best

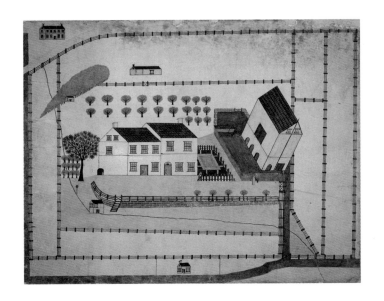

Possibly by Charles H. Wolf
American, about 1830–1900
Pennsylvania Farmstead with
Many Fences, early 19th century
Pen and watercolor on paper
18 x 23⅞ in. (45.7 x 60.6 cm)
Gift of Maxim Karolik for the M. and
M. Karolik Collection of American
Watercolors and Drawings, 1800–1875
56.740

remembered, for before them it had been generally assumed that there was almost no art worthy of
the name in mid-nineteenth-century America. The
Karoliks were among the first to champion Fitz Henry
Lane and, above all, Martin Johnson Heade, whom
Maxim called "the genius of our collection." Presented to the Museum in the late 1940s, the Karoliks's
paintings spurred a nationwide reassessment of
nineteenth-century American art, and a number of
the Karoliks's unknowns are today among the most
sought-after American artists.

The Karoliks themselves were almost extrava-
gantly modest, and Maxim refused to attend the
opening of the Museum's exhibition of the painting collection for fear his presence would distract
from the art. Most movingly, he saw the trilogy as a
celebration of his adopted country and the embodiment of its democratic spirit. In an open letter to the
Museum's director, he concluded: "We are not 'Patrons
of Art' or 'Public Benefactors.' We refuse to accept
these banal labels. We accept with pleasure only one
label: 'Useful Citizens.'"

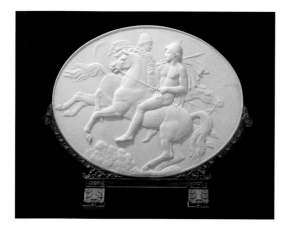

Horatio Greenough
American, 1805–1852
Castor and Pollux, about 1847

Bostonian Horatio Greenough was the first of many American sculptors to train in Italy, drawn there by its famed marble quarries; the inspiring examples of ancient Greek, Roman, and Renaissance sculpture; and a thriving, international community of artists eager to recapture the glories of classical art. This sculpture, carved in subtly modulated low relief and influenced by Roman architectural friezes and sarcophagi, depicts the famous warriors Castor and Pollux. According to one legend, Zeus rewarded the love of these brothers, separated by death, by joining them eternally in the sky as the constellation of the twins, Gemini.

Marble, with original black walnut frame
34⅝ x 45¼ x 1¾ in. (88 x 114.8 x 4.5 cm)
Bequest of Mrs. Horatio Greenough 92.2642

Sideboard
Pennsylvania (Philadelphia), 1850–60
Ignatius Lutz, American (born in France), 1817–1860

Concrete symbols of taste and social status change with changing times. In the mid-nineteenth century, massive sideboards—carved with fruit, vegetables, and animals and often laden with silver—adorned the dining rooms of the wealthy and style-conscious. In a period when much furniture was at least partly made by machine, handcrafted objects began to assume new status. The rich and complex carving that gives this massive piece its exciting silhouette could not have been achieved by machine. The sideboard bears the label of French-trained cabinetmaker Ignatius Lutz, who came to Philadelphia in 1844. One of many French and German furniture makers in American cities at this time, Lutz employed thirty craftsmen who mainly worked without power machinery in his successful shop.

Oak, yellow-poplar, marble
94 x 74 x 25 in. (238.8 x 188 x 63.5 cm)
Museum purchase with funds donated by the Estate of Richard Bruce E. Lacont 1990.1

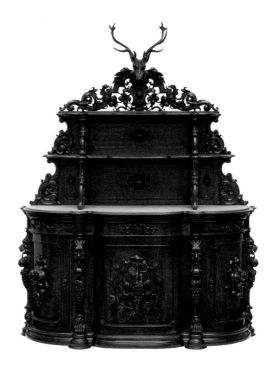

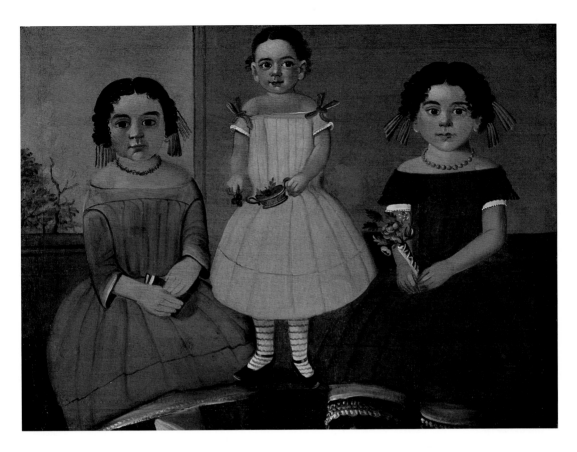

William Matthew Prior

American, 1806–1873

Three Sisters of the Copeland Family, 1854

While many nineteenth-century folk painters created works for their own enjoyment, William Matthew Prior made a handsome living as an artist. In 1841, he moved from Maine to East Boston, where his portrait business flourished. A staunch abolitionist, Prior had a number of African Americans as clients — including successful secondhand clothing dealer Samuel Copeland, from nearby Chelsea, whose daughters Prior portrays in this triple portrait. Unlike many images of African Americans of his day, Prior's display a seriousness and sympathy. The girls — Eliza (about six years old), Nellie (about two), and Margaret (about four) — wear fashionable off-the-shoulder dresses; their necklaces and hair ribbons also indicate their father's prosperity. The book, flowers, and fruit they hold indicate that they are educated. Their self-confidence is evident in their dignified poses. The book holds special poignancy, for Copeland, despite his business acumen, could neither read nor write.

Oil on canvas

26⅞ x 36½ in. (68.3 x 92.7 cm)

Bequest of Martha C. Karolik for the M. and M. Karolik Collection of American Paintings, 1815–1865   48.467

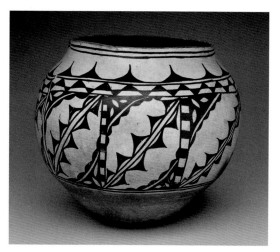

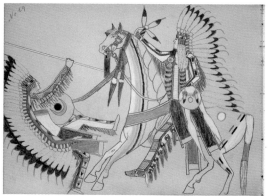

Storage jar
New Mexico (Cochiti or Santo Domingo Pueblo),
about 1860–80

This unusually large jar was created for use in the
home, not for the collectors' market. In this period,
women made the ceramic vessels necessary for ceremonial use and for the cooking, serving, and storage
of food and water. Jars of this size, intended to hold
grain, were highly valued and passed down from
mother to daughter. The bold decorations evoke rain
and water; they were painted with slip, a thin mixture
of clay and water colored with mineral pigments.

Earthenware with slip paint
H. 18 in. (45 cm)
Museum purchase with funds donated by Independence
Investment Associates, Inc.   1997.175

Silver Horn (Huangooah)
Kiowa Apache, 1860–1940
*Drawing No. 24. The Once-Famous Black Eagle
(Ka-et-te-kone-ke) of the Kiowa in Deadly Conflict
with Ute Chief. Ute Killed. From Ledger Book
Containing 33 Drawings*
1885

Over many centuries, Plains Indians painted records
of their battles, ceremonies, and tribal history on rock
walls, hide robes, and tipi coverings. In the reservation period, some Native American artists continued
this tradition using new materials—paper, pencils,
crayons, and inks. Such works as this one are called
"ledger drawings" because many were executed in
ledger, or account, books. This lively image of a battle
between Kiowa and Ute warriors is the work of Silver
Horn, a member of a family known for several generations of artists. The drawing is one of thirty-three in a
sketchbook annotated by Horace Pope Jones, a civil-
ian interpreter at Fort Sill, Oklahoma.

Graphite pencil and colored pencils on paper
10 1/8 x 14 in. (25.7 x 35.6 cm)
Gift of the Grandchildren of Lucretia McIlvain Shoemaker
and the M. and M. Karolik Fund   1994.429.24

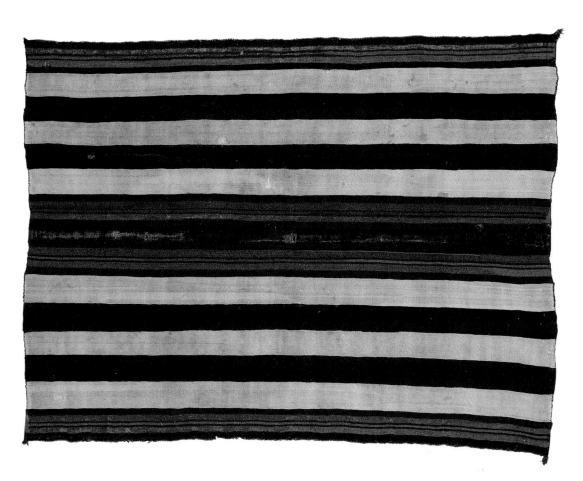

Wearing blanket
Navajo (Diné)
Arizona or New Mexico, 1840–60

Navajo women learn to weave from a young age, taught by their mothers and grandmothers in techniques that have been practiced for generations— from gathering plants to make the dyes, to spinning yarn from natural fibers, to weaving the final textiles. Finished blankets are thought to have a life force of their own, radiating a sense of vitality and harmony reflective of the Navajo philosophy of *hozho*, in which every individual strives to live in balance with the world. With its harmonious composition of line and color, this rare early wearing blanket is a masterpiece of the weaver's art. Such blankets were long prized as trade items among Native communities as far away as the Northern Plains and Great Basin. This example was given to the Museum in 1902 by Denman Waldo Ross, a professor of design at Harvard University and one of the first collectors to donate works of Native American art to the MFA.

Wool; weft-faced plain weave
73 x 53⅞ in. (185.5 x 137 cm)
Denman Waldo Ross Collection   02.80

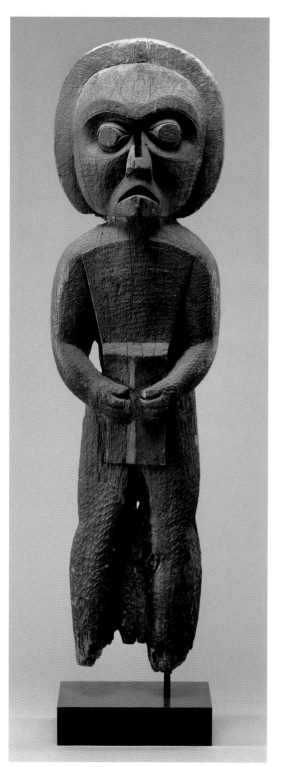

Potlatch figure
Kwakwaka'waku (Kwakiutl)
Canada, (Kwakwaka'waku, Northern Vancouver
Island), about 1840

A center of social and ritual life among the peoples
of the Northwest Coast, the potlatch was a feast in
which the host showered his guests with food, drink,
and gifts of blankets, masks, and valuable plaques of
decorated copper. In this way the potlatch host dem-
onstrated his wealth and ensured both the respect of
his neighbors and his own future gain, since at a later
time his guests would present him with even more
lavish gifts at their ceremonies. This monumental
figure would have been set up on the shore to welcome
guests to the potlatch. The trapezoidal shape over his
chest represents a copper plaque, symbol of the real
goods that guests would receive during the festivities.

Red cedar, paint
H. 67¾ in. (168 cm)
Museum purchase with funds donated by a friend of the
Department of American Decorative Arts and Sculpture
1998.3

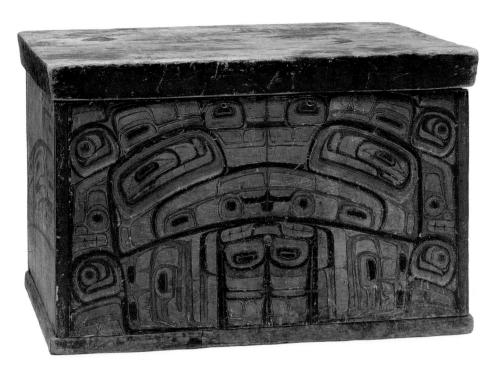

Bent-corner chief's chest
Probably Tsimshian
Canada (coastal British Columbia), about 1860

In traditional Tsimshian society, chests like this were used to store ritual objects such as masks and rattles, as well as the blankets and copper plaques that were indicators of wealth and status. The work of a highly skilled carpenter, the chest's four sides are made of a single piece of wood, which was steamed and bent into the shape of a box. Native people of the Northwest Coast believed in close and constant contact between the physical and spirit worlds, with humans and animals passing back and forth between the two realms, changing from one shape to another as they did so. Ravens, fish, and a mythical creature intermingle across the surface of this chest and defy any single interpretation.

Yellow cedar and red cedar with red (Chinese vermilion and red ochre) and black pigment
26¾ x 41⅜ x 24¼ in. (67.7 x 105.1 x 61.8 cm)
Museum purchase with funds donated by a friend of the Department of American Decorative Arts and Sculpture
1997.9

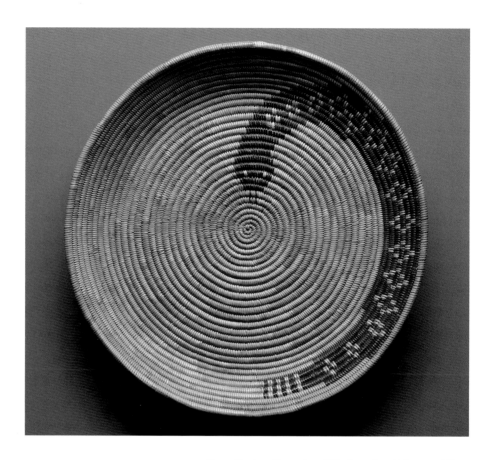

Tray

California (possibly Palm Springs), about 1900

Attributed to **Guadalupe Arenas,** Cahuilla, active
about 1900–1920

Basketry was the major art form of the Mission Indians (so named because they lived near the Spanish
missions along the California coast). Coiled baskets
and other objects were woven primarily of native
sumac that was often dyed and juncus grass, whose
stem changes naturally from deep brown to tan as it
grows. Fine Mission baskets such as this were made

for collectors from the 1890s into the 1930s, providing
much-needed income for the weavers and their families. This tray may be the work of Guadalupe Arenas,
who worked as a laundry woman in a Palm Springs
tuberculosis sanatorium. The rattlesnake, a favorite
motif on Mission baskets, was viewed as a symbol of
power, an avenging spirit, and a protective deity that
would bring good fortune to the weaver.

Coiled grass stems, juncus grass, sumac
Diam. 11½ in. (29.2 cm)
John Wheelock Elliot and John Morse Elliot Fund   1992.197

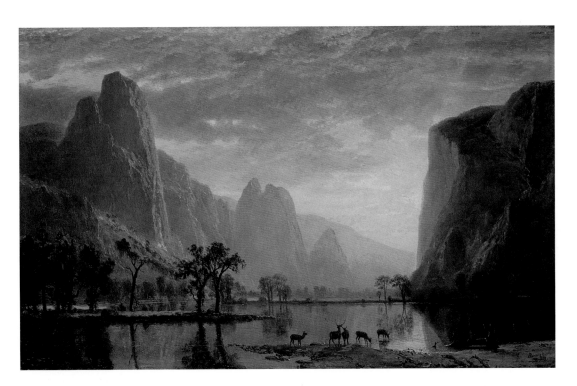

Albert Bierstadt
American (born in Germany), 1830–1902
Valley of the Yosemite, 1864

The unspoiled grandeur of the West was an endless source of fascination for armchair travelers in the eastern United States. Bierstadt, a canny business-man as well as a gifted painter, made several trips to the West. Back in his New York studio, he used the oil sketches and photographs from these journeys to create hundreds of paintings that range from the tiny to the gargantuan. These images celebrate the West's natural splendors, many of which would soon be altered forever by railroads, settlers, and tour-ists. The emotional charge that Americans found in the Western landscape — a charge similarly captured in Carleton Watkins's photographic vista from the same period (see page 226) — was conveyed by Bier-stadt's companion on a trip to the recently discovered Yosemite Valley in 1864: "Far to the westward, widen-ing more and more, it opens into the bosom of great mountain ranges, — into a field of perfect light, misty by its own excess, — into an unspeakable suffusion of glory created from the phoenix-pile of the dying sun."

Oil on paperboard
11⅞ x 19¼ in. (30.2 x 48.9 cm)
Gift of Martha C. Karolik for the M. and M. Karolik Collection
of American Paintings, 1815–1865   47.1236

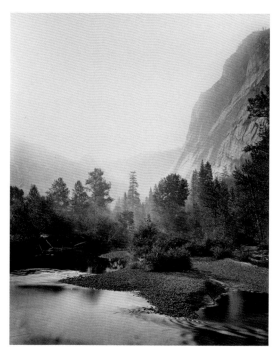

Carleton E. Watkins
American, 1829–1916
Mount Starr King and Glacier Point, Yosemite, No. 69, 1865–66
Photograph, mammoth albumen print from wet collodion negative
20 x 16⅛ in. (50.8 x 41 cm)
Ernest Wadsworth Longfellow Fund   2006.847

below
Thomas Moran
American (born in England), 1837–1926
Solitude, 1869
Lithograph
20⅝ x 16 in. (52.4 x 40.6 cm)
Gift of Sylvester Rosa Koehler   K3235

Best known as a painter, Thomas Moran spent his early career as an illustrator for *Scribner's Monthly*, carving and later drawing the publication's images for print. In 1871, he joined the Hayden Geological Survey as a guest artist on its exploration of Yellowstone—an expedition sponsored in part by *Scribner's*. Moran's sketches from that trip would capture the public imagination and, with the photographs of fellow survey member William Henry Jackson, help persuade Congress to establish Yellowstone as the first national park in 1872. (A proud Moran soon began signing his works TYM, for Thomas "Yellowstone" Moran.) But when he drew on stone to create this wild, atmospheric lithograph, Moran had not yet traveled to the West. He was likely inspired by the grandiose landscape paintings that his Hudson River School colleague, and fellow westward traveler, Albert Bierstadt, exhibited in New York beginning in the 1860s.

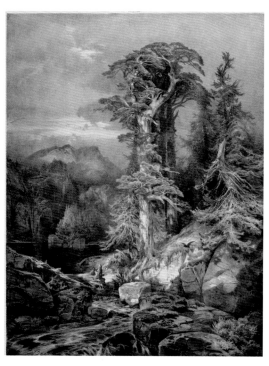

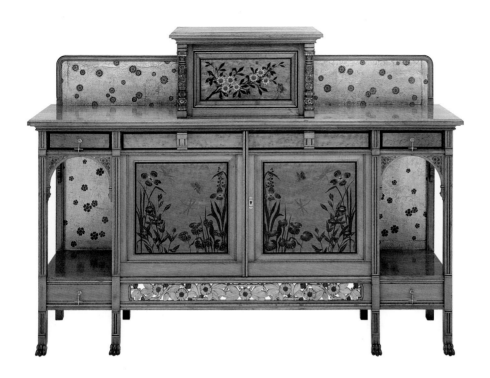

Cabinet
New York (New York), about 1880
Made by **Herter Brothers**, American, active 1865–1905

Spare and linear in form, this cabinet is enlivened
by a rich variety of carved and inlaid asymmetrical
ornament after the Japanese taste. Although probably
derived from Japanese screens and woodblock prints,
this ornament is free of any historical or symbolic
context. It features extraordinarily detailed insects
and plants, including tiny beetles chewing holes in
leaves. The pale wood and gilding reflect a movement
away from the prevalent taste for heavy, dark furniture. The cabinet is in superb original condition; notable is the embossed and stenciled gilt paper lining the
niches and splashboard—a rare survival. The cabinet
is the work of Herter Brothers, the fashionable firm
that produced some of New York's finest furniture in
the eclectic styles typical of the time. It may have been
made for railroad magnate Edward Henry Harriman,
one of the New York robber barons who were Herter
Brothers' frequent clients.

Maple, bird's-eye maple, oak or chestnut, stamped and gilt
paper; gilding, inlay, and carved decoration; original brass
pulls and key
52½ x 72¾ x 15⅛ in. (133.4 x 148.8 x 38.4 cm)
Museum purchase with funds donated anonymously and the
Frank B. Bemis Fund   2000.3

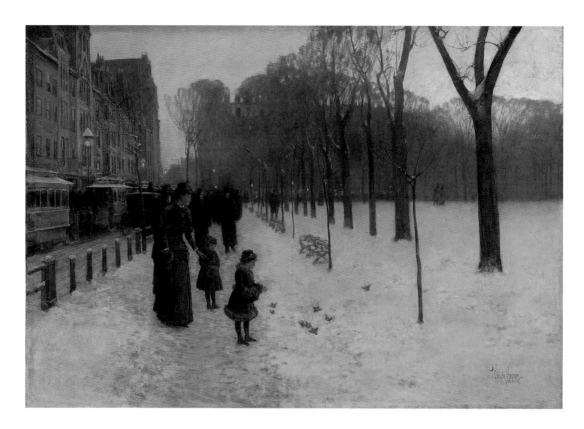

Childe Hassam
American, 1859–1935
At Dusk (Boston Common at Twilight), 1885–86

Along a snowy sidewalk, a fashionably dressed woman and her daughters, all wearing muffs against the cold, pause to feed some birds. Before them is the serene expanse of Boston Common; behind them, the streetlights are coming on and horse-drawn trolleys and cabs inch along crowded, and newly developed, Tremont Street. This painting, one of the most evocative of images of life in nineteenth-century Boston, is also an early example of Hassam's lifelong interest in the varied effects of light and in subjects drawn from the modern city; he later became one of the first American Impressionists.

Oil on canvas
42 x 60 in. (106.7 x 152.4 cm)
Gift of Miss Maud E. Appleton   31.952

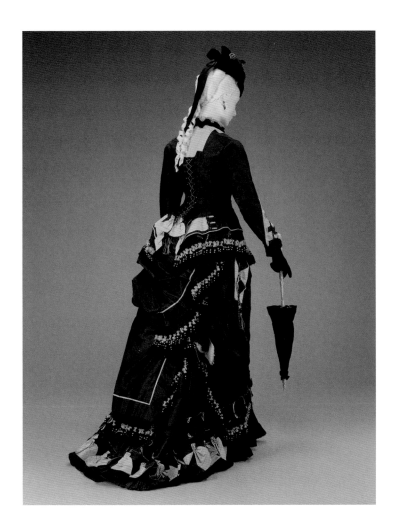

Woman's dress

Massachusetts (Boston), 1874–75

Labeled: "**John J. Stevens**/282 Washington Street, Boston"

Sarah Howe of Lowell, Massachusetts, had this dress made by the Boston dressmakers shop of John J. Stevens (1824–1902), who advertised his firm as "importers and dealers of Paris modes." Although designed as a "walking dress" for daytime strolls, it required the wearing of a corset and the cumbersome skirts would have been difficult to manage on the street. The dress reform movement, which had developed by the 1860s along with the women's suffrage movement, denounced such garments as restricting and unhealthy and scorned fashionable women as "upholstered bodies."

Silk; plain weave, trimmed with knotted net and tassels
Gift of Miss Ruth Burke   56.818a–b

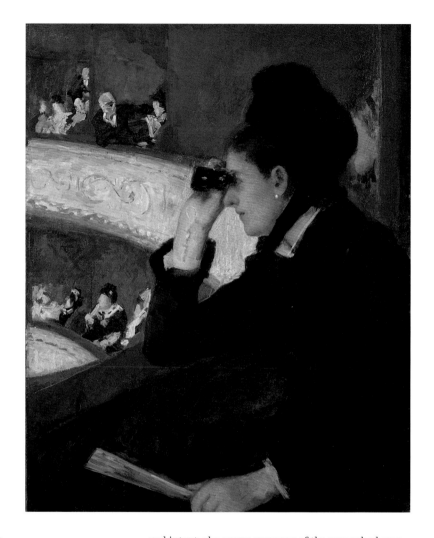

Mary Stevenson Cassatt

American, 1844–1926

In the Loge, 1878

Born and raised in Pennsylvania, Cassatt settled in Paris in 1875 and became the only American to exhibit with the Impressionist group. Like her friend Edgar Degas, she was a figure painter, attracted to detached and spontaneous views of modern life. Here, a woman in sober dress and hat uses her uptilted opera glasses to scan the occupants of other boxes. Self-contained and intent, she seems unaware of the man who leans out of another box, focusing his glasses on her. About the time this picture was painted, Cassatt began to carry a small sketchbook in which she swiftly recorded people and scenes that might later become subjects of paintings.

Oil on canvas

32 x 26 in. (81.3 x 66 cm)

The Hayden Collection — Charles Henry Hayden Fund   10.35

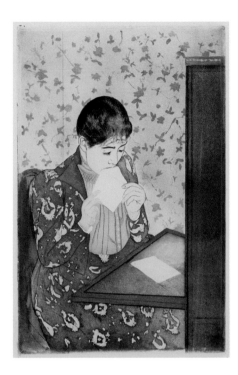

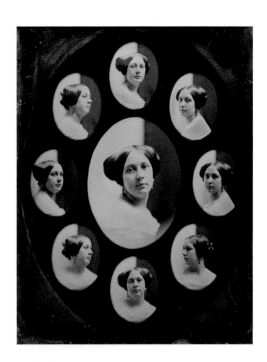

Mary Stevenson Cassatt
American, 1844–1926
The Letter, 1890-91

Southworth and Hawes
American, active 1843–1862
Portrait of a Woman in Nine Oval Views,
about 1855–61

After attending an 1890 Paris exhibition of more than 700 Japanese woodblock prints, Cassatt wrote: "You couldn't think of anything more beautiful. I dream of it." Like many of her contemporaries, Cassatt collected and admired Japanese prints for their modern-life subjects, emphasis on elegant line, unusual compositions, and barely modulated areas of color. This is one of a set of ten color prints in which Cassatt focuses on daily domestic life—women bathing and dressing, tending their children, out for a dress-fitting or a social call. The several plates required to produce the variety of colors were each inked by hand, and every one of Cassatt's sophisticated etchings with aquatint is a unique work of art.

The daguerreotype, introduced in 1839, was one of the earliest photographic processes. The Boston firm established by Albert Sands Southworth (1811–1894) and Josiah Johnson Hawes (1808–1901) was renowned for its ability to capture personality and expression in daguerreotype portraits—no mean feat in a medium that required the sitter to remain absolutely motionless for up to thirty seconds. In 1855 Southworth patented a device for making multiple exposures on the same plate, explaining that they might be used to select "the best for a locket; or they may be different views of the same face taken upon the same plate for the purposes of preserving them together." This is the finest of only two known examples of this adventurous technique.

Drypoint and color aquatint
Platemark: 13⅝ x 8⅞ in. (34.6 x 22.5 cm)
Gift of William Emerson and The Hayden Collection—
Charles Henry Hayden Fund 41.803

Photograph, daguerreotype
8½ x 6½ in. (21.6 x 16.5 cm)
Gift of Edward Southworth Hawes in memory of his father
Josiah Johnson Hawes 43.1405

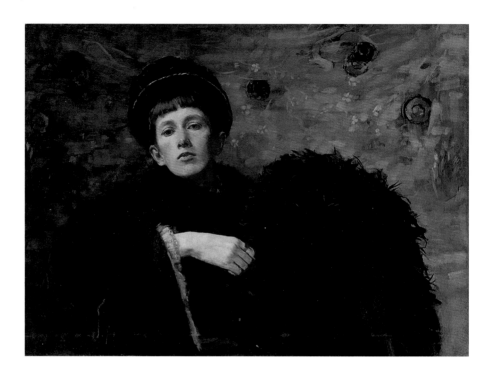

Ellen Day Hale

American, 1855–1940

Self-Portrait, 1885

Oil on canvas
28½ x 39 in. (72.4 x 99.1 cm)
Gift of Nancy Hale Bowers   1986.645

Hale studied in Boston, Philadelphia, and Paris and
supported herself by teaching art in Boston, by selling
her portraits and etchings, and by painting decorations in church interiors. This unconventional self-
portrait is unusually forthright for a woman painter.
Against a blue fabric background decorated with
swirling shapes and spots of bright color, her pur-
poseful, unsmiling face and capable hand stand out
from the surrounding soft blackness of dress, hat, and
ostrich-feather fan. A critic writing in 1887 acknowledged the artist's originality and skill: "Miss Ellen
Hale . . . displays a man's strength in the treatment
and handling of her subjects—a massiveness and
breadth of effect attained through sound training and
native wit and courage."

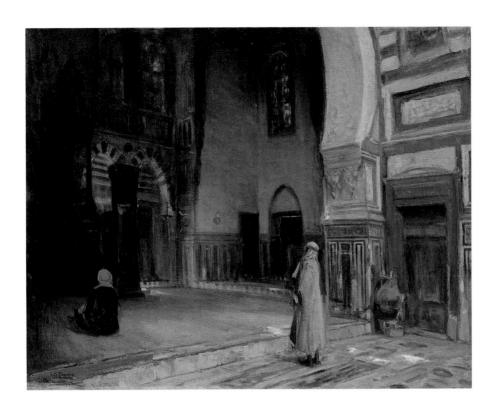

Henry Ossawa Tanner

American, 1859–1937

Interior of a Mosque, Cairo, 1897

Tanner, the foremost African American painter of the
late nineteenth century, was first trained in his native
Philadelphia but settled permanently in Paris in 1891.
There, he specialized in religious compositions, exhib-
iting many at the prestigious Salon exhibitions from
1894 to 1914. Sponsored by Philadelphia businessman
Rodman Wanamaker, Tanner traveled to the Near East
in 1897, following a stream of artists who had made
this trip since the 1830s. Like many individuals of his
time, Wanamaker believed that "one should go [to the
Near East] every two or three years, at least, to keep
in touch with the Orientalist spirit." Tanner visited
several mosques in Cairo; this loosely painted interior
depicts the madrasa of Sultan Qaitbey.

Oil on canvas
20½ x 26 in. (52.1 x 66 cm)
Museum purchase with funds
by exchange from The Hayden
Collection — Charles Henry Hayden
Fund, Bequest of Kathleen Rothe,
Bequest of Barbara Brooks Walker,
and Gift of Mrs. Richard Storey in
memory of Mrs. Bayard Thayer
2005.92

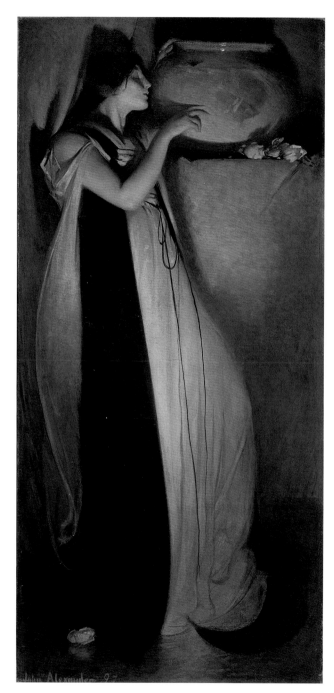

John White Alexander
American, 1856–1915
Isabella and the Pot of Basil, 1897

And she forgot the stars, the moon, and sun,
And she forgot the blue above the trees,
And she forgot the dells where waters run,
And she forgot the chilly autumn breeze;
She had no knowledge when the day was done,
And the new morn she saw not: but in peace
Hung over her sweet Basil evermore,
And moisten'd it with tears unto the core.

In John Keats's 1820 poem "Isabella; or, The Pot of Basil," the ambitious brothers of wealthy Isabella, determined that she marry a nobleman, murder her humble suitor Lorenzo. Isabella discovers Lorenzo's body buried in the woods, cuts off the head, and hides it in a pot planted with sweet basil, a symbol of undying love. Painted in Paris at the very end of the nineteenth century, this picture's theatricality and macabre theme reflect the decadent tastes of the period known as the fin de siècle.

Oil on canvas
75⅝ x 36⅛ in. (192.1 x 91.8 cm)
Gift of Ernest Wadsworth Longfellow   98.181

William Michael Harnett

American (born in Ireland), 1848–1892

Old Models, 1892

"As a rule," Harnett said, "new things do
not paint well." Here, fastidiously arranged
against a scuffed and cracked wooden door,
are a dented bugle that has lost its shine, an
old violin, volumes of Shakespeare and Homer
frayed and stained from many readings, tat-
tered scores of romantic songs, and a ceramic
jar from Europe. These are the models that
Harnett painted often—objects treasured
both for their textures and shapes and for
their evocation of past times. The American
master of the time-honored trompe l'oeil
("deceive the eye") style, Harnett rendered
his subjects with such minute precision that
viewers are led to wonder: "Is this really
only paint?" Scorned by the art establish-
ment as virtuoso trickery, Harnett's pictures
enchanted patrons in the hotels and saloons
where they most often hung. *Old Models* was
Harnett's last work, painted shortly before his
death at the age of forty-four.

Oil on canvas

54⅜ x 28¼ in. (138.1 x 71.8 cm)

The Hayden Collection—Charles Henry

Hayden Fund   39.761

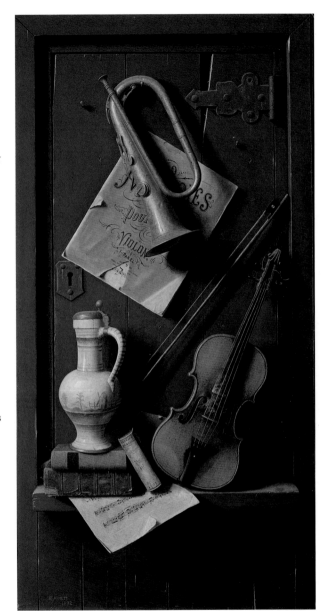

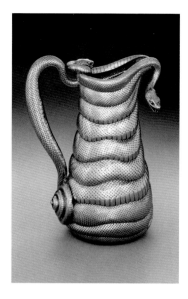

Snake pitcher
Rhode Island (Providence), 1885
Gorham Manufacturing Company

American mines were producing prodigious amounts of silver in the late
nineteenth century, and a flourishing market for silver objects encouraged innovation in both form and technique. To keep pace with the
demand, major silvermaking firms developed new production methods
and hired skilled craftsmen and designers from Europe. This startling
and seductive pitcher is a consummate expression of the period's love of
novelty, surprise, and virtuoso craftsmanship. The work of the silversmith alone took fifty-five hours. The bodies of the two entwined snakes
were embossed: pushed out or indented from the back. Another craftsman, the chaser, then articulated these basic snake forms from the front,
defining the scales of backs and bellies in a process similar to engraving—which took another eighty-six hours to complete.

Silver
H. 10 in. (25.4 cm)
Edwin E. Jack Fund   1983.331

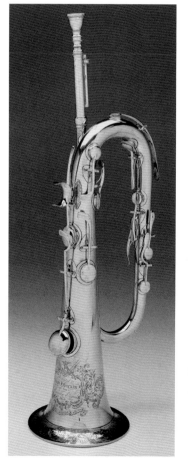

Keyed bugle in E-flat
Massachusetts (Boston), about 1854
Elbridge G. Wright, American, 1811–1871

By the time of the Civil War, virtually every American town had a brass
band that performed at dances, election-day parades, and outdoor summer concerts. The keyed bugle pitched in E-flat was usually the solo
instrument in such bands, and skilled bugle players could become celebri-
ties. Most bugles were copper; this costly silver instrument, as indicated
on the engraved bell, was a presentation piece given in 1854 to Joseph
J. Brenan, leader of the Marietta, Ohio, town band. By the 1860s, keyed
bugles had passed out of favor and become—like the one in William
Harnett's painting *Old Models*—sentimental reminders of days gone by.

Silver
H. 17½ in. (44.5 cm)
Gift of The Seminarians and Friends in memory of Warren C. Moffett   1990.85

John Frederick Peto
American, 1854–1907
The Poor Man's Store, 1885

Peto had more success as a cornet
player than as a painter and sold
his pictures for a few dollars—or
gave them away. Until about 1950,
Peto's paintings were often attributed to his friend and fellow Phila-
delphian William Harnett. This
colorful image of a tiny street-
front shop is Peto's masterpiece.
He used a canvas for the central
window area of the composition
and set it into a wooden "frame"
illusionistically painted to represent the wall, shelf, and door.
Multiple meanings and visual
jokes are characteristic of trompe
l'oeil painting. Here, the sign "Good
Board" below the window may
refer to the availability of lodging,
to the shelf from which the sign
hangs, or to the actual wood of the
painting's "frame."

Oil on canvas and panel
35½ x 25⅝ in. (90.2 x 65.1 cm)
Gift of Maxim Karolik for the M. and
M. Karolik Collection of American
Paintings, 1815–1865   62.278

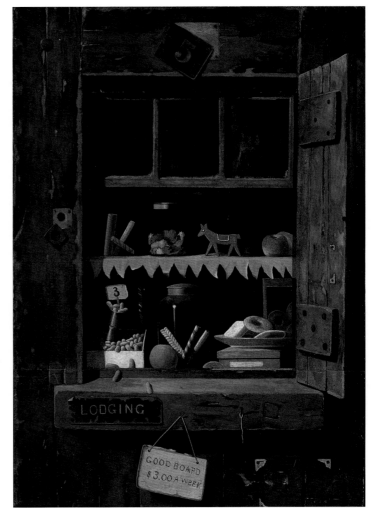

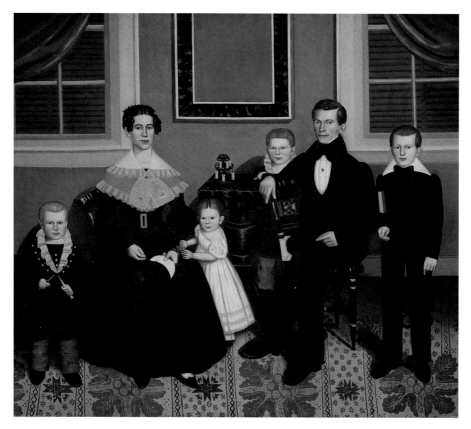

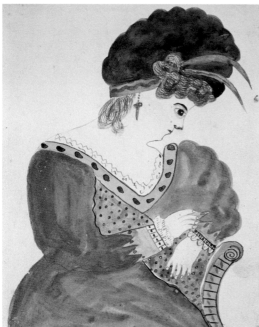

above

Erastus Salisbury Field

American, 1805–1900

Joseph Moore and His Family,

about 1839

Oil on canvas

82⅜ x 93⅜ in. (209.2 x 237.2 cm)

Gift of Maxim Karolik for the M. and M. Karolik Collection of American Paintings, 1815–1865   58.25

Mary Ann Willson

American, active 1800–1825

Young Woman Wearing a Turban,

between 1800–1825

Watercolor and graphite pencil on paper

7⅞ x 6½ in. (20 x 16.5 cm)

Gift of Maxim Karolik for the M. and M. Karolik Collection of American Watercolors and Drawings, 1800–1875   56.456

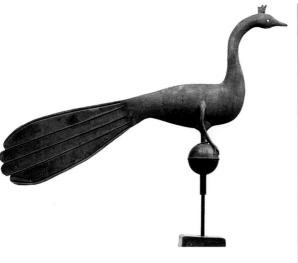

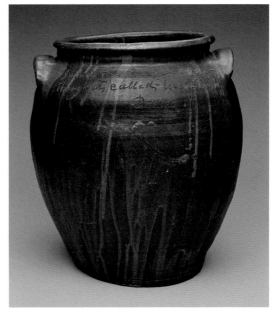

Peacock weathervane

Eastern United States, about 1860–75

Copper, painted gold; iron rod
H. 19¾ in. (50 cm), including ball
Gift of Mr. Maxim Karolik   54.1089

Storage jar

South Carolina (Edgefield County), 1857

Dave Drake (or Dave the Potter), American,
about 1800–about 1870, for the **Lewis J. Miles Factory**

Stoneware with alkaline glaze
H. 19 in. (48.3 cm)
Harriet Otis Cruft Fund and Otis Norcross Fund   1997.10

Although its extraordinary diversity resists generalization, much American folk art was made in rural
areas and small towns by artists who lacked formal
training in the fine arts. Some were professionals,
some amateurs; many of their names are lost. Most of
the objects they produced—like pottery and weather-
vanes—were primarily functional. Others were created for the pleasure of the artists and their friends,
family, and community.

At its best, American folk art is far more than the
unskilled imitation of work produced by trained practitioners in urban centers. Among its hallmarks is an
originality of conception unhampered by the desire to
be part of a recognized school or style. Although many
folk artists were somewhat limited by their lack of
training, they compensated for this with a directness

of expression emphasizing pattern, contour, color, and
simplified form in a way that is very pleasing to the
modern eye.

Maxim Karolik (see pages 216–217), who established the Museum's ever-increasing collection of
American folk art, once observed that folk artists
"sometimes lacked the ability to describe, but it certainly did not hinder their ability to express." Few
objects bear this out as eloquently as the storage jar
crafted by a slave known as Dave the Potter. Dave, who
fashioned the work in the pottery of his owner, was
literate, and was perhaps the only slave craftsman
permitted to sign his work. This jar is signed, dated
August 22, 1857, and inscribed: "I made this Jar for
Cash / Though its called lucre trash."

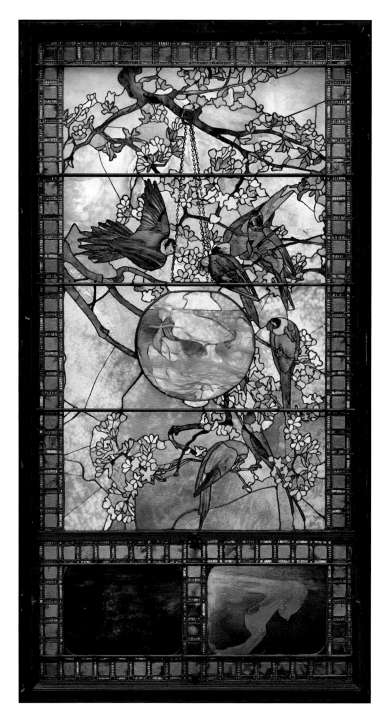

Louis Comfort Tiffany
American, 1848–1933
Tiffany Glass Company
Parakeets, about 1889

In a career that spanned five
decades, Louis Comfort Tiffany
worked in nearly every artistic
medium, but he became a household name for his work in stained
glass. Tiffany designed this window in late 1889, not for a specific
site but as an exhibition window.
Using it as an example of his
incomparable skills, he claimed
the window "illustrates most per-
fectly the possibilities of American
glass." Indeed, it highlights the two
major innovations of American-
style stained glass of the late
nineteenth century: the use of
opalescent glass, seen in the fishbowl, and plated glass, in which
multiple layers are stacked behind
one another to give the illusion of
depth. By carefully selecting and
manipulating his material—rough
or polished, opalescent or a mixture of colors—Tiffany was able
to create form, figure, shading, and
a sense of space. To heighten the
illusion, he used a real chain to
"suspend" the fishbowl.

Glass, lead, bronze chain
77 x 38½ in. (195.6 x 97.8 cm)
Gift of Barbara L. and Theodore B.
Alfond in honor of Malcolm Rogers
2008.1415

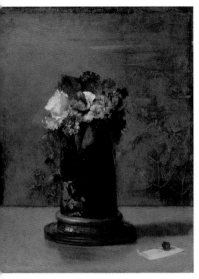

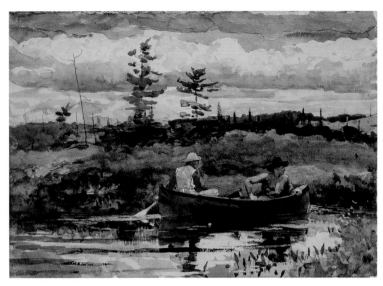

John La Farge
American, 1835–1910
Vase of Flowers, 1864

Winslow Homer
American, 1836–1910
The Blue Boat, 1892

Best known for his murals decorating Boston's Trinity Church
and for his stained-glass windows, La Farge was also a gifted
painter in watercolor and oil. His
images of flowers are evocative
rather than botanically accurate.
Here the spare composition and
background (which may represent a Japanese screen), as well as
the vessel, a Japanese brush pot,
reflect La Farge's fascination with
Asian art. The painting is given
a distinctive, personal quality
by the inclusion of a bent calling
card (inscribed "J. La Farge/1864")
lying beneath a wilting bachelor's
button.

In 1879 a critic stated that Winslow Homer had gone "as far as anyone
has ever done in demonstrating the value of watercolors as a serious
means of expressing dignified artistic impressions." Spontaneous in
effect, Homer's watercolors demonstrate an unequaled mastery of technique. He laid out his compositions with broad, overlapping washes of
color and then created a range of luminous coloristic and textural effects
by both adding pigment and subtracting it by blotting and scraping.
"You will see," Homer said, "in the future I will live by my watercolors."
Although most watercolors fade over time, *The Blue Boat*, painted on one
of Homer's frequent trips to the Adirondacks in New York State, is in pristine condition. Homer acknowledged his satisfaction with this masterwork by noting on the sheet: "This will do the business."

Watercolor over graphite pencil on paper
15¼ x 21½ in. (38.6 x 54.6 cm)
William Sturgis Bigelow Collection   26.764

Oil on gilded panel
18½ x 14 in. (47 x 35.6 cm)
Gift of the Misses Louisa W. and
Marian R. Case   20.1873

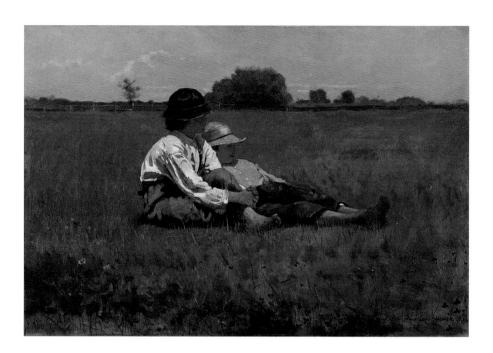

Winslow Homer
American, 1836–1910
Boys in a Pasture, 1874

Born in Boston, Homer was trained as a commercial printmaker, and
during the Civil War, he worked at the front for the illustrated journal
Harper's Weekly. In the 1870s, as America began to recover from the war,
Homer turned to painting sunny, optimistic pictures of young women
and children enjoying themselves outdoors. The boys in this painting—
companionable, idle, at peace—may be seen as emblems of America's
nostalgia for a simpler, more innocent time as well as of its hope for the
future. Their faces are shadowed and averted, a device Homer often used
to make his figures less individual and, therefore, more universal.

Oil on canvas
15⅞ x 22⅞ in. (40.3 x 58.1 cm)
The Hayden Collection — Charles Henry Hayden Fund   53.2552

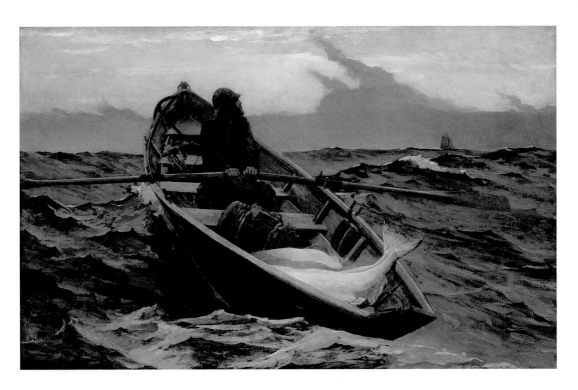

Winslow Homer

American, 1836–1910

The Fog Warning, 1885

Homer moved to Prout's Neck, near Portland, on the rocky coast of Maine by 1883. There, for the rest of his life, he painted the sea and those who made their living from it. *The Fog Warning* was inspired by Homer's trip with a fishing fleet to the Grand Banks off Nova Scotia. Here, the lone fisherman, his dory weighed down by enormous halibut, tries to reach the mother ship before it becomes enveloped in the dark fog bank on the horizon. The painting explores man's constant struggle with the sea — the source of livelihood but also of danger. This was the first painting by Homer to enter a public collection.

Oil on canvas
30¼ x 48½ in. (76.8 x 123.2 cm)
Anonymous gift with credit to the Otis Norcross Fund   94.72

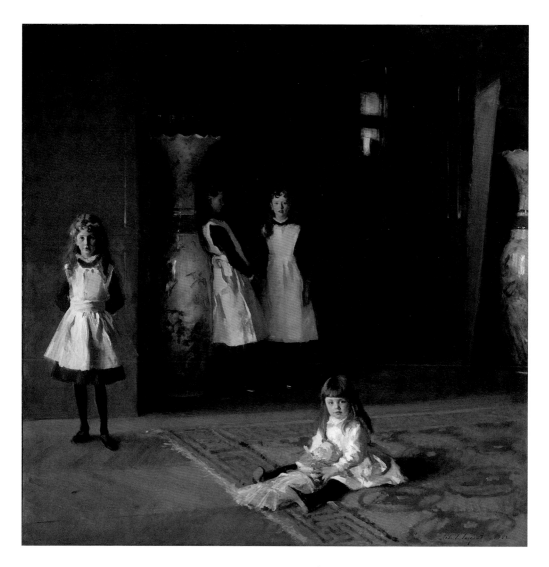

John Singer Sargent

American, 1856–1925

The Daughters of Edward Darley Boit, 1882

Sargent was a young painter of fashionable portraits when he created this unconventional image of his friend Edward Boit's daughters posing in the family's Paris apartment. The Boits, like Sargent, were often on the move, and the enormous Japanese vases in this picture survived multiple trips across the Atlantic (they were given to the Museum in 1997). The painting's square format is unusual, as is the isolated placement of the children within a shadowy, cavernous space described by one critic as "four corners and a void." Each girl is individualized, expressing her age and personality by subtleties of pose and gaze. And "when," mused American writer Henry James, "was the pinafore ever painted with that power and made so poetic?"

Oil on canvas
87⅜ x 87⅝ in. (221.9 x 222.6 cm)
Gift of Mary Louisa Boit, Julia Overing Boit, Jane Hubbard Boit, and Florence D. Boit in memory of their father, Edward Darley Boit   19.124

John Singer Sargent

American, 1856–1925

An Artist in His Studio,

about 1904

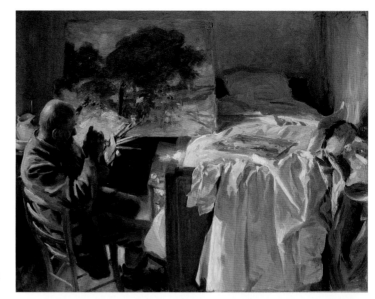

On a summer trip to the Italian Alps, Sargent depicted his friend, the artist Ambrogio Raffele, painting a bucolic landscape. The setting is a cramped hotel bedroom. Surrounded by sketches presumably made outdoors, Raffele holds a palette that bears actual gobs of thick, bright paint. Half the composition is given over to rumpled sheets and a discarded smock—an extraordinary display of brilliant brushwork that gave Sargent the opportunity (which he loved) of painting white on white.

Oil on canvas
22⅛ x 28⅜ in. (56.2 x 72.1 cm)
The Hayden Collection — Charles Henry Hayden Fund   05.56

John Singer Sargent

American, 1856–1925

Simplon Pass: The Tease,

about 1911

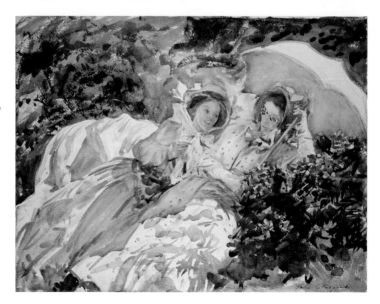

Sargent often produced more than twenty society portraits in a year; in the summer, he escaped to the freer, more personal, and more experimental medium of watercolor. He called his informal, anecdotal watercolors of friends and family "snapshots." Fluent and apparently spontaneous, they show a great mastery of complex techniques and are among Sargent's most admired works. Painted outdoors, they capture the colored shadows and the dappled effects of light; for this, watercolor—with its transparent washes of color over white paper—was the perfect medium. *The Tease* shows the artist's niece and a friend lounging on an outing at the Simplon Pass near the Italian-Swiss border.

Translucent and opaque watercolor, with wax resist, over graphite on paper
15¾ x 20⅝ in. (40 x 52.9 cm)
The Hayden Collection — Charles Henry Hayden Fund   12.216

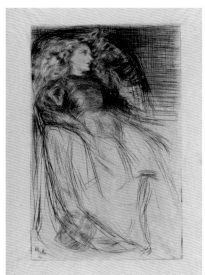

James Abbott McNeill Whistler
American (active in England), 1834–1903
Nocturne in Blue and Silver: The Lagoon, Venice, 1879–80

Whistler liked people to believe that he was born in Russia; in fact, although he made his career abroad, he was born in the mill town of Lowell, Massachusetts. Extraordinarily gifted and innovative, Whistler was determined to free his art from representation and narrative. "Art should be independent of all clap-trap," he asserted. "[It] should . . . appeal to the artistic sense of eye or ear, without confounding this with . . . devotion, pity, love, patriotism, and the like." In this night view of Venice, looking across still water to the church of San Giorgio Maggiore, Whistler painted the muted tones he loved. A friend who was with the artist when he created this image called it "possibly the most peace-bringing of Jimmy's pictures; certainly his finest night scene."

Oil on canvas
19¾ x 25¾ in. (50.2 x 65.4 cm)
Emily L. Ainsley Fund   42.302

James Abbott McNeill Whistler
American (active in England), 1834–1903
Weary, 1863

Whistler was a prolific and influential printmaker, particularly interested in etching and drypoint, techniques very similar to drawing with pen on paper. *Weary* was printed on silky Japanese paper to enhance the delicacy of its fine and swiftly rendered drypoint lines. The model was Whistler's mistress, a red-haired Irish beauty named Joanna Hiffernan who also appears in a number of the artist's most celebrated paintings. Her pose in *Weary* was inspired by "Jenny," a poem by Whistler's friend Dante Gabriel Rossetti about a prostitute "fond of a kiss and fond of a guinea."

Drypoint
Platemark: 7¾ x 5⅛ in. (19.7 x 13 cm)
Lee M. Friedman Fund   69.1178

Thomas Eakins
American, 1844–1916
Starting Out after Rail, 1874

"A boat is the hardest thing I know to put in
perspective," wrote Eakins. "It is so much like
the human figure, there is something alive
about it." This image of a boat skimming
across water enlivened by the play of wind
and light seems wonderfully immediate, but
most of Eakins's paintings were the result of
careful measurements, precise calculations,
and many preparatory studies. Although he
studied in Paris, he lived all his life in Philadelphia, and his family, friends, and the masculine world of sport were the subjects of his
art. Here, he depicts two friends setting off to
hunt for rail (a kind of bird) in the marshlands
along the Delaware River, near Philadelphia.

Oil on canvas mounted on Masonite
24¼ x 19⅞ in. (61.6 x 50.5 cm)
The Hayden Collection — Charles Henry Hayden
Fund   35.1953

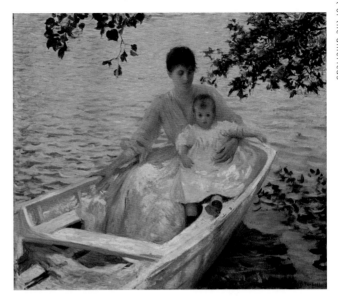

Edmund Charles Tarbell
American, 1862–1938
Mother and Child in a Boat, 1892

Boston artists played a major role in the recognition and
practice of Impressionism in America. Tarbell, who trained at
the School of the Museum of Fine Arts and later became one
of its most influential teachers, adopted a brilliantly colored
Impressionist technique after returning to Boston from studies in Paris. He was a founding member of The Ten, a group of
painters working in Impressionist styles whose exhibitions in
New York, beginning in 1898, helped make Impressionism the
most popular "modern" style in America.

Oil on canvas
30⅛ x 35 in. (76.5 x 88.9 cm)
Bequest of David P. Kimball in memory of
his wife Clara Bertram Kimball   23.532

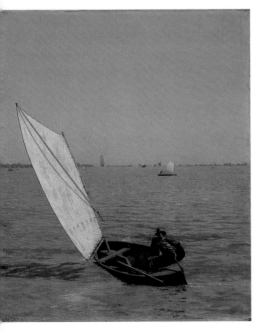

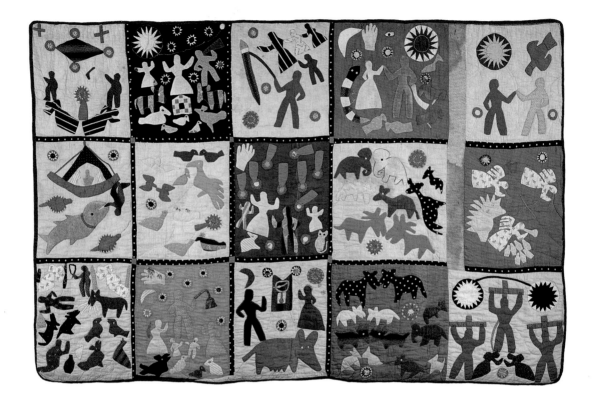

Pictorial quilt

Georgia (Athens), about 1895–98

Harriet Powers, American, 1837–1910

Described as "expressive in its every stitch of a most fiery imagination," this quilt was created at the end of the nineteenth century by an African American woman, born a slave, who lived on a farm near Athens, Georgia. The fifteen squares depict familiar biblical events—stories of Adam and Eve, Noah, Job, Jonah, Moses, and Christ—and record local legends and such fearful and marvelous natural phenomena as the Leonid meteor shower of 1833. Powers left a commentary on her work. The center panel, for instance, she explained as: "The falling of the stars on Nov. 13, 1833. The people were frightened and thought that the end had come. God's hand staid the stars. The varmints rushed out of their beds." Accounts of the eight-hour meteor shower of 1833, passed down through the generations, were part of the oral tradition from which Powers drew her imagery.

Cotton; plain weave, printed, pieced, and appliquéd; hand- and machine-embroidered with cotton and metallic yarns
69 x 105 in. (175 x 267 cm)
Bequest of Maxim Karolik   64.619

Renaissance revival neck ornament
New York (New York), 1900–1904
Designed by **G. Paulding Farnham,** American, 1859–1927, for **Tiffany & Co.**

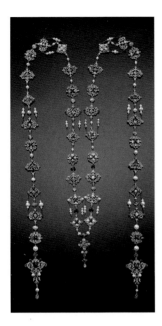

Tiffany & Co. is famous especially for its jewelry, an area in which the company emerged as an arbiter of taste and style by the mid-nineteenth century. Early on, founder Charles Lewis Tiffany recognized the possibilities of a new market among an emerging class of elite Americans for high-style jewels that would rival those owned by European aristocrats. To supply that market, Tiffany sought out and encouraged outstanding artists—including G. Paulding Farnham, who joined the firm as an apprentice in 1885. Farnham garnered acclaim for his revival-themed ornaments, many of which were shown at the 1901 Pan-American Exposition in Buffalo, New York. This extraordinary gold, gem-set, and enamel chain with arabesques and scrolling motifs takes as its reference point the jewels adorning women's dresses in Renaissance portraits. Among Renaissance-revival gems, the pastel palette of greens, orange, and pinks is unexpected, as is the design of a long chain rather than a connected necklace.

Platinum, gold, enamel, diamond, ruby, emerald, cat's-eye, chrysoberyl, sapphire, pearl
L. 58 in. (147.3 cm)
Gift of Susan B. Kaplan   2015.3184

Necklace
Massachusetts (Boston), 1910–18
Josephine Hartwell Shaw, American, 1865–1941

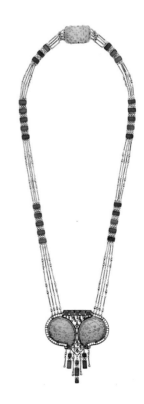

Like their colleagues working in other media, Arts and Crafts jewelry makers often favored unusual materials and finishes. Embracing novel combinations of color and texture, they often chose uncut, naturally shaped, semi- and non-precious stones, even pebbles, over faceted diamonds and rubies, and dull over polished surfaces. They sought to highlight the inherent beauty of each element within an overall harmonious composition. A prominent member of Boston's Society of Arts and Crafts, Josephine Shaw was widely admired for her outstanding jewelry. Often, she drew inspiration from the cultures and materials of Asia; she composed this necklace around two pieces of carved, eighteenth-century white Chinese jade. Shaw complemented these exotic (and presumably expensive) components with rectangles of common green glass, set in green-toned gold. The rhythmic repetition of the glass with the loops, rods, and balls of gold enhances the subtle tones and delicate carving of the jade.

Gold, jade, colored glass
Pendant: 4 x 3⅝ x ¼ in. (10.2 x 9.2 x 0.6 cm)
L. of chain: 33 in. (83.8 cm)
Gift of Mrs. Atherton Loring   1984.947

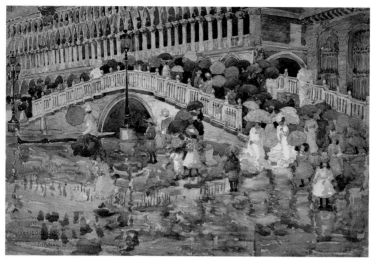

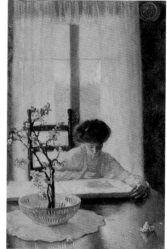

Maurice Brazil Prendergast
American (born in Newfoundland), 1858–1924
Umbrellas in the Rain, 1899

Lilian Westcott Hale
American, 1880–1963
L'Edition de Luxe, 1910

Prendergast was among the greatest American masters of watercolor. On a trip to Europe in 1898–99, he fell in love with Venice, painting watercolors that are among his finest works. Here, with the passing of a summer storm, a crowd of typically anonymous figures moves among famous Venetian monuments—the somber facade of the prison at right; the delicate arcades of the Doge's Palace; and the marble bridge, Ponte della Paglia. The bright shapes of umbrellas lead the eye through a composition that has the abstract, patterned quality of a mosaic. Although Prendergast shared the Impressionists' enthusiasm for outdoor subjects from modern life, his exploratory style and his use of watercolor rather than oil as his primary medium place him among American modernist artists of the early twentieth century.

Many women artists found support—and success—in Boston. Lilian Westcott Hale studied at the School of the Museum of Fine Arts under Edmund Tarbell, one of the leaders of the Boston School, a group of painters who favored tasteful, genteel subjects and an interest in light effects. Hale also believed in the importance of beauty and craftsmanship, but those traditional artistic ideals did not prevent her from rigorously pursuing a professional career. Her ethereal images of contemplative women earned her national recognition and were avidly sought by collectors. In this quiet image, a beautiful woman studies an illustration in a deluxe edition. As she reads, light streams in from the window behind her, bathing the room in a rosy glow. Those pink tones echo in the delicate flowers, the polished table, and the coppery hair of the figure—Rose Zeffler, a favorite model posed within Hale's studio. Carefully balanced and exquisitely rendered, the entire composition is an "edition de luxe"—an especially beautiful creation made for connoisseurs.

Watercolor over graphite pencil on paper
13⅞ x 20⅞ in. (35.4 x 53 cm)
The Hayden Collection — Charles Henry Hayden Fund
59.57

Oil on canvas
23 x 15⅛ in. (58.4 x 38.4 cm)
Gift of Miss Mary C. Wheelwright   35.1487

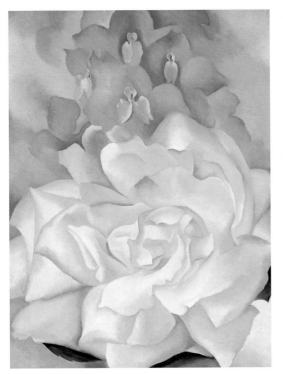

Alfred Stieglitz
American, 1864—1946
Georgia O'Keeffe, A Portrait (6), 1918

This photograph represents the long, dynamic inter-action of two great American artists. Stieglitz—a key figure in the promotion of modern art and in the acceptance of photography as art—began photo-graphing artist Georgia O'Keeffe in 1917, when she first came to New York. Fascinated with multiplicity, time, and change, Stieglitz believed that a single image was not sufficient to capture the complexity of a human personality. Over twenty years he made hundreds of photographs of the woman who became his lover and later his wife, a cumulative "portrait in time." This is one of the earliest photographs in a series of arrested moments that includes studies of her torso, feet, hands, and face. O'Keeffe remembered that Stieglitz photographed her with "a kind of heat and excitement." One scholar has called this "perhaps the most extraor-dinary series in the history of photography."

Photograph, palladium print
9¼ x 7⅜ in. (23.5 x 18.7 cm)
The Alfred Stieglitz Collection—Gift of the Georgia O'Keeffe
Foundation and M. and M. Karolik Fund   1995.692

Georgia O'Keeffe
American, 1887–1986
White Rose with Larkspur No. 2, 1927

O'Keeffe often painted objects from nature whose for-mal qualities attracted her. She once wrote: "Nobody sees a flower—really—it is so small—we haven't time—and to see it takes time, like to have a friend takes time. . . . So I said to myself—I'll paint what I see—what the flower is to me—but I'll paint it big. . . . I will make even busy New Yorkers take time to see what I see of flowers." One of O'Keeffe's favorite paint-ings, *White Rose* hung in the bedroom of her Abiquiu, New Mexico, home until 1979, when she selected it for the Museum.

Oil on canvas
40 x 30 in. (101.6 x 76.2 cm)
Henry H. and Zoe Oliver Sherman Fund   1980.207

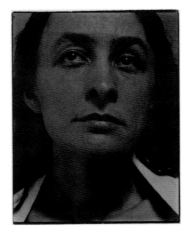

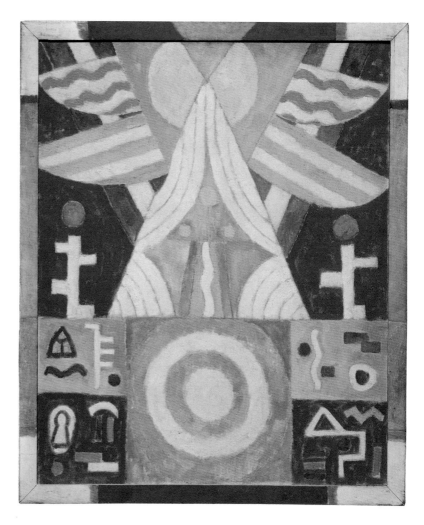

Marsden Hartley
American, 1877–1943
Arrangement—
Hieroglyphics
(Painting No. 2), 1914

In 1912 Hartley went abroad for the first time, but unlike many American modernists who traveled to France, he spent most of his time in Germany. There he came under the influence of the Blaue Reiter and other groups of young artists who were experimenting with new, basically abstract forms of expression. He adopted their use of bright, flat color, emphasis on geometric patterns, and interest in folk culture. *Arrangement—Hiero-glyphics* is one of several that make up Hartley's *Amerika* series, and it uses forms derived from Native American cultures, such as the triangular tipi and the geometric shapes evoking sand paintings. Hartley placed great emphasis on the presentation of his works, and he constructed and painted the frame of this picture to complement its design.

Oil on canvas
With frame: 42½ x 34¾ in.
(108 x 90.8 cm)
Gift of the William H. Lane
Foundation 1990.412

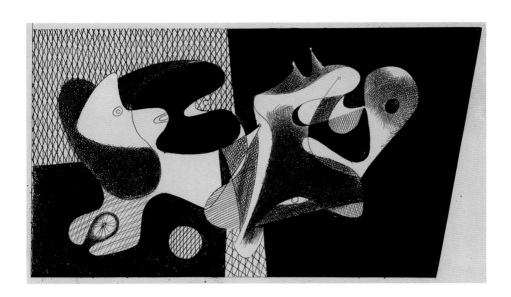

Arshile Gorky

American (born in Turkish Armenia), 1904–1948
Study for Nighttime, Enigma, and Nostalgia, about 1931–32

Gorky had little formal training; he learned by imitation and observation, taking the work of other artists as his point of departure. In this drawing, for example, the black trapezoid at right was derived from Giorgio De Chirico's 1913 painting *The Fatal Temple*, and scholars have noted the work's connection to Picasso's synthetic Cubist still lifes. Gorky, who stated that "drawing is the basis of art," was a skilled and prodigious draftsman. This drawing is from a series of more than fifty drawings and at least two paintings executed in the early 1930s, a time when Gorky's work was becoming increasingly abstract. What is the meaning of this series and its rather mysterious title? Gorky chose not to say. When curators at New York's Museum of Modern Art queried the subject matter of a similar drawing, the artist replied: "Wounded birds, poverty, and a whole week of rain."

India ink with underdrawing in graphite pencil, on paper
13 x 21¼ in. (33 x 54 cm)
Gift of Susan W. Paine in honor of Malcolm Rogers on the occasion of his tenth anniversary as Director of the MFA, Boston   2004.2256

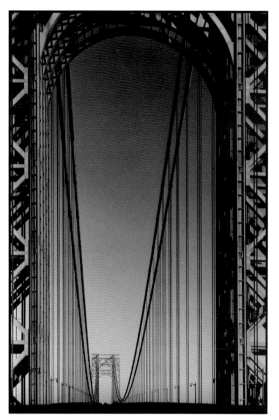

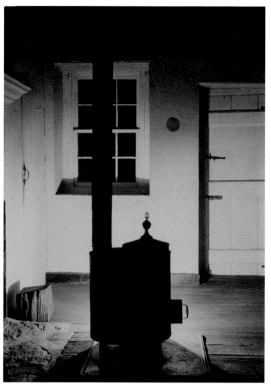

Margaret Bourke-White

American, 1904–1971

The George Washington Bridge, 1933

One of the original staff photographers at *Fortune*, *Life*, and *Time* magazines, Bourke-White is celebrated for her coverage of European battlefields and concentration camps during World War II as well as for her powerful images of the American South during the Depression, guerrilla warfare in Korea, and twentieth-century industry. This photograph—an icon of early, idealizing machine-age art—was made when the monumental George Washington Bridge was still under construction, for a *Fortune* essay on the Port of New York.

Photograph, gelatin silver print
13½ x 8⅞ in. (34.3 x 22.5 cm)
Charles Amos Cummings Fund   1988.2

Charles Sheeler

American, 1883–1965

Doylestown House—The Stove, 1916–17

Photograph, gelatin silver print
9⅜ x 6¾ in. (23.8 x 17.1 cm)
Gift of Saundra B. Lane in memory of William H. Lane   2002.886

opposite

Robert Rauschenberg

American, 1925–2008

Breakthrough II, 1965

Lithograph, printed from four stones
Printed and published by Universal Limited Art Editions, Inc.
Stone: 43½ x 29½ in. (110.5 x 74.9 cm)
Gift of Lewis P. Cabot   1970.515

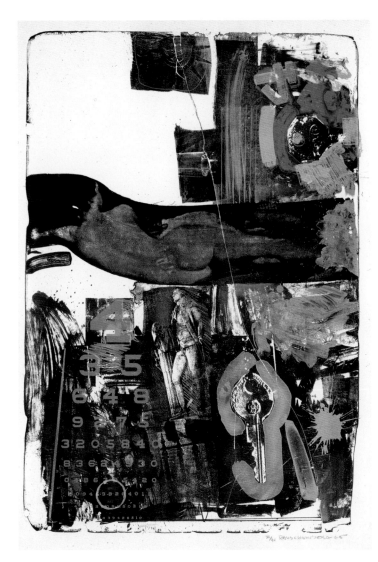

whitewashed, and pared down the house's interior to reflect his spare, modern vision. Photographed at night so that Sheeler could control the lighting, the dark silhouette of the iron stove is set off against the rectangles of window and door, the starkness modulated by the small, irregular details of stove handle and door hinges. Sheeler was also a painter (see page 260) but from this point on, photographs became central to his art.

In the second half of the twentieth century, photographic processes became less expensive and more accessible to artists and the general public. As photographic imagery became ubiquitous in popular and domestic culture, the uses to which artists put it changed as well. By the 1980s, a broader crossover existed between photography, painting, and printmaking. Some people no longer thought of themselves strictly as photographers but rather as artists in a larger sense who happened to work with images made with a camera. Such artists as Robert Rauschenberg and Andy Warhol used a variety of means to transfer photographic images from daily life and the mass media to the printing surface. Works in the Museum's collections reflect the many methods and processes in which photographic images are produced and reproduced, from the portraits of the 1840s to modern works on paper, glass, plastic, and other media.

By the end of the nineteenth century, photographers had recourse to faster, more easily managed processes such as gelatin silver prints, which use silver salts to produce a crisp image, favored by artists in the 1920s who renounced the painterly qualities of the earlier processes. This stunning Sheeler print is a pioneering image in the history of American photography—a highly modern, abstract, and Cubist-inspired photograph of a vernacular American subject. It is one of a series of twelve pictures that he took in his eighteenth-century farmhouse in Doylestown, Bucks County, Pennsylvania. Before beginning to photograph it, the artist arranged,

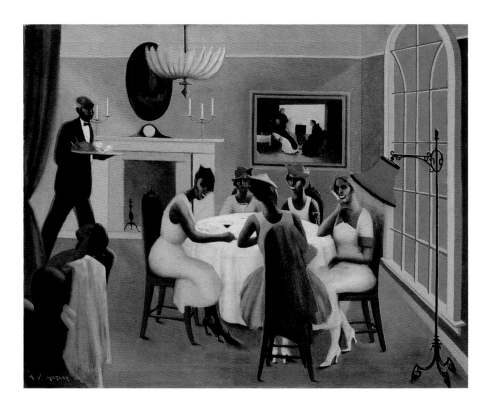

Archibald Motley

American, 1891–1981

Cocktails, about 1926

Archibald Motley was a major contribu-
tor to the Harlem Renaissance at a moment
when the black arts movement reached
new heights across the country, including in Motley's native Chicago. *Cocktails*,
painted during Prohibition, depicts a group
of well-dressed women enjoying drinks and
one another's company in an inviting room
bathed in warm pink light. By contrast,
the painting on the wall features a group
of monks—a detail that may identify the
women as Creoles, Catholic and upscale,
whose families, like Motley's, arrived in

Chicago from New Orleans. The portrait
over the mantel underscores the sense of
prosperity, but it also alludes to the importance of family and heritage. The woman at
the left in the armchair remains enigmatic.
There is no empty seat for her at the table:
is she not a part of the gathering? Or has
she fallen asleep? Shortly after completing
this work, in 1928 Motley became the first
African American artist to have a solo show
in New York.

Oil on canvas
32 x 40 in. (81.3 x 101.6 cm)
The John Axelrod Collection — Frank B. Bemis
Fund, Charles H. Bayley Fund, and The Heritage
Fund for a Diverse Collection   2011.1859

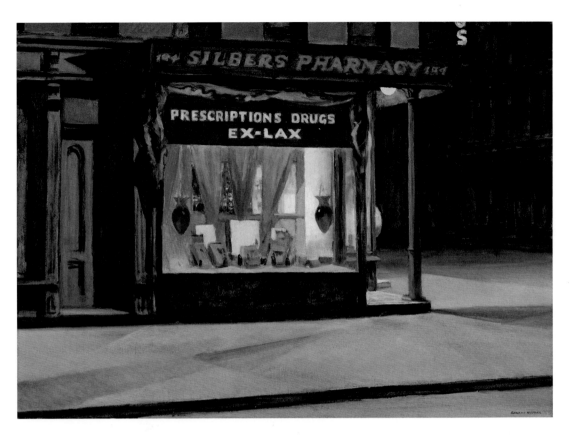

Edward Hopper

American, 1882–1967

Drug Store, 1927

Oil on canvas

29 x 40⅛ in. (73.7 x 101.9 cm)

Bequest of John T. Spaulding   48.564

Among the first of Hopper's paintings to illustrate what became a favorite theme, *Drug Store* depicts nocturnal solitude in the city. Eerily illuminated by electric light, the drugstore window (probably located near his studio in New York's Greenwich Village) is a bright spot in a picture otherwise made up of shadowy doorways and blank facades. The painting is full of subtle contradictions; for example, the patriotism expressed by the red, white, and blue bunting in the window display is undermined by the indelicacy of the product advertised above, and the acid colors and depopulated street discredit the window's ostensible welcome. Like much of Hopper's work, this painting is edgy and unsettling, creating a sense of melancholy and alienation.

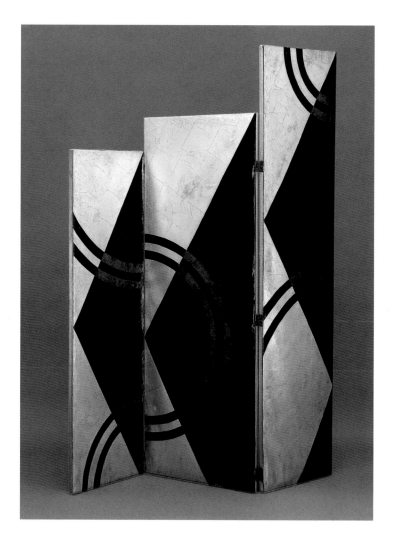

Screen

New York (New York), about 1930

Donald Deskey, American, 1894–1989

Trained as an architect, Donald Deskey became an artist and a pioneering industrial designer. Around 1927, he was hired by Paul Frankl—another architect-designer—to paint a series of decorative screens. Frankl, acclaimed for his modernist "Skyscraper" furnishings, was impressed by Deskey's furniture designs and wanted to encourage the young designer.

For this screen, Deskey combined the stepped silhouette of Frankl's Skyscraper line with sumptuous materials and shiny aluminum leaf. Thanks in part to Frankl's early support, Deskey became one of the country's best-known designers, responsible for, among other projects, the interiors in New York's Radio City Music Hall.

Wood, canvas, metal fittings, aluminum leaf, paint
76½ x 58½ in. (194.3 x 148.6 cm)
The John Axelrod Collection   2011.1648

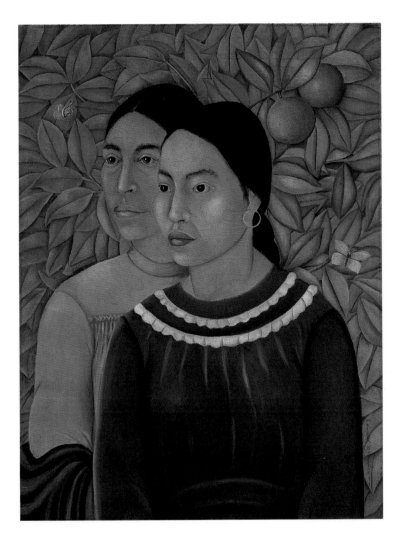

Frida Kahlo

Mexican, 1907–1954

***Dos Mujeres (Salvadora y Herminia)*, 1928**

One of the twentieth century's most compelling artists and storytellers, Frida Kahlo is known worldwide for her paintings that celebrate Mexican culture and give shape to dreams and the imagination. For this dignified double portrait, she captures the likenesses of two maids in her mother's household, women whom Kahlo had known in her youth. The painting is both a personal and political expression: it celebrates the ethnic diversity of Mexico's population, and it pays tribute to these working women as if they were Madonnas posed before a cloth of honor—in this case, a backdrop of dense, verdant foliage. Held privately in the United States since 1929, this painting is the first by Kahlo to enter a New England public collection.

Oil on canvas

27⅜ x 21 in. (69.5 x 53.3 cm)

Charles H. Bayley Picture and Painting Fund, William Francis Warden Fund, Sophie M. Friedman Fund, Ernest Wadsworth Longfellow Fund, Tompkins Collection—Arthur Gordon Tompkins Fund, Gift of Jessie H. Wilkinson—Jessie H. Wilkinson Fund, and Robert M. Rosenberg Family Fund

2015.3130

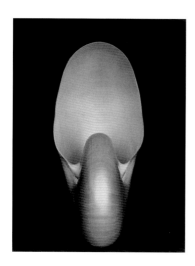

Edward Weston

American, 1886–1958

Chambered Nautilus, 1927

Among the most influential American photographers of the twentieth century, Edward Weston was also one of its most innovative. He pioneered a new, modern approach to the medium while embracing a range of subjects, including the human form, the landscape of the American West, and still lifes, which he first began photographing in Mexico in the mid-1920s. *Chambered Nautilus* represents his return to the genre and one of his earliest experiments photographing shells. In his still lifes, Weston embraced subjects that allowed him the heightened level of control that he sought in all his work, but which was much more difficult when photographing people. To create this extreme close-up, he used a large-format camera, photographing the nautilus shell against a plain backdrop in natural light, with a long exposure time. The resulting image is a masterpiece of sharp focus, streamlined sculptural form, and abstracted, anthropomorphic shape—characteristics that would define this phase of his career, often called his "high modernist" moment.

Photograph, gelatin silver print
9½ x 7⅜ in. (24.1 x 18.6 cm)
The Lane Collection   2017.1796

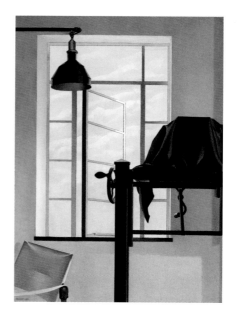

Charles Sheeler

American, 1883–1965

View of New York, 1931

Sheeler's ironically titled picture shows the interior of his own photography studio on an upper floor of a midtown New York apartment building and was painted at a pivotal time in his career. Through the 1920s he had enjoyed critical and financial success as a photographer while struggling to gain recognition as a painter. His difficult decision, made about 1931, to set aside photography and concentrate on painting is expressed through the studio's stillness and austerity—the camera is covered, the lamp turned off, and the chair vacant. Through the open window, we do not see the skyscrapers and bustling crowds normally associated with New York but instead a cloudy sky. Sheeler thus gave universal meaning to his image of personal transition by contrasting the precisely defined, if barren, interior with an undefined external world full of uncertainties. He called *View of New York* "the most severe picture I ever painted."

Oil on canvas
48 x 36⅜ in. (121.9 x 92.4 cm)
The Hayden Collection — Charles Henry Hayden Fund   35.69

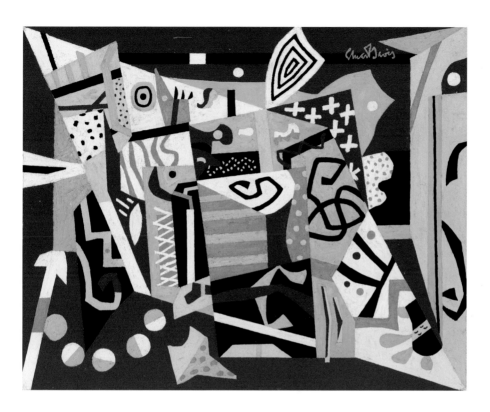

Stuart Davis

American, 1892–1964

Hot Still-Scape for Six Colors — 7th Avenue Style,
1940

Oil on canvas
36 x 44⅞ in. (91.4 x 114 cm)
Gift of the William H. Lane Foundation
and the M. and M. Karolik Collection,
by exchange   1983.120

From the time Davis moved to the city in his late
teens, New York was the principal subject of his art.
With a title evoking jazz (a great love of Davis's), his
"Still-Scape" combines still life and landscape, alluding both to the objects in his studio and to the world
outside, on Seventh Avenue. Davis wrote: "The subject
matter of this picture is well within the everyday
experience of any modern city dweller. Fruit and
flowers and kitchen utensils; fall skies; horizons; taxi
cabs; radio; art exhibitions and reproductions; fast
travel; Americana; movies; electric signs; dynamics
of city sights and sounds." The artist's impressions
of the city are captured with energy and flair by his
jaunty line, vibrant palette (the "six colors" of the
title), and the gritty texture of his paint.

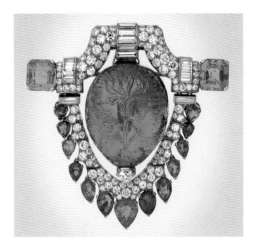

Marjorie Merriweather Post brooch
New York (New York), 1929
Made by **Oscar Heyman Bros.** for **Marcus & Co.**

The siblings who founded the jewelry firm Oscar Heyman & Bros. trained in the Fabergé workshops of Russia before immigrating to New York in the early twentieth century. Their company made a name for itself within the industry as a major "jeweler's jeweler," manufacturing iconic pieces for fine purveyors including Cartier, Tiffany & Co., Van Cleef & Arpels, and Marcus & Co., who retailed this glittering emerald and diamond brooch. Its centerpiece, a large emerald with carved designs from the seventeenth century, was purchased by a Marcus & Co. agent in Mumbai, India, in the 1920s. (In fact, the emerald was likely mined in Colombia and brought to India through trade with Spain and Portugal.) Completed on August 6, 1929, according to company records, the brooch was purchased by heiress and art collector Marjorie Merriweather Post, who had an affinity for emeralds. One of Post's prized possessions, it appears in no fewer than two painted portraits of her.

Platinum, diamond, emerald
2⅛ x 2⅛ x ⅜ in. (5.3 x 5.4 x 1.1 cm)
William Francis Warden Fund, Marshall H. Gould Fund, Frank B. Bemis Fund, Mary S. and Edward Jackson Holmes Fund, John H. and Ernestine A. Payne Fund, Otis Norcross Fund, Helen and Alice Colburn Fund, William E. Nickerson Fund, Arthur Tracy Cabot Fund, Edwin E. Jack Fund, Frederick Brown Fund, Elizabeth Marie Paramino Fund in memory of John F. Paramino, Boston Sculptor, Morris and Louise Rosenthal Fund, Harriet Otis Cruft Fund, H. E. Bolles Fund, Seth K. Sweetser Fund, Helen B. Sweeney Fund, Ernest Kahn Fund, Arthur Mason Knapp Fund, John Wheelock Elliot and John Morse Elliot Fund, Susan Cornelia Warren Fund, Mary L. Smith Fund, Samuel Putnam Avery Fund, Alice M. Bartlett Fund, Benjamin Pierce Cheney Donation, Frank M. and Mary T. B. Ferrin Fund, and Joyce Arnold Rusoff Fund   2008.179

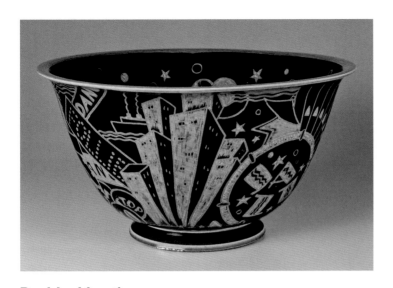

Punch bowl from the
Jazz Bowl series
United States (Rocky River, Ohio), 1931
Designed and decorated by **Viktor Schreckengost**, American, 1906–2008
Molded at **Cowan Pottery Studio**

In 1930 Schreckengost, a young potter working at the Cowan Pottery
near Cleveland, received an assignment to create a punch bowl with a
"New Yorkish theme." Covered with images of skyscrapers, cocktails, and
the lights of Broadway, his bowl captured the excitement and drama of
modern New York nightlife. Yet in design motif and function, the bowl
blatantly flaunted contemporary Prohibition laws that restricted alcohol
consumption. These rebellious connotations are all the more interesting when one learns that the original patron of the bowl was Eleanor
Roosevelt, whose husband Franklin ran for president two years later
on a platform calling for Prohibition's repeal.

Glazed porcelain with sgrafitto decoration
H. 9 in. (22.9 cm)
Gift of John P. Axelrod   1990.507

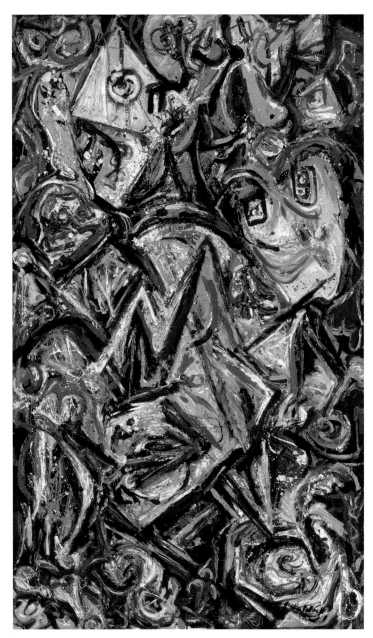

Jackson Pollock
American, 1912–1956
Troubled Queen, 1945

At once the most controversial and the most influential artist of his generation, Pollock was the leading figure of the Abstract Expressionist movement that made New York, in the late 1940s, the center of the international avant-garde. *Troubled Queen*, painted soon after Pollock moved from New York to rural Long Island, is a fascinating transitional work in which the suggestions of heads and faces—drawn from the artist's subconscious but echoing his earlier, figurative work—seem to struggle to assert themselves against the thick, slashing strokes and skeins of paint that became the hallmark of Pollock's revolutionary mature style. With its harsh, highly personal brushwork and startling, acidic colors, this turbulent painting, as one critic noted, "exudes raw power and psychic distress." Within a few years, all traces of the figure were gone from Pollock's work, and the act of painting itself became his subject.

Oil and alkyd (synthetic paint) on canvas
74⅛ x 43½ in. (188.3 x 110.5 cm)
Charles H. Bayley Picture and Painting Fund and Gift of Mrs. Albert J. Beveridge and Juliana Cheney Edwards Collection, by exchange   1984.749

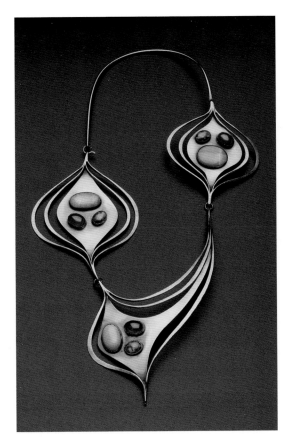

Necklace

New York (New York), about 1958

Art Smith, American (born in Cuba), 1917–1982

Art Smith, born to parents of Afro-Caribbean descent, was a seminal figure in the American studio jewelry movement. After training at the Cooper Union and with jeweler Winifred Mason, in 1948 Smith opened a shop in Greenwich Village, a vibrant art community where many leading modernist jewelers had studios within blocks of one another. His highly individual style takes cues from the large scale of East African dance regalia, the rhythms of jazz music, and the movement of contemporary African American dance. Smith designed stage jewelry for dance companies led by Talley Beatty, Pearl Primus, and Claude Marchant—likely influencing his sense of theatricality and interest in the relationship of jewelry to the body. This bold necklace demonstrates Smith's skill in manipulating positive and negative space, creating a sense of flowing movement in asymmetrical, biomorphic forms.

Silver, turquoise, rhodochrosite, chrysoprase, amethyst (or garnet)
17¼ x 10¼ x ¾ in. (43.8 x 26 x 1.9 cm)
The Daphne Farago Collection   2006.537

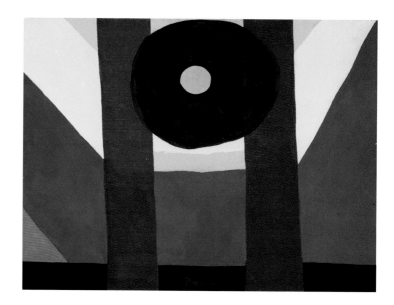

Arthur G. Dove
American, 1880–1946
That Red One, 1944

About 1910 Dove became the first American artist to experiment with pure abstraction. He painted in this style throughout his career, but always with reference to the natural world. These adventurous paintings were admired by his fellow artists but rarely sold, and Dove's whole life was marked by financial struggle; *That Red One* was produced while the artist was living in an abandoned post office in Centerport, Long Island, New York. Despite Dove's personal difficulties, this painting is triumphant in mood, with the sunlike form in the center (a favorite Dove motif) dominating a design of broad shapes painted in clear, flat colors. Although the inspiration for the scene was characteristically commonplace—probably a view through trees across a pond at daybreak—the vision is monumental and heroic.

Oil and wax on canvas
27 x 36 in. (68.6 x 91.4 cm)
Gift of the William H. Lane Foundation   1990.408

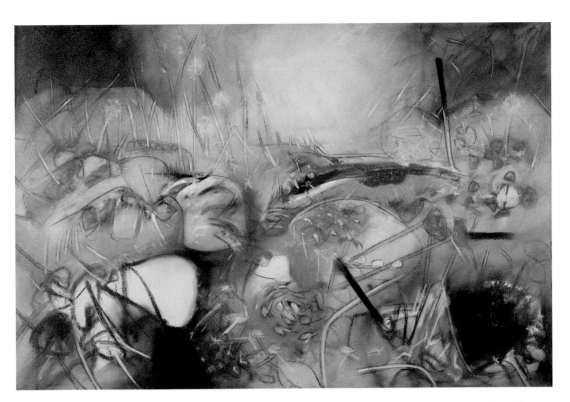

Matta (Roberto Sebastián Matta Echaurren)
Chilean, 1911–2002
Cercle du Blé, 1953

Born in Chile, Matta spent much of his professional life in Europe, where the violence of the Spanish Civil War helped shape his vision. During World War II, he fled Europe for the United States, returning to Paris in 1948. As the full horrors of the war (including the Holocaust) became known, Matta grew increasingly interested in depicting collective struggles. Painted in 1953, *Cercle du Blé* presents a primordial landscape of violence and conflict. Its spear-like shapes conjure ancient armies clashing in battle; the painting's title, which means "Circle of Wheat," suggests the scything of crops at harvesttime, a metaphor for the loss of life in war. Rubbed and abraded lines appear throughout—a reflection of Matta's affiliation with the Surrealists and his particular adoption of "automatic drawing," a method of working without planning or forethought. Typically, Matta would apply thin washes of pigment to his canvases before improvisationally rubbing and smearing them with a hand or cloth. Using a brush, Matta then further defined the forms he discerned in the smeared paint.

Oil on canvas
44½ x 68 in. (113 x 172.7 cm)
Gift of Susan W. and Stephen D. Paine   1981.666

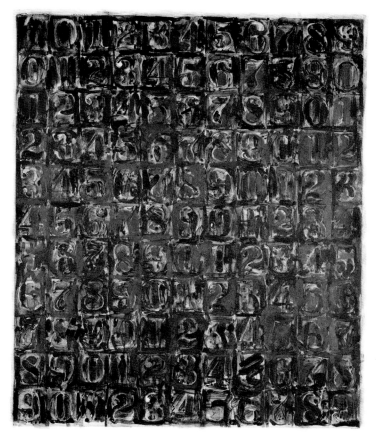

opposite

Norman Lewis
American, 1909–1979
Untitled, about 1960–64

Norman Lewis was the only African American painter among the first generation of Abstract Expressionists. Yet throughout his career and for years after, Lewis was conspicuously absent from most histories of modern art. Early in his career, he participated in the Federal Art Program of the Works Progress Administration (WPA), working alongside artists such as Jackson Pollock. In the 1930s, Lewis joined Harlem's 306 Group, which encouraged emerging African American artists, and in 1963 he helped found Spiral, an artists' discussion group dedicated to the civil rights movement.

With its subtle contrasts between opaque and nearly transparent areas of paint and its "allover" composition, *Untitled* epitomizes Lewis's elegant approach to abstraction. His use of thin, dry brushwork lends a mysterious but seductive depth and dimension, drawing the viewer in while leaving ample room for interpretation. The painting tells no explicit story, but the clusters of marks can be read as small figures that may hint at questions about individuals, groups, and the relationships between them. This work was painted for prominent African American collectors—the Honorable Edward R. Dudley, the first African American man to run

Jasper Johns
American, born 1930
Black Numbers, 1960

Johns heralded the Pop Art movement in New York in the 1950s with his transformation of everyday objects into art. This drawing is one of a number of works in several media in which Johns took simple numbers and then pursued a game of art and illusion, exploring spatial and formal relationships through the layering of transparent and opaque imagery. The drawing is made even more subtle by the artist's use of a wash created from powdered graphite, which produces an ambiguously shimmering surface.

Graphite wash on pale cream paper mounted on white paper
21 x 18 in. (53.3 x 45.7 cm)
Gift of Susan W. and Stephen D. Paine   1996.362

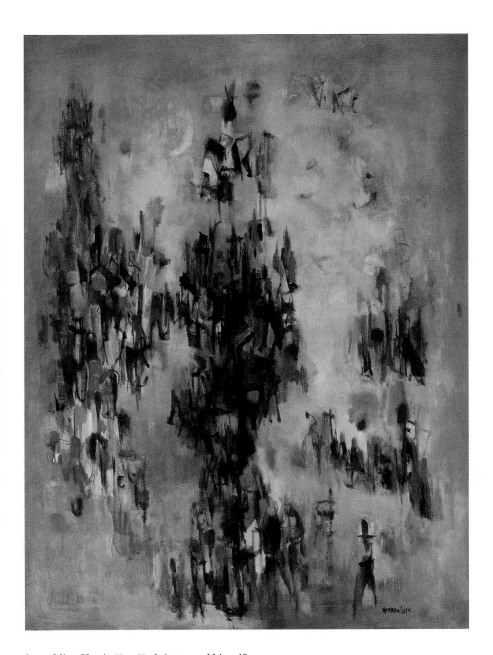

for public office in New York State, and his wife,
Rae Oley Dudley, an artist—for their Harlem home.

Oil on canvas
64 x 49 in. (162.6 x 124.5 cm)
Juliana Cheney Edwards Collection and
Emily L. Ainsley Fund   2008.1403

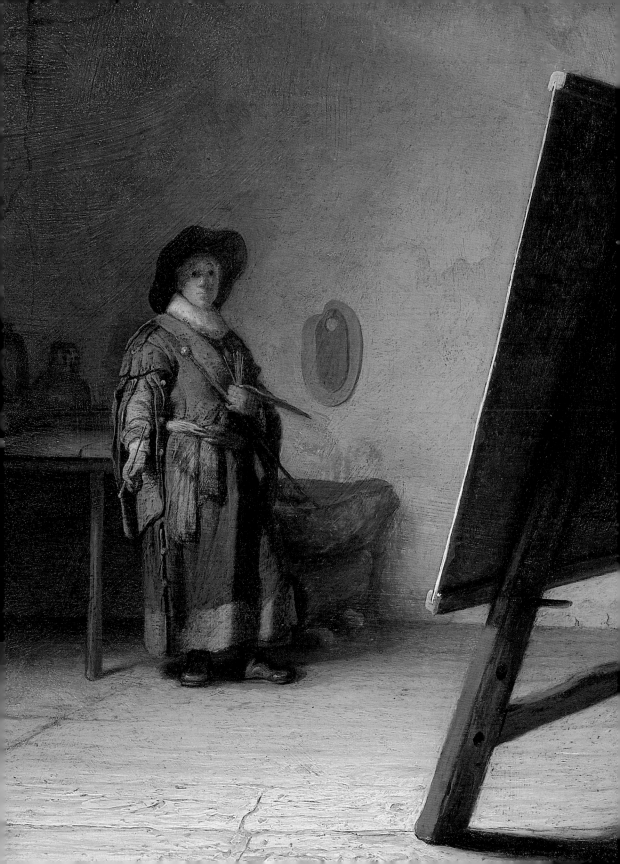

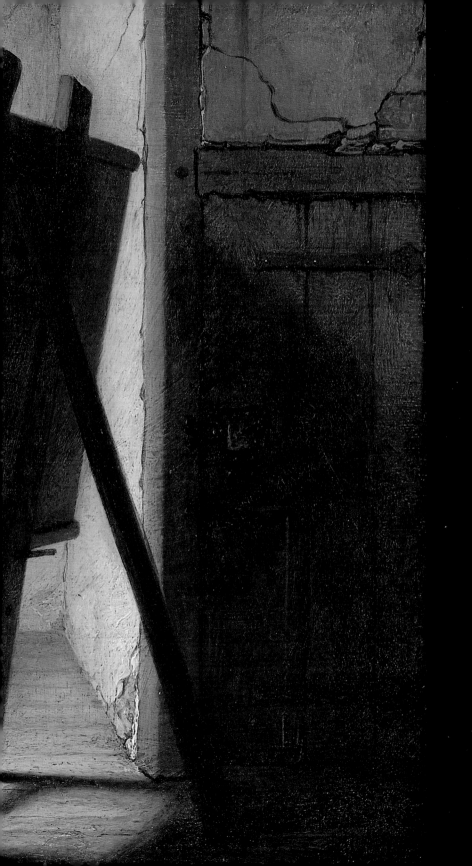

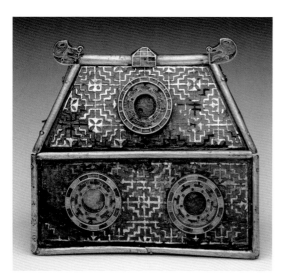

Fragment of a shroud
Southern Spain (probably Almería), early 12th century

Important individuals in the Middle Ages were often buried wrapped in precious fabrics, and this silk weaving brocaded with gold thread is believed to have been part of the shroud of a bishop of Burgo de Osma, a city in central Spain. Its design is Islamic and within the small circles is the Arabic inscription "This was made in Baghdad, may God protect it." Luxury goods from Baghdad were highly prized in Europe, but this cloth was probably made in the Muslim city of Almería in Spain; the false inscription was intended to increase the value of the cloth.

Silk; lampas with supplementary metallic patterning wefts
17 x 19¾ in. (43 x 50 cm)
Ellen Page Hall Fund   33.371

Reliquary shrine (Emly Shrine)
Ireland, late 7th or early 8th century

Made to hold the sacred relics of a saint (often parts of the saint's body), Irish house-shaped reliquaries have been discovered as far away as Norway and Italy—carried there by Irish pilgrims or Viking raiders. This one, however, was found in Ireland and is named for its nineteenth-century owner, Lord Emly of Limerick. It is quite tiny and was prob-ably hung from the neck or shoulder of its owner as a source of protection and spiritual strength.

Champlevé enamel on bronze over yew wood; gilt bronze moldings, inlay of lead-tin alloy
3⅝ x 1⅝ x 4⅛ in. (9.2 x 4.1 x 10.5 cm)
Theodora Wilbour Fund in memory of Charlotte Beebe Wilbour   52.1396

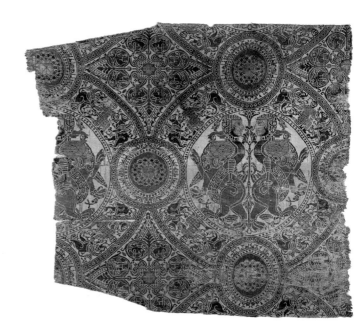

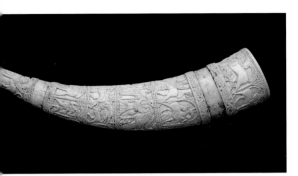

Oliphant
Southern Italy (probably Amalfi), about 1100

Horns called oliphants (from the Old French word for elephant) were carved from elephant tusks acquired from the East Africa coastline. Amalfi, where this oliphant was probably made, was one of several southern Italian ports that traded with Africa in the twelfth century. Although horns were used for hunting, drinking, and in battle, large and intricately carved examples such as this were prized as luxury objects and symbolic statements of wealth and status. Sometimes they were exchanged ceremonially as part of the transfer of land, which included the right to hunt on that land—a carefully guarded marker of feudal privilege, as only the nobility was allowed to hunt. Some nobles gave their oliphants to the Church, and most surviving examples were preserved through the centuries in the treasuries of cathedrals or monasteries.

Ivory
L. 21 in. (53.4 cm)
Maria Antoinette Evans Fund   57.581

Madonna and Child
Northern Italy (probably province of Piacenza), second quarter of the 12th century

Made of stone instead of the more typical wood, and with most of its original paint intact, this sculpture of the Madonna and Child is extremely unusual. It was probably made for placement on or over an altar. While many twelfth-century sculptures of the Madonna are frontal and austere, this one, with its tenderly entwined figures, invites viewing from oblique angles. The striking depiction of Mary holding a son who is more man than baby powerfully foreshadows Jesus's death and increases the emotional intensity of this extraordinary work.

Limestone with polychromy
29⅛ x 15¾ x 8⅞ in. (74 x 40 x 22 cm)
Maria Antoinette Evans Fund   57.583

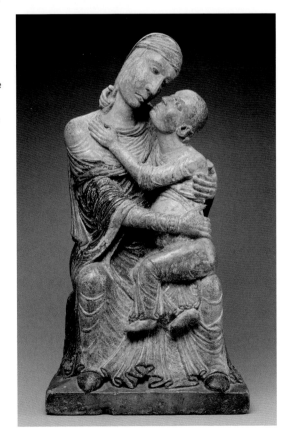

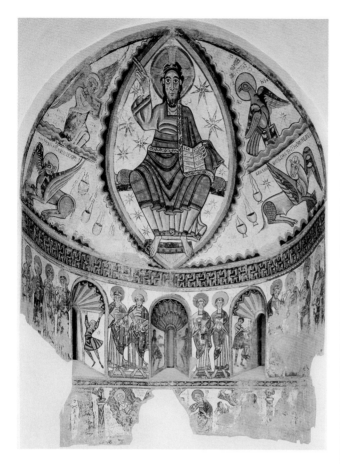

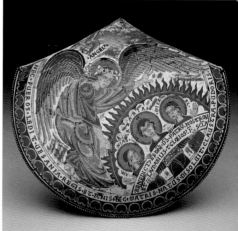

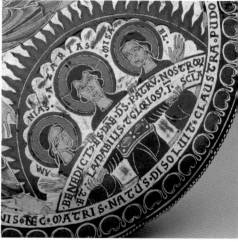

Christ in Majesty with Symbols of the Four Evangelists
Spain (Catalonia), 1150–1200

This fresco once decorated the apse of Santa Maria del Mur, a small church in the foothills of the Spanish Pyrenées. Huge-eyed and solemn, the imposing figure of Christ in Majesty dominates the composition. He is surrounded by symbols of the four Evangelists, whose writings form the core of the Bible's New Testament, and he holds a book inscribed "I am the way, the truth, and the life; no man cometh unto the Father but by me." Below are images of Christ's original disciples, the twelve Apostles, and scenes from the Bible. More than twenty feet high, the fresco was sold from the church in 1919. The process of removing it from the wall was a delicate and difficult one. First, craftsmen glued to the front of the painting layers of cotton muslin that, when dry and hard, kept the paint in place. Next, a thin layer of plaster was chiseled away behind the fresco to separate it,

in sections, from the wall on which it was painted. The fresco was then backed with canvas, waterproofed with a mixture of lime and Parmesan cheese, and transported to Barcelona, eventually coming to Boston.

Fresco secco transferred to plaster and wood
254 x 150⅜ in. (645 x 382 cm)
Maria Antoinette Evans Fund   21.1285

opposite, right

Three Worthies in the Fiery Furnace

Southern Netherlands (Meuse region, Maastricht?), 1150–75

Composition, color, and technical precision place this large plaque among the finest examples of medieval enamelwork to survive. It tells the Old Testament story of the Three Worthies who refused to worship a golden image and were cast into a furnace where they "walked about in the midst of the flames, singing hymns to God and blessing the Lord. Then Azariah stood and offered this prayer: 'Blessed art thou, O Lord, God of our fathers, and worthy of praise; and thy name is glorified for ever.'" Hearing this, an angel "drove the fiery flame out of the furnace . . . so that the fire did not touch them at all or hurt or trouble them." In the Middle Ages, many Old Testament stories were viewed as precursors of New Testament ones; the Three Worthies prefigured the purity of the Virgin, as the encircling inscription here makes clear: "Neither the fury of the King nor the fire can harm the youths, nor can the birth of the Mother destroy the seal of her Virginity."

Champlevé enamel and gilding on copper
8¼ x 8¾ in. (20.8 x 22.7 cm)
William Francis Warden Fund   51.7

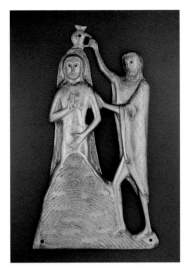

Baptism of Christ

France (Limoges), mid-13th century

This relief was originally one of several scenes from the life of Christ that were mounted on a flat plaque that decorated an altar. It is of exceptional quality, with the gilded-copper surface skillfully worked to capture the textures of hair, fur, and water. The relief is unusual in showing John the Baptist baptizing Jesus in two ways— by pouring water from an ewer over his head and by immersing him in the river Jordan. Jesus, his hand raised in blessing, stands in water whose ripples are suggested by curved segments of white enamel interspersed with shapes of swimming fish.

Champlevé enamel and gilding on copper
14½ x 8¼ x 1⅛ in. (36.8 x 21.1 x 2.8 cm)
Francis Bartlett Donation of 1912
50.858

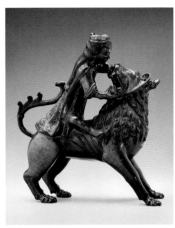

Samson and lion aquamanile

Northern Germany, late 13th– early 14th century

In the Old Testament's book of Judges, the young Samson met a lion that "roared against him; and the Spirit of the Lord came mightily upon him, and he tore the lion asunder as one tears a kid." Here, Samson has just leaped onto the lion's back and confronts its fearsome jaws. The story often appears in medieval art and literature as a prefiguration of Christ's conquest of the devil. Here, it is presented in the form of an aquamanile, a vessel used for ritual hand-washing during the Mass that was later adapted for use in monasteries and princely residences. The aquamanile was filled through an opening on Samson's head; there is a spout below the lion's left ear and its tail makes a handle.

Leaded latten (a copper alloy)
13⅜ x 14½ x 4½ in. (34 x 36.8 x 11.4 cm)
Benjamin Shelton Fund   40.233

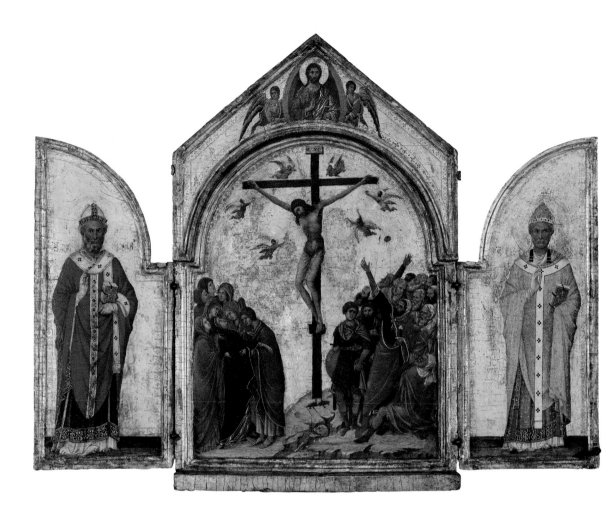

Duccio di Buoninsegna
Italian (Siena), active in 1278, died by 1319
*Triptych: The Crucifixion: The Redeemer with
Angels; Saint Nicholas; Saint Clement*, 1311–18

Duccio's ability to weave groups of figures into moving and compelling pictorial narratives was unprecedented in Italian painting. His jewel-like color and elegant, linear style dominated Sienese painting for two hundred years. Here, beneath the poignant, subtly modeled body of Christ, mourners gathered around the Virgin Mary melt together in shared grief; on the other side of the cross, the poses and gesticulations of soldiers and onlookers suggest confusion and disarray. A sumptuous object for private devotion, it was undoubtedly commissioned by a wealthy individual whose patron saints were probably Nicholas and Clement. Designed to be portable, the triptych is beautiful even when closed; the backs of the wings are painted in imitation of marble and semiprecious stones.

Tempera on panel
Center panel: 24 x 15½ in. (60 x 39.5 cm)
Left wing: 17¾ x 7⅝ in. (45 x 19.4 cm)
Right wing: 17¾ x 7⅞ in. (45 x 20.2 cm)
Grant Walker and Charles Potter Kling Funds   45.880

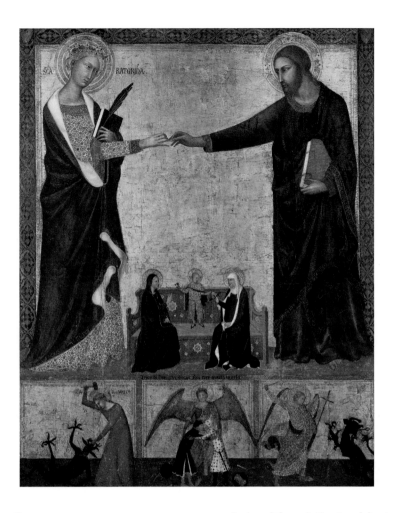

"Barna da Siena"

Italian (Siena), active about 1330–1350

The Mystic Marriage of Saint Catherine, about 1340

The legendary Saint Catherine of Alexandria had
a vision in which Christ took her as his spiritual
bride, placing a ring on her finger. In this painting,
the union symbolized by this event is echoed in the
central scenes below: the Christ Child grouped with
his mother and his grandmother, Saint Anne, and two
enemies reconciled by an archangel. The triumph of
good over evil is represented in the lower scenes to
right and left by saints Margaret and Michael subdu-
ing demons. These images suggest that the donor
named in the inscription, Arigo di Neri Arighetti,

commissioned the painting to celebrate the end
of a feud. Many aspects of the painting seem to be
unique in fourteenth-century Italian art, including
the representation of Saint Catherine of Alexandria
with the adult rather than the infant Christ and the
topical scene of enemies discarding their weapons
and embracing. This is one of the largest and most
unusual fourteenth-century Sienese paintings, but
the identity of the artist known as "Barna da Siena"
remains a mystery.

Tempera on panel
54⅝ x 43¾ in. (138.9 x 111 cm)
Sarah Wyman Whitman Fund 15.1145

Virgin and Child on the crescent moon

Lower Austria, about 1440–50

This refined and graceful sculpture was once part of an elaborate altar shrine (now lost) in the parish church of Krenstetten in Lower Austria. It is carved from a single piece of wood, except for the piece from which the face at the bottom is carved, which may be a later addition or repair. It is hollowed out behind to prevent cracking. The quality of the carving is remarkable, as seen in the deep, looping folds of the Virgin's mantle. Crowned as the Queen of Heaven, the Virgin—with her gently swaying posture and delicate features—represents the epitome of idealized beauty.

Poplar with polychromy and gilding
69½ x 22 x 12 in. (176.5 x 55.9 x 30.5 cm)
Centennial Purchase Fund   65.1354

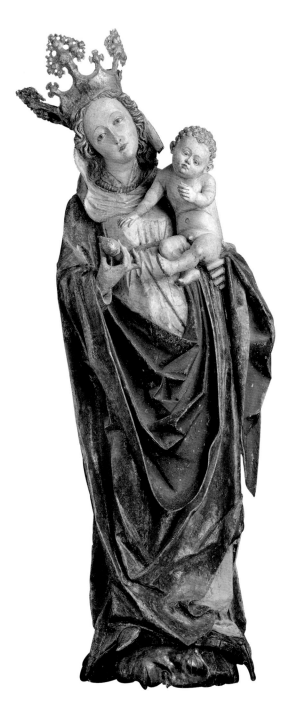

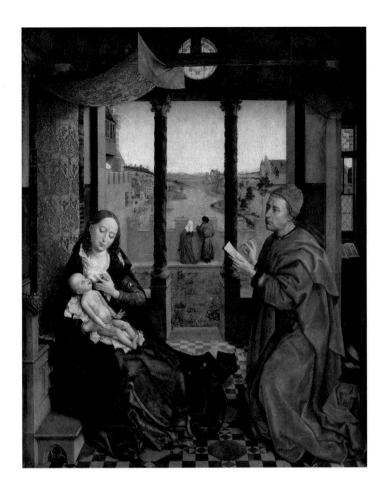

Rogier van der Weyden
Flemish, about 1400–1464
Saint Luke Drawing the Virgin, about 1435–40

Saint Luke is the patron saint of artists, and this altar-piece, a masterwork of fifteenth-century painting, may have been made for the chapel of the painters' guild in Brussels. Rogier van der Weyden made at least three full-size copies of this original version, evidence of the high regard in which the composition was held in its time. Tests using infrared reflectography, which can reveal the underdrawing or preparatory sketches hidden below a painting's surface, show that van der Weyden redrew the head of Saint Luke and other details many times before settling on the final composition. The other versions of the painting do not have this evidence of developing ideas, indicating that they were derived from the Museum's example.

It was once popularly believed that Saint Luke was the first to record the Virgin's likeness, and here the saint reverently makes a preliminary drawing for his portrait of her. Among the meticulously rendered, real-world details, the enclosed garden beyond the room symbolizes the Virgin's purity, the couple gazing out at a river and a Flemish town may represent the Virgin's parents, and tiny carvings of Adam and Eve on Mary's throne allude to Christ and his mother as the new Adam and Eve come to redeem mankind from original sin.

Oil and tempera on panel
54⅛ x 43⅝ in. (137.5 x 110.8 cm)
Gift of Mr. and Mrs. Henry Lee Higginson   93.153

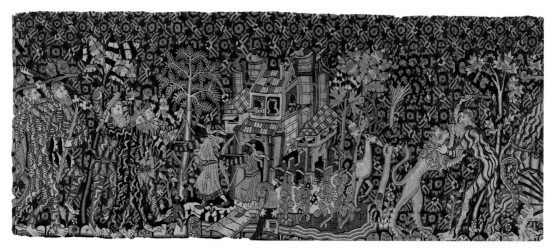

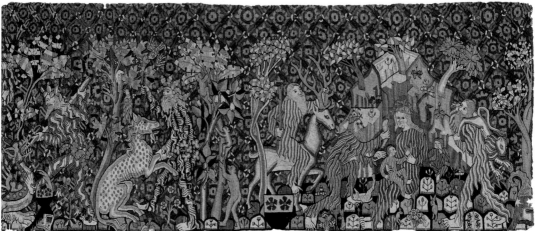

Wild Men and Moors
Southern Germany (possibly Strasbourg), about 1440

Hairy "wild men," neither entirely man nor beast, were popular subjects in medieval art and literature. On the left of this tapestry (top detail), wild men attack a castle defended by Moors, whose king and queen look out from a window. In the center are wild men with a unicorn, a dragon, and a lion, and on the right (bottom detail), men return from the hunt and pay homage to a mother with her children. This spectacular tapestry probably hung along the back of a choir stall in a church or above a row of benches. Against the latticework background, fanciful plants and animals and the patterned, hairy coats of wild men create a magical world.

Linen and wool; tapestry weave
39¼ x 193 in. (100 x 490 cm)
Charles Potter Kling Fund   54.1431

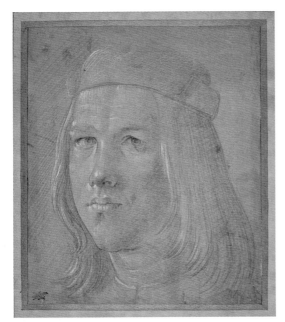

Lorenzo di Credi
Italian, 1456/59–1537
Head of a Youth, about 1500

Like the one Saint Luke makes in Rogier van der Weyden's painting (see page 279), this is a silverpoint drawing. Such drawings, common from the late fourteenth to the early seventeenth century, were made with a sharp, silver instrument on paper specially coated so that the metal would leave a mark. The son of a goldsmith, Lorenzo di Credi was a fellow pupil of Leonardo da Vinci in the Florentine workshop of painter and sculptor Andrea del Verrocchio. Credi later inherited and became the master of that studio and, although a fine portraitist, is best known for his religious paintings.

Silverpoint, highlighted with white, on gray prepared paper
8⅞ x 7¾ in. (22.5 x 19.5 cm)
Denman Waldo Ross Collection   17.592

Spoon
Southern Netherlands, about 1430

On the bowl of this spoon, a fox dressed as a monk and carrying three dead geese in his cowl holds a document bearing the word *pax* (peace). He is preaching to a flock of geese while another fox seizes one of the congregation. The perceived hypocrisy of the clergy was frequently mocked in the late Middle Ages, and the inspiration for the decoration of this spoon may have been a well-known proverb: "When the fox preaches, beware your geese." Or the scene may be drawn from a Flemish version of the immensely popular *Roman de Renart*, a collection of stories (featuring Renart the fox) in which animals live in a society modeled on that of medieval France. The spoon is one of a group of luxury objects that are believed to have been made for Philip the Good, Duke of Burgundy, a great patron of the arts who amassed large collections of tapestries, paintings, metalwork, illustrated books, and jewels.

Painted enamel and gilding on silver
6⅞ x 1⅞ x 1 in. (17.6 x 4.9 x 2.6 cm)
Helen and Alice Colburn Fund   51.2472

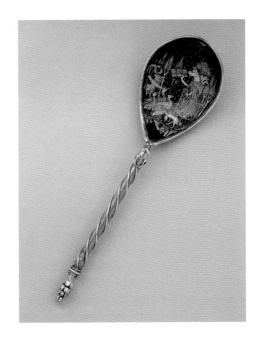

Fra Carnevale (Bartolomeo di Giovanni Corradini)

Italian (School of the Marches), active by 1445, died in 1484

Presentation of the Virgin in the Temple, about 1467

Fra Carnevale most likely painted this work as part of a monumental altarpiece for the church of Santa Maria della Bella in Urbino, and the repainted area along the top edge reveals the shape and placement of the original frame. The figures stand before a vast basilica whose facade, with its triumphal arch based on those of Constantine and Septimus Severus in Rome, is an important early instance of Renaissance fascination with classical architecture. The painting's precise spatial organization allows the viewer to gaze deep into the temple, discovering painted altarpieces and a glimpse of the street. Although traditionally identified as a Presentation of the Virgin in the Temple (with the young Virgin, dressed in blue, standing in the center foreground), the painting's unusually secular aspects and lack of specific focus make it uncertain what event in the Virgin's life is actually depicted.

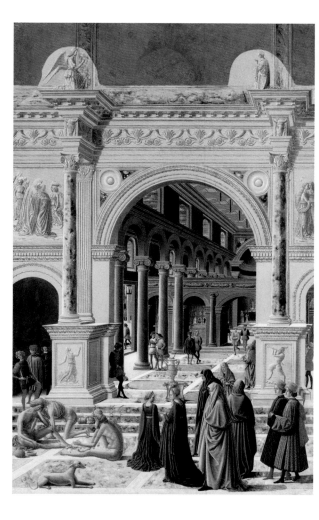

Oil and tempera on panel
57⅝ x 38 in. (146.5 x 96.5 cm)
Charles Potter Kling Fund   37.108

opposite, left

Length of velvet

Italy (possibly Florence), about 1450–1500

During the Renaissance, Florence and Venice were centers for innovation in all the arts, including textiles. Weavers perfected the complex technique of making patterned silk velvets, often in two or three heights of cut and uncut pile that produced a sculptural, three-dimensional quality. Patterns were made even more complex when gold wefts were raised by a small hook to form loops, or *bouclé*, which were thought to enhance the color of the velvet and so were known poetically as *allucciolature*, a term meaning "to throw forth light." Such velvets are often seen in tapestries and paintings and were used to make altar cloths, religious vestments, and luxury clothing worn by aristocrats. The popular motif of the pomegranate seen here was a symbol of immortality and fertility in Middle Eastern and Asian religions and was introduced to Italy through trade with the Ottoman Empire.

Silk; velvet with supplementary metallic patterning wefts
77½ x 29 in. (197 x 73.5 cm)
Julia Knight Fox Fund   31.140

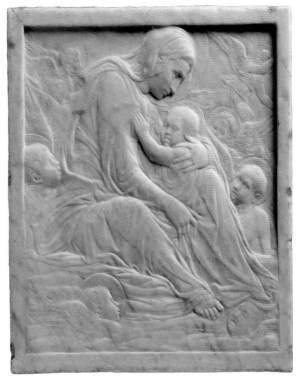

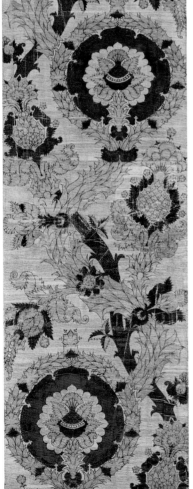

Donatello
Italian, 1386–1466
Madonna of the Clouds, about 1425–35

One of very few works in the United States by the preeminent
sculptor of the early Italian Renaissance, this exquisite marble
relief was probably commissioned as an object of private devotion
and may have been framed in a wooden tabernacle with painted
wings. The relief depicts the Madonna of Humility, surrounded
by angels and seated on a bank of clouds. The extremely shallow
carving, measurable in millimeters, relies on soft, raking light that
creates shadows to delineate the edges of the forms. This subtle
and exacting relief technique is called *rilievo schiacciato* (flattened
relief). Possibly inspired by the classical art of cameo carving (see
page 83), schiacciato relief was invented by Donatello, and few
other sculptors attempted it.

Stone; marble
13 x 12⅝ in. (33.1 x 32 cm)
Gift of Quincy Adams Shaw through Quincy Adams Shaw, Jr. and Mrs.
Marian Shaw Haughton   17.1470

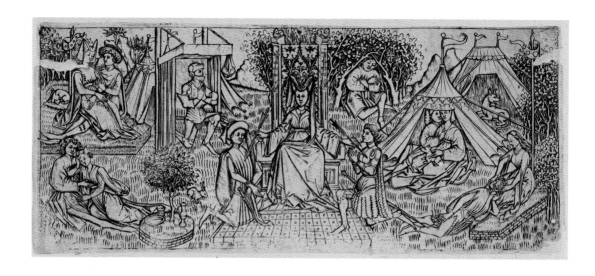

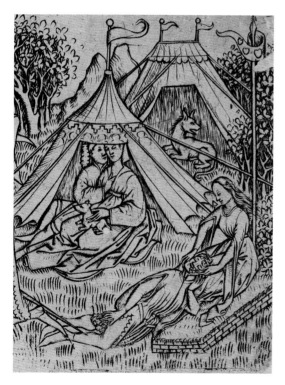

Master of the Gardens of Love
Netherlandish, active 1440–1450
The Small Garden of Love, 1440–50

The first prints from engraved plates were made in the mid-fifteenth century by armorers and other metal-workers who decorated their wares with sharp tools. To record and preserve their patterns, these crafts-men filled the indented lines with ink and printed the design onto paper. The Master of the Gardens of Love, one of the first engravers for whom a body of work can be identified, was perhaps trained as a goldsmith. This image is an allegory of courtly love: enthroned in a pastoral and romantic setting, the Queen of Love casts her spell on a knight and a nobleman. Around her are a variety of courting couples as well as a knight who kneels reverently and a sad young man in a bower of trees, suffering pangs of love.

Engraving
Platemark: 3¼ x 7¾ in. (8.4 x 19.6 cm)
Katherine E. Bullard Fund in memory of Francis Bullard
65.594

Master of the Boccaccio Illustrations

Netherlandish, active about 1470–1490

Adam and Eve, 1476

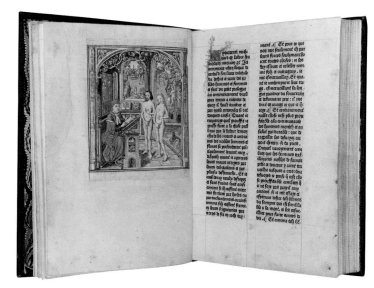

Published in 1476 in the prosperous Flemish town of Bruges, this is the earliest known printed book illustrated with engravings, which were printed separately and pasted into the volume. In the Museum's copy (the finest and most complete surviving example), the engravings were also colored by hand. The text, written in the later fourteenth century by Giovanni Boccaccio, consists of a series of imaginary interviews with celebrated sufferers of misfortune. Translated from the original Latin into French in the fifteenth century, the book was admired throughout Europe. In the engraving illustrated here, Boccaccio sits in his study interviewing Adam and Eve. Beyond the windows, vignettes recall events from their lives, including, on the left, the two pleading for mercy from God, who is dressed as a bishop.

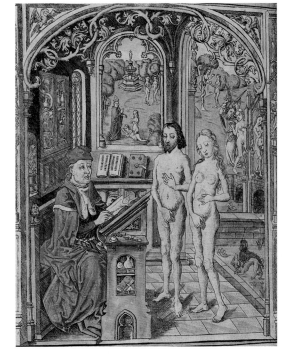

Engraving, hand-colored
From *De la ruine des nobles hommes et femmes* (Of the ruin of noble men and women) (Bruges: Colard Mansion, 1476)
Page: 14½ x 10½ in. (36.8 x 26.6 cm)
Image: 8¼ x 6¼ in. (21 x 15.9 cm)
Maria Antoinette Evans Fund   32.458

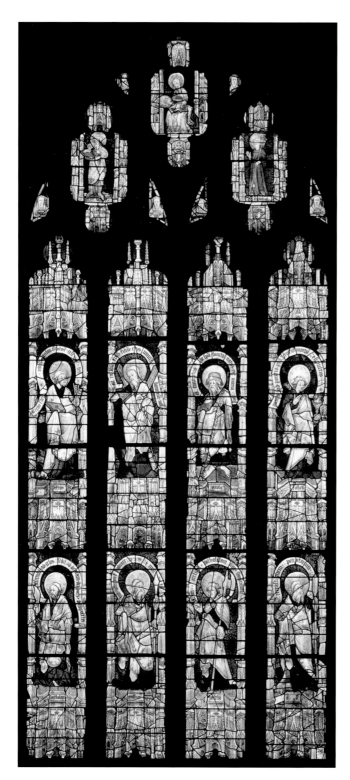

Window with eight Apostles and other saints

England, about 1420–35

This imposing stained-glass window is one of the finest produced in England in the early fifteenth century. Possibly made for Hereford Cathedral, it was moved to the chapel at Hampton Court, in Herefordshire, and sold from there in 1924. Once part of a larger window, this portion depicts eight of the twelve Apostles, the original disciples of Jesus; all but one has his name inscribed on the dais below his feet. Above their heads are long scrolls with Latin inscriptions from the Apostles' Creed, a fundamental statement of Christian belief. A Pietà, John the Baptist, and Saint Francis are depicted in the three tracery lights (uppermost windows). The figures are softly modeled and delicately detailed, silhouetted against backgrounds of deep red and blue.

Pot-metal glass, flashed glass, and white glass with silver-oxide stain; modern limestone tracery
221½ x 103½ in. (563 x 263 cm)
Maria Antoinette Evans Fund
25.213.1–21

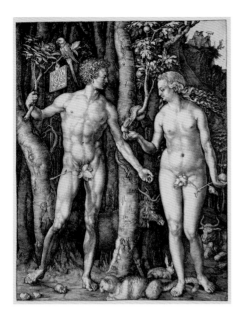

Albrecht Dürer
German, 1471–1528
The Fall of Man (Adam and Eve), 1504

In the sixteenth century, prints increasingly were appreciated as works of art in their own right, and Dürer's engravings provided him with a considerable income. On one level, his *Fall of Man*, produced shortly after his return from Italy, was intended to present the perfect human body as represented in the ideals of the Italian Renaissance. On another level, the image is dense with late-medieval symbolism. For example, the animals in the foreground represent characteristics of the four "humors"—melancholy (the elk), sensuality (the rabbit), cruelty (the cat), and sluggishness (the ox). It was believed that these "humors" had been in perfect equilibrium within the human body until Adam ate the forbidden fruit. Afterward, this balance was destroyed, and individual men and women were controlled by different "humors," resulting in defects of character and in sin, illness, and death.

Engraving
Platemark: 9⅞ x 7⅝ in. (25.1 x 19.4 cm)
Museum purchase with a centennial gift from Landon T. Clay
68.187

Hendrick Goltzius
Dutch, 1558–1617
Nox (from the series *Demogorgon and the Deities*), designed about 1588–89

Printmaker, draftsman, and painter Hendrick Goltzius was the hero of Dutch art in the late sixteenth century. Known especially for his masterful engravings, he occasionally worked in the technique of chiaroscuro woodcut, using two or more blocks to print lines and tone separately. This print belongs to a series of oval woodcuts depicting gods and goddesses. Nox, primordial Greek goddess of the night (and mother of Sleep and Death), appears seated in a bat-powered coach, a passenger traversing the night sky. Rats parade over the wicker canopy that obscures the sun, while a rooster awaits the dawn. Sleep-inducing poppy heads adorn the goddess's hair.

Chiaroscuro woodcut
13⅝ x 10⅜ in. (34.7 x 26.2 cm)
Fund in memory of Horatio Greenough Curtis   53.7

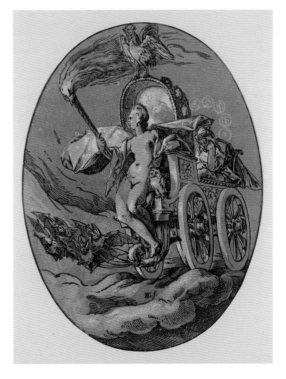

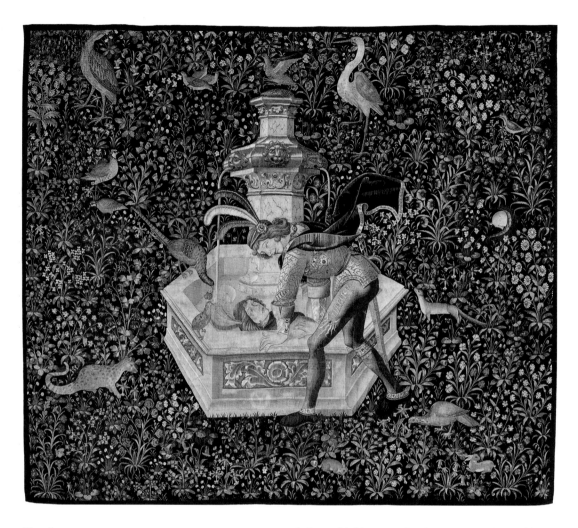

Narcissus
France or the Franco-Flemish territories, 1480–1520

In northern Europe, tapestries were prized and costly works of art. Used to decorate walls in both religious and secular spaces, large tapestries served much the same function as fresco paintings in Italy and Spain. This example shows Narcissus admiring himself in a fountain. According to myth, Narcissus angered the goddess Juno when he spurned the love of a nymph, Echo; as punishment, Juno made him fall helplessly in love with his own reflection, staring at it until he pined away. After his death, Narcissus was changed into the flower that bears his name. The story was particularly appropriate for tapestries like this one, called "millefleurs" because their backgrounds are densely strewn with flowers.

Wool and silk; tapestry weave
111 x 122½ in. (282 x 311 cm)
Charles Potter Kling Fund   68.114

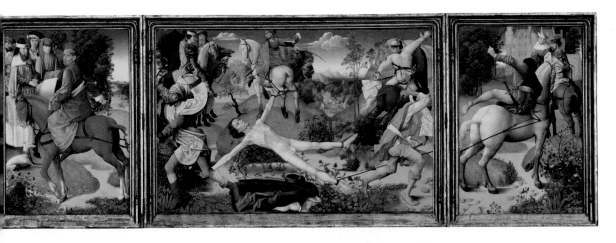

Unidentified artist

Flemish, 1475–1500

Martyrdom of Saint Hippolytus

In legend, Hippolytus was a Roman soldier who was
present at the martyrdom of Saint Laurence and soon
after converted to Christianity. Refusing to renounce
his new faith, Hippolytus was condemned to be torn
apart by horses. The explosive drama of this painting is heightened by two elements not usually found
in representations of the subject: the men who whip
the horses to pull still harder and the way the scene
is spread across all three panels, intensifying the
viewer's experience of the saint's torment. The wings
of this large, exceptionally well-preserved altarpiece
would have been opened or closed according to the
liturgical cycle of the year; when the altarpiece is
closed, these panels reveal figures of saints painted in
grisaille (monochrome gray) to simulate sculpture.

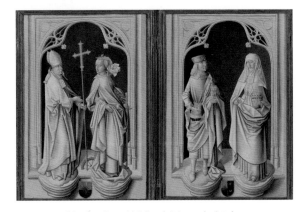

Appearance of the altarpiece with left and right panels closed

Tempera and oil on panel
34½ x 99⅝ in. (87.6 x 253.1 cm)
Walter M. Cabot Fund   63.660

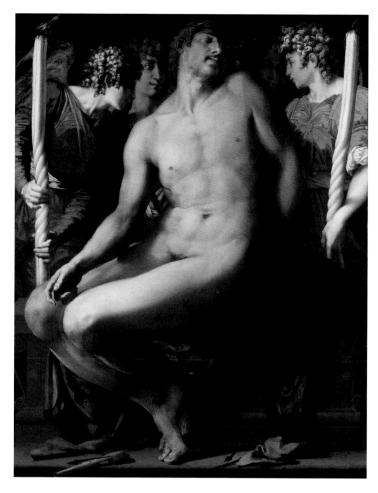

Rosso Fiorentino (Giovanni Battista di Jacopo)
Italian (Florence), 1494–1540
The Dead Christ with Angels, about 1524–27

At once intensely spiritual and physical, this painting
is one of few surviving works by Rosso Fiorentino,
a major practitioner of the Mannerist style, characterized by the use of contrasting colors, ambiguous
space, and sinuous, elongated figures. Most depictions of the dead Christ show him at the moment
of being taken down from the cross or held by his
grieving mother. Here, however, Christ's body—which
seems on the brink of resurrection—is attended only
by four adolescent angels.

A belligerent redhead from Florence, Rosso ("red"
in Italian) painted this altarpiece for the bishop of the
town of Borgo San Sepolcro. The picture's relatively
small size and unusual depiction of a traditional
subject suggest that it was intended for the bishop's
private chapel. Rosso painted the altarpiece in Rome,
and his profound admiration of Michelangelo's
recently painted frescoes in the Sistine Chapel is evident in the colors of the angels' garments and in the
idealized, muscular nude body of Christ.

Oil on panel
52½ x 41 in. (133.5 x 104.1 cm)
Charles Potter Kling Fund   58.527

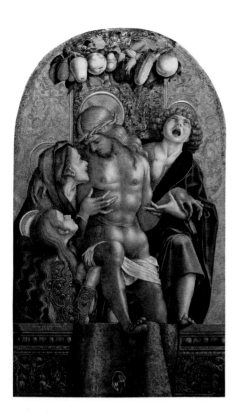

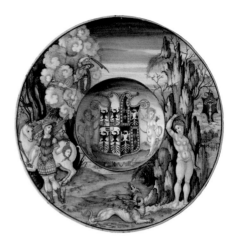

Carlo Crivelli
Italian (Venice), born 1430–35, died about 1495
Lamentation over the Dead Christ, 1485

Crivelli spent his career along the Adriatic coast of Italy, away from his native Venice, and there developed a highly personal artistic style in which splendor of ornament is combined with intense emotion. In this painting, Christ's body is supported by the mourning figures of the Virgin, Mary Magdalene, and Saint John. Suffering is powerfully conveyed by the boldly foreshortened head of Saint John and the intertwined hands of Saint John and Christ, one tense with grief, the other rigid in death. At the same time, the illusionistic swag of fruits and vegetables and the profusion of tooled and embossed gold give this devotional image the quality of a precious object. The shape of the painting and the implied point of view (well below the level of the figures) suggest that it once may have been the center of the upper tier of a large altarpiece.

Tempera on panel
34¾ x 20⅞ in. (88.3 x 53 cm)
Anonymous Gift and James Fund   02.4

Plate
Italy (Urbino), about 1524
Nicola da Urbino, Italian, active by 1520, died in 1537–38

This plate is one of twenty-two surviving pieces of a splendid service made for Isabella d'Este, Marchioness of Mantua; it bears her coat of arms in the center. In spite of being constantly short of money, Isabella was an ambitious patron of the arts with, as she admitted, an "insatiable desire" for ancient Greek and Roman art.

Tin-glazed earthenware, known as maiolica, was often decorated during this period with scenes from classical mythology. This plate features the exploits of the mythological Greek hero Perseus who beheaded the snake-haired gorgon Medusa (whose head he holds, at left) and rescued the princess Andromeda, chained to a rock by a monster. The composition is derived from a woodcut in a 1497 edition of Ovid's *Metamorphoses*.

Tin-glazed earthenware (maiolica)
Diam. 10⅝ in. (26.8 cm), h. 2 in. (5.1 cm)
Otis Norcross Fund   41.105

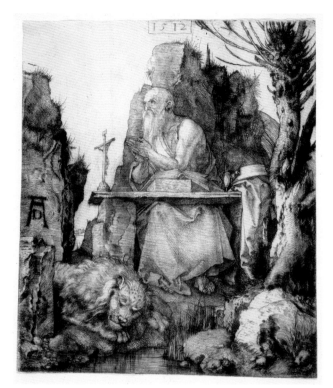

Albrecht Dürer

German, 1471–1528

Saint Jerome Seated by the Pollard Willow, 1512

In the fourth century, Saint Jerome renounced his passion for ancient Greek and Latin literature in favor of the Bible and an ascetic, Christian life. He spent many years translating the Old and New Testaments into Latin, and Dürer shows him in a mood of intellectual and religious intensity, seated with his books in a harsh landscape. The lion sleeping at his feet became his life-long companion after Saint Jerome pulled a thorn from the animal's paw.

Dürer excelled in the uncommon medium of drypoint, in which a sharp metal instrument is used to scratch lines directly into the copper plate from which the image will be printed. This process raises, along the incised line, a ragged edge of copper called burr that holds ink and thus gives softness and depth to the print's tonal range. Because the burr is very delicate and usually wears away after fewer than twenty printings of the plate, drypoint impressions of this superb quality are extremely rare.

Drypoint
Platemark: 8¼ x 7¼ in. (20.8 x 18.5 cm)
Anna Mitchell Richards Fund   37.1296

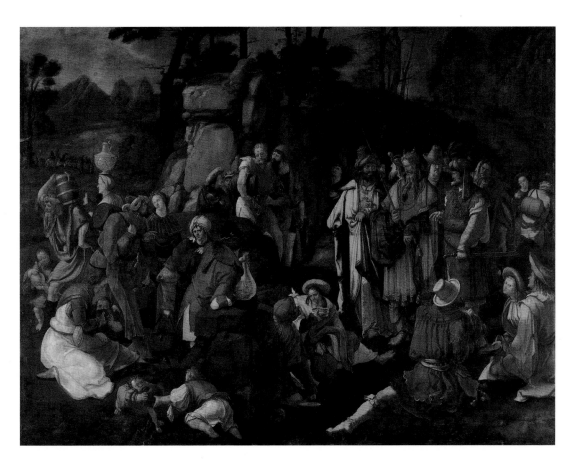

Lucas van Leyden

Netherlandish, 1494–1533

***Moses and the Israelites after the Miracle of
Water from the Rock***, 1527

In the Old Testament, as Moses led the Israelites
through the desert, they complained: "Why have you
made us come up out of Egypt, to bring us to this
evil place? It is no place for grain, or figs, or vines,
or pomegranates; and there is no water to drink."
Advised by God, Moses struck a rock with his staff,
bringing forth a spring of water. This painting depicts
the aftermath of the miracle, as the Israelites eagerly
quench their thirst.

Like Albrecht Dürer, Lucas van Leyden is best
known as a printmaker although he was also a painter
of distinction. This dramatic composition is his only
work painted in tempera on linen, instead of the more
usual panel. Canvases of this large size may have been
intended to decorate rooms as a less expensive alternative to woven tapestries.

Glue tempera on linen
71⅝ x 93½ in. (181.9 x 237.5 cm)
William K. Richardson Fund   54.1432

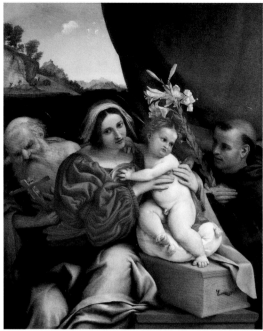

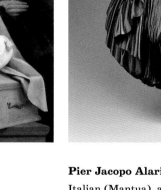

Lorenzo Lotto
Italian (Venice), about 1480–1556
Virgin and Child with Saints Jerome and Nicholas of Tolentino, 1523–24

Vibrant colors and deep, atmospheric landscapes are hallmarks of the work of Lotto, a Venetian contemporary of Titian, who worked as both a portraitist and a religious painter. Here, in a characteristically clear and straightforward way, Lotto presents a visual statement of fundamental Christian beliefs. The table that supports both the Christ Child and his mother represents the altar. The small coffin beneath the Child foretells his death, as does the crucifix held by the weeping Saint Jerome. But the Child turns away from the cross and toward the lily that evokes both the Annunciation, when Mary learned she was to bear a child, and Christ's triumphant Resurrection after his death.

Oil on canvas
37⅛ x 30⅝ in. (94.3 x 77.8 cm)
Charles Potter Kling Fund   60.154

Pier Jacopo Alari Bonacolsi, called **Antico**
Italian (Mantua), about 1460–1528
Bust of Cleopatra, about 1519–22

The Roman Empire fell but never disappeared. The languages, literature, art, and architecture of the ancient world have provided Europe with models—to be imitated or rejected—for the last fifteen hundred years. Latin remained the language of religion and intellectual life through the Middle Ages, and in the fifteenth and sixteenth centuries, a wild enthusiasm for antiquities encouraged the close study and copying of Roman art. The bust of Cleopatra, commissioned by Isabella d'Este, is by a sculptor who became so skilled at capturing the spirit of ancient art that his contemporaries gave him the nickname "Antico."

Bronze, with traces of gilding
H. 25⅜ in. (64.5 cm)
William Francis Warden Fund   64.2174

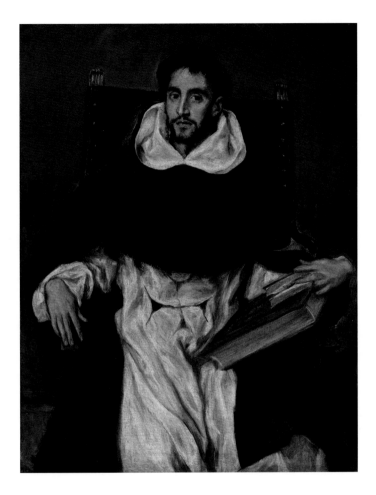

El Greco (Domenikos Theotokopoulos)
Greek (active in Spain), 1541–1614
Fray Hortensio Félix Paravicino, 1609

Born on the Greek island of Crete, Domenikos Theotokopoulos spent most of his career in Spain where he
became known as El Greco, the Greek. Celebrated for
religious subjects painted in a passionate, strikingly
individual style, El Greco was also a portraitist who
looked beyond likeness to probe his sitter's inner life.
The brilliant young man depicted here—a close friend
of the artist—was a monk of the Trinitarian Order, a
poet much influenced by Luis de Góngora (see page
306), and a professor of rhetoric. Paravicino loved this
portrait and wrote El Greco a sonnet praising it. The
poem begins:

Divine Greek, in your work, be not amazed,
That in the image, art surpasses being,
But rather that the heavens, to temper you,
Took away the life bestowed by your brush.
The sun does not spin through the heavenly sphere
As on your canvas.

In later years, Paravicino became preacher to the
king and the most celebrated orator of his time. The
painting's restrained color range and its focus on
Paravicino's dark eyes, sensitive mouth, and long
fingers are compelling; the swift, broad brushstrokes
give the portrait vitality and immediacy.

Oil on canvas
44⅛ x 33⅞ in. (112 x 86.1 cm)
Isaac Sweetser Fund   04.234

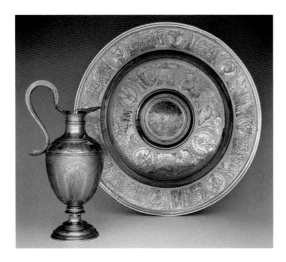

Ewer and basin

England (London), 1567–68

Maker's mark: a pick or scythe;

monograms of engraver: *P* over *M*

The lavish display of valuable objects on a sideboard near the dining table was central to social and ceremonial events in the courts of Europe. On occasion, this ewer and basin may also have been passed around the table with scented water for washing hands. The set stands out among silver of the Tudor period for the quality of its engraved decoration. Finely detailed scenes from the Old Testament are interspersed with portraits of every English sovereign from William the Conqueror to Elizabeth I, suggesting that the set may have been commissioned as a gift to or from Queen Elizabeth herself.

Silver, parcel gilt
Ewer: 13¼ x 4¼ in. (33.8 x 10.9 cm)
Basin: 2⅛ x 19¾ in. (5.4 x 50 cm)
John H. and Ernestine A. Payne Fund, Theodora Wilbour Fund in memory of Charlotte Beebe Wilbour and funds by exchange from an Anonymous gift in memory of Charlotte Beebe Wilbour (1833–1914), Bequest of Frank Brewer Bemis, the M. and M. Karolik Collection of 18th-century American Arts, Gift of G. Churchill Francis, Gift of the Trustees of Reservation, Estate of Mrs. John Gardner Coolidge, Gift of Phillips Ketchum in memory of John R. Macomber, Gift of Mrs. Richard Cary Curtis, Gift in memory of Dr. William Hewson Baltzell by his wife, Alice Cheney Baltzell, Gift of Mr. and Mrs. Richard Storey in memory of Mr. Richard Cutts Storey, Gift of Mrs. John B. Sullivan, Jr., Gift of Mrs. Heath-Jones, Bequest of Charles Hitchcock Tyler, Gift of Miss Caroline M. Dalton, Bequest of Clara Bennett, Maria Antoinette Evans Fund, Gift of Miss E. E. P. Holland   1979.261–262

Sofonisba Anguissola

Italian, about 1532–1625

Self-Portrait, about 1556

Sofonisba Anguissola was one of six sisters, all painters, from a wealthy Italian family. Because women were not permitted to study anatomy or draw from live, nude models, the sisters were inadequately trained to attempt complex religious or historical compositions. Therefore, they primarily painted portraits, including many of one another and themselves.

The art historian Giorgio Vasari wrote that Anguissola "has shown greater application and better grace than any other woman of our age in her endeavors at drawing . . . [and] by herself has created rare and very beautiful paintings." In this miniature self-portrait, the artist holds a medallion inscribed in Latin around the rim: "The maiden Sofonisba Anguissola, depicted by her own hand, from a mirror, at Cremona." Inside the circle is a cryptogram whose entwined letters are included in the name of Anguissola's father, Amilcare, also a painter. The full meaning and original purpose of this enigmatic portrait remain a mystery.

Varnished watercolor on parchment
3¼ x 2½ in. (8.2 x 6.3 cm)
Emma F. Munroe Fund   60.155

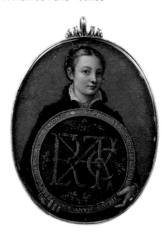

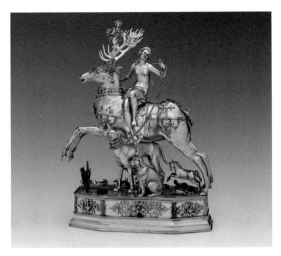

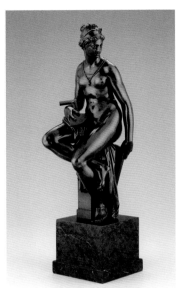

Diana and Stag automaton
Germany (Augsburg), about 1610–20
Marked by **Joachim Fries**

Intricate silver automata were among the most
marvelous works of art in Kunstkammers, German
princely collections of artistic and natural wonders.
Craftsmen in the city of Augsburg, a major European artistic center, specialized in objects for courtly
Trinkspiele (drinking games). This superbly made
figure represents Diana, classical goddess of the hunt,
riding on a leaping stag. The base contains a mecha-
nism that, when wound with a key, moved the piece
across the banquet table on concealed wheels. The
gentleman near whom it stopped removed the stag's
head and drank the wine that filled the hollow body. If
the closest diner was a lady, she drank from the body
of the largest dog. This automaton—unusual in that
its movements have survived—may have been a tour-
nament prize at the celebrations accompanying the
coronation, in 1612, of Holy Roman Emperor Matthias.

Cast-and-chased silver, partially gilded
H. 13 in. (33 cm)
Museum purchase with funds donated anonymously and the
William Francis Warden Fund, Frank B. Bemis Fund, Mary
S. and Edward J. Holmes Fund, John Lowell Gardner Fund,
and by exchange from the Bequest of William A. Coolidge
2004.568a-d

Giambologna (Jean Boulogne)
Flemish (worked in Italy), 1529–1608
Architecture, about 1600

Born in Flanders, Giambologna traveled to Italy to
study sculpture and remained there for the rest of his
life. By the early 1560s he was employed by the Medici
dukes in Florence, and he soon became admired as the
foremost sculptor in Europe. His bronze statuettes
were sometimes offered as prestigious diplomatic
gifts and became part of many important collections,
including that of Emperor Rudolph II.

This beautifully finished figure was inspired by
ancient Greek and Roman bronzes. Compared to
classical examples, however, this sculpture exhibits greater complexity and sense of movement in
the graceful bends and turns of body and limbs. The
figure, who personifies Architecture, holds a framing
square, protractor, and compass. This cast is distinguished by the artist's signature, which appears on
the drawing board behind her.

Bronze; marble base
17¾ x 4¾ x 6 in. (45.1 x 12.1 x 15.2 cm)
Maria Antoinette Evans Fund and 1931 Purchase Fund   40.23

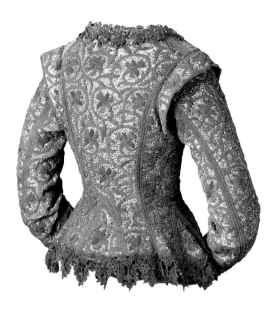

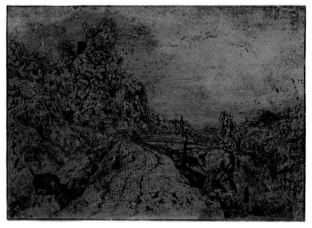

Hercules Segers
Dutch, 1589/90–about 1638
Rocky Landscape, a Church Tower in the Distance, 1610-20

Woman's jacket
England, about 1610–15 with later alterations

The stylized daffodils (or "daffadillies," as they were called) exquisitely embroidered on this jacket reflect Elizabethan England's love of botany and gardening. According to family tradition, the jacket was given by Queen Elizabeth I to a member of the Wodehouse family, following a royal visit to their estate in 1578. However, the style of the embroidery and the cut of the jacket indicate that it was made at least thirty years later.

Linen; plain weave embroidered with silk, metallic threads, and spangles
H. 17 in. (43 cm)
The Elizabeth Day McCormick Collection   43.243

Segers's etchings are remarkable for their experimental use of color and innovative combinations of techniques. *Rocky Landscape*, for example, was printed with blue ink on paper prepared with a pink ground; after printing, the image was washed over with olive-green pigment. At a time when artists often made several hundred identical impressions from a single etched plate, each of Segers's prints is a unique work of art. Not even Rembrandt—who greatly admired Segers's work—employed so many techniques in such unprecedented ways. Etched with tangled, snaking lines, Segers's landscapes are haunting and otherworldly. The contemporary painter and theorist Samuel van Hoogstraten wrote that Segers was "pregnant with whole provinces, which he gave birth to in immeasurable spaces."

Etching and drypoint
Platemark: 5⅛ x 7⅜ in. (13.3 x 18.7 cm)
Kate D. Griswold Fund, Ernest Wadsworth Longfellow Fund, Gift of Jessie H. Wilkinson–Jessie H. Wilkinson Fund, Katherine E. Bullard Fund in memory of Francis Bullard, and M. and M. Karolik Funds
1973.208

Jacques Bellange

French (active in Lorraine), about
1575–1616

***The Holy Women at the
Sepulchre***, about 1613

The New Testament's Gospel of
Saint Mark describes three female
followers of Christ who came,
the day after his Crucifixion, to
the cave where his body had been
placed. There, the women found
only an empty tomb and an angel
who told them that Christ had
risen from the dead. Bellange's
depiction of this event (including
another appearance of the three
women entering the cave at upper
left) is wonderfully artificial and
theatrical with its dramatic light
effects and unsettling, tilted space.
The attenuated figures, posed like
modern-day fashion models with
affected gestures and sweeping gowns, are characteristic of
Bellange's style, which was much
appreciated by the worldly dukes
of Lorraine, for whom he also
painted religious subjects and
portraits. Working at a time when
few French painters were making
prints, Bellange's mastery of etching is particularly notable.

Etching and engraving
Sheet: 17¾ x 11½ in. (44 x 29.1 cm)
Otis Norcross Fund   40.119

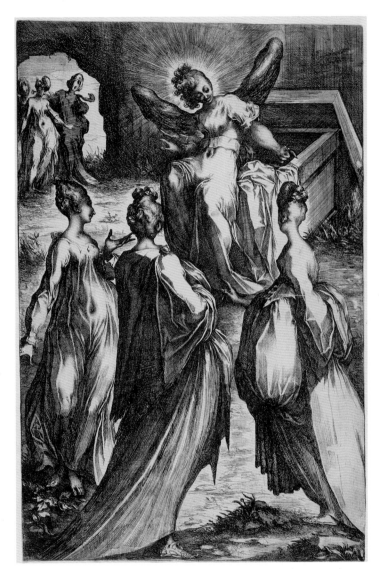

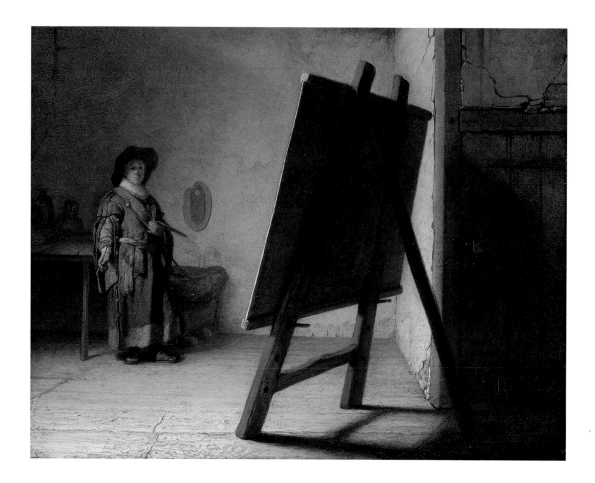

Rembrandt Harmensz. van Rijn
Dutch, 1606–1669
Artist in His Studio, 1628

Within the cracked plaster walls of his modest studio, an artist holds his brushes and the mahlstick he will use to steady his hand as he paints. Beside him are his palette and a stone for grinding pigments. The easel's worn rung suggests that the artist sits when he paints, resting his feet, but here he stands back, readying himself. The drama is one of thought rather than action, and it is intensified by contrasts of light and shadow and by bold juxtapositions of near and far. The painter is dwarfed by his panel—a darkened, looming object that appears to challenge, even threaten him. This moving image transcends visual reality to explore the daunting experience of artistic creation. It is not about painting itself but about when, where, and how to begin.

Oil on panel
9¾ x 12½ in. (24.8 x 31.7 cm)
Zoe Oliver Sherman Collection given in memory of
Lillie Oliver Poor 38.1838

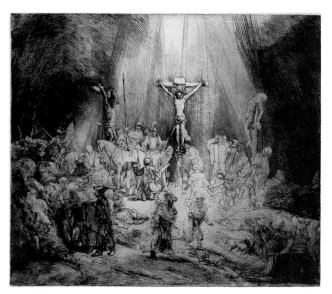

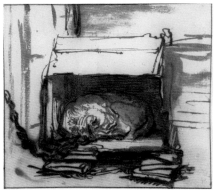

Rembrandt Harmensz. van Rijn
Dutch, 1606–1669
Christ Crucified between the Two Thieves
(The Three Crosses), 1653

Rembrandt was one of the greatest printmakers of all time, and his hundreds of prints reflect his endless struggle to find new forms of graphic expression. This scene of anguish and confusion, executed in the fragile medium of drypoint, shows his bold experimentation. It illustrates the moment when, according to the biblical account, "There was a darkness over all the earth. . . . And when Jesus had cried with a loud voice, he said, Father, into thy hands I commend my spirit." Before printing the image, Rembrandt shrouded much of the copper plate with a heavy veil of ink that would print as an almost impenetrable darkness. He then wiped the central area so that Christ appears to be illuminated by a great cone of supernatural light.

Drypoint
Platemark: 15⅛ x 17⅞ in. (38.5 x 45 cm)
Katherine E. Bullard Fund in memory of Francis Bullard and
Bequest of Mrs. Russell W. Baker   1977.747

Rembrandt Harmensz. van Rijn
Dutch, 1606–1669
Sleeping Watchdog, 1637–40

In his paintings and prints, Rembrandt brilliantly delved into the depths and complexities of human experience. In this drawing (on which he later apparently based a small etching), the artist records a much more humble subject with the same sureness and sensitivity to the potential of a few swift lines and a wash of color.

Pen and brown ink with brush and brown wash, with touches of opaque white watercolor on cream laid paper
5⅝ x 6⅝ in. (14.3 x 16.8 cm)
John H. and Ernestine A. Payne Fund   56.519

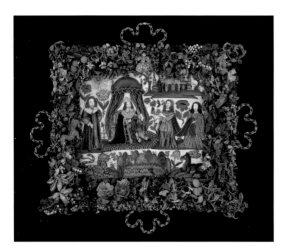
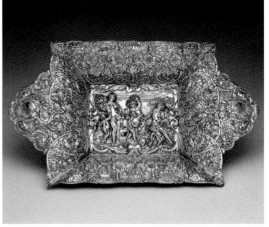

Gift basket
England, 1668

Whimsical baskets such as this, composed of beads threaded on wire and embroidered on silk, were the prized handiwork of amateur needleworkers. Most likely presented as gifts at weddings and christenings, they imitate silver baskets, such as the one illustrated at right, made to display a child's clothes before a christening. On this basket, the figures may depict England's king Charles II and his queen, Catherine of Braganza. However, biblical figures were often shown in contemporary dress on English needlework of this period, and the figures may represent King Solomon and the queen of Sheba.

Wire, silk, wood; embroidered with silk, glass beads, seed pearls, and feathers; raised work
L. 25 in. (63 cm)
The Elizabeth Day McCormick Collection   43.530

Layette basket
The Netherlands (The Hague), 1666–67
Marked by **Adrien van Hoecke**, Dutch, 1635–1716

Layette baskets such as this one—uniquely Dutch in form—were intended for the ceremonial presentation of an infant's christening garments. This opulent silver example, one of only five known today, is enriched by exquisite and varied floral decoration on the sides and handles. The central scene depicts Venus, goddess of love, accepting gifts of wine and fruit from Bacchus, god of wine, and Ceres, goddess of agriculture. An outstanding example of seventeenth-century Dutch silver, the basket is worked in the embossed or repoussé technique. The decoration was first shaped by hammering from the back, and the ornament was then chased—defined and finished on the front with hammers and punchers—to achieve surface textures and decoration without removing any metal.

Silver
28⅜ x 17 x 5 in. (72 x 42.1 x 12.8 cm)
John H. and Ernestine A. Payne Fund   1982.617

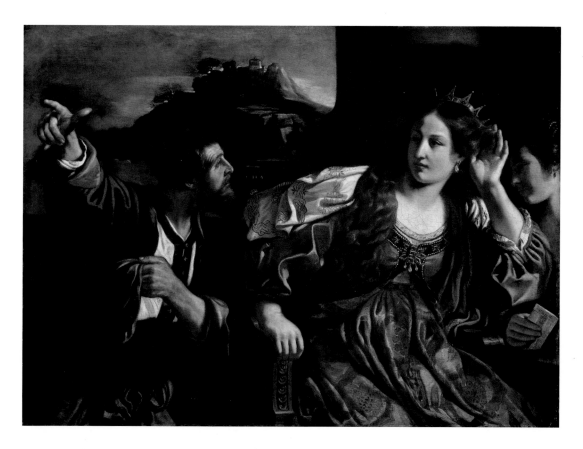

Guercino (Giovanni Francesco Barbieri)
Italian (Bologna), 1591–1666
Semiramis Receiving Word of the Revolt of Babylon, 1624

Interrupted at her toilette by a messenger bringing news of a revolt, Semiramis, the legendary queen of Babylon, refused to finish combing her hair until
she had personally led her army to crush the rebels. In Guercino's theatrical
rendering of the story, the figures appear like actors on a shallow stage, with
the maid, holding a comb, boldly cropped at one side. Gestures are exaggerated and emphatic, particularly that of the messenger, who seems to reach
out of the painting into the viewer's space. Giovanni Francesco Barbieri
(nicknamed Guercino because of his squint) was greatly admired by his
contemporaries. This painting, once owned by King Charles II, was a gift
from the Dutch state in 1660 on the occasion of his restoration to the English
throne after the Civil War and subsequent period of parliamentary rule.

Oil on canvas
44¼ x 60⅞ in. (112.5 x 154.4 cm)
Francis Welch Fund   48.1028

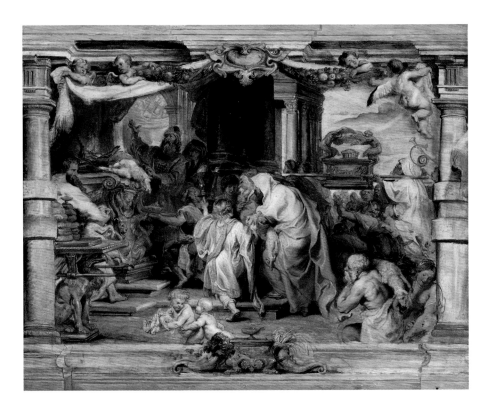

Peter Paul Rubens

Flemish, 1577–1640

The Sacrifice of the Old Covenant, about 1626

Courtier, diplomat, and among the foremost artists of his age, Rubens painted this fresh and vibrant oil sketch as a design for a tapestry in a cycle known as the *Triumph of the Eucharist.* Commissioned by a daughter of Spain's King Philip II for a convent in Madrid, the tapestries were woven in Brussels and remain in the convent today. On the left, an Old Testament priest sacrifices a lamb in a ceremony foreshadowing the sacrifice of Christ that is commemorated in the Christian sacrament of the Eucharist, or Holy Communion. The cornucopias of wheat and grapes in the foreground allude to the bread and wine of that sacrament. Delighting in pictorial illusionism, Rubens painted the scene as if it were a tapestry held up by cherubs, so that the final, woven version would suggest a tapestry within a tapestry.

Oil on panel
27¾ x 34½ in. (70.8 x 87.6 cm)
Gift of William A. Coolidge   1985.839

Jacob Jordaens
Flemish, 1593–1678
Portrait of a Young Married Couple, about 1621–22

Jordaens, a prolific painter and printmaker, worked
for a time in the studio of Rubens, and after Rubens's
death he became the leading painter of Antwerp.
Although the couple in this portrait remains unidentified, Jordaens's sitters were primarily members
of Antwerp's prosperous middle class, and both
husband and wife are handsomely and expensively
dressed. Some details may have a symbolic significance, such as the ivy, an emblem of love and fidelity,
that climbs over a broken column, a symbol of forti-
tude in adversity.

Oil on panel
49 x 36⅜ in. (124.5 x 92.4 cm)
Robert Dawson Evans Collection   17.3232

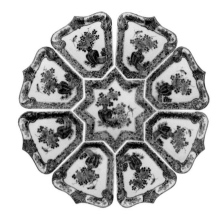

Sweetmeat set
Netherlands (Delft), about 1680
Marked by **Samuel van Eenhoorn**, Dutch, 1655–1686
Made at the **Greek A Factory**

Potters in the Dutch city of Delft perfected glazes
that rivaled the brilliance of Chinese porcelain and
allowed them to compete successfully with Asian
imports. This impressive ensemble of serving dishes
is a masterpiece of Delft pottery, created at the Greek
A Factory, one of the leading manufactories of the day,
known for its work for the royal court. Eight lappet-
shaped dishes surround an eight-pointed star-shaped
central dish; blue decorations on each include imagery of large vases with birds perched on flowering
branches. Based on Chinese examples, the set may
have held sweet and savory preserves or candied fruit
to accompany dinner or dessert. Household inventories of the period refer to "preserve sets," which
probably served as centerpieces in wealthy homes—
though today, complete sets such as this one are rare.

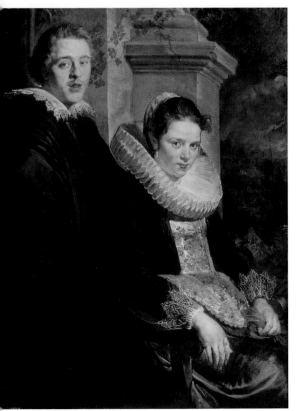

Tin-glazed earthenware
Diam. 28½ in. (72.4 cm)
The G. Ephis Collection — Museum purchase with funds
donated anonymously, Charles Bain Hoyt Fund, John H. and
Ernestine A. Payne Fund, Mary S. and Edward J. Holmes
Fund, William Francis Warden Fund, Tamara Petrosian Davis
Sculpture Fund, John Lowell Gardner Fund, Seth K. Sweetser
Fund, H. E. Bolles Fund, and funds by exchange from the Kiyi
and Edward M. Pflueger Collection-Bequest of Edward M.
Pflueger and Gift of Kiyi Powers Pflueger   2012.576.1-9

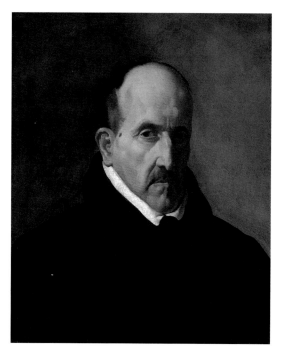

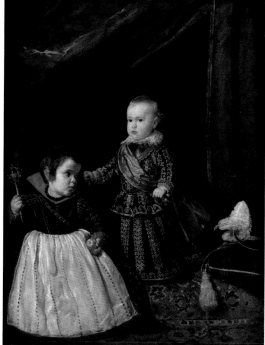

Diego Rodríguez de Silva y Velázquez

Spanish, 1599–1660

Luis de Góngora y Argote, 1622

One of Velázquez's most incisive psychological studies, this portrait was painted during the artist's first
trip to the court in Madrid. It was commissioned by
Velázquez's teacher and father-in-law, who wanted
it as a model for his own series of paintings of celebrated writers. Góngora is now considered among
Spain's leading poets, but in his lifetime, although
his light verse was much appreciated, his serious
poetry was considered obscure and pedantic. When
Velázquez painted him, the poet was sixty years old
and in frail health, embittered by his long years and
lack of recognition at court. This acclaimed portrait
may well have led to Velázquez's appointment as a
court painter at the age of twenty-four.

Oil on canvas

19¾ x 16 in. (50.3 x 40.5 cm)

Maria Antoinette Evans Fund 32.79

Diego Rodríguez de Silva y Velázquez

Spanish, 1599–1660

Don Baltasar Carlos with a Dwarf, 1632

Born in 1629, Baltasar Carlos was the first son of King
Philip IV. This portrait, at once majestic and tender,
may commemorate the ceremony in which the nobility
swore allegiance to the two-year-old prince as heir to
the throne. The baby is dressed as he was at that ceremony, with the sash, sword, and baton of command.
The lively pose of one of the dwarfs employed as com-
panions to royal children provides a foil to the regal
immobility of the very young prince. The dwarf holds
an apple and a rattle, trifles that may allude playfully
to the orb and scepter that Baltasar Carlos would
wield as king of Spain (in fact, the prince died at the
age of seventeen without succeeding to the throne).

Oil on canvas

50⅜ x 40⅛ in. (128.1 x 102 cm)

Henry Lillie Pierce Fund 01.104

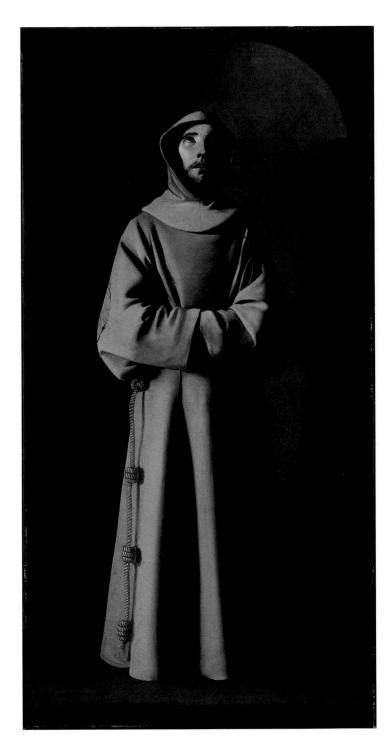

Francisco de Zurbarán
Spanish, 1598–1664
Saint Francis, about 1640–45

Zurbarán was renowned as a painter of austere religious images for churches and monasteries throughout Spain. Muted colors, rigorously simple compositions, and theatrical lighting give the artist's sacred figures an almost mystical presence. This painting, one of the artist's many depictions of monastic saints, apparently illustrates a ghostly legend invented to promote a belief that the body of Saint Francis had never decomposed. According to the story, in 1449 Pope Nicholas V visited the church where Saint Francis had been buried for more than two hundred years. There, in the darkness of the crypt, the pope saw the saint, standing in a shallow niche and showing no sign of decomposition. Zurbarán captures the moment when the pope first saw the body, illuminated by torchlight that throws an eerie shadow on the wall.

Oil on canvas
81½ x 42 in. (207 x 106.7 cm)
Herbert James Pratt Fund   38.1617

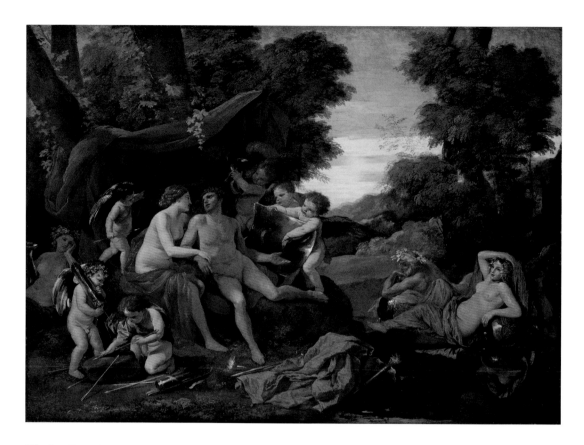

Nicolas Poussin

French (active in Rome), 1594–1665

Mars and Venus, about 1630

Although he spent most of his career in Rome, the French artist Poussin's intellectual, idealizing style influenced the course of painting in his native land for three hundred years. This allegory of the triumph of Love over War shows Mars, god of war, enraptured by Venus, goddess of love, while her attendant cherubs make playthings of his weapons and armor. Intended for a circle of erudite collectors and connoisseurs in Rome, Poussin's paintings were inspired by the art and literature of classical antiquity and the Renaissance. *Mars and Venus* was based on a passage from the ancient Roman poet Lucretius, and many elements of the composition derive from an antique sarcophagus relief. However, in its warm color, harmonious landscape, and sensuous mood, the painting also demonstrates Poussin's early admiration for Titian and other Venetian painters of the Renaissance.

Oil on canvas
61 x 84 in. (155 x 213.5 cm)
Augustus Hemenway Fund and
Arthur William Wheelwright Fund   40.89

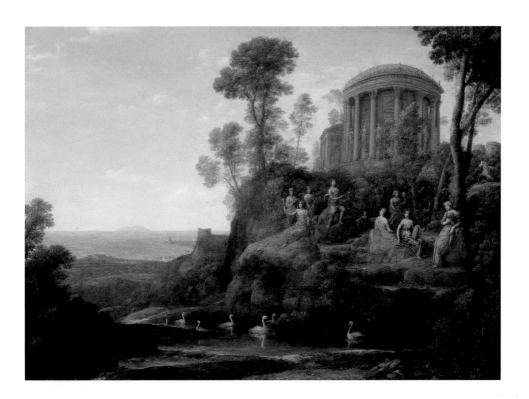

Claude Lorrain (Claude Gellée)
French (active in Rome), about 1600–1682
Apollo and the Muses on Mount Helicon, 1680

Claude Lorrain, born Claude Gellée in the Lorraine region of France,
lived (like Poussin) most of his life in Rome, painting the countryside—
redolent with associations of classical antiquity—around the city and
along the Bay of Naples. Painted when the artist was almost eighty, this
work represents Apollo, god of poetry and music, surrounded by the nine
Muses, embodiments of the arts. At the upper right, the winged horse
Pegasus has dislodged a rock, thus releasing the waters of Hippocrene,
the fountain of the Muses and the source of artistic inspiration.

Oil on canvas
39¼ x 53¾ in. (99.7 x 136.5 cm)
Picture Fund   12.1050

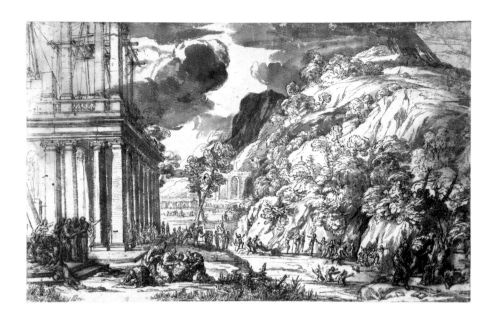

Pietro da Cortona
Italian (Rome), 1596–1669
Landscape with the Construction of a Classical Temple, 1630s

Cortona—ranked with Gian Lorenzo Bernini and Francesco Borromini
as one of the most important artists of the Roman Baroque—was a leading painter of frescoes. He also was an architect, an interest evident in
the building that rises in this large and accomplished work. An early
drawing, this is the first major Cortona landscape to enter an American
public collection. Using tightly arranged pen lines and very loose strokes
of wash applied with a brush, Cortona conjured an idealized vision of
antiquity, balancing the skilled work of man against the voluminous,
light-filled hillside and dramatic, cloudy sky. The drawing's exuberance and virtuosity make it a touchstone for understanding the art of
seventeenth-century Italy.

Pen and brown ink with brush and brown wash, over black chalk on paper
8⅞ x 16½ in. (22.5 x 41.9 cm)
Charles Potter Kling Fund   2000.996

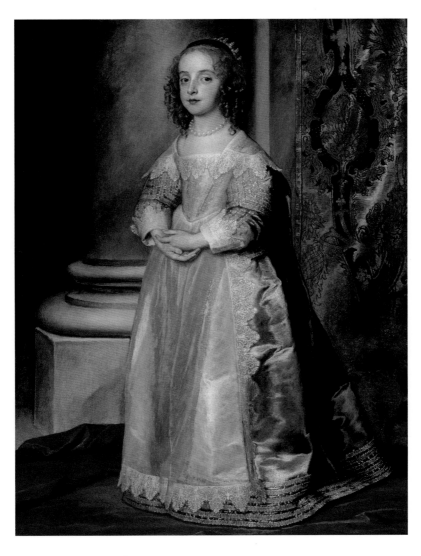

Anthony van Dyck

Flemish, 1599–1641

Princess Mary, Daughter of Charles I, about 1637

This portrait of Mary, Princess Royal (the daughter, sister, and eventually mother of kings of England), was possibly a gift to her bridegroom, the Dutch prince William of Orange, on the occasion of their marriage in 1641. Poised beyond her years, six-year-old Mary is richly dressed, her gown densely orna-mented with embroidery and lace, although still with her child's leading strings hanging down behind.

Described by Peter Paul Rubens as "the best of my pupils," van Dyck was in the service of James I of England by the age of twenty and later became court painter to James's son and Mary's father, King Charles I. He produced a series of portraits of the king, his family, and the court that are of almost unparalleled elegance and distinction.

Oil on canvas
52 x 41⅞ in. (132.1 x 106.3 cm)
Given in memory of Governor Alvan T. Fuller by the
Fuller Foundation   61.391

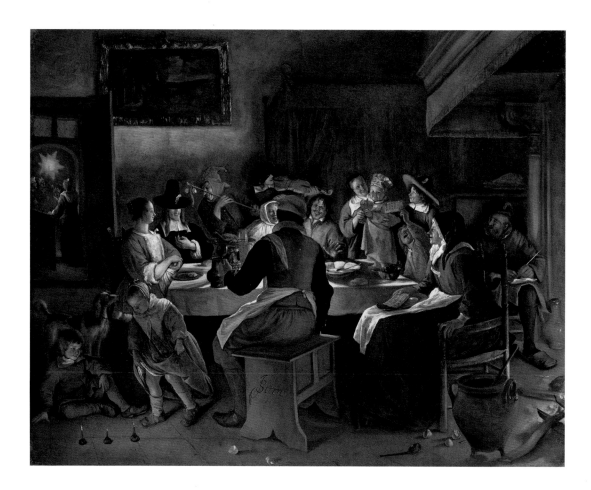

Jan Havicksz. Steen
Dutch, 1626–1679
Twelfth-Night Feast, 1662

Twelfth Night, the sixth of January, was the day when the three kings, led by a star, are believed to have arrived in Bethlehem to honor the birth of Jesus. Although the celebration of this and other Catholic holidays was condemned in the Protestant Netherlands, many people continued to observe it at home with festive gatherings. Steen was a gifted and lively storyteller, and this painting, originally owned by a Catholic family in Leiden, is crowded with convivial detail. A baby (wearing a paper crown) has been chosen by lottery to be king. Children play a jumping game over candles symbolizing the three kings, and in the background, a servant greets the "star singers" who traveled from house to house. The revelers are individualized and yet drawn together by the light (whose source we do not see) emerging from the table.

Oil on canvas
51⅝ x 64¾ in. (131.1 x 164.5 cm)
1951 Purchase Fund   54.102

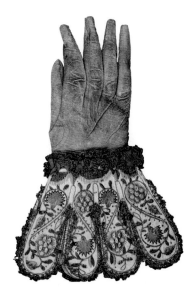

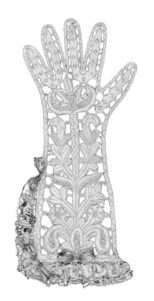

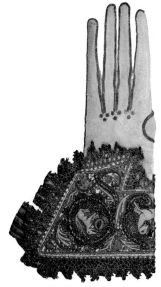

Glove

England, early 17th century

Leather, embroidered with silk, metallic threads, and spangles; metallic
bobbin lace
H. 15 in. (38 cm)
Gift of Philip Lehman in memory of his
wife Carrie L. Lehman   38.1356a–b

Glove

Italy, late 17th century

Linen bobbin lace with silk ribbons
H. 15 in. (38 cm)
Gift of Philip Lehman in memory of his
wife Carrie L. Lehman   38.1271

Glove

England, early 17th century

Leather; embroidered with silk, seed
pearls, metallic threads, and spangles;
metallic bobbin lace; woven silk and
metallic ribbon
H. 13 in. (33 cm)
Gift of Philip Lehman in memory of his
wife Carrie L. Lehman   38.1351a–b

An Italian visitor to London in 1618 observed: "The fashion of gloves is so
universal that even the porters wear them very ostentatiously." Indeed,
throughout Europe, delicate lace or splendidly decorated leather gloves
(sometimes perfumed at extra expense) were a mark of wealth and style
and frequently presented as prestigious gifts. Most gloves were made
in one size, and the extremely long fingers reflect fashion more than the
actual size of the wearer's hands. Although these gloves show signs of
occasional use, the fact that they have survived is evidence of the esteem
in which they were held.

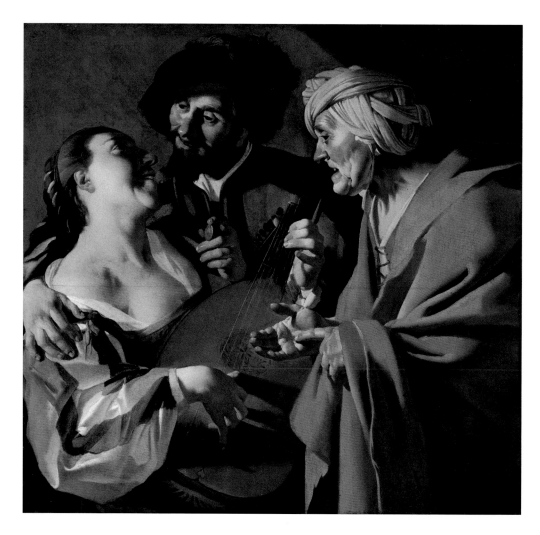

Dirck van Baburen

Dutch, born 1590–1595, died 1624

The Procuress, 1622

The city of Utrecht was the center of Catholic life in the otherwise Protestant Dutch republic, and Baburen was one of a group of Utrecht painters who, unlike most of their Dutch contemporaries, had studied in Catholic Rome. Influenced by the Italian master Caravaggio, these artists specialized in painting large half-length figures, brought close to the picture surface and solidly modeled in strongly contrasting light and shadow. In this spirited image of mercenary love,

an amorous client bargains with a procuress (one who solicits clients for a prostitute) for the favors of a voluptuous young woman. The figures' colorful costumes, so different from the modest black-and-white dress favored by respectable burghers of Utrecht, suggest street entertainers or characters in a play. A lute, symbol of love, occupies the center of the composition and the gestures of the hands that surround it tell the painting's story.

Oil on canvas

40 x 42⅜ in. (101.5 x 107.6 cm)

M. Theresa B. Hopkins Fund   50.2721

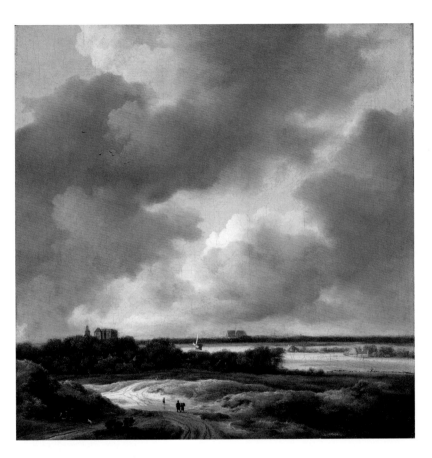

Jacob Isaacksz. van Ruisdael

Dutch, 1628 or 1629–1682

View of Alkmaar, about 1670–75

Early Northern landscape painting generally had as its subject either imaginary views or picturesque scenes of Italy and other foreign lands. But seventeenth-century Dutch artists invented a new form of landscape painting that captured without embellishment the low horizons and expansive skies of their native country. Understood as proud emblems of the prosperous Dutch republic, such paintings were eagerly purchased by people of all social classes. An English visitor wrote in 1641: "The faires are full of pictures, especially Landscips." However, even though Dutch painters enjoyed the most active patronage in Europe, they often had to supplement their income with other occupations: Jan Steen worked as a brewer and an innkeeper, and it is believed that Ruisdael was a doctor.

View of Alkmaar is dominated by a vast, cloud-filled sky that patterns the countryside below with sun and shadow. Although modest in size, the painting's effect is monumental.

Oil on canvas

17 ½ x 17 ⅛ in. (44.4 x 43.4 cm)

Ernest Wadsworth Longfellow Fund   39.794

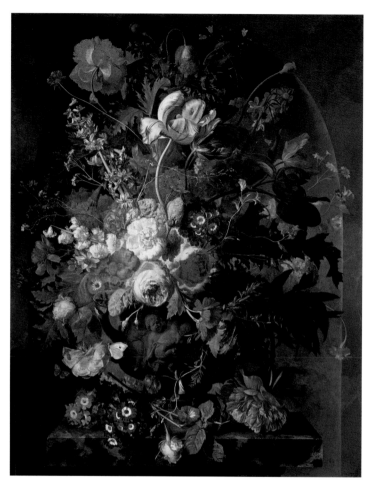

Jan van Huysum

Dutch, 1682–1749

Vase of Flowers in a Niche, about 1732–36

Although flowers had traditionally enlivened portraits and other paintings, Dutch artists of the seventeenth century developed the independent flowerpiece. This specialty later reached its peak in van Huysum's exuberant paintings, which are unsurpassed in their illusionism and dazzling color. Although apparently real, this composition is of an imaginary bouquet, combining flowers that bloom in different seasons. Yet, to the delight of the botanist and gardener alike, each blossom is a faithful record of a living specimen, some of which were much sought after, including the hybrid striped tulip, the hyacinth, the yellow rose, and the *Rosa huysumiana*, named for the artist and now known only from his paintings. The artist traveled every summer to Haarlem, a center of flower cultivation, to make studies of rare flowers. Van Huysum's determination to paint blossoms from life could delay a work's completion; in 1742 he wrote to an impatient client: "The flowerpiece is very far advanced; last year I couldn't get hold of a yellow rose, otherwise it would have been completed."

Oil on panel
35 x 27½ in. (88.9 x 70 cm)
Bequest of Stanton Blake   89.503

Cistern and fountain

England (London), about 1708–9
Marked by **David Willaume I**,
British, 1658–about 1741

Almost six feet tall, this monumental cistern and fountain were made
for the earls of Meath, an ancient
noble family with extensive holdings
in England and Ireland. They were
subsequently acquired by George
Augustus, Prince of Wales, who later
became England's George II (reigned
1727–60). The objects were kept in Germany, at Hanover, the ancestral home
of the English Hanoverian kings. The
cistern and fountain are distinguished
by their superb quality and condition, confident and sensitive modeling,
royal provenance, and massive size.
They were made by London silversmith David Willaume, who counted
the most wealthy and powerful among
his clients. These pieces would have
been displayed on the buffet, a dramatic display of silver and an essential component of elaborate court
dining rituals. The fountain, holding
water, was placed on a table above the
cistern. Footmen filled glasses of wine
from bottles cooling in the cistern and
rinsed drained glasses with water
from the fountain so that they might
be used again.

Silver
Cistern: 26 x 45 x 27 in. (66 x 114.3 x 68.6 cm)
Fountain: H. 42½ in. (108 cm)
Museum purchase with funds donated
anonymously, Theodora Wilbour Fund in
memory of Charlotte Beebe Wilbour,
Harriet J. Bradbury Fund, and other funds,
by exchange   1999.98.1, 1999.98.2a–b

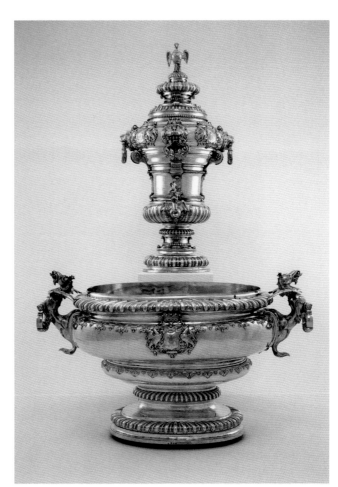

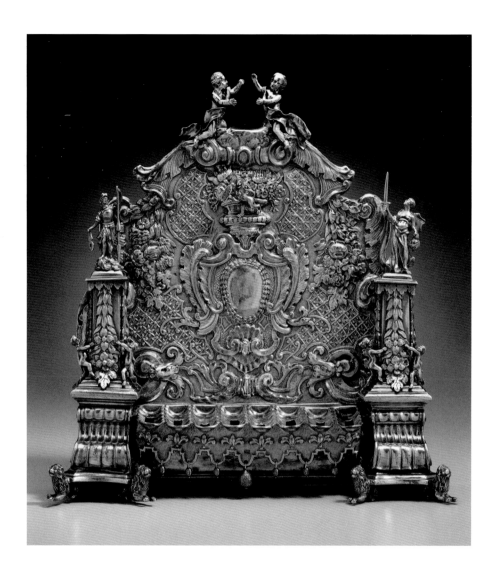

opposite

Hanukkah lamp

**Germany (probably Augsburg),
about 1750**

Hanukkah, the Jewish festival of
lights, commemorates the rededi-
cation of the Temple in Jerusalem
following the defeat of the Seleucid
kingdom by the Maccabees in the
second century B.C. According to
tradition, a small amount of olive
oil burned miraculously for eight
days; today, the eight-day holiday
is celebrated with the lighting
of one flame each night. With its
elaborate Rococo decoration, this
splendid lamp features eight reservoirs on its base; each would have
held oil and a wick for lighting. The
two figures standing on the side
pilasters are Judith and David,
two ancient Jewish heroes who
rebelled against a stronger enemy.
The two figures at the top and the
lion just below, holding the tablets
of the Ten Commandments, were
added later—testaments that the
work was used, embellished, and
ultimately valued over time.

Silver gilt

13 x 12⅜ in. (33 x 31.4 cm)

Museum purchase with funds donated by Lizbeth and George Krupp, Joyce
and Edward Linde, Scott Nathan and Laura DeBonis, Barbara L. and Theodore
B. Alfond, Cordover Family Foundation, Judith P. and S. Lawrence Schlager,
Anonymous gift, Susan B. Kaplan, Clay Barr, and Irving W. Rabb, and by exchange
from an Anonymous gift in memory of Charlotte Beebe Wilbour (1833–1914),
William Francis Warden Fund, made possible by the generous assistance of John
Axelrod, Bequest of Charles Cobb Walker, General Funds, The John Axelrod
Collection, Bequest of Maxim Karolik, Gift of Mrs. Sidney T. Allen, Given in memory
of Dr. William Hewson Baltzell by his wife, Alice Cheney Baltzell, John Gardner
Coolidge Collection, Bequest of Frank Brewer Bemis, Gift of Mrs. Dows Dunham,
Gift of Edward Jackson Holmes, Gift of Mrs. Forsyth Wickes, Gift of Mrs. George
Linder, Juliana Cheney Edwards Collection, Gift of the Walpole Society, Gift of Mr.
and Mrs. Stephen C. Greene, Gift of Mrs. Albert J. Beveridge, Bequest of Helen
S. Coolidge, Gift of Mr. and Mrs. John Templeman Coolidge, Bequest of Charles
Hitchcock Tyler, Gift of Miss M. H. Jewell, Gift of Mrs. Joseph Newhall Smith in
memory of her husband, Gift of the Western Art Visiting Committee, Gift of the
John Gardner Greene Trust, Otis Norcross Fund, Gift of Mrs. Francis B. Lothrop,
Gift of the Trustees of the Reservation Estate of Mrs. John Gardner Coolidge, Gift of
Dr. Henry J. Bigelow, Gift of Mrs. Albertine W. F. Valentine, residuary legatee under
the will of Hervey E. Wetzel, Denman Waldo Ross Collection, Gift of Mrs. Henrietta
Page, Gift of Frank Gair Macomber, The Elizabeth Day McCormick Collection, Gift
of the Estate of Gertrude T. Taft, Susan Greene Dexter Fund, Bequest of Maxim
Karolik, Bequest of Miss Amy M. Sacker, Gift of Mrs. Frances E. Perry, Gift of
Mrs. Horatio Appleton Lamb in memory of Mrs. Winthrop Sargent, Gift of Mr.
Edward Jackson Holmes, Bequest of George Nixon Black, Gift of Mrs. Frederick
T. Bradbury, Gift of Mr. and Mrs. William de Forest Thomson, Bequest of Susan
Greene Dexter in memory of Charles and Martha Babcock Amory, Gift of Francis H.
Bigelow, Gift of Bloomingdale's, John Wheelock Elliot and John Morse Elliot Fund,
Bequest of Forsyth Wickes — The Forsyth Wickes Collection, Swan Collection —
Gift of Miss Elizabeth Howard Bartol, Gift of Mrs. H. P. Sturgis, Gift of Mrs. Abbott
Lawrence, Bequest of George Washington Wales, Alfred Greenough Collection, Gift
of Mrs. Guy Lowell in memory of her husband, Guy Lowell, Gift of the Collection
of Edward Jackson Holmes, Bequest of Gertrude T. Taft, Bequest of James W.
Paige, Gift of Mrs. Henry Mason, Bequest of Mrs. John H. Thorndike, Gift of Richard
Edwards, Gift of Miss Louise M. Nathurst, Jessie and Sigmund Katz Collection, The
Phillip Leffingwell Spalding Collection — Given in his memory by Katharine Ames
Spalding, Philip Spalding, Oakes Ames Spalding, and Hobart Ames Spalding, Gift
of Roland Nickerson, Gift of George E. Cabot in memory of Eliza Hemenway Cabot,
Bequest of Mrs. M. A. Elton, Turner Sargent Collection — Bequest of Mrs. Turner
Sargent (Amelia J. Holmes), Gift of Dr. George L. Walton, Bequest of Emma M.
Dimond, Gift of Mrs. Thomas P. Rich, Gift of Misses Catharine Langdon Rogers and
Clara Bates Rogers, Bequest of Mrs. Edna H. Howe, and funds from Mary S. and
Edward Jackson Holmes Fund and William Francis Warden Fund   2009.5022

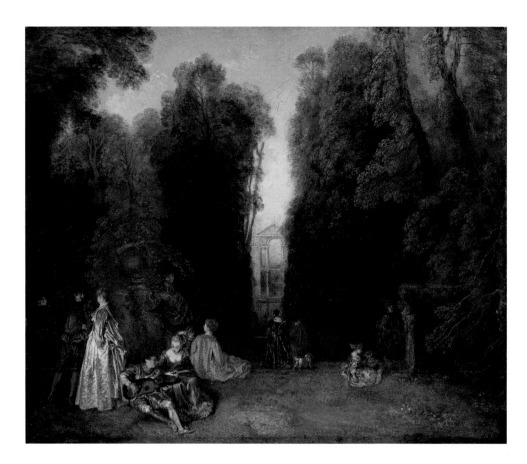

Antoine Watteau

French, 1684–1721

***La Perspective (View through the Trees in the Park
of Pierre Crozat),*** about 1715

Watteau was famous for a specific type of painting
he developed, the *fête galante*, in which ladies and
gentlemen converse, flirt, and make music in idyllic
landscapes. Although he lived in Paris from the age of
eighteen, Watteau's roots were Flemish. And it is from
Flemish paintings, like Rubens's depiction of lovers in
gardens, as well as the outdoor scenes of lovers and
musicians painted by the Venetians Titian and Gior-
gione, which he saw in Parisian collections, that Watteau created his poetic vision of love and artifice.

   This is Watteau's only *fête galante* with an identifiable setting: the Château de Montmorency near Paris,

home of Watteau's patron, the art collector and financier Pierre Crozat. The artist often visited Montmorency where he observed firsthand the aristocratic
delight in artifice and ambiguity that his paintings
capture with such perfection. Here, the marble facade
of the house (originally built for Charles Le Brun, First
Painter to King Louis XIV) appears in the distance
beyond a reflecting pool. Seamlessly blending reality
and fantasy, Watteau transformed Crozat's park into
a dreamlike world where fashionably gowned women
and men in costumes are arranged like actors on a
stage framed by towering trees.

Oil on canvas

18⅜ x 21¾ in. (46.7 x 55.3 cm)

Maria Antoinette Evans Fund   23.573

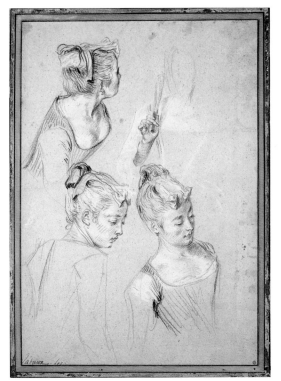

Antoine Watteau
French, 1684–1721
Three Studies of a Woman and a Study of Her Hand Holding a Fan, about 1717

Drawing from life, Watteau made sheets of figure studies that he often incorporated into paintings, bringing a sense of naturalness and spontaneity to his romantic and idealized canvases. Such sheets, however, are also harmoniously composed works of art in their own right, as in this example with its three views of a young model and her hand holding a fan. Watteau used red chalk (his favorite drawing medium) to shape and model the figures, combining it with black to define and emphasize the forms and white for the planes of eyelids, cheeks, and chest.

Red, black, and white chalk on tan paper
13½ x 9½ in. (34.1 x 24.1 cm)
Bequest of Forsyth Wickes–The Forsyth Wickes Collection
65.2610

Guitar
France (Paris), 1680
Nicolas Alexandre Voboam II
French, after 1633–about 1693

King Louis XIV played the guitar, and the instrument was a feature of aristocratic French social gatherings. (Note the man in the foreground in Watteau's painting *La Perspective*.) One contemporary observed: "Everyone at court wanted to learn, and God alone can imagine the universal scraping and plucking that ensued." Enjoyed both as solo instruments and to accompany singers, many guitars were beautifully decorated. Here, the graceful outline of the instrument's body is accentuated with a border of inlaid ivory and ebony that contrasts handsomely with the spruce top. Guitars made by the Voboam family, active in Paris between 1650 and 1730, were much in demand, but only about thirty examples survive today.

Ebony, red cedar, spruce, ivory
H. 36¼ in. (91.9 cm)
Otis Norcross Fund, Gift of
Mr. and Mrs. Richard M. Fraser and Bequest
of Gertrude T. Taft, by exchange   1993.576

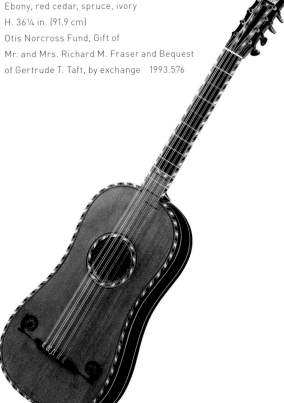

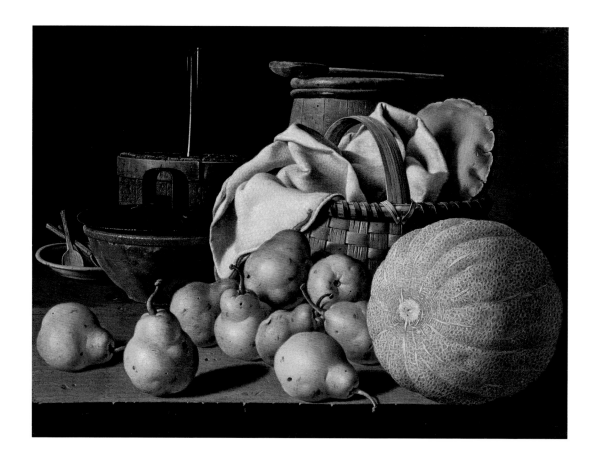

Luis Meléndez

Spanish, 1716–1780

Still Life with Melon and Pears, about 1770

Like his French contemporary Chardin, Meléndez favored arrangements of everyday objects painted with sober yet sensuous realism. He savored shapes, surfaces, and colors—from the webbed rind of the melon to the glint of a wine bottle cooling in a cork bucket—and despite the profusion of objects, his paintings convey a satisfying sense of balance and measure. This still life is based on one from a series of forty-five, said to represent "every species of food produced in Spain," that Meléndez created for the king's New Cabinet of Natural History in the Royal Palace in Madrid. Ironically, many were painted at a time when poor harvests had produced severe food shortages. The artist himself had no money to buy food, claiming that his brush was his only asset.

Oil on canvas
25⅛ x 33½ in. (63.8 x 85 cm)
Margaret Curry Wyman Fund 39.41

Sauceboat and stand
France (Paris), about 1756–59
Made by **François-Thomas Germain**
French, 1726–1791

After the 1755 earthquake that devastated Lisbon, Portugal's King Jose I ordered four new table services to replace the extensive holdings of royal silver that had been lost. As did many European royalty, he turned to a Parisian silversmith, in this case François-Thomas Germain, who employed 120 workers to execute the commission. This is one of a pair of sauceboats with a rockwork base and handles formed of branches of celery. A vivid document of the artistic and technical mastery of the French silversmith, the sauceboat is one of about 300 pieces of silver that came to the Museum from the estate of Elizabeth Parke and Harvey S. Firestone, whose collection of rare French domestic silver is one of the most magnificent in an American museum.

Silver
5½ x 15⅜ x 8⅞ in. (13.8 x 39 x 22.6 cm)
Elizabeth Parke Firestone and
Harvey S. Firestone, Jr. Collection   1993.515.2

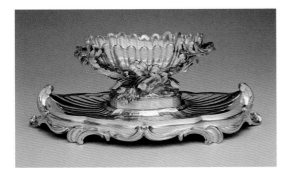

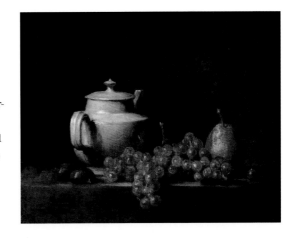

Jean Siméon Chardin
French, 1699–1779
Still Life with Teapot, Grapes, Chestnuts, and a Pear, 17[64?]

Chardin celebrated the commonplace. There is an air of informality and intimacy about his still lifes, as if he were working in his kitchen rather than his studio. In fact, inventories reveal that he owned most of the objects that he painted so meticulously, balancing form and texture. He also loved the pure, sensuous quality of paint, as the patch of brilliant orange brushed on the pear attests. The critic Denis Diderot enthused: "O Chardin! It's not white, red, or black pigment that you crush on your palette: it's the very substance of the objects, it's air and light that you take up with the tip of your brush and fix onto the canvas."

Oil on canvas
12⅝ x 15¾ in. (32 x 40 cm)
Gift of Martin Brimmer   83.177

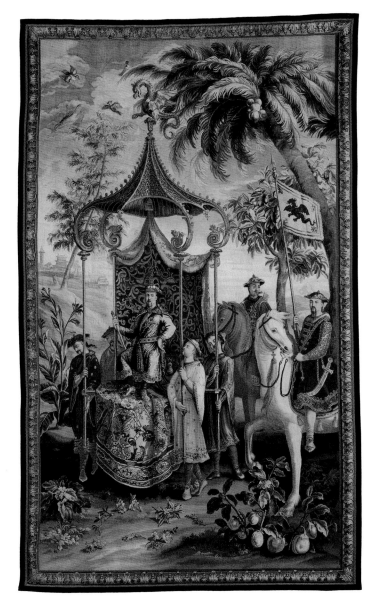

The Emperor on a Journey
France (Beauvais), late 17th
or early 18th century
Designed by **Guy Louis Vernansal,
Jean-Baptiste Belin de Fontenay,**
and **"Batiste"** (probably **Jean-
Baptiste Monnoyer**)

During the reign of Louis XIV, the
French tapestry industry enjoyed a
brilliant period. At this time, there
was a passion for what has come
to be called "chinoiserie"—depictions of Asian life and landscape
that reflect a little knowledge and
a great deal of imagination. For
many years, the manufactory at
Beauvais wove a series of chinoiserie tapestries called *The Story
of the Emperor of China*, perhaps
inspired by the accounts of a
French Jesuit priest who returned
from China in 1697. On this panel,
the emperor—enthroned beneath
a fanciful canopy with his feet on
a Near Eastern rug—is probably
Kang Xi, who reigned from 1661 to
1721. The tapestry has survived in
particularly fine condition, with its
vibrant colors intact.

Wool and silk; tapestry weave
152 x 94 in. (386 x 239 cm)
Gift of Mr. and Mrs. Henry U. Harris in
the name of Mrs. Edwin S. Webster and
Mr. and Mrs. Henry U. Harris   65.1352

Giovanni Battista Tiepolo
Italian (Venice), 1696–1770
Time Unveiling Truth,
about 1745–50

One of the last great international
court artists, Tiepolo is best known
for huge frescoes that decorate
the walls and ceilings of palaces
in Italy, Germany, and Spain. This
complex allegory depicts Truth
as a proud young woman whose
opulent beauty is set off by the
dark, winged figure of Time. Time's
scythe denotes death, and Cupid,
whose quiver of arrows remains
on the ground, symbolizes earthly
love rendered powerless by Time.
The parrot at right represents
the enemies of Truth: vanity and
deceit. Truth's emblem, the sun,
shines above, while earthly things,
represented by the globe, lie subject beneath her foot.

Oil on canvas
91 x 65¾ in. (231 x 167 cm)
Charles Potter Kling Fund   61.1200

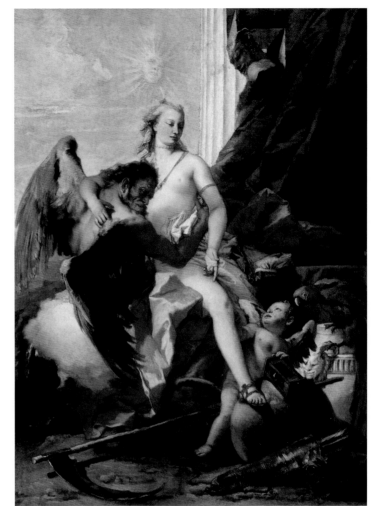

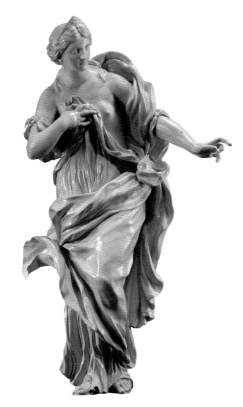

opposite, *left*

Modeled by Johann Joachim Kändler

German, 1706–1775

Macaw, about 1732

Made at the **Meissen Manufactory**

Augustus II, elector of Saxony and king of Poland, was obsessed with Asian porcelain and (successfully) sponsored the efforts by chemists and alchemists to decode its secrets, enabling European manufacture. Around 1725, Augustus conceived of a plan to convert a Dresden palace into a magnificent setting for the royal ceramics collection. The ground level would display more than 20,000 examples of Chinese and Japanese ceramics, while the upper floor was reserved for porcelain produced at his own factory at nearby Meissen. The most spectacular space would be a long gallery decorated with nearly 600 porcelain birds and animals, meant to impress visitors seeking an audience with the ruler. In 1732, modeler Johann Joachim Kändler created this dynamic and expressive life-sized Brazilian macaw climbing down the trunk of a tree. The astonishing naturalism stems from the artist's insistence on using live examples in the royal zoos as the basis for his work.

Hard-paste porcelain

H. 49 in. (124.5 cm)

Kiyi and Edward M. Pflueger Collection. Bequest of Edward M. Pflueger and Gift of Kiyi Powers Pflueger   2006.922

After a sculpture by Giuseppe Piamontini

Juno, about 1745–55

Made by the **Doccia Manufactory**, Italy

Under its founder, Carlo Ginori, the Doccia Manufactory of Florence set out on a highly ambitious program to create a museum of porcelain works based on models by great Italian artists past and present. This sculpture, one of only a handful of large-scale Doccia works known today, represents the Roman goddess Juno, protector and special counselor of the state. Painstakingly executed in hard-paste porcelain, Juno's rarity is matched by her beauty—and by the sheer technical feat of firing and assembling the various pieces that constitute her. The figure is based on a model by the Florentine sculptor Giuseppe Piamontini (1663–1744); her swirling draperies and extended limbs exhibit the grace and animation of the master's style. According to factory archives, which list the molds used for Piamontini's sculptures, Juno would have been paired with a figure of Jupiter, her husband and king of the gods.

Glazed hard-paste porcelain

H. 38½ in. (97.8 cm)

Partial gift in memory of I. W. Colburn by Frances H. Colburn, Clarissa Colburn Hunnewell, and Oliver C. Colburn, and museum purchase with funds from the John Lowell Gardner Fund, John H. and Ernestine A. Payne Fund, Russell B. and Andrée Beauchamp Stearns Fund, Otis Norcross Fund, and Tamara Petrosian Davis Fund   2008.1414

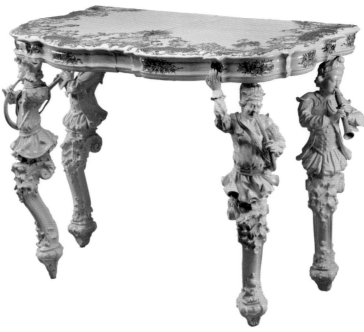

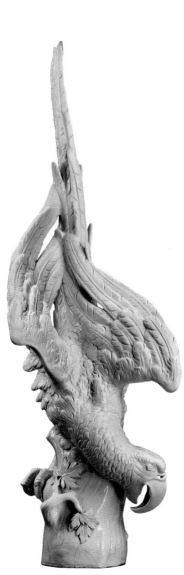

Console table
Spain (Alcora), about 1761–63
Made at the **Alcora Manufactory**

In Spain, the Alcora factory was the leading producer of fine ceramics in the eighteenth century. In the mind of the Count of Aranda, the factory's chief patron, a thriving ceramics industry was an essential step toward elevating the arts of Spain in order to glorify the kingdom. This unusual masterpiece represents one of the few successful attempts to create ceramic furniture in Europe. It consists of two halves, each supported by musicians playing horns and trumpets. It was probably conceived of as part of a "porcelain room," perhaps to rival one recently commissioned by King Carlos III for the royal palace at Aranjuez. Factory archives mention such a table in combination with large wall plaques, small figures on brackets, and even a ceramic chandelier. Combined, the impact of the richly modeled forms and painted decoration must have been spectacular—a fitting tribute to Spain's ceramics ambitions, as well as the count's.

Tin-glazed earthenware, enamels
38 x 52¼ x 27 in. (96.5 x 132.7 x 68.6 cm)
Henry H. and Zoe Oliver Sherman Fund   2010.585

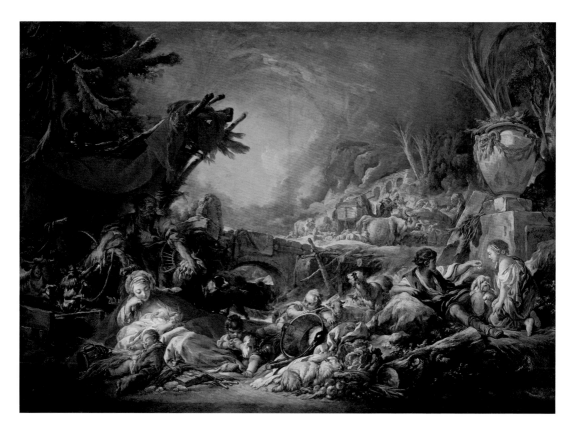

François Boucher

French, 1703–1770

Halt at the Spring, 1765

Boucher, possibly the most influential French artist of the eighteenth century, was also one of the most versatile. He not only decorated palaces and private residences but also painted portraits, landscapes, and mythological scenes and designed opera sets, porcelains, and tapestries. He enlarged and reworked this painting (originally a depiction of the Rest on the Flight into Egypt, with Mary, Joseph, and Jesus at left) into a fantasy of peasant life enlivened by dashing brushwork, lighthearted sensuousness, and pastel colors punctuated by vibrant red. Attracted to the fanciful and artificial, Boucher objected to the natural world as "too green and badly lit." When this painting was exhibited in Paris in its earlier form in 1761, the critic Denis Diderot wrote: "What colors! what variety! what richness of objects and of ideas! This man has everything except truth." Acquired in the mid-nineteenth century for a house in Boston's South End, *Halt at the Spring* and its companion, *Return from Market*, subsequently became the first European paintings to enter the Museum's collection.

Oil on canvas
82⅛ x 114⅛ in. (208.5 x 290 cm)
Gift of the heirs of Peter Parker   71.2

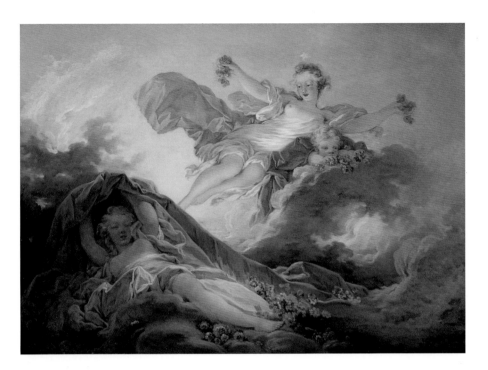

Jean-Honoré Fragonard
French, 1732–1806
Aurora Triumphing over Night, about 1755–56

Fragonard's paintings embody the gracious sensuality, exuberance, and soft pastel colors of the eighteenth-century French Rococo style. In this early work, the artist shows his indebtedness to his master François Boucher, who specialized in amorous mythological paintings that delight in the pleasure of artifice. The poet Homer called Aurora "rosy fingered." Here, Fragonard paints the goddess of dawn (identified by the morning star on her head) sprinkling rose petals from the morning sky onto the sleeping figure of Night below. The painting once had a different shape: traces of its original rounded and scalloped edges indicate that it was made to fit within ornamental paneling (*boiserie*) above a door frame, perhaps in a bedroom. In the nineteenth century, restorers added canvas inserts to square the corners, turning it into an independent gallery picture.

Oil on canvas
37½ x 51¾ in. (95.3 x 131.4 cm)
Museum purchase with funds by exchange by contribution, and by exchange from a Gift of Laurence K. and Lorna J. Marshall   2013.62

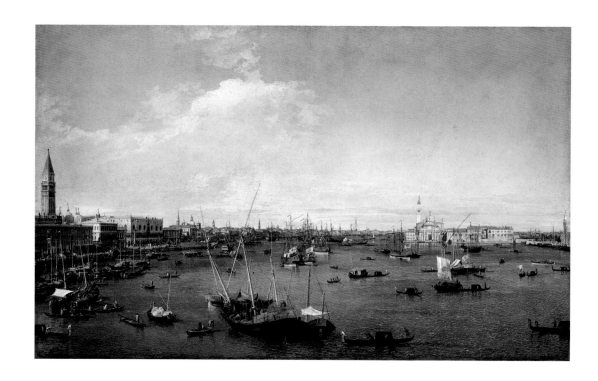

Canaletto (Giovanni Antonio Canal)
Italian (Venice), 1697–1768
Bacino di San Marco, Venice, about 1738

Giovanni Antonio Canal, known as Canaletto, was the foremost painter
of *vedute*, or views, of Venice, and his works were much in demand
among eighteenth-century travelers on the "Grand Tour" of Europe. This
painting, purchased by the Earl of Carlisle for his home, Castle Howard
in Yorkshire, England, is among Canaletto's masterpieces. The expanse
of the lagoon, or *bacino*, is animated with gondolas, work boats, and
ships flying the flags of England, France, and Denmark. Famous landmarks include the Doge's Palace at left and the church of San Giorgio
Maggiore at right. The clear light and the drifting clouds that dapple
the water unite all this activity into a grand, unified whole. Canaletto
composed his paintings from several viewpoints so as to encompass
more buildings than actually could be seen from one place. A contemporary wrote: "He paints with such accuracy and cunning that the eye
is deceived and truly believes that it is reality it sees, not a painting."

Oil on canvas
49 x 80½ in. (124.5 x 204.5 cm)
Abbott Lawrence Fund, Seth K. Sweetser Fund, and Charles Edward French Fund
39.290

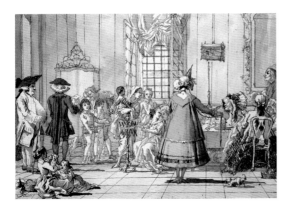

Giovanni Domenico Tiepolo
Italian (Venice), 1727–1804
The Milliner's Shop, about 1791

Son and chief assistant of a famous and successful
father (see page 325), Tiepolo was an accomplished
artist in his own right: a masterful draftsman with a
special talent for acutely observed images of Venice's
upwardly mobile middle class going about their daily
business. In this drawing, one in a series depicting
scenes of contemporary life, employees of a fashionable shop mingle with customers and their children.
Amid the bustle, the motionless woman in yellow
(seen from behind) provides the composition's focal
point; her sweeping gesture leads the eye to the all-
important bonnet displayed on the table at right.

Pen and brown ink, with brown, ocher, and yellow washes,
over black chalk on white paper
14⅞ x 19¾ in. (37.6 x 50 cm)
William E. Nickerson Fund   47.2

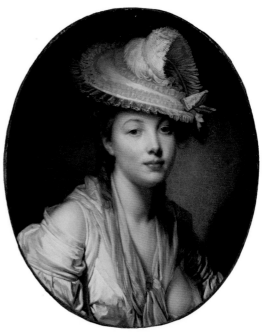

Jean-Baptiste Greuze
French, 1725–1805
The White Hat, about 1780

Best known for his moralizing scenes of middle-class
domestic life, Greuze also painted accomplished
portraits. "I don't like faces that are painted already,"
Greuze declared, and this image of an unidentified
young woman captures the combination of sensuality and innocence much admired in prerevolutionary
France. The sitter's artfully dishevelled dress reflects
a "natural" fashion favored by Queen Marie Antoinette,
and her glowing skin is enhanced by the painting's
palette of soft blues and grays. The oval shape, which
Greuze often employed for images of beautiful women,
is echoed in the curves of the woman's shoulder and
breast—and in the remarkable feathered hat that
dominates the composition.

Oil on canvas
22⅜ x 18¼ in. (56.8 x 46.5 cm)
Gift of Jessie H. Wilkinson–Jessie H. Wilkinson Fund,
Grant Walker Fund, Seth K. Sweetser Fund, and
Abbott Lawrence Fund   1975.808

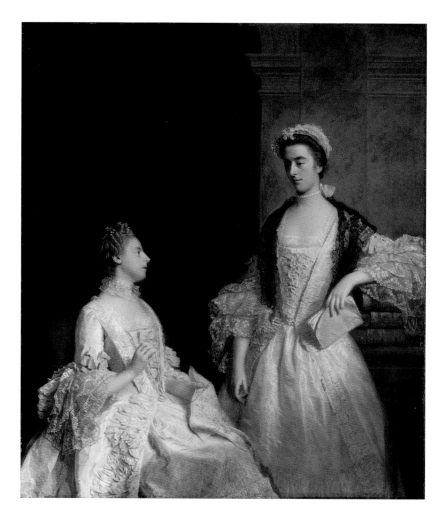

Allan Ramsay

Scottish, 1713–1784

Portrait of Horace Walpole's Nieces: The Honorable Laura Keppel and Charlotte, Lady Huntingtower, 1765

Ramsay, a Scotsman who studied for three years in Italy, infused his portraits with Italian elegance and lightness. He returned home to Edinburgh in 1738 but soon settled in London, becoming the city's leading portrait painter. Following his appointment as painter to King George III in 1761, Ramsay exclusively painted royal subjects. In this portrait, the artist captures the delicate attire and natural conversation between sisters Laura (in blue) and Charlotte (in pink), daughters of Sir Edward Walpole and granddaughters of Prime Minister Robert Walpole. Their uncle, the writer Horace Walpole, commissioned the portrait, and letters between Walpole and Ramsay discuss such details as dimensions, payments, and a sitting for Laura. In fact, the sisters did not sit for Ramsay at the same time: he painted each of their heads separately, and they were then sewn together with additional pieces of canvas to expand the composition.

Oil on canvas
61½ x 54 in. (156.2 x 137.2 cm)
Bequest of Eleanor B. Winthrop in memory of Nathaniel T. Winthrop   2009.2783

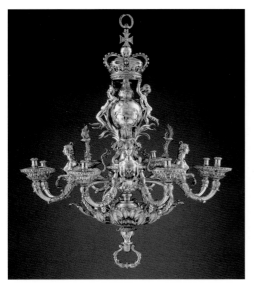

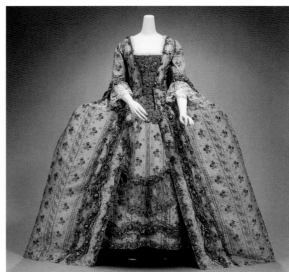

Chandelier

Germany (Hanover), 1736

Designed by **William Kent**, English, 1685–1748;
marked by **Balthasar Friedrich Behrens**, German,
1701–1760

George II was the second Hanoverian king of England.
This chandelier is one of five that he commissioned,
probably for the Leineschloss, the royal palace in
Hanover; the figure of a horse on the globe beneath
the sovereign's crown is the emblem of the House of
Hanover. The chandelier was designed in England by
William Kent and executed in Germany by the gold-
smith of the court of Hanover, who worked from a
wooden model carved after Kent's original design.

Kent was the first and most influential of the great
eighteenth-century English architect-designers, and
received many important commissions from the court
and the aristocracy, designing not only buildings but
also gardens, furniture, silver, paintings and their
frames, book illustrations, and theatrical productions.

Silver
H. 46½ in. (118.1 cm)
William Francis Warden Fund, Anonymous gift in memory of
Zoë Wilbour, Gift of Henry H. Fay, and Gift of W. K. Flint, by
exchange   1985.854

Woman's formal dress

France, about 1770

Opulent dress epitomized status and taste in the eighteenth century, when textiles and decorative trims
made from precious materials were extremely costly.
This extravagant French gown literally reshaped the
body of the woman who wore it. Tightly laced, boned
stays (corset) supported the bust and imposed an elegant posture, while wide side hoops (paniers) under
the skirt extended the hips by as much as four feet.

Silk and metallic thread; plain weave (tafetta) with warp float
patterning, brocaded with silk; applied metallic bobbin lace
and silk flowers
Overdress center front height: 58 in. (147.3 cm); Petticoat
center front height: 40⅛ in. (102 cm)
The Elizabeth Day McCormick Collection   43.643a–b

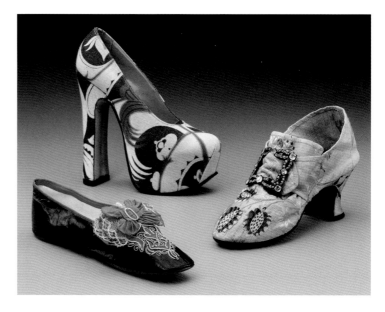

top left

Woman's shoe

England, 1991

Designed by **Vivienne Westwood,**
English, born in 1941

Cotton; printed twill

7⅞ x 3⅛ x 3⅜ in. (20 x 8 x 8.5 cm)

Textile Income Purchase Fund

2002.672.1–2

lower left

Woman's slipper

England (worn in America),
about 1850

Leather, silk plain weave (taffeta) and
lace, machine embroidery, silk satin,
cotton plain weave, metal buckle
(probably gold-plated brass)

2½ x 2¾ x 9¼ in. (6.5 x 7 x 23.7 cm)

Gift of Emily Welles Robbins (Mrs.
Harry Pelham Robbins) and the
Hon. Sumner Welles, in memory of
Georgiana Welles Sargent   49.1020a–b

right

Woman's buckle shoe

England, about 1770

Silk; plain weave with supplementary
patterning wefts; silk ribbon; leather;
linen lining

5 x 3⅛ x 9½ in. (12.5 x 8 x 24.2 cm)

Gift of Emily Welles Robbins (Mrs.
Harry Pelham Robbins) and the
Hon. Sumner Welles, in memory of
Georgiana Welles Sargent   49.1007a–b

Shoes have long been among the most important of women's fashion
accessories. These examples, dating from three different centuries, share
a use of luxurious materials and elaborate decoration that makes it clear
they were not made simply to protect feet from cold and wet. Made in
about 1770 of ribbed yellow silk brocaded with polychrome silk yarns,
the buckle shoe was worn in America by Mehetable Stoddard (Hylsop),
1719–1792. The flat slipper at lower left, made in England in the 1850s,
was called a "Chameleon shoe," a style that became popular in the middle
of the nineteenth century. Vivienne Westwood took the abstract pattern
on her 1991 platform shoe at top left directly from an eighteenth-century
brocaded silk damask fabric, known as a "bizarre silk," transforming the
elegant and exotic silk into a modern printed cotton denim.

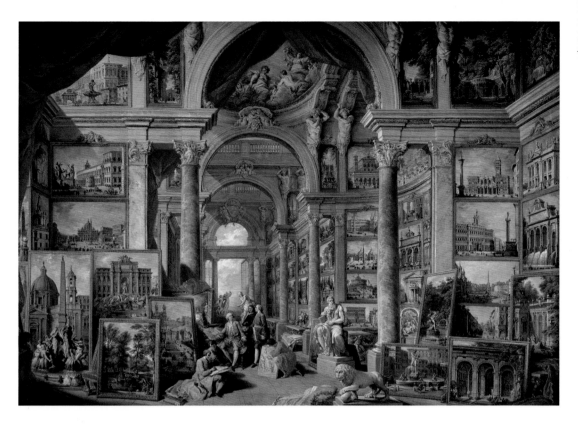

Giovanni Paolo Pannini
Italian (Rome), 1691–1765
Picture Gallery with Views of Modern Rome, 1757

Pannini, like his contemporary Canaletto in Venice, was trained as a stage
designer and became extremely successful painting images of Rome for
foreign visitors on the "Grand Tour." This enormous painting is one of
four views of ancient and modern Rome commissioned by the Duc de
Choiseul to commemorate his four years as French ambassador to the
Vatican. Here, in a theatrical and totally imaginary gallery, the duke sits
surrounded by plaster casts of sculptures by Michelangelo and Bernini
and detailed views (all painted, of course, by Pannini) of Saint Peter's
Square, the Trevi Fountain, the Spanish Steps, and other famous Roman
buildings, fountains, and monuments.

Oil on canvas
67 x 96¼ in. (170 x 244.5 cm)
Charles Potter Kling Fund   1975.805

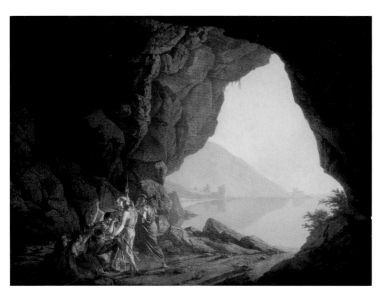

Joseph Wright of Derby
English, 1734–1797
***Grotto by the Seaside in the Kingdom of Naples with Banditti, Sunset**, 1778*

The first major English artist to make a successful career outside London, Wright painted portraits, landscapes, and images of contemporary life for the affluent middle class in his native Derby, who derived their wealth from the Industrial Revolution. In 1773, Wright made an extended trip to Italy where he sketched, in meticulous detail, the grottoes off the coast of Salerno, near Naples. After his return to England in 1775, he used these drawings to create paintings, like this one, that combine powerful observation and spectacular light effects with a sense of the sublime. The mysterious, moody figures (which the artist identified as "bandits") enhance this painting's haunting blend of reality and imagination.

Oil on canvas
48 x 68 in. (121.9 x 172.7 cm)
Charles H. Bayley Picture and Painting Fund and other Funds, by exchange   1990.95

The Richmond Race Cup
England (London), 1764
Designed by **Robert Adam**, Scottish, 1728–1792; marked by **Daniel Smith** and **Robert Sharp**, English, in partnership about 1763–1788

The form and ornament of this opulent trophy reflect the enthusiasm for classical antiquity sparked by mid-eighteenth-century excavations at the Roman sites of Herculaneum and Pompeii, which provided a wealth of previously unknown information about ancient architecture and decoration. This winner's cup was designed by Robert Adam, whose style—inspired and shaped by two years in Rome—introduced Neoclassicism to England. Commissioned by the stewards of the prestigious Richmond Gold Cup Race, this trophy was won by Silvio, a horse owned by John Hutton of Yorkshire.

Gilded silver
H. 19⅛ in. (48.6 cm)
Theodora Wilbour Fund in memory of Charlotte Beebe Wilbour and Frank Brewer Bemis Fund   1987.488a–b

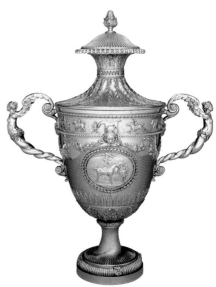

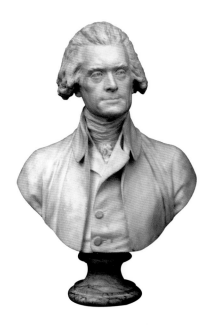

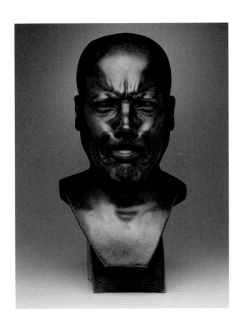

Jean-Antoine Houdon
French, 1741–1828
Thomas Jefferson, 1789

One of the greatest portrait sculptors, Houdon is
most celebrated for his psychologically acute and
technically superb images of famous contemporaries.
Thomas Jefferson (1743–1826) had recommended the
sculptor for a statue of George Washington in the Virginia state capitol years before. Jefferson was serving as American minister to France when he sat for
Houdon in Paris. Houdon first modeled the likeness in
clay, and then made a plaster cast that he used as the
model from which he created this marble version, the
most recognizable and enduring image of Jefferson. It
was the source of the presidential portrait on the 1801
Indian Peace Medal, for the Jefferson dollar (minted
in 1903), and for the nickel, as it was issued in 1938.

Marble
H. 22¼ x 18⅞ x 10¼ in. (56.5 x 48 x 26 cm)
George Nixon Black Fund 34.12

Franz Xaver Messerschmidt
Austrian, 1736–1783
A Hypochondriac, about 1775–80

Late in his life, Austrian sculptor Franz Xaver
Messerschmidt began a series of "Character Heads." His
goal was to record all the various grimaces and expres-
sions the human face was capable of making, and he
used himself as the template. Pinching himself below
the rib, Messerschmidt would observe his reaction in
a mirror and set out to capture it, working in alabaster
and metal alloys including lead, as is the case with this
head. Among the most enigmatic and moving works of
sculpture from the eighteenth century, Messerschmidt's
forty-nine surviving heads reflect both contemporary
fascination with physiognomy—the theoretical art of
judging character through the reading of facial expres-
sions—and the artist's own fragile emotional state. (He
had long been suffering from an undiagnosed ailment.)
A Hypochondriac was the first Messerschmidt work to
enter an American museum collection.

Lead
H. 16¾ in. (42.6 cm)
William E. Nickerson Fund, No. 2 57.117

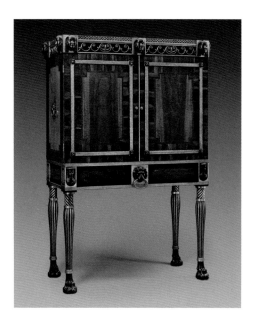

Cabinet on stand

England (London), about 1805
Attributed to **James Newton**, English, 1773–1821

In the late eighteenth and early nineteenth centuries, James Newton was among London's most fashionable cabinetmakers. His Neoclassical-style furniture appealed to aristocratic clients, who purchased his works for their homes in London and beyond. This imposing cabinet on stand was designed for a collector, for inside it features two banks of graduated drawers—particularly well suited to hold antique coins, medals, gems, and other small-scale works of art. In its decoration, it reflects up-to-the-moment taste for Egyptian motifs, inspired by Napoleon's recent campaign in Egypt and the flood of new information on Egyptian antiquities and monuments that entered Europe through illustrated publications in the first decades of the nineteenth century.

Oak, pine, and mahogany, veneered with satinwood, rosewood, tulipwood, ebony, and boxwood; partially ebonized and gilded; ivory, and brass
64 x 42½ x 19 in. (162.6 x 108 x 48.3 cm)
Gift of Horace Wood Brock in memory of George "Peabo" Gardner, Jr. 2006.1927

Grand piano

England (London), 1796
Manufactured by **John Broadwood and Son,** English, active 1795–1808
Case designed by **Thomas Sheraton**, English, 1751–1806
Satinwood, purpleheart, tulipwood, with cameos and medallions by **Josiah Wedgwood** and coin casts by **James Tassie**

Unequaled in its sumptuous Neoclassical ornamentation, this instrument was commissioned from England's leading piano maker by Manuel de Godoy, prime minister of Spain. It is the earliest extant piano with a range of six full octaves and the only piece known to have been specifically designed by the influential cabinetmaker Thomas Sheraton. The piano's decoration includes inlays of rare tropical woods, opaque glass-paste casts of ancient Greek coins, and cameos and medallions made of jasperware, a white porcelain invented by Josiah Wedgwood, the artist who raised English ceramics to an unprecedented level of artistic and commercial success.

97⅞ x 43⅞ x 3⅞ in. (248.7 x 111.5 x 91.2 cm)
From the George Alfred Cluett Collection, given by Florence Cluett Chambers 1985.924

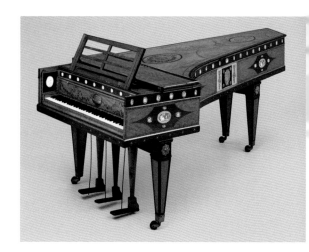

Bergère

France (Paris), 1787
Made by **Jean-Baptiste-Claude Sené**, French,
1747–1803

This bergère (an armchair with fully upholstered arms) is part of a suite of ten pieces of bedroom furniture purchased by Marc-Antoine Thierry de Ville d'Avray, administrator of the Garde-Meuble de la Coronne, the office responsible for furnishing royal residences. Intended for his bedroom, Thierry placed the order with craftsmen patronized by King Louis XVI and, for the upholstery, requisitioned yardages left over from the silk woven for the King's Gaming Room at Fontainebleau. Boston merchant James Swan, official agent for the French revolutionary government in the United States, acquired the set in exchange for grain, munitions, and other things the cash-poor French government desperately needed. This is the only complete suite of eighteenth-century French furniture in the United States.

Gilded beech, with reproduction silk upholstery
37¾ x 28¼ x 25½ in. (95.88 x 71.75 x 64.77 cm)
Bequest of Susan Howard Pickering   36.640

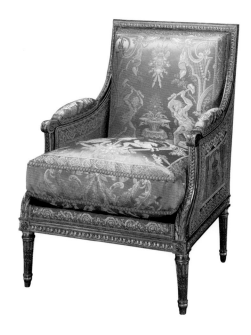

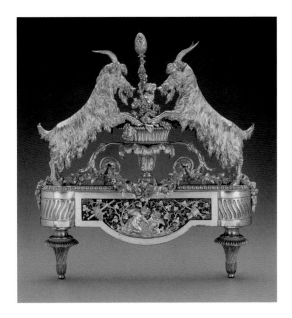

Andiron

France (Paris), about 1785
Attributed to **Pierre-Philippe Thomire**,
French, 1751–1843

This andiron (one of a pair in the Museum's collection) evokes the splendors of prerevolutionary France. It is made of bronze and coated with a thin layer of gold, a process involving the application of mercury that burned off in the firing, unwittingly exposing workers to the deadly effects of this toxic element.

These refined andirons are the work of Thomire, a prominent French bronzeworker, and the collaborative effort of many individual specialists in modeling, casting, chiseling, and gilding. The design features goats eating grapes from a basket while below them, against a background originally covered with blue enamel, two cherubs shear a ram. The andirons may have been made for the dining room of the Queen's Billiards House, part of Marie Antoinette's "rustic" village near the Palace of Versailles.

Gilt bronze, silver-plated copper plaque decorated with oil-based paint containing Prussian blue pigment
H. 19 in. (48.3 cm)
Bequest of Miss Elizabeth Howard Bartol   27.521.1–2

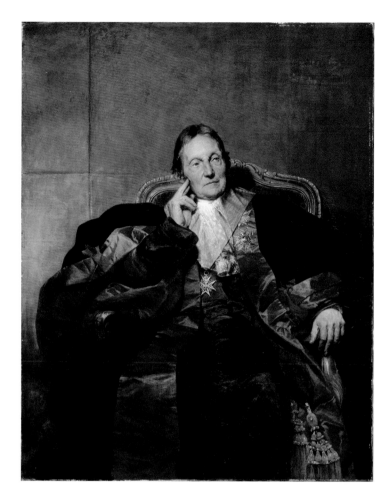

Hippolyte Delaroche
French, 1797-1856
Marquis de Pastoret, 1829

When Delaroche painted Pastoret (1756–1840), the marquis had just become chancellor of France, the culmination of a long career in public life. Commissioned by Pastoret's son from an artist best known for his detailed paintings of highly charged historical events, this image recalls aristocratic portraits of the seventeenth century in its scale and emphasis on Pastoret's voluminous robes. The marquis wears the insignia of a Grand Officer of the Order of Saint-Esprit and two medals (the Saint Andrew Cross and the Legion of Honor) on his lapel. This opulence is strikingly contrasted with the sitter's thoughtful pose and austere, unidealized face.

About a year after his portrait was painted, Pastoret was stripped of his honors for refusing allegiance to the new constitutional monarch, Louis Philippe. The change in political climate may explain why Pastoret's coat of arms (still faintly visible in the upper left corner) was removed from the painting.

Oil on canvas
61⅛ x 48¼ in. (155.3 x 122.6 cm)
Susan Cornelia Warren Fund and the Picture Fund   11.1449

Claude Michel, called **Clodion**

French, 1738–1814

The Flood, 1800

Clodion, who had benefited from royal patronage, fell out of favor during the French Revolution. Determined to reestablish his career,
the aging artist, who had previously specialized in small terra-cotta statues, exhibited
at the Paris Salon of 1801 a life-sized plaster
sculpture for which this superb terra-cotta
was a preparatory model. Balanced on a rocky
ledge surrounded by water, a man struggles
to save his son; behind him (not visible here)
is the half-submerged figure of a drowned
woman and her child. In conceiving a human
drama caused by a flood, Clodion was being
deliberately "modern," for recent scientific
discoveries suggested that earthquakes and
floods had played a major role in the forma-
tion of the planet.

Terra-cotta

21½ x 11 x 9 in. (54.5 x 27.9 x 22.9 cm)

John H. and Ernestine A. Payne Fund   1981.398

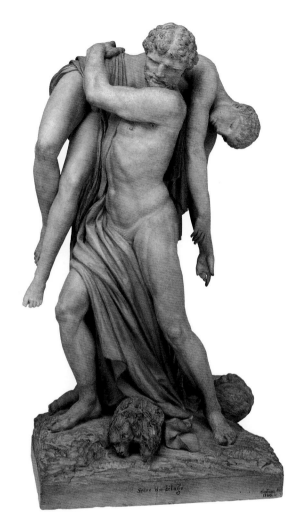

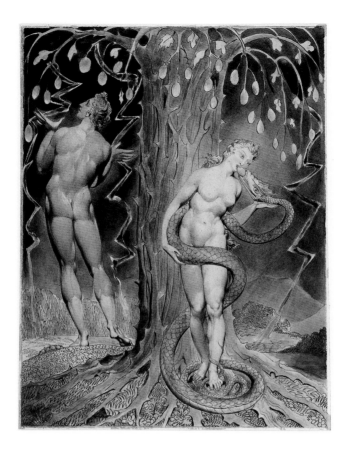

William Blake

English, 1757–1827

***The Temptation and Fall of Eve* (illustration to Milton's *Paradise Lost*)**, 1808

Living in a time he viewed as excessively confused and materialistic, Blake expressed his mystical, theological, and philosophical beliefs in visionary poetry, prints, and paintings. This watercolor illustrating a scene from John Milton's epic poem *Paradise Lost* is one of a set commissioned by Blake's loyal patron Thomas Butts. In the Bible, Adam and Eve were forbidden by God to eat fruit from the tree of the knowledge of good and evil. Like Milton, Blake specifically identifies the Fall of Man with the moment when Eve succumbs to temptation and takes the fruit from the mouth of the evil serpent. The sky is rent by lightning and the tree covered with thorns, as Blake expresses Milton's words: "Earth felt the wound, and Nature from her seat / Sighing through all her Works gave signs of woe / That all was lost."

Pen and watercolor on paper
19½ x 15¼ in. (49.7 x 38.7 cm)
Museum purchase with funds donated by contribution   90.99

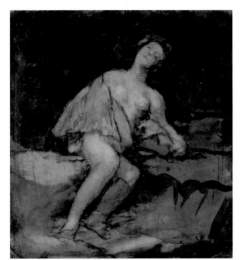

Francisco Goya y Lucientes
Spanish, 1746–1828
Reclining Nude, 1824–25

Goya's paintings, drawings, and prints, which range from official royal portraits to bitter satire on the foibles and atrocities of contemporary society, reflect the dramatically changing world in which he lived. Near the end of his life, Goya left Spain for France, arriving "deaf, old, clumsy, and weak . . . and so happy and wanting to experience life." It was during the winter of 1824 that he painted a group of tiny yet extraordinarily innovative paintings on thin sheets of ivory. According to a contemporary description, Goya "blackened the ivory plaque and let fall on it a drop of water which removed part of the black ground as it spread out, tracing random light areas. Goya took advantage of these traces and always turned them into something original and unexpected."

Carbon black, with watercolor and scratching, on ivory
Overall: 3½ x 3⅜ in. (8.7 x 8.6 cm)
Ernest Wadsworth Longfellow Fund   63.1081

Antonio Canova
Italian, 1757–1822
Bust of Beatrice, about 1819–22

Canova was arguably the greatest Neoclassical sculptor and the most famous artist of his day. He invented the "ideal head" about 1811 to capture his conception of perfect, timeless beauty. This bust began as a portrait of his friend, the famous beauty Juliette Récamier; her celebrated portrait by Jacques-Louis David is in the Louvre. Canova's original plaster bust did not please Récamier, and he abandoned the idea of carving the final marble. Instead, he idealized Récamier's features, transforming the bust into an imagined portrait of Beatrice, mythical muse of the medieval Italian poet, Dante. This precise and delicate bust—technically brilliant in the carving of spiraling hair, translucent veil, and softly textured flesh—is a work of evolutionary mastery, as the portrait of a real woman became an imaginative personification of a literary figure and the expression of Canova's ideal of beauty.

Marble
23 x 11 x 10 in. (58.4 x 27.9 x 25.4 cm)
William Francis Warden Fund, Edward J. and Mary S. Holmes Fund, John Lowell Gardner Fund, Russell B. and Andrée Beauchamp Stearns Fund, Helen B. Sweeney Fund, Frank B. Bemis Fund, Seth K. Sweetser Fund, H. E. Bolles Fund, Arthur Mason Knapp Fund, and Benjamin Pierce Cheney Donation 2002.318

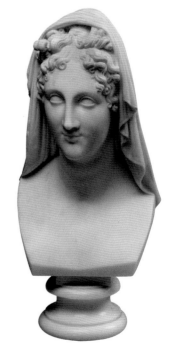

Mask fan

England, made for the Spanish market, 1740s

Paper leaf (double), patched with skin, etched, engraved, and painted in watercolor; ivory sticks, pierced, partially painted, varnished and gilded; mother-of-pearl buttons on brass rivet

Maximum open: 19 ⅛ in. (48.5 cm)

Oldham Collection   1976.179

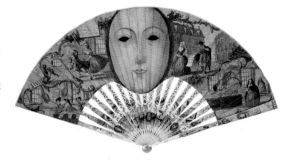

Brisé fan depicting Gothic church ruins

England, about 1825

Horn blades, painted in watercolor and gilded; silk connecting ribbon; paste studs at rivet

Maximum open: 13 in. (33 cm)

Oldham Collection   1976.317

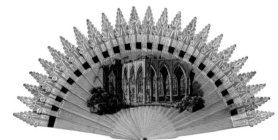

Brisé fan

Possibly Italy, 1810–30

Silver filigree blades with silk connecting ribbon; silver washer and filigree ring

Maximum open: 14 ⅜ in. (36.5 cm)

Oldham Collection   1976.354

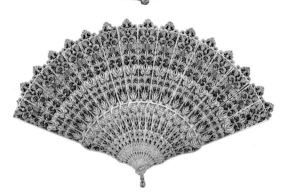

The fan, more than all other fashion accessories to elegant dress, was an essential part of the rituals of the arts of conversation and flirtation. The English writer James Addison commented in 1711: "Women are armed with fans as men with swords and sometimes do more execution with them." First introduced into European court circles in the late sixteenth century, fans are wonderfully varied both in the materials of which they are made and their decoration, which ranges from biblical scenes to famous architectural landmarks and the words of popular songs. Some examples feature masks with eye openings and can be held to provocatively conceal the user's identity. Brisé (broken, in French) fans, constructed without connecting leaves of paper or skin, were inspired by Japanese examples. The intricate, silver brisé fan shown here belonged to Marie Louise, second wife of Napoleon I. It survives with its original leather case, stamped with a crown and its owner's initials.

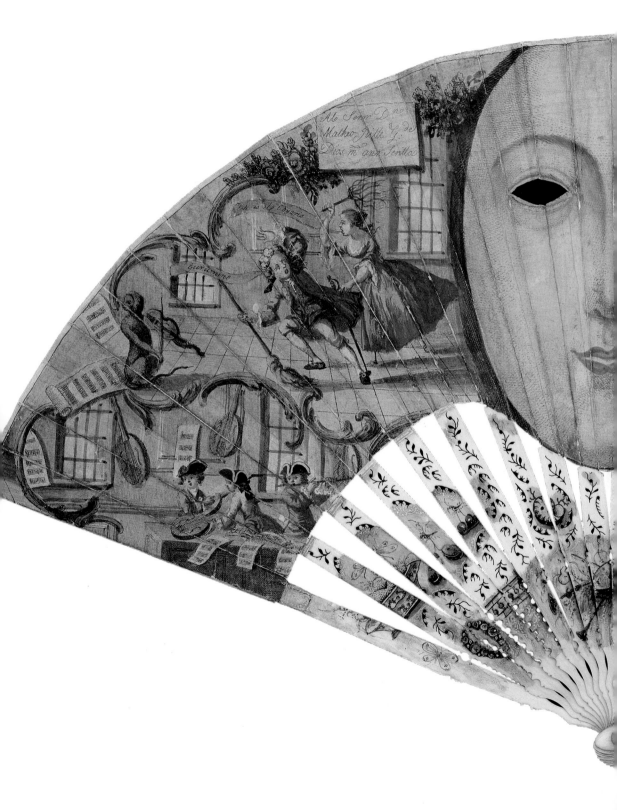

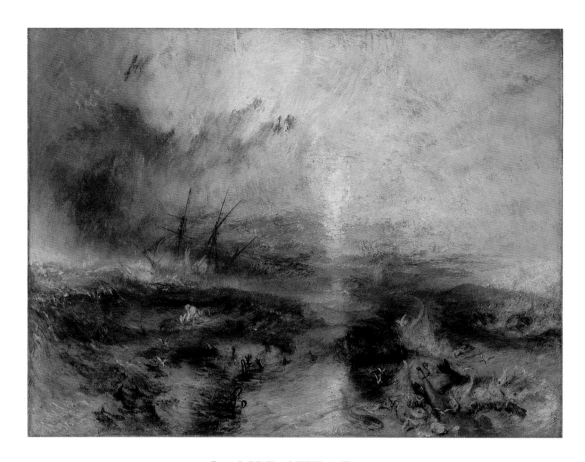

Joseph Mallord William Turner

English, 1775–1851

Slave Ship (Slavers Throwing Overboard the Dead and Dying, Typhoon Coming On), 1840

One of Turner's most celebrated paintings, *Slave Ship* was inspired by an eighteenth-century poem and by the true story of an English ship, traveling in 1781 from Africa to Jamaica. The captain of this ship threw overboard 132 sick slaves because he could collect insurance money for slaves "lost at sea," but not for those who died from disease. Although the limbs and chains of the victims are discernible in the foreground, Turner focuses on the terrifying power of nature and the merging of churning sea and livid sky. The painting was owned for almost thirty years by art critic John Ruskin who stated: "If I were reduced to rest Turner's immortality upon any single work, I should choose this."

Oil on canvas
35¾ x 48¼ in. (90.8 x 122.6 cm)
Henry Lillie Pierce Fund   99.22

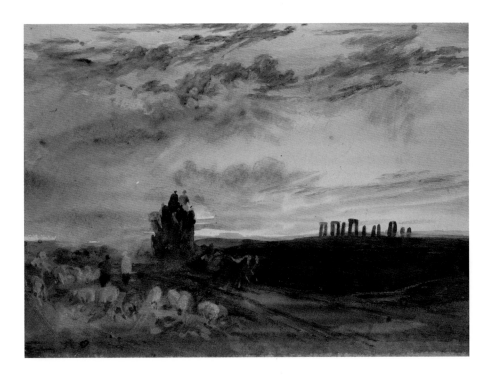

Joseph Mallord William Turner
English, 1775–1851
Stonehenge at Daybreak, about 1811

Turner had equal command of oil and of watercolor but favored the latter
when working outdoors, rendering directly and spontaneously the changing qualities of atmosphere and light. This drawing is one of many studies
he made specifically to be engraved for his *Liber studiorum*, a compila-
tion of landscapes—long regarded as his most important achievement—
which occupied the artist for over a decade. Here, dramatically silhouetted
on the horizon, is Stonehenge, a mysterious circle of massive, ancient
stones on Salisbury Plain in southern England. Turner loved such picturesque and romantic subjects, and he captured the essence of Stonehenge's
grandeur and monumentality in this small image.

Brush and brown wash over graphite pencil on paper
7⅝ x 10⅝ in. (19.4 x 27 cm)
Anonymous gift   59.795

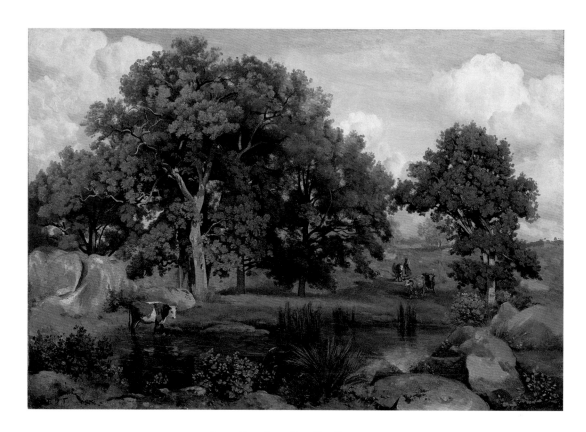

Jean-Baptiste-Camille Corot
French, 1796–1875
Forest of Fontainebleau, 1846

Beginning in the 1820s, Corot spent summers sketching in the vast Forest
of Fontainebleau, south of Paris. He based this painting on such informal
sketches, reworking them to create a more structured composition, with
the horizontals of foreground and background balanced by the verticals
of trees and the cows positioned to mark recession into space. Nevertheless, as a depiction of a familiar local site without the "justification" of
a biblical or mythological subject, this painting became a pivotal work
in the development of French landscape painting when it was accepted
for the Salon of 1846. Corot believed that artists "must . . . never lose the
first impression that quickened our emotion." His work formed a bridge
between traditional, idealizing landscapes and those of the Impressionists, to whom Corot was a mentor and an inspiration.

Oil on canvas
35½ x 50¾ in. (90.2 x 128.8 cm)
Gift of Mrs. Samuel Dennis Warren   90.199

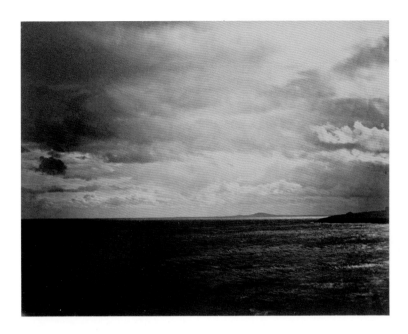

Gustave Le Gray
French, 1820–1884
Cloudy Sky—The Mediterranean with Mount Agde, 1857

Gustave Le Gray's majestic ocean views stunned his contemporaries.
Early photographers had struggled to record the lighter tonalities of sky
and the darker earth in the same picture. Le Gray, a pioneer of photographic techniques, solved this problem by adding a second negative,
carefully piecing it into the image along the horizon line in the printing
process. Printed on a scale that was large for the time, photographs such
as this view of Mount Agde, taken along France's Mediterranean coast,
possess a visual power that brought Le Gray international praise. They
also reflect the photographer's interest in the painterly possibilities of
his medium, with an intensity and drama that evoke the sense of awe
found in Late Romantic art.

Photograph, albumen print from two wet collodion-on-glass negatives
12¼ x 15⅝ in. (31.1 x 39.7 cm)
Gift of Charles W. Millard III in honor of Clifford S. Ackley   1997.241

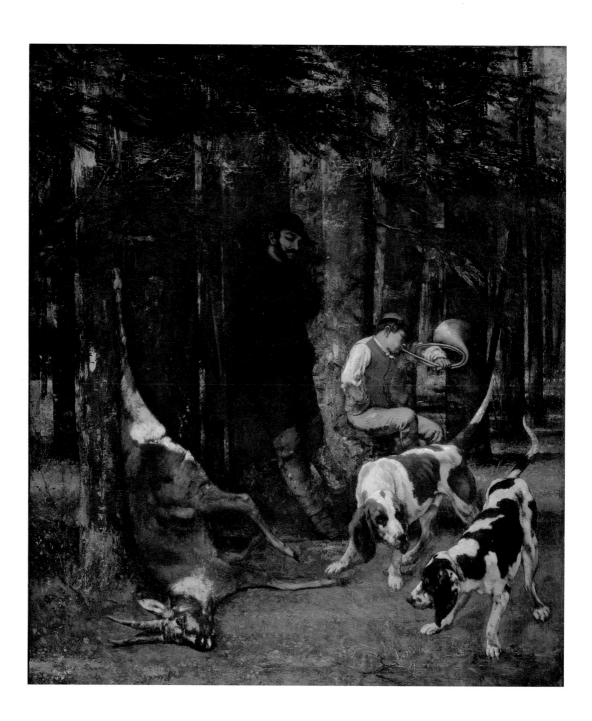

opposite
Gustave Courbet
French, 1819–1877
The Quarry (La Curée), 1856

Courbet was the self-styled
leader of the Realist movement in
French art. Most of his paintings
of modern life were condemned
as offensively ordinary, but *The
Quarry* was well received when it
was exhibited at the Salon of 1857.
Probably set in the Jura Mountains
along the French-Swiss border,
the painting features the artist
himself, posed as a huntsman.
He enlarged the original canvas
as he worked, adding one piece
across the top above the hunter's
head and others to include the
horn blower and the dogs. In 1866
when he learned that *The Quarry*
had been purchased by a group
of young Boston artists, Courbet
exclaimed: "What care I for the
Salon, what care I for honors, when
the art students of a new and great
country know and appreciate and
buy my works?"

Oil on canvas
82¾ x 72¼ in. (210.2 x 183.5 cm)
Henry Lillie Pierce Fund   18.620

Eugène Delacroix
French, 1798–1863
The Lamentation (Christ at the Tomb), 1848

Against a deep and somber landscape, desolate mourners gather around
the body of Christ. Delacroix's use of resonant color and expressive,
sketchy brushwork had a profound influence on later painters, including the Impressionists. Although Delacroix constantly struggled with
his personal spiritual beliefs, American writer and critic Henry James
called this "the only modern religious picture I have seen that seemed to
me to be painted in good faith." Delacroix himself wrote that "the whole
arouses an emotion that astonishes even me."

Oil on canvas
64 x 52 in. (162.6 x 132.1 cm)
Gift by contribution in memory of Martin Brimmer   96.21

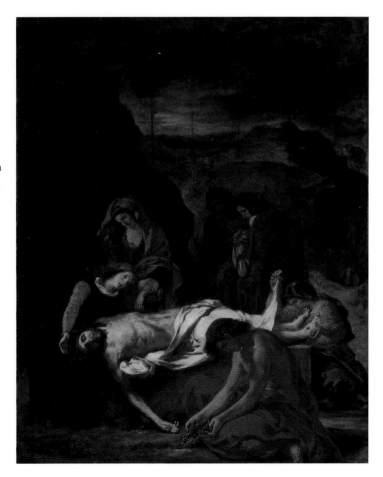

Jean-François Millet

French, 1814–1875

The Sower, 1850

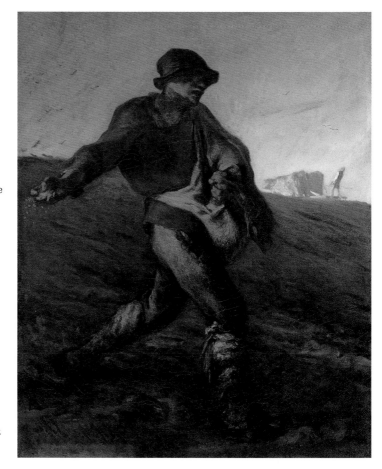

Striding across broken ground, a peasant sows winter wheat in the cold November twilight. Behind him, an ox-drawn harrow closes the soil over the grain. This painting's dark, heavily worked surface inspired one critic to write that the artist "seemed to paint with the very earth that is being planted." Millet said that he was "driven to make pictures that mattered," and his art was revolutionary in its assertion that the commonplace activities of ordinary people were worthy subjects for serious art. France's Revolution of 1848 had granted the vote to all male citizens, including the landless peasants who vastly outnumbered landowners. Although Millet insisted that his art was not political, many Parisians found this powerful, shadowed figure threatening when the painting was exhibited at the Salon of 1850. One writer saw the peasant as sowing not wheat but "the seeds of discord and revolution." In the 1850s, long before Millet was widely appreciated in his homeland, Boston artists and collectors traveled to France to meet the artist and purchase his works. The Museum acquired its world-famous holdings of Millet's work through the generosity of these foresighted collectors, in particular Martin Brimmer, the Museum's first president; local artist William Morris Hunt; and collector Quincy Adams Shaw.

Oil on canvas
40 x 32½ in. (101.6 x 82.6 cm)
Gift of Quincy Adams Shaw through Quincy Adams Shaw, Jr. and Mrs. Marian Shaw Haughton   17.1485

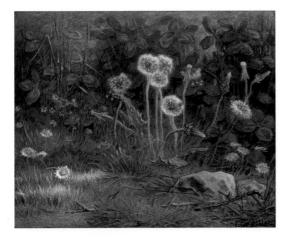

Jean-François Millet
French, 1814–1875
Dandelions, 1867–68

Millet frequently worked in pastel, which allowed him to combine his love of drawing and painting. Indeed, after 1865 he made almost as many pastels as oil paintings, thanks to an admiring patron, Parisian architect and financier Emile Gavet, who was prepared to buy every pastel that Millet produced. Here, against a richly variegated green background, Millet presents the life of a common wildflower, from tight buds to airy bursts of white-plumed seeds. Not a conventional still life, *Dandelions* is a landscape—a close-up view of a small patch of meadow that might otherwise be overlooked.

Pastel on tan wove paper
16 x 19¾ in. (40.6 x 50.2 cm)
Gift of Quincy Adams Shaw through
Quincy Adams Shaw, Jr. and
Mrs. Marian Shaw Haughton   17.1524

Dante Gabriel Rossetti
English, 1828–1882
Bocca Baciata (Lips That Have Been Kissed), 1859

Rossetti was a founding member, in 1848, of the Pre-Raphaelite Brotherhood, which sought to counteract the eclecticism and excess of the mid-nineteenth century by returning to the simplicity of medieval art. His works in the new style are detailed, story-telling images drawn from the Bible, the writings of Dante, or the legends of King Arthur. This painting, however, represents a turning point in Rossetti's career—the first example of the subject that was to occupy him for the rest of his life. The painting depicts a sensual young woman with loosened hair and a distant, unfocused gaze. There is no story here, no clue to the painting's meaning. The poet Algernon Swinburne declared that *Bocca Baciata* was "more stunning than can be decently expressed," and many others recognized it as an assertion that a work of art might be only beautiful, without any obligation to moralize or instruct.

Oil on panel
12⅝ x 10⅝ in. (32.1 x 27 cm)
Gift of James Lawrence   1980.261

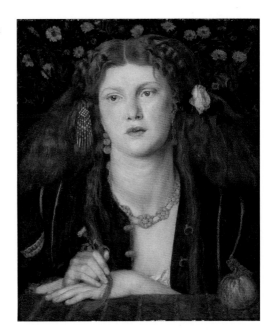

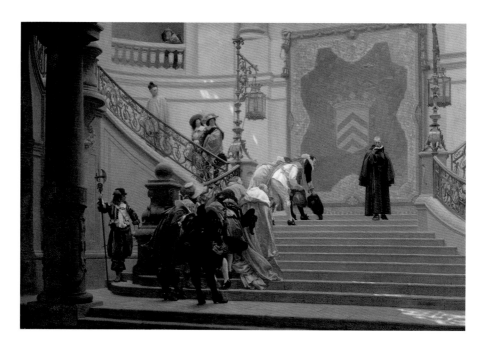

Jean-Léon Gérôme
French, 1824–1904
L'Eminence Grise, 1873

Gérôme's paintings—with their precise detail, imperceptible brushwork, and brilliant effects of color and light—epitomized the admired and officially sanctioned academic style that prevailed throughout Europe in the later nineteenth century. This wonderfully theatrical painting recreates the grand staircase of the palace of Cardinal Richelieu (the Red Cardinal) who ruled France during the childhood of Louis XIII in the early seventeenth century. Descending the staircase is Richelieu's secretary and confidant, François LeClerc du Trembly, a friar known as *l'éminence grise* (the Gray Cardinal), a term that has come to mean "the power behind the throne." Framed by a huge tapestry bearing Richelieu's coat of arms, the friar reads his prayer book, ignoring the obsequious bows and resentful glances of the courtiers, whose opulent dress contrasts strikingly with his own sober garments.

Oil on canvas
27 x 39¾ in. (68.5 x 101 cm)
Bequest of Susan Cornelia Warren   03.605

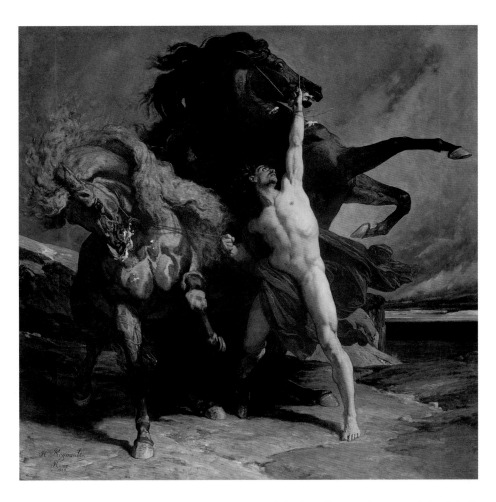

Henri Regnault
French, 1843–1871
Automedon with the Horses of Achilles, 1868

Full of youthful fire and passion, this mammoth painting—more than ten feet square—was painted while Regnault, the son of the director of the Sèvres porcelain manufactory, was a student in Rome. Several years later, the artist returned home to fight in the Franco-Prussian War and was killed during the siege of Paris at the age of twenty-seven. Derived from Homer's epic, the *Iliad*, the painting depicts Automedon, chariot driver for Achilles, struggling to control Xanthos and Balios, the horses that will carry the Greek hero into his final, fatal battle. Exhibited around the United States in the 1870s and 1880s, the painting was called both "the grandest painting in America" and "highly seasoned and unhealthful food which renders the palette insensitive to the milder flavors of what is wholesome." Following petitions by Boston artists and art students, this work was purchased by public subscription and presented to the Museum in 1890.

Oil on canvas
124 x 129½ in. (315 x 329 cm)
Museum purchase with funds donated by contribution 90.152

All encyclopedic collections of prints are measured both by the depth of their holdings and by individual works of superb artistic quality or rarity. These drypoints (below) are by the printmaker known as the Master of the Amsterdam Cabinet, one of the first to explore the medium for artistic purposes. These images, which demonstrate a remarkable ability to create natural poses and a convincing illusion of three-dimensional form, are among very few surviving examples. Similarly, the Museum's fine impression of Goya's *The Giant*, among the most enigmatic and compelling of the Spanish artist's graphic works, is a highlight of the collection.

On the other hand, one of the primary characteristics of printmaking is that many images — subtly or dramatically different — can be made by inking, printing, or otherwise altering the same woodblock, etching or engraving plate, lithographic stone, or silkscreen. Many printmakers value this ability to create variations on a theme, printing a composition and then modifying it by adding or removing lines, or by simply changing the colors of the ink, printing the image on papers of contrasting colors or textures, or wiping the ink in different ways to alter the balance of light and dark.

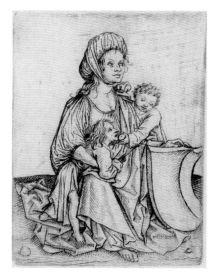
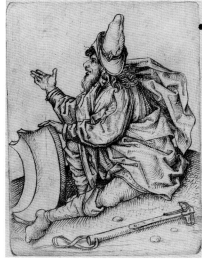

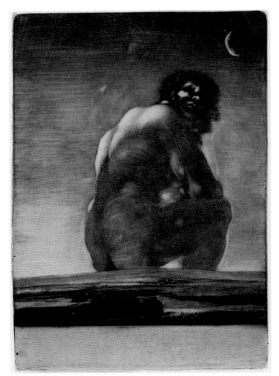

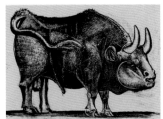

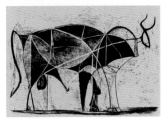

From works by Dürer and Rembrandt to Jim Dine, the Museum's collection embraces this evidence of the creative process. Many examples of individual prints allow viewers to explore, evaluate, and learn by comparison. As an example, at right are six images of a bull that Pablo Picasso created on the same lithographic stone. Each one is beautiful and interesting in its own right; together, they provide the opportunity, in a sense, to look over the artist's shoulder as he worked reductively from a detailed rendering of the animal's outward appearance to its essential structure, captured in a few swift lines.

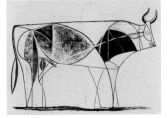

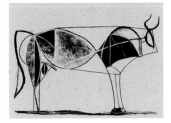

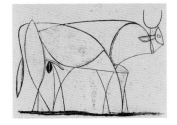

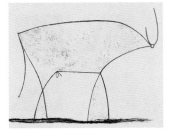

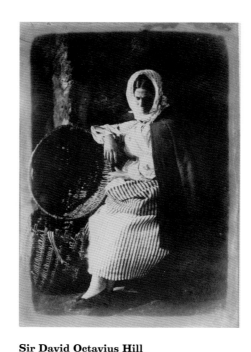

Sir David Octavius Hill
Scottish, 1802–1870
Robert Adamson
Scottish, 1821–1848
Elizabeth Johnstone, Seated Newhaven Fishwife, 1843–48

The early photographic process of calotype, unstable and difficult to control, was nevertheless capable of effects of great beauty. Intrigued by its possibilities, Hill and Adamson formed a remarkable collaboration, and in less than four years they produced three thousand calotypes described by a contemporary as "the wonder of every gathering of scientific or artistic men." Their most innovative project—which effectively invented social documentary photography—was a series of photographs of the fishermen and -women in the village of Newhaven, just north of Edinburgh. The fishwives, famous for their good looks and picturesque dress, cleaned the catch and carried it to market in huge baskets. In portraits like this one, where broad areas of light and dark are skillfully juxtaposed, the photographers created small works that are nevertheless monumental in feeling.

Photograph, salt print from calotype negative
8⅜ x 6¼ in. (21.3 x 15.9 cm)
Purchased with funds given by David Bakalar   1974.469

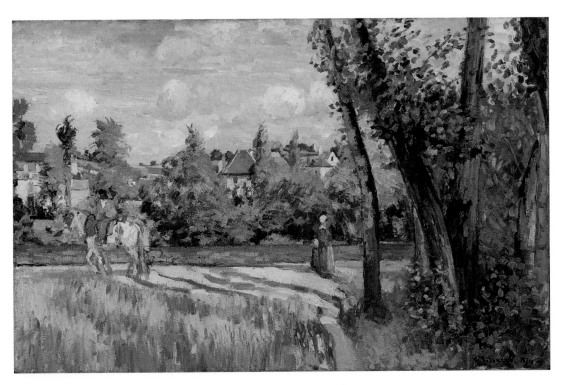

Camille Pissarro

French (born in the Danish West Indies), 1830–1903

Sunlight on the Road, Pontoise, 1874

Somewhat older than the other French Impressionists, Pissarro was an early leader of the group and later an important mentor to Cézanne and Gauguin. This serene view of a village near Paris, with its fresh palette and broad brushwork, exemplifies Impressionist painting at the time of the group's first exhibition in 1874. Typical of Pissarro, the painting is not only direct and spontaneous but carefully structured around a series of horizontal bands punctuated by the verticals of the trees and animated by the woman and horseman making their way along the road.

Oil on canvas

20⅝ x 32⅛ in. (52.4 x 81.5 cm)

Juliana Cheney Edwards Collection   25.114

Edouard Manet

French, 1832–1883

Street Singer, about 1862

Manet was one of the first great painters of modern urban life. One day, while walking through the streets of Paris, he saw a woman with a guitar emerging from a modest café. He asked her to pose for him, but she laughed and ran away. Although *Street Singer* was ultimately created in the studio using a professional model (eighteen-year-old Victorine Meurent), it retains the impact of Manet's initial experience— including the swiftly brushed glimpse of a petticoat as the woman lifts her skirt, her enig-matic expression, and the blurred impression of an aproned waiter beyond the swinging doors.

In this large painting, Manet gave a humble member of the working class great dignity, but most contemporary critics found the work vulgar and offensive.

Oil on canvas
67⅜ x 41⅝ in. (171.1 x 105.8 cm)
Bequest of Sarah Choate Sears in memory of her husband, Joshua Montgomery Sears   66.304

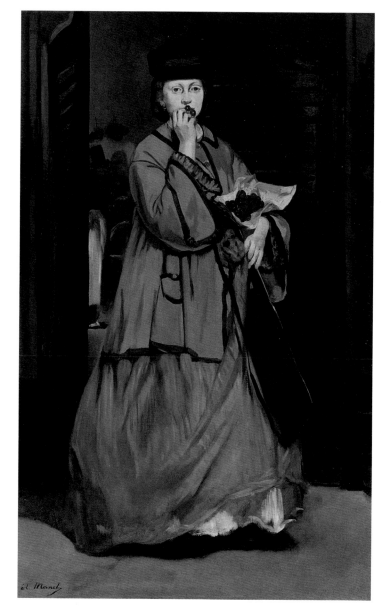

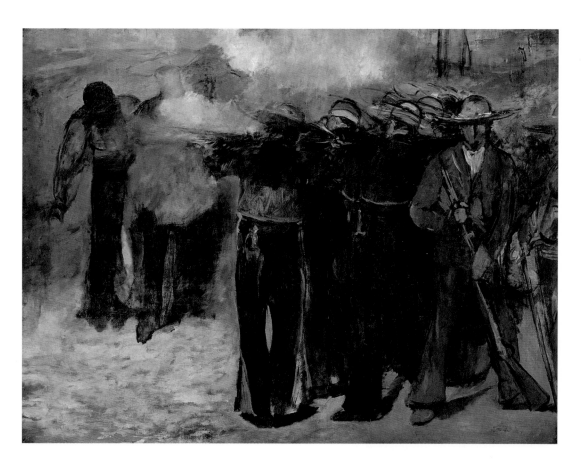

Edouard Manet
French, 1832–1883
***Execution of the Emperor Maximilian**, 1867*

In 1864 Maximilian, brother of the emperor of Austria, was installed as emperor of Mexico under the protection of the French emperor Napoleon III and a French army of occupation. In 1867, however, Napoleon suddenly withdrew his support and his troops, and Maximilian was captured and executed by Mexican forces loyal to their former government. When the shocking news reached Paris, Manet—a republican and fervent critic of the French empire—decided to immortalize this event on a scale traditionally reserved for scenes from history or the Bible. Basing his composition on photographs and eyewitness accounts, the artist worked for almost two years, producing four oil paintings and a lithograph of the subject. This immediate and impassioned painting is the first, unfinished version.

Oil on canvas
77⅛ x 102¼ in. (195.9 x 259.7 cm)
Gift of Mr. and Mrs. Frank Gair Macomber   30.444

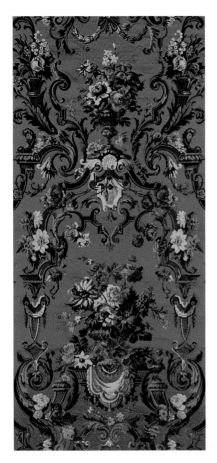

Furnishing panel
France (Lyon), about 1860–80

This is one of thirty-three woven silk furnishing panels in the Museum's collection that were made in the nineteenth century at the Mathevon et Bouvard factory. Founded in 1750, Mathevon et Bouvard was the most prestigious silk-weaving company of Lyon, France's center of textile production during the 19th century. The firm provided interior decoration for palaces throughout Europe; for royalty in Germany, Denmark, Spain, Russia, Britain, Egypt, and Morocco; and for private clients that included Sarah Bernhardt and members of the Rothschild family. The designs of these textiles reflect the period's fascination with historical styles, but the fabrics also reflect the burgeoning industrial era in which they were made. The remarkable colors are the result of chemical dyes, and these were among the outstanding productions of the innovative Jacquard loom, introduced about 1800, which allowed increasingly complex patterns and subtle shading.

Silk; velvet
25¾ x 61½ in. (65.5 x 156.2 cm)
John H. and Ernestine A. Payne Fund   1987.110

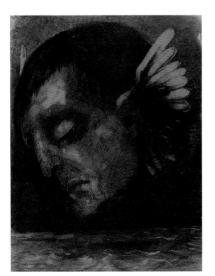

Odilon Redon
French, 1840–1916
Tears (Les pleurs), 1878

During the late 1870s, Redon—a foremost Symbolist artist—began to work with charcoal to express and exorcise the visions and dreams that haunted him. He was drawn to charcoal's extensive tonal range and to its rich black, which he called "the most essential color." Redon referred to his large, elaborately worked charcoal drawings as his *noirs* (blacks). This powerful, mysterious work is a major example of the *noirs*, many of which depict floating heads or eyes, which seem to be images of the artist's inner, seeking self.

Charcoal with touches of white watercolor on paper
17½ x 14 in. (44.5 x 35.6 cm)
Sophie M. Friedman Fund and funds donated by Ruth V. S. Lauer in memory of Julia Wheaton Saines, and Susan Bennett, Claire and Richard Morse, and partial gift of Elizabeth Marshall Thomas and John K. Marshall   2005.199

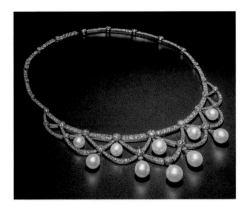

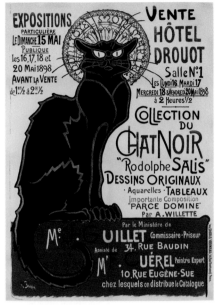

Pearl and diamond necklace
Europe, about 1880

This necklace represents the height of fashion during the late nineteenth century. It features ten extraordinary natural pearls — large, immensely costly, matched for color, shape, and size. It likely took years, if not decades, to assemble them for this necklace. Each pearl is removable, so the ornament can also be worn as an all-diamond necklace.

A personal and portable treasure, as well as a family heirloom, it was owned in the twentieth century by Baroness Clarice de Rothschild, a member of the Vienna branch of the important banking family. At the time of the Anschluss, Nazi Germany's annexation of Austria, in 1938, Rothschild was in London with her husband, Alphonse. She had taken this necklace with her on the voyage, and as a result it was not confiscated by the Nazis. A quintessential example of the Rothschild taste, it is, surprisingly, not signed by its maker or retailer.

Silver, gold, pearls, diamonds
7¼ x 5⅞ x ½ in. (18.5 x 15 x 1.2 cm)
Gift of the heirs of Bettina Looram de Rothschild
2013.1774

Théophile-Alexandre Steinlen
French (born in Switzerland), 1859–1923
Collection of the Chat Noir, 1898

In the 1890s Le Chat Noir (The Black Cat) was an innovative Montmartre cabaret, famous for its shadow plays, poetry readings, and concerts that attracted both Parisian artists and members of high society. Rodolphe Salis was the owner of Le Chat Noir, and Steinlen — who lived in Montmartre and made many posters for its artists, entertainers, and cabaret owners — first designed this bold and arresting poster to advertise the shows that brought Montmartre to Europe and North Africa every summer. Like many such ventures, Le Chat Noir could not survive the death of its founder, and it folded in 1897 after sixteen years. This poster is Steinlen's reworking of the original to announce the sale of Salis's art collection. The integration of text and image is particularly striking. Steinlen had a strong (but not sentimental) affection for cats, as is clear in this iconic image. In the cat's halo are the words "Montjoye Montmartre."

Poster, color lithograph
54⅞ x 39⅓ in. (139.4 x 99.1 cm)
Ernest Wadsworth Longfellow Fund and partial gift of James
A. Lapides 2002.62

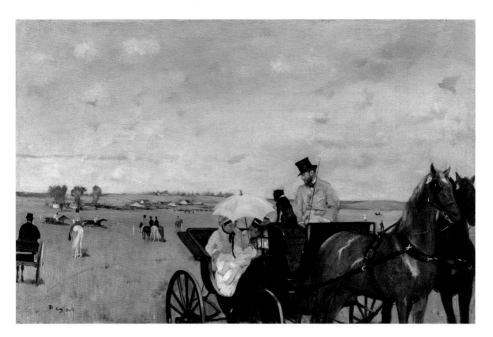

Edgar Degas

French, 1834–1917

At the Races in the Countryside, 1869

Degas's paintings were often inspired by the amuse-
ments that he enjoyed as a well-to-do Parisian: the
opera, the ballet, art exhibitions, and horse racing. Like many of his compositions, this painting
of a racecourse in Normandy, shown at the first
Impressionist exhibition in 1874, is artfully structured so as to appear as casual as a snapshot.
Grouped informally in the foreground are Degas's
friend Paul Valpinçon, his wife, and their infant son in
the arms of his wet nurse. Their carriage and horses
are cut off at the edges of the canvas in a radical
crop of the scene. The abrupt juxtaposition of objects
near and far away and the contrast of indistinct and
sharply focused forms are other features that give this
painting its revolutionary effect of spontaneity.

Oil on canvas
14⅜ x 22 in. (36.5 x 55.9 cm)
1931 Purchase Fund   26.790

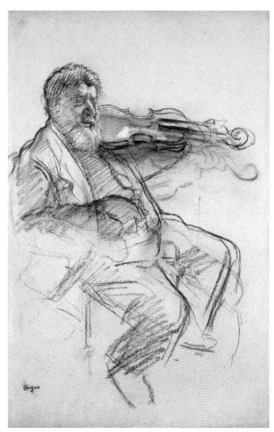

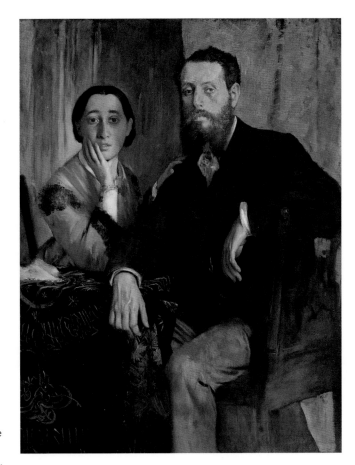

opposite, bottom

Edgar Degas

French, 1834–1917

The Violinist, about 1879

Degas's father was an accomplished organist, and the artist
had a deep love and appreciation
of music. During the 1870s he frequently attended rehearsals of the
orchestra and ballet of the Paris
Opéra, sketching the performers at
work, often as preparatory studies for paintings. This study is for
the violinist in *The Rehearsal,* a
painting of a ballet practice now
in the Frick Collection, New York.
Although sketchy and spontaneous, the drawing is rich in tonal
variations and bold line, the fall
of light rendered with accents of
white chalk. Degas captures with
remarkable facility the progression of arms and instrument as
they move from one position to
the next.

Charcoal heightened with white chalk
on blue-gray paper
18⅞ x 12 in. (47.9 x 30.5 cm)
William Francis Warden Fund 58.1263

Edgar Degas

French, 1834–1917

Edmondo and Thérèse Morbilli, about 1865

This intriguing double portrait shows Degas's sister Thérèse and her
husband, Edmondo Morbilli, their first cousin, whom she married in 1863.
While never a professional portraitist, Degas created numerous images of
family and friends in which he explored personality through pose, gesture,
and the subtleties of facial expression. Here, Edmondo, self-assured and
at ease, physically dominates the composition, while Thérèse, more intro-
spective, one hand resting on her husband's shoulder, is partly in shadow,
the details of her clothing a little blurred, as if out of focus. Although the
composition suggests the formal, sixteenth-century portraits Degas had
studied in Italy, the neutral background, shallow space, and overlapping
poses are typical of contemporary daguerreotype photographs.

Oil on canvas
45⅞ x 34¾ in. (116.5 x 88.3 cm)
Gift of Robert Treat Paine, 2nd 31.33

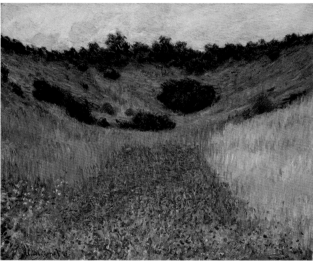

Claude Monet

French, 1840–1926

***Rouen Cathedral Facade and Tour d'Albane
(Morning Effect)**, 1894*

Monet's series paintings of the 1890s—multiple
variations of a single motif conceived, executed, and
exhibited as a group—are among his most inventive and remarkable works. In the winter of 1892 the
artist spent several months studying and painting
the facade of Rouen Cathedral in his native Normandy. From rooms facing the cathedral across a
square, Monet concentrated on the analysis of light
and its effects on the forms of the facade, changing
from one canvas to another as the day progressed.
Later he extensively reworked the thirty paintings
of the cathedral series in his studio at Giverny. Their
encrusted surfaces of dry, thickly layered paint evoke
the rough texture of weathered stone, absorbing and
reflecting light like the walls of the cathedral itself.

Oil on canvas
41¾ x 29⅛ in. (106.1 x 73.9 cm)
Tompkins Collection — Arthur Gordon Tompkins Fund   24.6

Claude Monet

French, 1840–1926

***Poppy Field in a Hollow near Giverny**, 1885*

Monet and his fellow Impressionists believed that
art should express its own time and place and that
it should do so in an appropriately modern style. In
the 1860s and 1870s, working primarily outdoors, the
Impressionists observed that objects seen in strong
light lose definition and appear to blend into one
another. No clear outlines exist in this sunny landscape. Its forms and textures are suggested by the
size, shape, and direction of the brushstrokes, and the
juxtaposition of complementary reds and greens gives
the painting a vibrant intensity. By the mid-1880s,
most members of the original group had turned away
from Impressionism, but Monet declared: "I am still
an Impressionist and will always remain one."

Oil on canvas
25⅝ x 32 in. (65.2 x 81.2 cm)
Juliana Cheney Edwards Collection   25.106

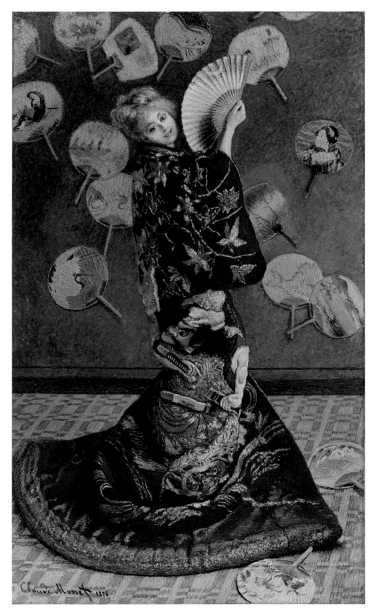

Claude Monet

French, 1840–1926

La Japonaise (**Camille Monet in Japanese Costume**), 1876

The quintessential Impression-ist landscape painter, Monet executed only a handful of major figure paintings. This life-size portrait, a great success at the second Impressionist exhibition in 1876, is a virtuoso display of color and texture as well as a witty comment on the current enthusi-asm—which Monet shared—for all things Japanese. The seemingly coy model is Monet's wife, Camille, who wears a blond wig to empha-size her Western identity and holds a fan with the colors of the French flag. On one of the Japanese fans decorating the background wall, a woman in traditional cos-tume casts the impostor a startled look, while the clever arrangement of the splendid robe animates the fierce warrior embroidered on it.

Oil on canvas
91¼ x 56 in. (231.8 x 142.3 cm)
1951 Purchase Fund   56.147

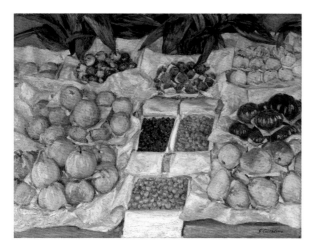

Gustave Caillebotte
French, 1848–1894
Fruit Displayed on a Stand, about 1881–82

Although less well known than other French Impressionists, Caillebotte was one of the style's most original practitioners and a major promoter and collector of Impressionist art. Often attracted by unusual vantage points and innovative manipulation of space, his close-up view of a fruit vendor's wares enticingly arranged on rumpled paper was described by a contemporary critic as "still life freed from its routine." It is a memorable composition of complementary shapes and colors that gives an immediate sense of a display glimpsed along a Parisian street.

Oil on canvas
30⅛ x 39⅝ in. (76.5 x 100.6 cm)
Fanny P. Mason Fund in memory of Alice Thevin   1979.196

opposite, left
Gustave Caillebotte
French, 1848–1894
Man at His Bath, 1884

A member (and major patron) of the Impressionist circle of artists, Gustave Caillebotte tended to paint real Parisian men and women—out and about on the streets of the city or, as here, in more private realms. A lone bather stands with his back to us in a sparse room with only a few ordinary furnishings: bathmat and tub, chair with clothes on it and boots nearby. A dressing gown lies on the floor near his feet. In contrast to the heroic male nudes of earlier generations of painters, Caillebotte's man is starkly unidealized; fresh from his bath, he dries himself vigorously, leaving his hair standing on end. With robust brushstrokes, Caillebotte celebrates the here and now of modern life and emphasizes the immediacy of sensation. Nearly life-size, the painting was intended by the artist as an exhibition picture, something to be seen and to garner attention. In 1888, he sent it to Brussels for a group exhibition, but few were able to see it: the organizers sequestered the unusual modern nude in a closet-like space.

Oil on canvas
57 x 45 in. (144.8 x 114.3 cm)
Museum purchase with funds by exchange from an Anonymous gift, Bequest of William A. Coolidge, Juliana Cheney Edwards Collection, and from the Charles H. Bayley Picture and Painting Fund, Edward Jackson Holmes Fund, Fanny P. Mason Fund in memory of Alice Thevin, Arthur Gordon Tompkins Fund, Gift of Mrs. Samuel Parkman Oliver — Eliza R. Oliver Fund, Sophie F. Friedman Fund, Robert M. Rosenberg Family Fund, and funds donated in honor of George T. M. Shackelford, Chair, Art of Europe, and Arthur K. Solomon Curator of Modern Art, 1996–2011   2011.231

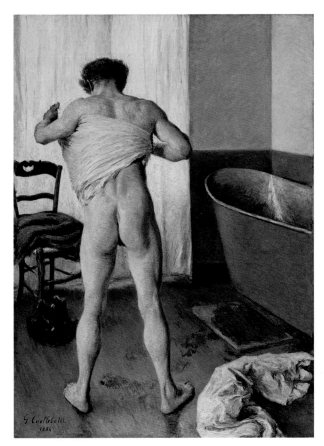

Auguste Rodin
French, 1840–1917
Eternal Springtime
Modeled about 1881; cast about 1916–17

Rodin modeled *Eternal Springtime* while planning his monumental project *The Gates of Hell*, the bronze doors inspired by Dante's *Inferno* that were commissioned in 1880 for a planned museum of decorative arts. *The Gates of Hell* were never finished; the original plaster version is now in the Musée d'Orsay, Paris. Although Rodin ultimately did not include *Eternal Springtime* in his composition for the doors, it is among his most celebrated works, daring in the precarious pose of the figures, their lean bodies extended into space, and in the complexity of convex and concave curves as the bodies intertwine.

Bronze
H. 24¾ in. (62.9 cm)
Bequest of William A. Coolidge   1993.50

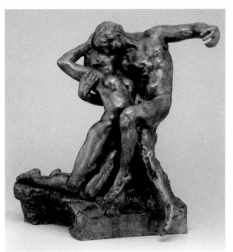

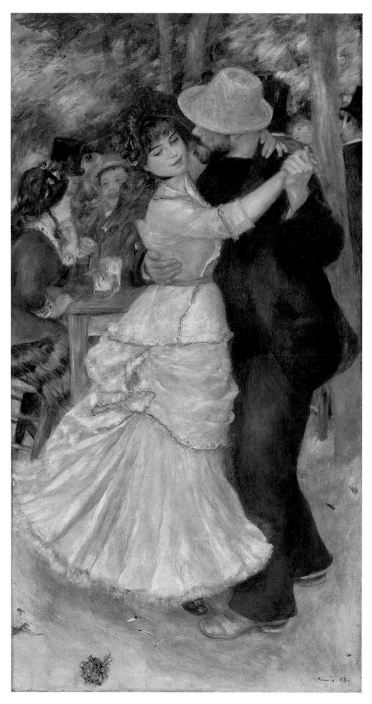

Pierre-Auguste Renoir
French, 1841–1919
Dance at Bougival, 1883

One of Renoir's most ambitious and beloved works, this painting was executed in the studio but captures with delightful immediacy a sunny afternoon at Bougival. Close to Paris and frequented by city dwellers, Bougival's open-air cafés were described as "quite select and expensive, and girls go there without particular expectations." Renoir's young woman was modeled by Suzanne Valadon, a trapeze artist turned professional model who became well known as a painter and was the mother of artist Maurice Utrillo. The male figure may have been posed by Hippolyte-Alphonse Fournaise. The motion of the dancing couple is conveyed by the swirl of the woman's skirt and by the blurred focus of the revelers in the background. The painting is timeless in the pleasure it conveys but modern in its setting and details—Valadon's dress, bonnet, and haircut, for example, were the latest summer fashions in 1883.

Oil on canvas
71⅝ x 38⅝ in. (181.9 x 98.1 cm)
Picture Fund   37.375

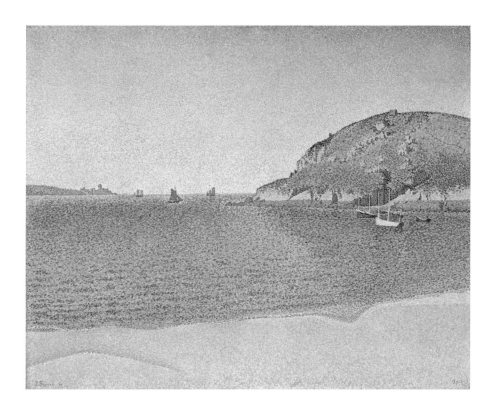

Paul Signac
French, 1863–1935
Port of Saint-Cast, 1890

Signac was profoundly inspired by Georges Seurat (1859–1891), who developed the style of painting called Pointillism (or Divisionism), in which color and form are rendered in tiny touches of paint. Signac became the chief theorist of the new style and also devoted himself to the scientific study of optics, publishing his findings on the relationship of light and color in 1898. This austere, luminous seascape is one of a series of four paintings depicting different views of the coast of Brittany, France, that Signac exhibited in 1891 as *The Sea*. The large, simplified forms of the spare design may reflect Signac's admiration for the Japanese woodblock prints that influenced many French painters in the later nineteenth century.

Oil on canvas
26 x 32½ in. (66 x 82.5 cm)
Gift of William A. Coolidge   1991.584

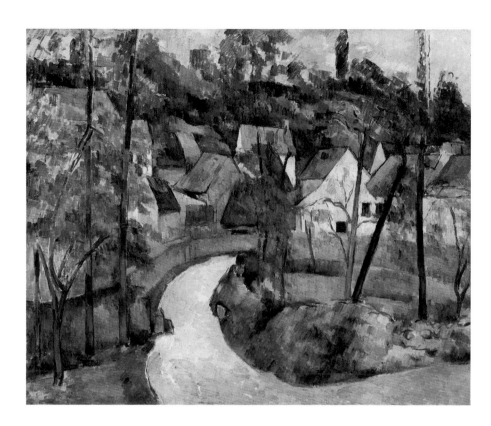

Paul Cézanne
French, 1839–1906
Turn in the Road, about 1881

During the 1870s, Cézanne worked closely with Camille Pissarro, who taught him to paint outdoors using the bright colors and broken brush-strokes of Impressionism. Cézanne, however, was always less interested in the changing face of nature than in its permanent aspects. Here, the artist shows his preference for clearly outlined shapes and for three-dimensional forms modeled with squarish brushstrokes of changing colors. While the road draws us back into space, it exists at the same time as a flat, yellowish shape: Cézanne is asserting that, although his painting gives the illusion of recession and of depth, it is first and foremost a work of art that actually exists only on the surface of the canvas. *Turn in the Road* was owned for many years by Claude Monet.

Oil on canvas
23⅞ x 28⅞ in. (60.6 x 73.3 cm)
Bequest of John T. Spaulding   48.525

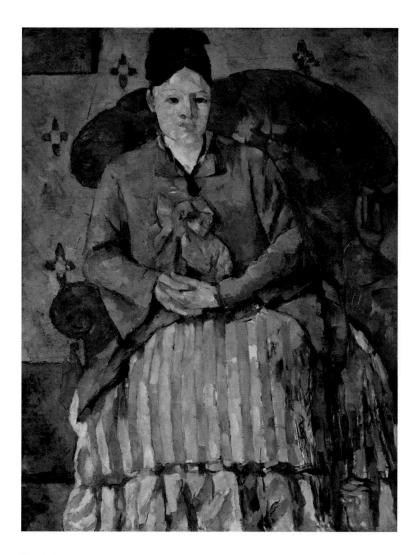

Paul Cézanne

French, 1839–1906

Madame Cézanne in a Red Armchair, about 1877

Cézanne said: "I want to make Impressionism into an art as solid and lasting as the art of the museums." Whether painting landscapes, still lifes, or people, the artist spent many painstaking hours studying and analyzing his subjects, and some of his portraits required up to one hundred sittings. More than two dozen portraits exist of Hortense Fiquet, who lived with Cézanne for almost twenty years before they married in 1886. Painted in the couple's Paris

apartment, this early portrait has a serene and timeless monumentality; its many small blocks of subtly varied color, describing shadows and volume, are locked into a harmonious whole. After seeing this painting in a 1907 exhibition, the German poet Rainer Maria Rilke wrote: "In this red armchair, which is a personality, a woman is seated. . . . It seems that each part [of the painting] knows of all the other parts."

Oil on canvas

28½ x 22 in. (72.5 x 56 cm)

Bequest of Robert Treat Paine, 2nd   44.776

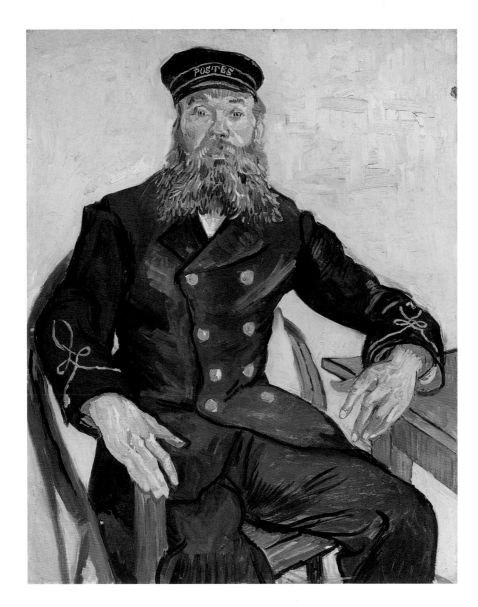

Vincent van Gogh
Dutch (worked in France), 1853–1890
Postman Joseph Roulin, 1888

In 1886 van Gogh left his native Holland for Paris, where he learned from the Impressionists to look closely at nature and to lighten his dark palette. Unlike the Impressionists, however, he became less interested in capturing visual reality than in exploring color and line as a means of personal expression. In 1888 he went south to Arles, where he made six portraits of the local postman, Joseph Roulin. Wanting to "paint the postman as I feel him," he rendered the figure in intense, brilliant color, the forms—notably the hands—distorted for expressive effect. The artist described his subject as "a man who is neither embittered, nor sad, nor perfect, nor happy, nor always irreproachably right. But such a good soul and so wise and so full of feeling and so trustful."

Oil on canvas
32 x 25¾ in. (81.3 x 65.4 cm)
Gift of Robert Treat Paine, 2nd   35.1982

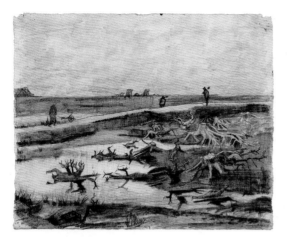

Vincent van Gogh
Dutch (worked in France), 1853–1890
Landscape with Bog Trunks (Work in the Fields),
1883

Van Gogh studied for the ministry and worked as a
lay preacher among coal miners before deciding to
become an artist. The work of his early Dutch period,
inspired by the art of French painter Jean-François
Millet, is imbued with his intense sympathy for the
harsh life of the working poor. This early drawing of
workers digging peat in a bleak landscape anticipates
the emotional power of van Gogh's mature style. The
artist wrote to his brother about it: "Yesterday I drew
some decayed oak roots, so-called bog trunks (that is,
oak trees that have perhaps been buried for a century
under the bog . . .). Some black ones were lying in the
water in which they were reflected, some bleached
ones were lying on the black earth. A little white path
ran past it, behind that more peat, pitch-black. . . . it
was absolutely melancholy and dramatic."

Graphite pencil with pen and brown ink on paper
13½ x 16⅝ in. (34.3 x 42.4 cm)
Gift of John Goelet   1975.375

Vincent van Gogh
Dutch (worked in France), 1853–1890
Houses at Auvers, 1890

Van Gogh moved in 1890 to the village of Auvers, near
Paris, placing himself in the care of Dr. Paul Gachet,
who had long been interested in both psychiatry and
the arts. Here, van Gogh depicted the street not far
from Dr. Gachet's house, creating a flattened tapestry
of shapes in which the tiled and thatched roofs form
a patchwork of texture and color. Although based on
observation, *Houses at Auvers*—with its swirling,
stabbing brushstrokes and sinuous contours—is
a landscape of emotions, charged with energy and
passionate feeling. Not long after this painting was
finished, van Gogh committed suicide at the age of
thirty-seven.

Oil on canvas
29¾ x 24⅜ in. (75.6 x 61.9 cm)
Bequest of John T. Spaulding   48.549

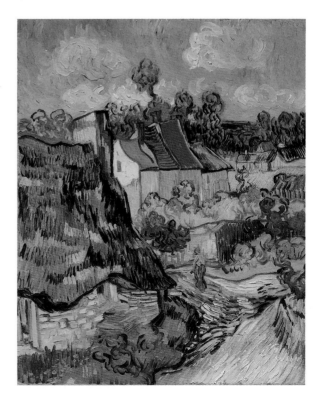

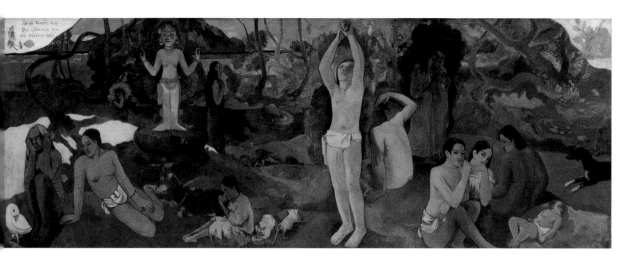

Paul Gauguin

French, 1848–1903

Where Do We Come From? What Are We? Where Are We Going?, 1897–98

Gauguin wrote, "The Impressionists look for what is near the eye, and not at the mysterious centers of thought." He, in contrast, sought to capture an inner world of fantasy and dream and considered this enormous canvas, created in Tahiti, his masterpiece. He indicated that the painting should be read from right to left, with the three major figure groups illustrating the questions posed in the title. The three women with a child represent the beginning of life; the central group symbolizes the daily existence of young adulthood; and in the final group, according to the artist, "an old woman approaching death appears reconciled and resigned to her thoughts"; at her feet "a strange white bird . . . represents the futility of words." Yet, as so often in Gauguin's work, the whole remains mysterious: "Explanations and obvious symbols would give the canvas a sad reality," Gauguin wrote. "And the questions asked [by the title] would no longer be a poem."

Oil on canvas
54¾ x 147½ in. (139.1 x 374.6 cm)
Tompkins Collection—Arthur Gordon Tompkins Fund   36.270

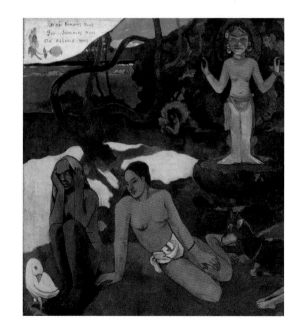

Paul Gauguin

French, 1848–1903

Soyez amoureuses vous serez heureuses
(Be In Love and You Will Be Happy), 1889

A stockbroker by profession, Gauguin began painting as a hobby in the early 1870s and soon became
part of the Impressionist circle. In 1883 he lost his job
and decided to become a full-time artist. Three years
later he made his first trip to Brittany, in France — the
beginning of his lifelong search for places untainted
by the materialism of modern urban society, which
Gauguin saw as "morally and physically corrupt."

Carved in Brittany, this extraordinary relief
addresses the theme of love with bitterness and sar-
casm. Gauguin wrote: "I have carved something . . .
remarkable. Gauguin (as a monster) seizing the hand
of a protesting woman and telling her: 'Be in love and
you will be happy.'" The fox at lower right is an Indian
symbol of perversity and reappears in the work
Gauguin executed in Tahiti.

Carved and painted lindenwood
37⅜ x 28⅜ x 2½ in. (95 x 72 x 6.4 cm)
Arthur Tracy Cabot Fund   57.582

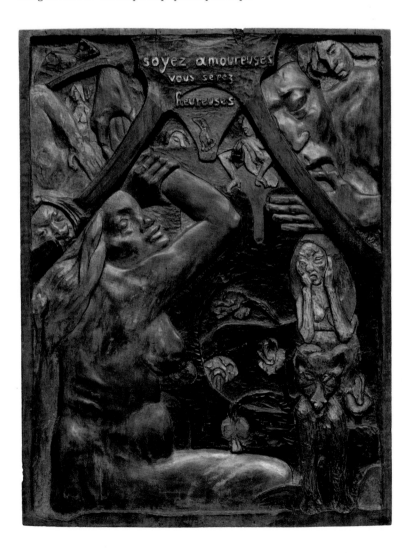

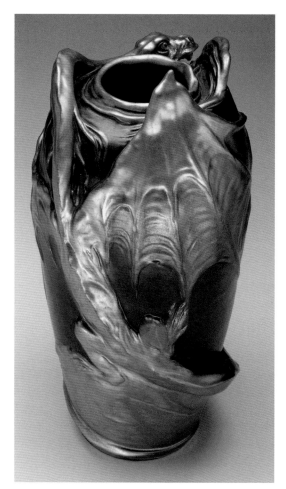

Vase

Hungarian (Pécs), about 1900
Produced by the **Zsolnay
Manufactory** after a model by
Lajos Mack

This vase molded with a winged
dragon was made at the factory
founded by Vilmos Zsolnay in
1855 in Pécs, a Hungarian town
near the Austrian border. Beginning with earthenware vessels
in traditional styles, the Zsolnay
factory expanded production in
the 1870s to include more refined
and decorative wares, some
inspired by Turkish, Chinese, or
ancient American ceramics. Luster
glazes imitating contemporary
iridescent glass were developed at
the factory in the 1890s. A range of
subtly colored luster glazes creates the rich surface effect of this
fanciful vase whose asymmetrical,
curving forms and stylized naturalism typify the influential Art
Nouveau style.

Earthenware with luster glazes
13¾ x 7⅝ in. (34.9 x 19.4 cm)
European Decorative Arts Curator's
Fund   1990.173

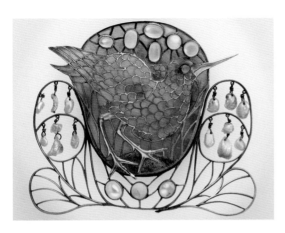

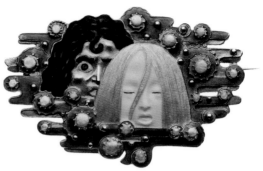

Apparitions brooch
France (Paris), about 1899
Henri Vever, French, 1854–1942
Designed by **Eugène Samuel Grasset**, French
(born in Switzerland), 1841–1917

Marsh bird brooch
England, 1901–2
Charles Robert Ashbee, English, 1863–1942

Ashbee was a leader of the Arts and Crafts movement in Britain, and one of the first in the group to design jewelry. In 1888, he founded the Guild of Handicraft in London, dedicating it to the design and fabrication of decorative objects and running it as a cooperative enterprise. In 1902, around the time this ornament was made, the guild moved north to Gloucestershire to create an artists' commune. Like many of his colleagues, Ashbee embraced socialist ideals and emphasized teamwork. For this piece, he collaborated with fellow guild members Adolf Gebhardt to fabricate it and William Mark to enamel it. (Originally, Ashbee designed the marsh bird as a hair ornament; it was converted shortly after being made.) Unusually, it features backless *plique-à-jour* enamel, which allows light to pass through the metal cells, mimicking the effect of stained glass. Six polished moonstones shimmer in the space above the bird's head and wings. At each side, freshwater pearls dangle elegantly from wire loops.

At the turn of the twentieth century, the female figure was a popular motif among avant-garde Art Nouveau jewelers. In contrast to the empowered "New Woman," figures in jewelry tended to be ethereal, sexualized, or a bit of both. This brooch's ghostly subject—and the look of horror on the man's face—are said to relate to a Japanese tale about a female ghost who lures young men to their graves. But it also relates to the era's anxiety over shifting gender roles.

Vever and Grasset were awarded the Grand Prix for their collaborative work at the 1900 Exposition Universelle in Paris, where they exhibited a version of this brooch. At the time, Maison Vever was a well-known Parisian jewelry house, and Grasset, who trained as a sculptor, was an established designer and illustrator. Four versions of the *Apparitions* brooch are known to exist; this is the only one to survive with its original box intact.

Gold, enamel
L. 2 in. (5 cm)
William Francis Warden Fund   2015.2162

Gold, silver, enamel, moonstone, topaz, freshwater pearl
H. 3½ in. (9 cm)
Museum purchase with funds donated by Susan B. Kaplan, Marshall H. Gould Fund, John H. and Ernestine A. Payne Fund, Linda Fenton, Dorothy-Lee Jones Fund, Penny Vinik, and Adrienne Iselin Gilbert Memorial Fund   2007.827

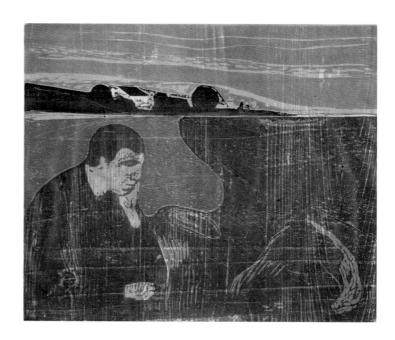

Edvard Munch
Norwegian, 1863–1944
Evening (Melancholy), 1896

Munch's first attempts at printmaking, of which this is an example, were made in Paris, a center of experimentation in printmaking methods. At first working in color lithography (which required extensive collaboration with a professional printer), Munch soon turned to woodcut, a technique that enabled him to prepare the block himself up to the moment of printing. In his woodcuts, the artist innovatively included the grain of the wood into his designs. He also developed a unique jigsaw-puzzle technique of sawing the wooden blocks into pieces, inking them individually, then reassembling and printing them as a single block. Composed of simplified shapes and curving, expressive line, this image, derived from his *Frieze of Life* paintings, universalizes human experience while depicting a specific subject—a friend, infatuated with an older woman, who mourns alone on a beach while his lover and her husband embark on a boat trip on a midsummer night.

Color woodcut, printed from two blocks on thin Asian paper
Block: 14¾ x 17⅞ in. (37.6 x 45.5 cm)
William Francis Warden Fund   57.356

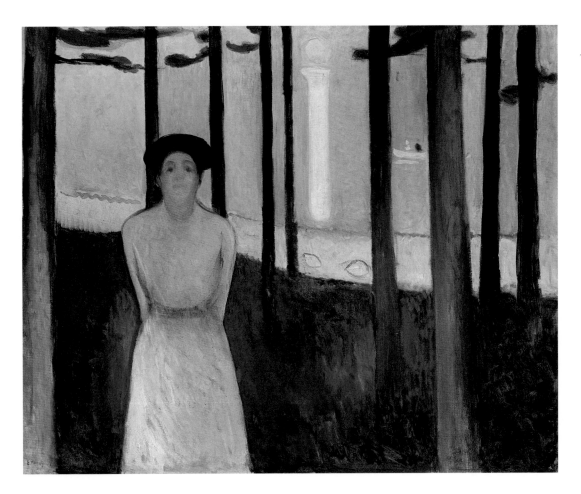

Edvard Munch
Norwegian, 1863–1944
Summer Night's Dream (The Voice), 1893

Many of Munch's most memorable paintings are from the series called *The Frieze of Life*, which deals symbolically with themes of love and death. *Summer Night's Dream* presents a gently melancholy evocation of adolescent sexual awakening, in which the still figure of the girl both offers herself to and holds back from the viewer, whom the artist has placed in the position of her anticipated lover. The setting is probably the Borre woods on the Oslo Fjord, a site of ancient Viking graves and a traditional place for courtship during Norway's softly illuminated summer nights. Munch's notes reveal that this painting recalls his first, ultimately painful love affair: "What a deep mark she left on my mind, so deep that no other image can ever totally drive it away."

Oil on canvas
34⅝ x 42½ in. (87.8 x 108 cm)
Ernest Wadsworth Longfellow Fund   59.301

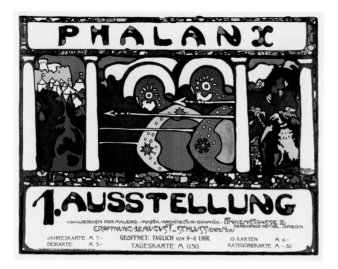

Wassily Kandinsky

Russian (worked in Germany), 1866–1944

Poster for the First Phalanx Exhibition, 1901

Kandinsky, widely regarded as the originator of
purely abstract art, abandoned a legal career in
his native Russia at the age of thirty to study art in
Munich, the center of modern German art, music,
literature, and theater. This poster, in the Art Nouveau
style, is imbued with graphic energy and charged
with symbolic meaning. It was one of Kandinsky's
first public graphic works and advertised the initial
exhibition of the Phalanx society, an organization
of avant-garde artists that he helped to found. The
armor-clad warriors who form an interlocked battle
line, or phalanx, allude to the members of this tightly
knit and militant group.

Poster, color lithograph
19½ x 26⅜ in. (49.6 x 67.1 cm)
Gift of Susan W. and Stephen D. Paine   1984.959

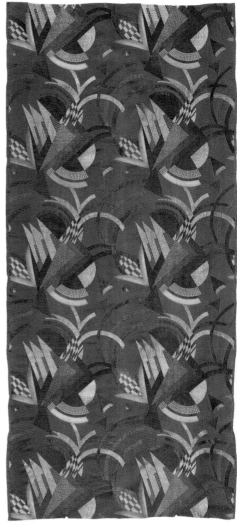

opposite, right

Furnishing fabric

France (Paris), about 1927

Designed by **Maurice Dufrène**, 1876–1955

In the 1920s France was the undisputed leader of the luxury-goods market. Major Paris department stores were influential arbiters of taste, often establishing their own art studios to design and manufacture household goods in the most modern styles. Dufrène— who designed furniture, glassware, ceramics, wallpaper, and silverware as well as textiles—was artistic director of La Maîtrise, the art studio of the Paris department store Galeries Lafayette. This stunning and dramatic furnishing fabric is a superb example of the beauty and dynamism of Art Deco textiles and is influenced as well by both Cubist and Futurist art. The textile was woven on the mechanized Jacquard loom that made possible intricate designs and subtle variations in texture, giving this fabric a complex, reflective surface that is a tribute to the sophistication of French fabrics in the early twentieth century.

Rayon and cotton jacquard
51½ x 114½ in. (130.8 x 290.8 cm)
Museum purchase with funds donated by The Textile and
Costume Society, Museum of Fine Arts, Boston   2000.673

Flower basket

Austria (Vienna), 1906–13

Designed by **Josef Hoffmann**, 1870–1956

Manufactured by the **Wiener Werkstätte**

In 1903 the Austrian architect Josef Hoffmann cofounded the Wiener Werkstätte (Viennese Workshops) to "produce good and simple articles of everyday use." The Workshops made metalwork, jewelry, leatherwork, and furniture according to principles that emphasized function, proportion, and the appropriate use of materials. Wishing to eliminate all historical references from his work, Hoffmann created a new vocabulary of modular, geometric design to replace the lush, curvilinear Art Nouveau style then current in Europe. Made from prefabricated, perforated metal sheets, this imposing flower basket employs pure geometry with cylinders and rectangles formed by repeated squares. Only thirteen of these baskets were manufactured by the Wiener Werkstätte between 1906 and 1913.

Painted metal
27½ x 12 in. (69.8 x 30.4 cm)
Bequest of the Estate of Mrs. Gertrude T. Taft, Gift of Edward
Perry Warren, Gift of Alex Cochrane, Anonymous gift, Gift of
Charles Loring, and Estate of Mrs. William Dorr Boardman
through Gift of Mrs. Bernard C. Weld, by exchange   1994.238

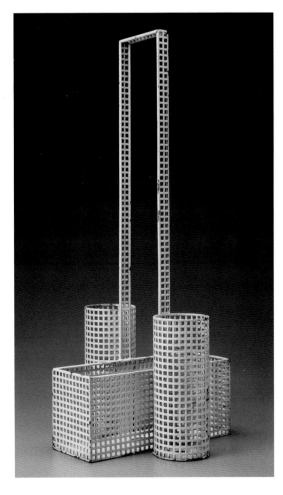

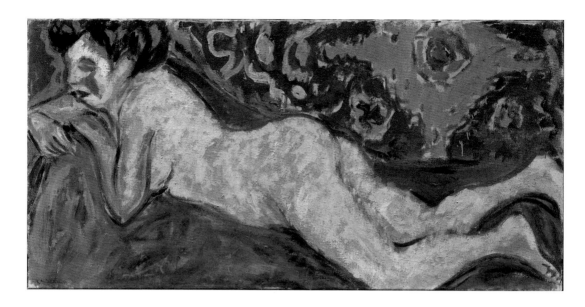

Ernst Ludwig Kirchner
German, 1880–1938
Reclining Nude, 1909

Determined to "revitalize German art," Kirchner joined with three other
architectural students to found, in 1905, the idealistic artistic brotherhood called Die Brücke (The Bridge). The group was active in Dresden
and Berlin until 1913 and strove to form a bridge between art and life.
Inspired by the psychological intensity and expressive form and color
of van Gogh, Gauguin, Munch, and Matisse (although Kirchner vehe-
mently denied the impact of these artists), Die Brücke developed the
widely influential style known as German Expressionism. Here, Kirchner
rendered a traditional studio nude in a forceful Expressionist style with
rough brushwork, bold outlines, and strong acid colors that evoke feelings of tension and isolation.

Oil on canvas
29 1/8 x 59 5/8 in. (74 x 151.5 cm)
Tompkins Collection — Arthur Gordon Tompkins Fund   57.2

Henri Matisse

French, 1869–1954

Carmelina, 1903

"What interests me most," Matisse wrote, "is neither still life nor landscape but the human figure. It is through it that I best succeed in expressing the nearly religious feeling that I have towards life." Here, in this rigorously balanced composition, the curves of the model's body are accentuated by the interlocking rectangles of the background, where the artist himself and the model's back are reflected in a mirror. Matisse declared that "the whole arrangement of my pictures is expressive. The place occupied by figures or objects, the empty spaces around them, the proportions, everything plays a part." In this early work, Matisse is already a master of color, playing off vibrating reds and blues against the blocks of warm earth tones representing furniture, walls, picture frames, and blank canvases.

Oil on canvas
32 x 23¼ in. (81.3 x 59 cm)
Tompkins Collection — Arthur Gordon
Tompkins Fund   Res.32.14

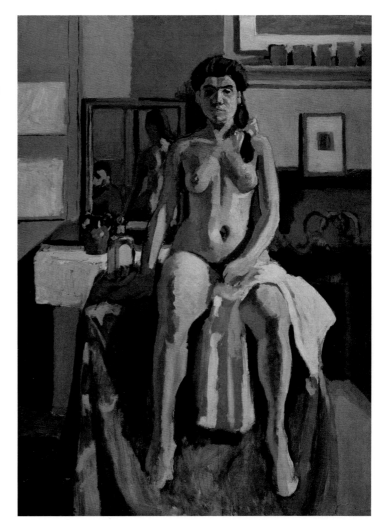

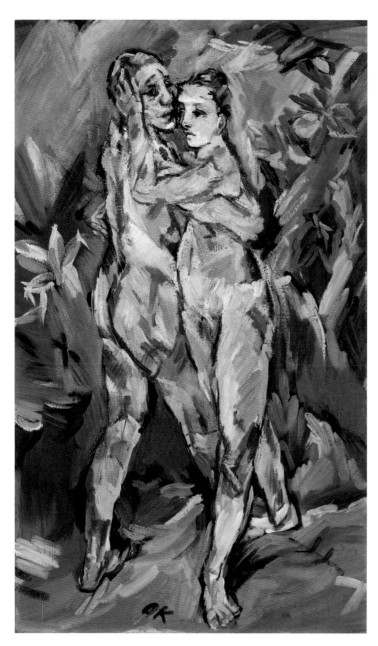

Oskar Kokoschka
Austrian, 1886–1980
Two Nudes (Lovers), 1913

Painted in Vienna on the eve of
World War I, Kokoschka's self-
portrait with Alma Mahler—
widow of the composer Gustav
Mahler—is a monument to their
intense and stormy love affair.
Powerfully evoking the artist's
tumultuous feelings, the painting is filled with restless, dynamic
movement. Its brushwork is agi-
tated and expressionistic, with
light carefully manipulated to
enliven the surface and create a
sense of depth. There is, in addition, a tenderness to the image,
evoked by the interlocked pose
of the lovers, which suggests the
formal intimacy of a dance.

Oil on canvas
64¼ x 38⅜ in. (163 x 97.5 cm)
Bequest of Sarah Reed Platt   1973.196

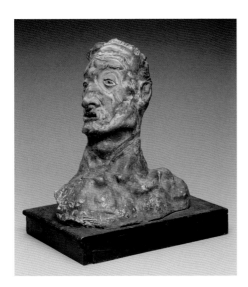

Oskar Kokoschka
Austrian, 1886–1980
Self-Portrait as a Warrior, 1909

Kokoschka is best known for his psychologically intense paintings of people and landscapes. This bust—made from unfired clay—is extraordinarily rare, given that only on a few occasions did the artist work in sculpture. A self-portrait, it also marks the very moment when Kokoschka began working in his highly personal Expressionist style. He presents his own features brutally distorted with suffering; his skin seems to be peeled back to reveal nerves and raw flesh. When it was first displayed, the work was greeted with shock and ridicule in early twentieth-century Vienna, where the sinuous, graceful style of Art Nouveau dominated. Later, it became associated with Nazi "degenerate art," its photograph appearing in numerous publications; however, it was never officially shown as such, for its owner had taken it to the United States in 1937.

Unfired clay painted with tempera
H. 14⅜ in. (36.5 cm)
John H. and Ernestine A. Payne Fund   60.958

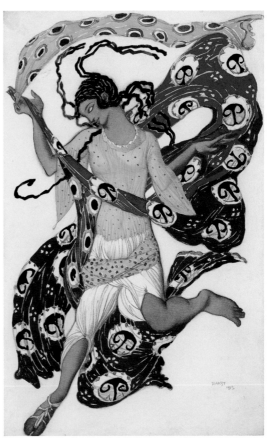

Léon Nikolaievitch Bakst
Russian, 1866–1924
The Butterfly (Costume design for Anna Pavlova), 1913

Bakst dazzled early twentieth-century Europe with his opulent designs for the ballet and theater. His feeling for exotic styles, voluptuous color, and sensuous line profoundly influenced contemporary fashion, interior design, and jewelry. Bakst created many costumes for performances by the great Russian ballerina Anna Pavlova (1881–1931) at the Imperial Ballet and the Ballets Russes. After she started her own troupe, the dramatic solo *The Butterfly* was one of Pavlova's most popular works.

Opaque and translucent watercolor with graphite pencil on paper
17¾ x 11 in. (45 x 28 cm)
Gift of Mrs. John Munro Longyear and Mrs. Walter Scott Fitz   14.701

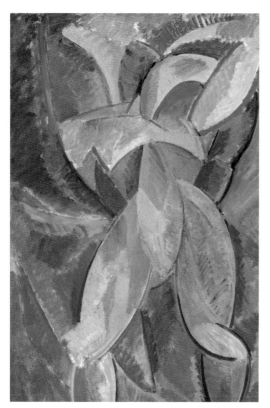

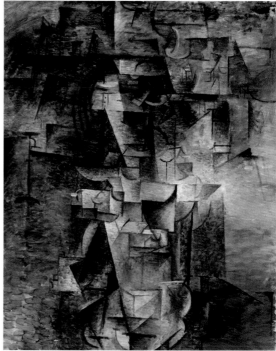

Pablo Picasso

Spanish (worked in France),

1881–1973

Standing Figure, 1908

Oil on canvas

59 ⅛ x 39 ½ in. (150.2 x 100.3 cm)

Juliana Cheney Edwards

Collection 58.976

Pablo Picasso

Spanish (worked in France),

1881–1973

Portrait of a Woman, 1910

Oil on canvas

39 ⅝ x 32 in. (100.6 x 81.3 cm)

Charles H. Bayley Picture and Painting

Fund, and Partial gift of Mrs. Gilbert W.

Chapman 1977.15

These two works mark milestones in the early development of Cubism, possibly the most influential movement in twentieth-century art. The result of a unique collaboration between Pablo Picasso and Georges Braque, Cubism was an attempt to render three-dimensional forms on a two-dimensional surface in a radically new way—by breaking up the volumes into flat, angular facets or planes that imply multiple, simultaneous views of an object or a figure.

In *Standing Figure*, Picasso took a time-honored subject—the female nude—and divided the body into simplified components that interact so that the figure seems to turn on the surface of the canvas. Painted two years later, *Portrait of a Woman* is much more systematically fragmented, its forms opening out into flat planes that dissolve into one another. Only a few details such as the hair at top left are readily identifiable; the background suggests a studio setting with canvases stacked against a wall. Picasso used a nearly monochromatic palette to distance this image from real-world associations and to focus more clearly on the painting's compositional structure.

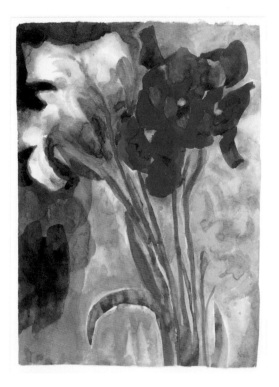

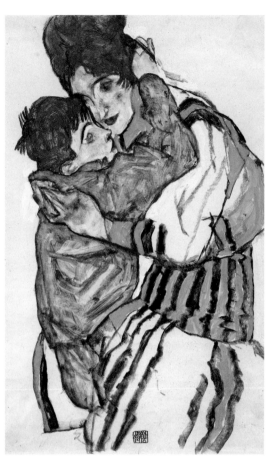

Emil Nolde

German, 1867–1956

Irises

Nolde was among the most original painters and printmakers of his time, and his inventive and rapidly executed watercolors are among his greatest works. He favored simple subjects and bold forms that fill the entire sheet, and he used damp, highly absorbent Japanese paper that gave extraordinary depth and luminosity to his colors.

Watercolor on white Asian paper
18½ x 13½ in. (47 x 33.5 cm)
Seth K. Sweetser Fund   57.667

Egon Schiele

Austrian, 1890–1918

Schiele's Wife with Her Little Nephew, 1915

Schiele's distinctive style is characterized by an almost neurotic intensity of feeling, a love of pattern, and a magnificent energy of line. Here, he combines two media—broadly drawn charcoal and opaque watercolor. The woman's tight embrace and the yellow-and-black striping of her dress evoke a tigress fiercely protecting her cub. Since his early death in the influenza epidemic of 1918, Schiele has come to be regarded as one of the greatest Expressionist artists.

Charcoal and opaque and translucent watercolor on paper
19 x 12½ in. (48.3 x 31.8 cm)
Edwin E. Jack Fund   65.1322

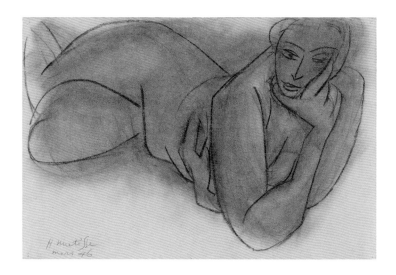

Henri Matisse

French, 1869–1954

Reclining Nude, 1946

Among the most powerful and innovative artists of the twentieth century, Matisse influenced generations of artists through the vast and varied output of a career that spanned more than sixty years. Throughout his exploration of drawing, painting, sculpture, printmaking, book illustration, and paper cutouts, his stated goal was to unearth "the essential character of things" and to produce an art "of balance, purity, and serenity." For Matisse, drawing was like "making an expressive gesture with the advantage of permanence." In this masterful late work, the artist's efforts to capture his subject remain clearly visible in the smudged, half-obliterated strokes of charcoal that underlie firm, sure outlines that define — in the most economical way — the voluptuous body and complex pose of his model.

Charcoal on cream laid paper
16 ¼ x 24 in. (41.3 x 61 cm)
Charles H. Bayley Picture and Painting Fund   2004.70

Max Beckmann

German (1884–1950)

Double Portrait, 1946

Persecuted by the Nazis, Beckmann fled his native Germany in 1937, staying in Amsterdam for ten years before settling in the United States. He painted this double portrait of Curt Valentin, an émigré art dealer living in New York, and Hanns Swarzenski (later a curator at the MFA) as a gesture of gratitude and friendship. Both men had known Beckmann in Berlin in the 1920s, and they became lifelong supporters of the artist and his work.

Both Valentin and Swarzenski visited Beckmann in Holland in 1946, but their stays did not overlap. In this painting, Beckmann imagines them together: Swarzenski at left, Valentin at right. The deep colors and thick black strokes outlining the figures and describing their features are signatures of Beckmann's highly expressive and powerful personal style. The glass of wine in Swarzenski's hand might refer to a gift of several bottles he gave Beckmann during his visit; Valentin holds a candle, as "keeper of the flame" of avant-garde European artists who struggled through the dark Nazi era.

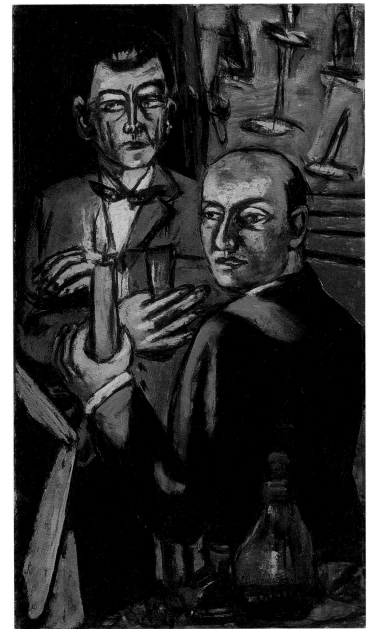

Oil on canvas

51½ x 29¾ in. (130.8 x 75.6 cm)

Gift of Dr. Hanns Swarzenski   1989.348

Piet Mondrian

Dutch, 1872–1944

***Composition with Blue, Yellow and Red**, 1927*

Beginning in 1917, Mondrian became associated with the De Stijl (The Style) movement, an international group of like-minded artists who advocated for pure abstraction in painting, architecture, and design. Adherents believed that carefully balanced and simple compositions had a broader social function, restoring order and harmony to modern life. In 1920, Mondrian produced the first of the abstract paintings for which he is best known, with rectangular fields of white and primary colors divided by black lines. For the artist, these canvases expressed the fundamentals of painting—color, line, and form—in their essential states. Like all of his mature compositions, this work, from 1927, was the result of a long process of searching for perfect equilibrium. Small areas of intense red, yellow, and blue are countered by larger fields of neutral whites to harmonious effect. Despite the painting's strict order, Mondrian maintains a sense of rhythm and movement by arranging the lines and rectangles asymmetrically and by leaving evidence of the physical brushstroke on the painted surface.

Oil on canvas
15¾ x 19⅞ in. (40 x 50.5 cm)
Gift of Maria and Conrad Janis in memory of Sidney and Harriet Janis, with gratitude to Arne Glimcher   2009.5042

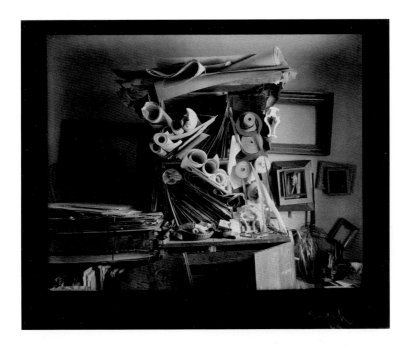

Josef Sudek
Czechoslovakian, 1896–1976
Labyrinths, 1969

One of the most quietly original photographers of the twentieth century, Sudek lived a withdrawn and frugal existence in Prague, a city marked for most of his lifetime by political upheaval and repression. His photographs document a world of private feeling and experience, drawn from the most commonplace materials and subjects. "I believe that photography loves banal objects," he said, "And I love the life of objects." Many of his photographs are focused explorations of themes. *Labyrinths*, one of his last series, captures the chaos of his small, cramped studio, but the photographs are much more. This image is a carefully arranged composition of straight edges and rounded shapes, each articulated by the magical and evocative natural light that Sudek revered.

Photograph, gelatin silver print
11½ x 15¼ in. (22.9 x 29.2 cm)
The Sonja Bullaty and Angelo Lomeo Collection of Josef Sudek Photographs,
The Saundra B. Lane Photography Purchase Fund   2003.196

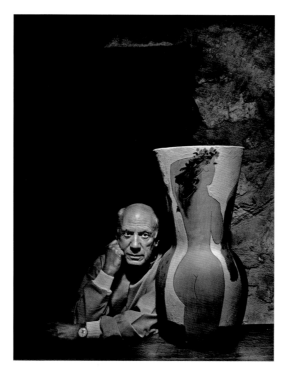

Yousuf Karsh
Canadian (born in Turkish Armenia), 1908–2002
Pablo Picasso, 1954
Photograph, gelatin silver print
40⅛ x 29½ in. (101.9 x 74.9 cm)
Gift of Estrellita and Yousuf Karsh   2002.59

opposite
Pablo Picasso
Spanish (worked in France),
1881–1973
Rape of the Sabine Women, 1963

Painted when Picasso was eighty-two, this is his last major statement about the horrors of war, and is said to have been inspired by the Cuban missile crisis. In it, Picasso transforms a familiar subject from the art of the past—the story of early Romans who, suffering a shortage of marriageable women, invited the neighboring Sabines to Rome and then carried off all their young women. Against a sunny background of blue sky and green fields, the grotesquely distorted figures are compressed into the foreground space, the horses and soldiers trampling a woman and her child. Purchased by the Museum the year after it was painted, this powerful image of outrage and despair bears testimony to Picasso's productivity and energy in the last decade of his life.

Oil on canvas
76⅞ x 51⅝ in. (195.3 x 131.1 cm)
Juliana Cheney Edwards Collection,
Tompkins Collection—Arthur
Gordon Tompkins Fund, and Fanny
P. Mason Fund in memory of Alice
Thevin   64.709

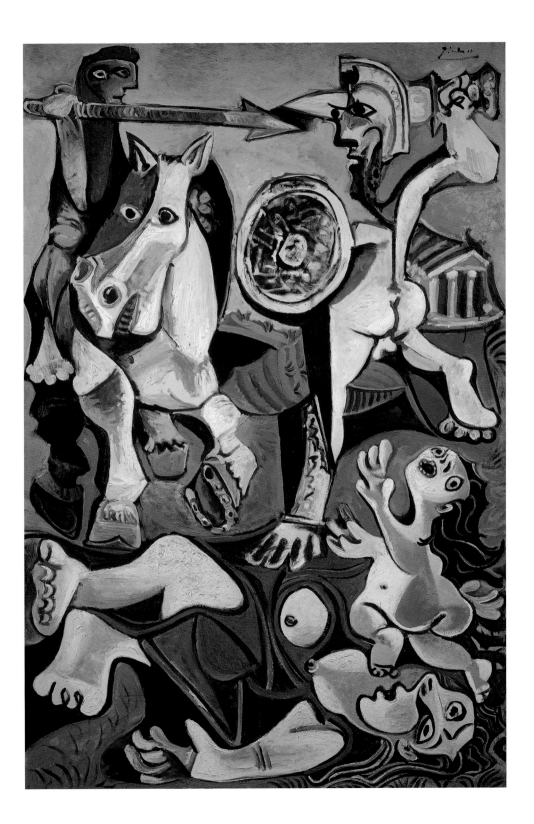

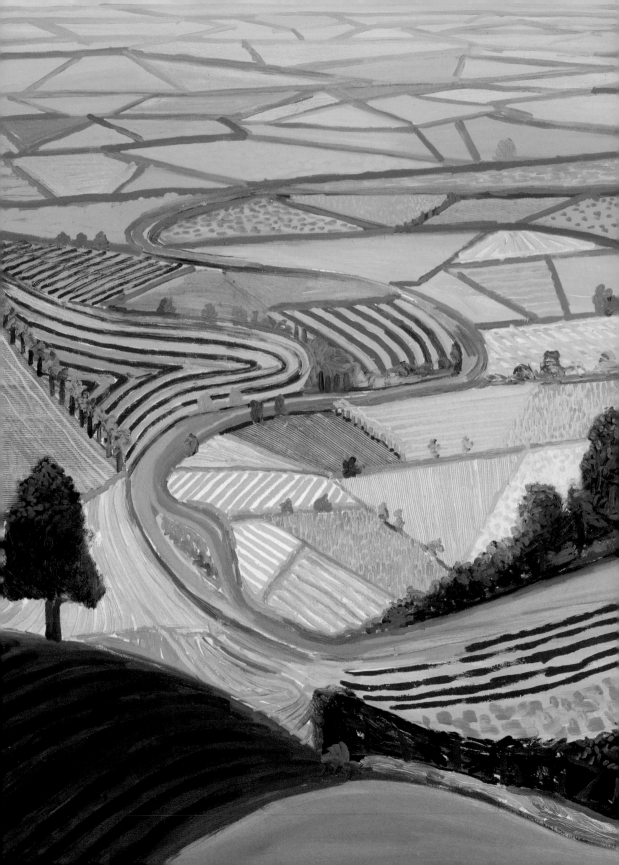

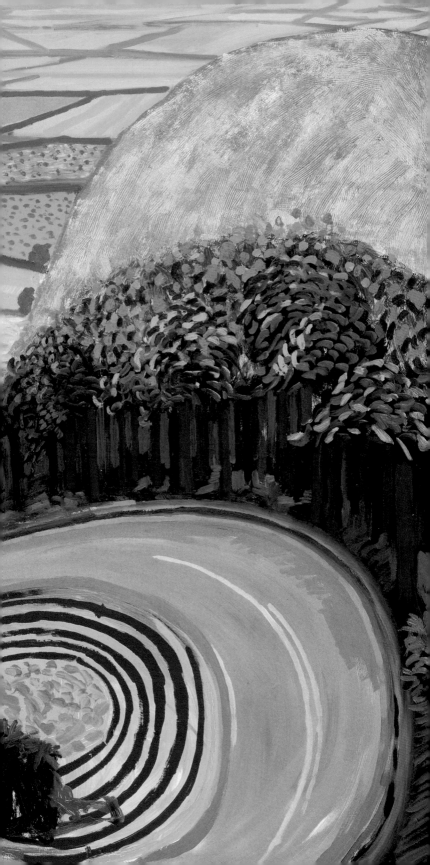

Andy Warhol
American, 1928–1987
Red Disaster, 1963, 1985

Beginning his career as a successful commercial artist, Warhol became, in the early 1960s, an underground filmmaker and a painter who sought to mechanize painting by including photographic images reproduced by the silkscreen process. In 1962 his main subjects were soup cans, soda bottles, Elvis Presley, and Marilyn Monroe. The following year—a time of enormous social and political change—he began to explore death in modern American society. The electric chair was the first subject in his series of "disasters" that also included car crashes and images of police brutality. *Red Disaster,* derived from a photograph of the death chamber at Sing Sing Prison, may be viewed as a grave and haunting plea against capital punishment; some, however, see its grim repetitiveness as an embodiment of callousness and inhumanity.

Silkscreen ink on synthetic polymer paint on canvas
Each panel: 93 x 80¼ in. (236.2 x 203.8 cm)
Charles H. Bayley Picture and Painting Fund
1986.161a–b

Stephen Shore
American, born 1947
Trail's End Restaurant, Kanab, Utah, August 10, 1973, 1973

When Stephen Shore was fourteen, Edward Steichen selected his work for New York's Museum of Modern Art, and at twenty-three, he became just the second living photographer to have a solo exhibition at New York's Metropolitan Museum of Art. (Steichen was the first.) A pioneer of the use of color in American photography, Shore is best known for his road-trip photographs from the 1970s, which capture commonplace details of American culture from an uninflected point of view. *Trail's End Restaurant, Kanab, Utah* depicts Shore's breakfast at a quintessential small-town diner, with glasses of milk and ice water, cantaloupe, and a plate of pancakes set against a Western-themed placemat. One of Shore's most iconic images, it highlights the diaristic nature of his approach. Yet, despite its snapshot-like appearance, the photograph was, in fact, deliberately set up and took hours to make, using a 4 x 5 camera on a tripod.

Photograph, chromogenic print
13¾ x 17⅜ in. (35 x 44.2 cm)
Museum purchase with funds donated by Scott Offen
2016.185

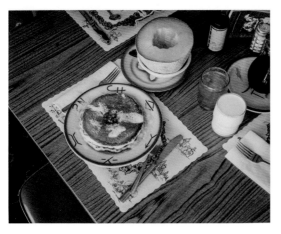

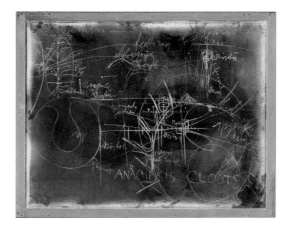

Joseph Beuys
German, 1921–1986
Untitled (Blackboard), 1973

Sculptor, printmaker, performance artist, and impassioned teacher, Beuys created the images on this blackboard during his presentation of "12 Hour Lecture—An Homage to Anachrsis (Anacharasis) Cloots" at the Edinburgh Arts Summer School. This was one of a series of public lectures in which Beuys used blackboards to illustrate what he termed his "expanded concept of art," which incorporated science and economics and related social order to a living organism evolving toward freedom. He was inspired by Anacharasis Cloots (whose name is written across the bottom), an eighteenth-century radical born near Beuys's hometown of Kleves, who became an important figure in the French Revolution and whose idealistic belief in liberty, equality, and fraternity meant a great deal to the artist. With its complex visual layering of images, text, and diagrams, this blackboard is especially rare; most other early examples were considered merely teaching tools and wiped clean after use.

White and colored chalks on blackboard with wooden frame
Framed: 41½ x 53½ in. (105.4 x 135.9 cm)
Catherine and Paul Buttenwieser Fund   2000.979

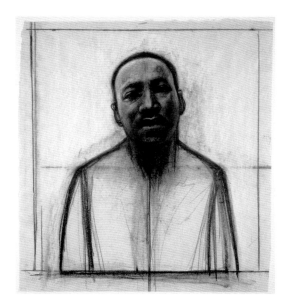

John Wilson
American, 1922–2015
Dr. Martin Luther King, Jr., 1985

In 1985, Wilson was awarded a commission from the National Endowment for the Arts to create a bronze bust of Martin Luther King, Jr., for the U.S. Capitol building in Washington, D.C.—the first representation of an African American in the Capitol rotunda. Wilson made this sensitive drawing in preparation for the sculpture, using black and white pastel. In the drawing, as in the sculpture, Wilson aimed to create an idealization of King, rather than a photographic likeness, in order to better convey his universal significance. King's head, tilted slightly, is carefully modeled, while the torso remains flat and schematic. Wilson's use of vertical and horizontal lines to divide the composition suggests both a Christian martyr's cross and the crosshairs of the assassin's rifle. According to Wilson, it was his intention to "use shapes, lines, and colors like Dr. King used words, to change how people looked at others who were different from them."

Black and white pastel on cream Japanese paper
21⅞ x 20⅞ in. (55.7 x 52.9 cm)
Richard Florsheim Art Fund and Anonymous Gift   1997.102

Kiki Smith
American, born 1954
Lilith, 1994
Edition 2 of 3

Smith's art is devoted to the exploration of the human body, inside and out. This deliberately unsettling sculpture was created from life casts of a female model, and in accordance with the artist's instructions, it is hung so that *Lilith* clings to the wall upside down, staring up at the viewer with glass eyes. The title refers to an ancient Sumerian demon, a creature of the air who, in postbiblical Hebrew legend, is identified as Adam's intended first wife, who flew away when he refused to accept her as his equal. Long relegated to the realms of superstition and viewed as an evil spirit dangerous to men and children, Lilith has been reinterpreted in recent decades as an ideal of female strength and independence.

Silicon bronze and glass
33 x 27½ x 19 in. (83.8 x 69.9 x 48.3 cm)
Contemporary Art Support Group Fund, Robert L. Beal, Enid L. Beal and Bruce A. Beal Acquisition Fund, Barbara Fish Lee, and the Lorna and Robert M. Rosenberg Fund   1996.60

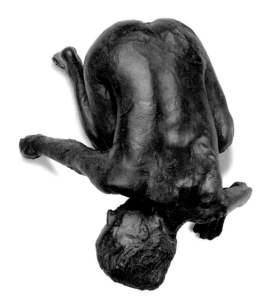

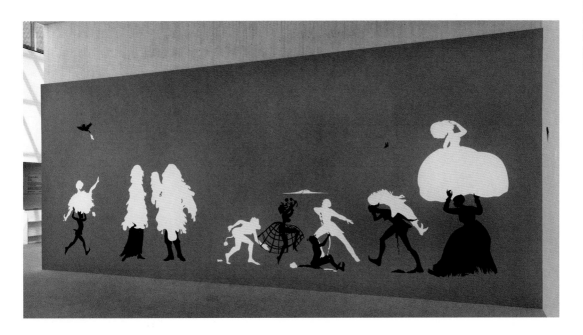

Kara Walker
American, born 1969
The Rich Soil Down There, 2002

Across an expanse of more than thirty feet, a dozen black-and-white silhouettes are paired in mysterious ways, all of which evoke struggle. Often violent and erotic, Walker's work addresses issues of racial and sexual stereotypes, of power and its abuse. "Silhouettes are reductions," the artist says, "and racial stereotypes are also reductions of actual human beings." Exploring black history is central to Walker's art, and she acknowledges the inspiration of earlier black artists whose work dealt with racial and cultural issues. In *The Rich Soil Down There*, many figures are exaggerated African stereotypes, and costumes seem to be of the nineteenth century, perhaps the antebellum South. Following the artist's instructions, assistants created the piece on a Museum wall, using templates to paint the precise borders of each image and then adhering the paper cutouts within the borders.

Cut paper and adhesive on painted wall
Overall: 180 x 396⅛ in. (457.4 x 1006.2 cm)
Museum purchase with funds donated by members of the 2004–2005 Contemporary Art Visiting Committee: Audrey and Jim Foster, Barbara Lee Endowment for Contemporary Art by Women, Robert and Jane Burke, Henry and Lois Foster Contemporary Purchase Fund, Ann and Graham Gund, Elizabeth and Woody Ives, Joyce and Edward Linde, JoAnn McGrath, Davis and Carol Noble, John and Amy Berylson, Lorraine and Alan Bressler, Catherine and Paul Buttenwieser, Robert and Esta Epstein, The Fine Family Foundation, Sandra and Gerald Fineberg, Eloise and Arthur Hodges, Ellen and Robert Jaffe, Richard and Nancy Lubin, Susan W. Paine, Elizabeth and Samuel Thorne, Gail and Ernst von Metzsch, Stephen and Dorothy Weber, Rhonda and Michael Zinner, Karin and David Chamberlain, Marlene and David Persky, Ann Beha and Robert Radloff, Jan Colombi and Jay Reeg, Marcia Kamentsky, Alexandra and Max Metral, Joan Margot Smith, Marvin and Ann Collier, Jerry Scally, Martin and Deborah Hale, Katherine R. Kirk, Allison D. Salke, Gwendolyn DuBois Shaw, Robert and Bettye Freeman, Joan and Michael Salke, and Lois B. Torf   2005.339

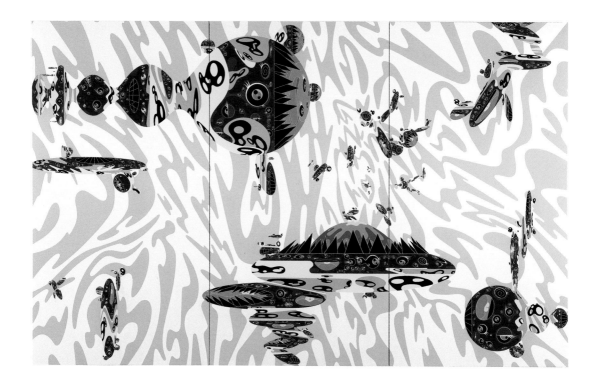

Takashi Murakami
Japanese, born 1962
If the Double Helix Wakes Up . . . , 2002

Known for his colorful paintings, sculpture, and commercial merchandise—T-shirts, watches, key chains, mouse pads—Murakami combines his deep knowledge of traditional Japanese art with contemporary cartoons (*manga*) and animation (*anime*). His work is produced in factory-style studios in Japan and New York, with numerous assistants creating objects from the artist's sketches. Murakami skillfully blends high and low culture, recognizing this as a factor of modern life. Although he says that he is "always looking to what lies beyond Pop," Murakami is particularly attracted to the anti-narrative, anti-emotional work of Andy Warhol, whose signature camouflage background appears in this painting. The title refers to a structural arrangement of DNA, and the painting contains Murakami's famous, mouselike, cartoon figure Mr. Dob—morphed almost beyond recognition. As Murakami firmly states: "I am surrounded by cute images and figures from cartoons and comic books, and so that is what I paint."

Acrylic on canvas mounted on wood
Overall: 98½ x 157¼ in. (250.2 x 399.4 cm)
3 panels, each 98½ x 52¼ in.
Catherine and Paul Buttenwieser Fund   2002.108

Cindy Sherman
American, born 1954
Untitled #282, 1993

Sherman usually works in series,
photographing herself in a range
of guises that explore contemporary culture—from actresses in
old black-and-white films to a new
perception of Renaissance portraits to clowns. In 1993 *Harper's
Bazaar* invited Sherman to select
and photograph high-fashion
clothes from the Spring collections, publishing the results in the
magazine. Here Sherman wears
clothing designed by Jean-Paul
Gaultier, the *enfant terrible* of
French fashion, known—among
other things—for his use of older
and full-figured models. Like much
of Sherman's work, the image is
both humorous and disturbing,
with the slightly bulging belly and
the awkwardly protruding knee
balanced by an elegantly posed
hand. "I try to get something going
with the characters so that they
give more information than what
you see," Sherman has said. "I'd
like people to fantasize about this
person's life."

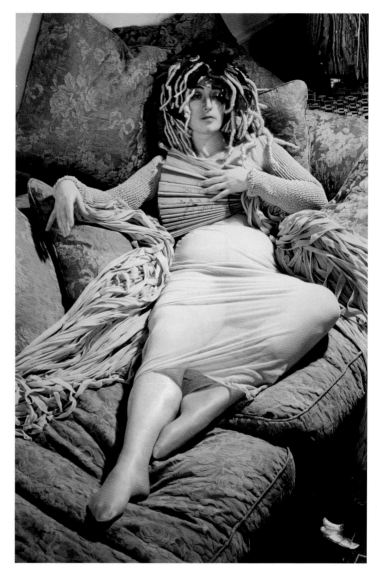

Photograph, chromogenic print
Edition 3 of 6
91 ¼ x 61 ⅛ in. (231.6 x 155.3 cm)
Ernest Wadsworth Longfellow
Fund   1993.687

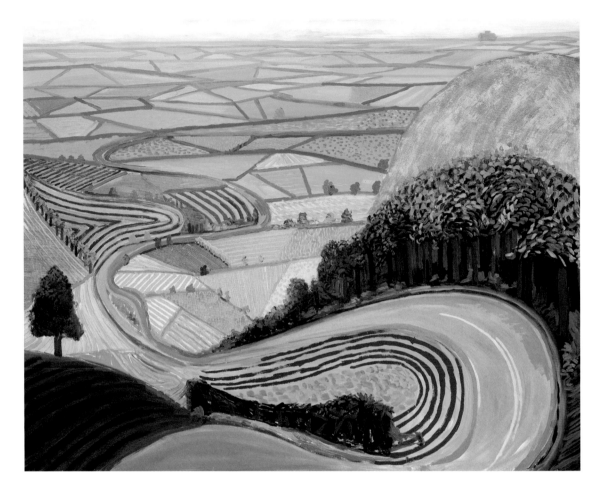

David Hockney
English, born 1937
Garrowby Hill, 1998

Coming to prominence as part of the British Pop Art
movement in the early 1960s, Hockney is a painter
and printmaker who has also worked innovatively as
a photographer and stage designer. With the brilliant
palette characteristic of many of his works, *Garrowby
Hill* is one of a series of soaring, panoramic landscapes of his native Yorkshire, in northern England,
begun in 1997. Hockney has long worked with painting and photography together, and this painting's
multiple perspectives are the result of photographs
that the artist made while traveling in an open car
and later synthesized in his Los Angeles studio.

Oil on canvas
60 x 76 in. (152.4 x 193 cm)
Juliana Cheney Edwards Collection,
Seth K. Sweetser Fund, and Tompkins
Collection — Arthur Gordon Tompkins
Fund   1998.56

Philip Guston
American, 1913–1980
The Deluge, 1969

During the 1950s and early 1960s, Guston worked in a sensuous and
luminous Abstract Expressionist style. In 1968, however, he began to
introduce caricatural images into his freely painted abstract works, a
movement from abstraction to representation that had a profound influence on many younger contemporaries. *The Deluge* is an early example of
Guston's new direction. Both the image and the title suggest the aftermath of some cataclysmic event, with the objects on the horizon seeming
about to be engulfed by the formless darkness below.

Oil on canvas
77 x 128 in. (195.6 x 325.1 cm)
Bequest of Musa Guston   1992.509

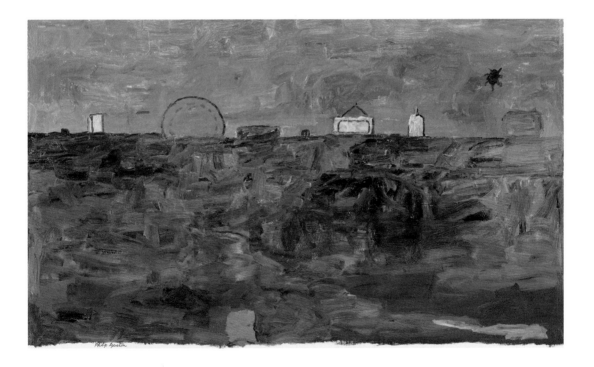

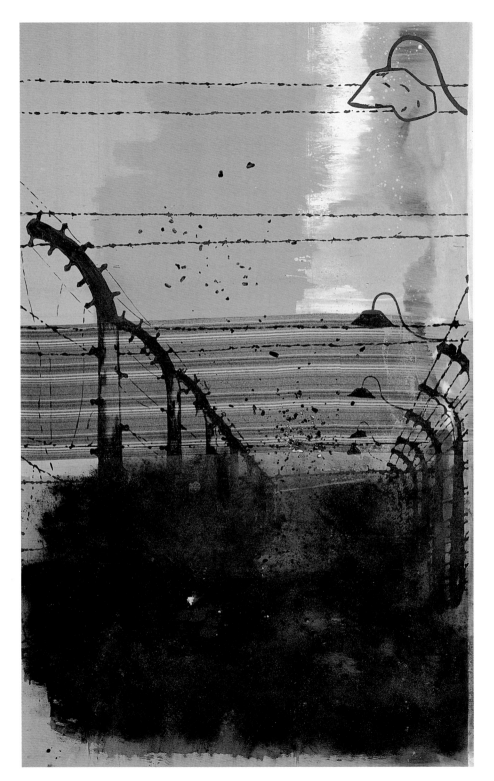

opposite
Sigmar Polke
German, 1941–2010
Lager, 1982

Polke, who grew up in communist East Germany, escaped to West Germany in 1953. Working in collaboration with such artists as Gerhard Richter, Polke founded a German variation of Pop Art and often includes found objects in his work. His huge, multimedia *Lager*, which means "camp" in German, is one of a series of paintings in which the artist addressed the Holocaust. At the center is an image from a photograph of the electrified fences inside the concentration camp at Auschwitz, while the canvas is divided by an actual blanket that tangibly evokes the experience of the camp's prisoners. While *Lager* powerfully recalls the horrors of the Holocaust, the orange light of the sun in the background may symbolize the artist's hopes for an end to human atrocities.

Acrylic and spattered pigment on pieced fabric support
158 x 98¾ in. (401.3 x 250.8 cm)
Gift of Charlene Engelhard   1993.961

Kikuji Kawada
Japanese, born 1933
Hinomaru, Japanese National Flag, 1962,
printed 1989

Born in 1933, Kikuji Kawada has long held a prominent place in postwar Japanese photography. This image belongs to a series of photographs Kawada made to illustrate his acclaimed 1965 photobook *Chizu (The Map)*, which examines, through text and image, Japan in the era after the atomic bombings of Hiroshima and Nagasaki. He began the deeply reflective project in the early 1960s, "using the notion of the map as a clue to the future and to question the whereabouts of my spirit." Gritty, highly symbolic, this image presents a rumpled and soiled Japanese flag lying on the ground. Praised for its powerful, evocative exploration of a defining moment in Japanese history, *Chizu*, with its striking black-and-white photographs, conveys the artist's feelings—and those of many of his compatriots—on the subject of national identity in the years of reckoning after the end of the Second World War.

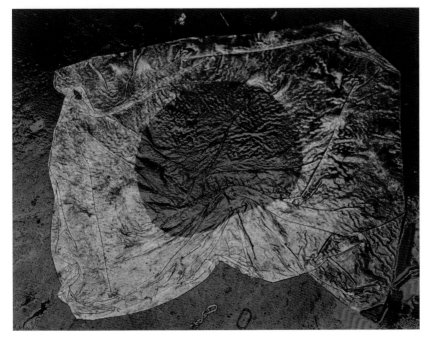

Photograph, gelatin silver print
16⅛ x 20⅞ in. (41 x 53 cm)
Museum purchase with funds donated by Willard and Elizabeth Clark
2014.1129

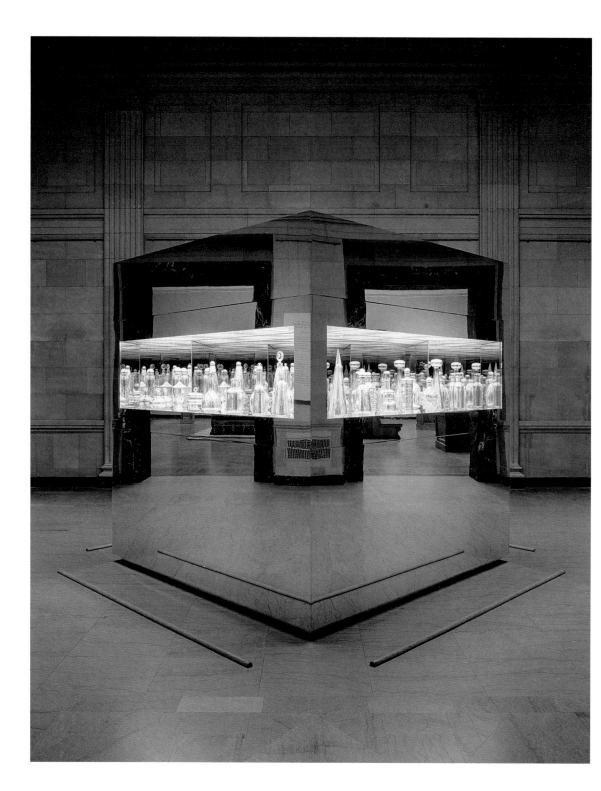

opposite

Josiah McElheny
American, born 1966
Endlessly Repeating Twentieth Century Modernism, 2007

McElheny has stated that he aims to explore how "the act of looking at a reflective object could be connected to the mental act of reflecting on an idea." In his sculptures and installations, McElheny deploys the most sophisticated and virtuoso glass working techniques, combined with conceptual rigor, to explore crucial moments in the development of modernity's visual and theoretical undercurrents. *Endlessly Repeating Twentieth Century Modernism* belongs to a series of works based on a conversation that took place in 1929 between sculptor Isamu Noguchi and designer/architect Buckminster Fuller. Their discussion imagined a world of form without shadow: a reflective, self-enclosed environment, filled with reflective objects; a perfect utopia. Set within the monumental, mirrored environment are decanters, vases, boxes, and bottles, based on twentieth-century European models and handblown by McElheny from mirrored glass. Their reflections repeat, seemingly infinitely—a portrayal of the capitalist notion that all objects are eternally repeatable, that everything can be remanufactured endlessly without regard to era, geography, or culture.

Handblown mirrored glass, low iron and transparent mirror, metal, wood, electric lighting
94½ x 92¾ x 92¾ in. (240 x 235.6 x 235.6 cm)
Museum purchase with funds donated by the Linde Family Foundation   2007.600

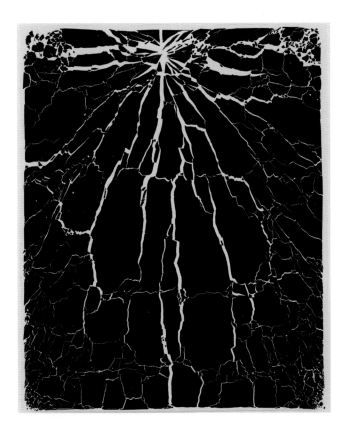

Tara Donovan
American, born 1969
Untitled, 2008

In drawings, sculptures, and large-scale installations, Donovan transforms ordinary commercial objects like Styrofoam cups, sewing pins, drinking straws, and Scotch tape into patterns that echo natural forms. To make this "glass drawing," she rolled ink on a large pane of glass, shattered it, and then pressed the inked pattern of the loose breaks onto paper. For Donovan, form follows material; her work results from a process of experimentation and discovery, as she comes to know and understand at a fundamental level the behaviors, and possibilities, of her media. A monotype, or one-of-a-kind print, *Untitled* can be read as what it literally is—an impression of broken glass—but also some kind of force field, such as lightning bolts against a night sky.

Broken glass inked and impressed on paper (glass drawing)
51¾ x 42½ in. (131.4 x 108 cm)
The Virginia Herrick Deknatel Purchase Fund   2008.1525

Kehinde Wiley

American, born 1977

John, 1st Baron Byron, 2013

Wiley often quotes European "masters" in his highly stylized portraits while exploring issues of race, economic disparity, gender, and sexuality. For *John, 1st Baron Byron*, he took inspiration from a painting of the same name, made in the seventeenth century by British painter William Dobson. That work portrays the English cavalier John Byron, 1st Baron Byron, who points out of the frame while, behind him, a black page boy tends his white stallion. In Wiley's composition, a muscular, rosy-lipped black man takes Byron's place, wearing designer sportswear and pointing in the opposite direction against an ornate textile backdrop. The image carries an overt homoeroticism—a challenge to the ways male sexuality has been portrayed throughout history, but also to the difficulties that many black gay men face in gaining acceptance within their own communities. Between the powerful gaze of Wiley's model and our own looms the question of what it means to participate in, or to be excluded from, wider society or culture.

Oil on canvas

72 x 60 in. (182.9 x 152.4 cm)

Juliana Cheney Edwards Collection, The Heritage Fund for a Diverse Collection, and funds donated by Stephen Borkowski in honor of Jason Collins   2013.633

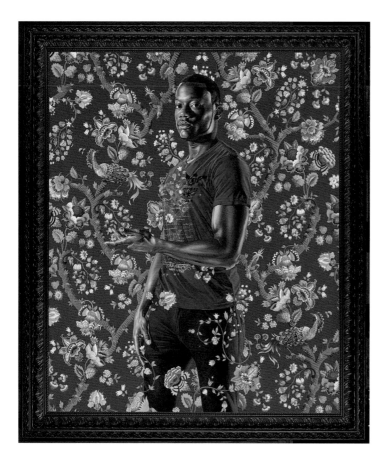

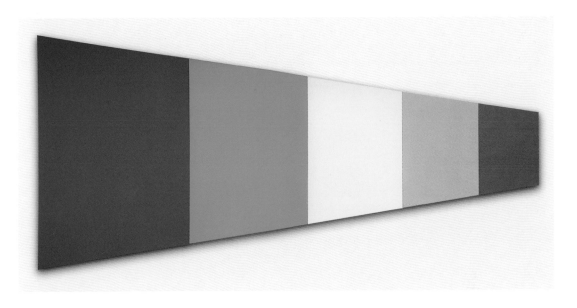

Ellsworth Kelly

American, 1923–2015

***Blue Green Yellow Orange Red**, 1968*

Oil on canvas
120 x 272 in. (304.8 x 690.9 cm)
Gift of the Bank of America Corporation   2011.93.1-5

While studying at the School of the Museum of Fine Arts from 1946 to 1948, Kelly painted and drew from life. His mature, abstract works, too, are rooted in things that he saw: shadows, plants, architectural details. Kelly captured their essence by distilling them into pure line, shape, and, above all, color. Throughout his career, Kelly brought to bear an intense engagement with the nature of—and relationships between—colors, in works that challenge traditions of painting and push beyond the conventional perimeter of the canvas. The trapezoidal *Blue Green Yellow Orange Red* represents a "half-spectrum": five solid canvases of graduated sizes, adjoined, are hung banner-like together. Tapering at one side, the work seems to recede into space, recalling perhaps the principles of one-point perspective, used by painters to create an illusion of depth. At the same time, the very basic structure and color continually emphasize the painting's surface and assert its relationship to the wall on which it hangs.

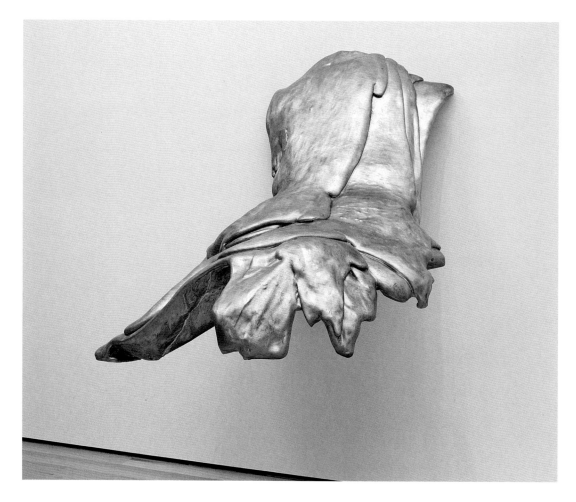

Lynda Benglis

American, born 1941

Wing, 1970

Lynda Benglis was a pioneering member of the process-driven and feminist art movements of the late 1960s and early 1970s. Originally, she trained as a painter, and her sculptures reflect the influence of Jackson Pollock's drip methods, as well as Color Field painters Morris Louis and Helen Frankenthaler—artists whose unorthodox techniques of pouring, soaking, and staining their canvases were fundamental to their works' meanings. *Wing* shifts the conversation about the liquid, flowing medium of paint into three dimensions. To create the work, Benglis poured polyurethane that hardened, capturing a gesture in air. Organic in form, it evokes the curves of the body; cast in solid aluminum, *Wing* also represents a comment on the hefty, often geometric metal works popular among male artists at the time. Seeming to leap from the wall, *Wing* stands as evidence of an artistic process, a moment frozen in time.

Cast aluminum
67 x 59¼ x 60 in. (170.2 x 150.4 x 152.4 cm)
Museum purchase with funds from the Catherine and Paul Buttenwieser Fund, Joyce Linde, Frank B. Bemis Fund, Barbara Lee Endowment for Contemporary Art by Women, Towles Contemporary Art Fund, and the Vance Wall Foundation   2011.1

Joan Jonas
American, born 1936
Ice Drawing, 2012

Since the late 1960s, Joan Jonas has traversed
boundaries between media, combining sound, text,
and drawing in video performances and installations. A pioneer of performance and video art, she has
addressed our complex relationship to the natural
world in her recent projects. *Ice Drawing* is a video and
sculptural installation and one component of her live-
performance, multichannel installation *Reanimation*.
In *Ice Drawing*, video footage shows the artist creating
an abstract drawing using ink and ice (a gesture that
she carries out live during the performance). The video
is presented by way of a projector, whose light refracts
through a set of hanging crystals, spilling colored light
throughout the gallery and onto the bodies of viewers. Implicated in the moment and connected by the
refracted constellation, we watch as ink spills onto a
pristine white surface and ice melts.

Installation consisting of video (color, silent, projected
through structure) and structure with metal armature and
hanging crystals
Museum purchase with funds donated by members of the
2014–15 Contemporary Art Visiting Committee: Bruce and
Shelly Eckman, James and Audrey Foster, Joyce Linde, Erica
Gervais Pappendick and Ted Pappendick, Carolyn Fine and
Jeremiah E. Friedman, Ashley and Jamie Harmon, Steven
Rogowski, Robert and Esta Epstein, John F. Cogan, Jr.,
and Mary L. Cornille, Davis and Carol Noble, Nicholas and
Marjorie Greville, Leigh Braude, Lorraine Bressler, Robert
and Jane Burke, Ronald and Ronni Casty, John and Bette
Cohen, Woody and Elizabeth Ives, Joy and Douglas Kant,
Katherine Kirk, Susan Kohn and Philip Markell, Barbara
Krakow, Richard and Nancy Lubin, Beth and Richard
Marcus, Susan Paine, Marc Plonskier, Amy and Jonathan
Poorvu, Ellen Poss, Robert Radloff, Carol Wall, Eloise
Hodges, Lizbeth and George Krupp, Marjory Jacobson,
Timothy Phillips, Allison Salke, Lois Torf, Bruce and Judy
Eissner, and the Barbara Lee Endowment for Contemporary
Art by Women   2015.3375

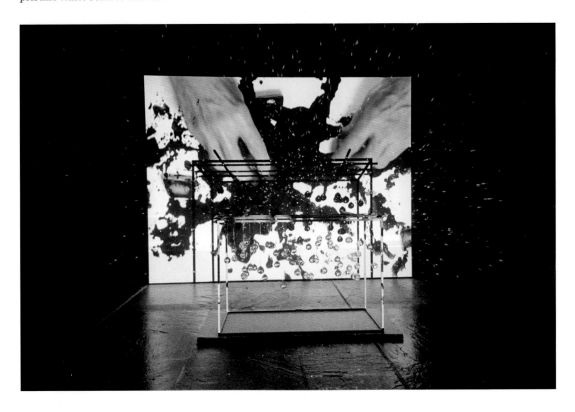

Amalia Pica
Argentinean, born 1978
Now Speak!, 2011

Born in Argentina and based in
London and Mexico City, Amalia
Pica creates works that often foreground participation to examine
communication, in particular the
ways messages are delivered and
received. "I am interested in what
brings us together," Pica has said,
"and so communication and its
difficulties are for me a sign of
how much we need each other."
According to myth, upon completing his exceptionally lifelike
sculpture of Moses, Michelangelo
commanded the marble, "Now,
speak!" Pica updates that legendary quote as contemporary "social
sculpture." *Now Speak!* is both
a physical object and a symbolic
platform—an invitation to share
one's voice and perspective pub-
licly. A cast-concrete lectern, it
is activated when people step up
behind it and make their procla-
mations in the form of inspired,
spur-of-the-moment declara-
tions, invocations of historical
speeches, programmed performances, and more.

Cast concrete, live performance
59½ x 40⅛ x 32 in. (151 x 101.8 x 81.2 cm)
Museum purchase with funds donated
anonymously   2013.1829

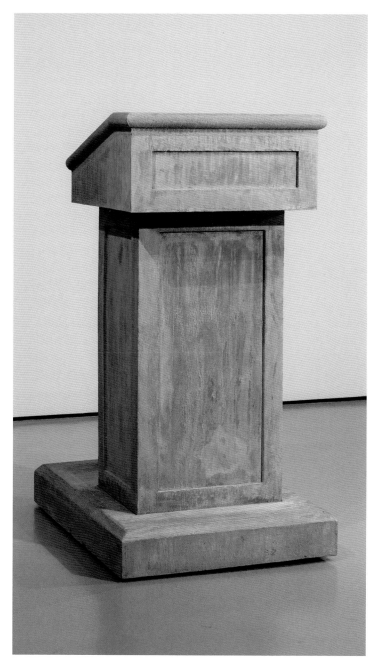

Carmen Herrera
Cuban, born 1915
Blanco y Verde (#1), 1962

Trained as an architect in her native Havana, Cuba, Herrera went on to study painting in New York. She transformed her work in the late 1940s in Paris, where she worked and exhibited alongside a number of international abstract artists. "I began a lifelong process of purification," Herrera has said, "a process of taking away what isn't essential." Icons of balance and counterbalance, paintings like *Blanco y Verde (#1)* reduce imagery to mirrored, colored forms. Two slim, triangular flashes of green barely touch at the center, like cuts in the white plane of the canvas. Foreground and background are ambiguous; the green shapes create what might be read as a hard-edged abstraction or a horizon line in an austere landscape. As the artist noted in 1994, "I like straight lines, I like angles, I like order. In this chaos that we live in, I like to put order."

Acrylic on canvas
60 x 72 in. (152.4 x 182.9 cm)
Museum purchase with funds donated by Barbara L. and Theodore B. Alfond through The Heritage Fund for a Diverse Collection   2014.1009

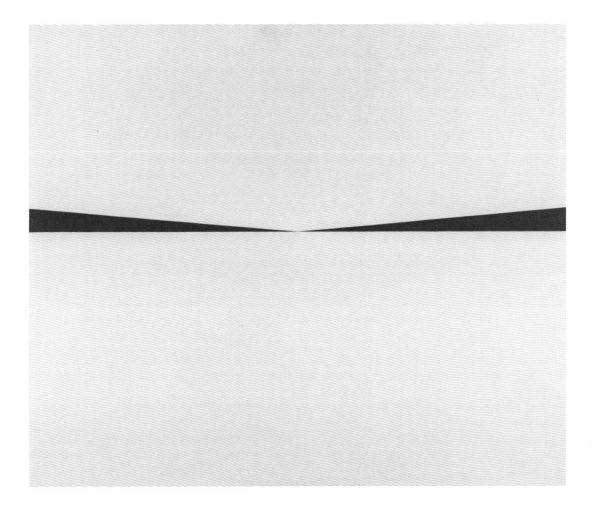

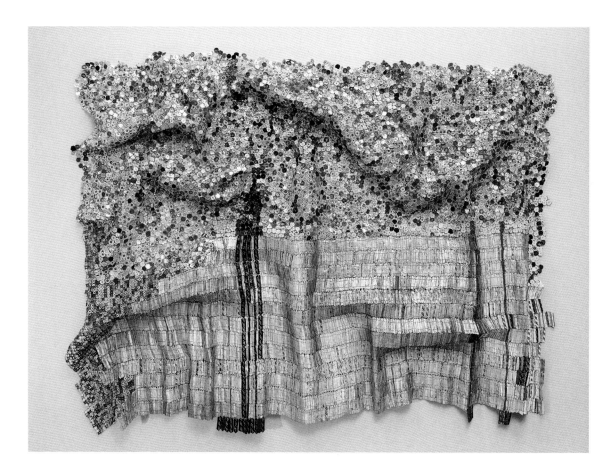

El Anatsui
Ghanaian, born 1944
Black River, 2009

Born in Ghana and active for most of his career in
Nigeria, El Anatsui assembles large-scale works
from found and recycled materials. To create *Black
River*, Anatsui worked with a team of assistants to
"weave" discarded liquor-bottle caps and wrappers
into a metallic tapestry. Historical African forms and
aesthetics inform his process, including traditional
Ghanaian *kente*-cloth weavings, in their juxtaposition of color and shape. Connecting to those traditions, Anatsui refers to works like *Black River* as
"cloths" rather than as "installations" or "sculptures."
When pinned to the wall, its hills and valleys recall

a topographical map; at center, a "black river" seems
to seep across a border. Liquor wrappers with names
like "Dark Sailor" and "Black Gold" hint at Africa's
long history of slavery and colonialism, as well as
today's conflicts over natural resources, especially
oil. Embracing an artistic process that unites the
past and the present, Anatsui speaks to the legacy of
European colonization and how it has shaped contemporary African life.

Aluminum, bottle caps, copper wire
105 x 140 in. (266.7 x 355.6 cm)
Towles Fund for Contemporary Art, Robert L. Beal, Enid
L. Beal and Bruce A. Beal Acquisition Fund, Henry and Lois
Foster Contemporary Purchase Fund, Frank B. Bemis Fund,
and funds donated by the Vance Wall Foundation   2010.586

Alice Neel
American, 1900–1984
Linda Nochlin and Daisy, 1973

Working from life, Alice Neel
established a powerful empathy
and identification with her sitters,
capturing them with disarm-
ing frankness using her signature deliberate brushstrokes and
vibrant palette. Today considered
among the foremost figurative
painters of the twentieth century,
Neel spent most of her career
in New York working in relative
obscurity, receiving the acclaim
of critics and curators only late in
her life. Her subjects were usually
friends or acquaintances; in this
painting, she portrays pioneering
art historian Linda Nochlin and
Nochlin's six-year-old daughter,
Daisy. Shortly after the publication
of Nochlin's seminal essay "Why
Have There Been No Great Women
Artists?" in 1971, Neel invited
her to sit for a portrait. Long an
advocate for women's rights,
Neel felt a strong sympathy with
Nochlin's text, which provoked
a reevaluation of the conditions
and prejudices that historically
caused so many female artists to
be overlooked. Neel chose to depict
Nochlin as a writer and a mother.
Blunt and revealing, the gazes of
both figures confront the viewer:
one shrewd and knowing, the other
wide open to a different future.

Oil on canvas
55⅞ x 44 in. (141.9 x 111.8 cm)
Seth K. Sweetser Fund   1983.496

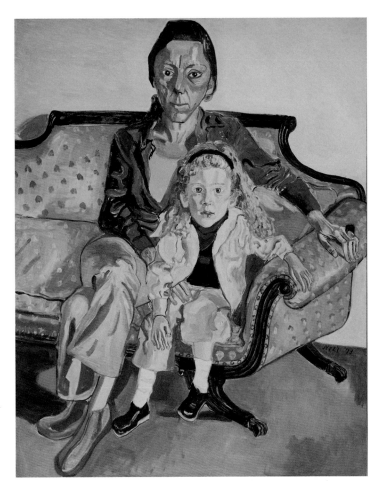

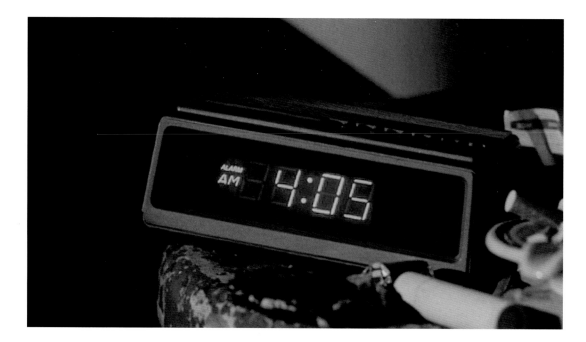

Christian Marclay
Swiss-American, born 1955
The Clock, 2010

Hailed as a masterpiece of media art, Christian Marclay's *The Clock* is a twenty-four-hour film composed of thousands of clips spanning cinematic and television history. Each brief clip references time through a verbal mention, the blare of an alarm clock, or a glance at a watch, among myriad examples. Synchronized to the time zone in which it is exhibited, the work is also, in practical terms, a functioning timepiece, marking the minutes as they go by.

While *The Clock* does not feature any one overarching story or "look," it embraces strong narrative elements. Activities take place on-screen (and in real time) at their socially prescribed moments: characters eat dinner in the evening and rise for work early in the morning. Weaving together these clips, Marclay casts a critical eye on the social construction of time and the ways in which the mass media establishes norms and structures our day-to-day lives. For viewers, the experience of time and space is divided: drawn into the momentary fictions before them, they are also aware of their place in the gallery as the minutes — or hours — pass in real time.

Single-channel video (color, sound)
Edward Linde Fund — jointly owned by the Museum of Fine Arts, Boston, and the National Gallery of Canada   2011.473

Lorna Simpson
American, born 1960
She, 1992

Simpson first gained attention in the 1980s for works that combine image and text to challenge dominant notions of race, identity, culture, and history. She has noted the influence of the feminist movement—especially black feminism—in shaping works like *She*, which examines how everyday language and imagery can perpetuate misconceptions and prejudices about gender and race. This four-panel work confronts the reliance on stereotypes in our definition of identity. Masculine gestures, body language, and the tailored suit might suggest one gender for the subject; the title and the plaque above the photographs declare the opposite. At the same time, Simpson has created a faceless portrait—undermining the traditional definition of the genre while underscoring just how much we might rely on that feature to determine identity. The effect is an unexpected guessing game: do we place more trust in the word or in the image?

Photograph, dye-diffusion photographs (Polaroid prints), plaque
29 x 85¼ in. (73.6 x 216.5 cm)
Ellen Kelleran Gardner Fund   1992.204a-e

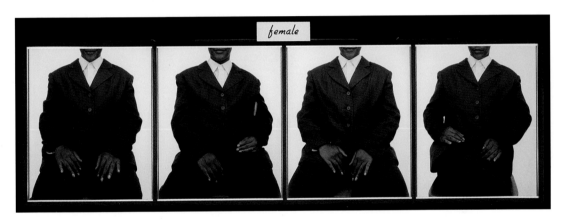

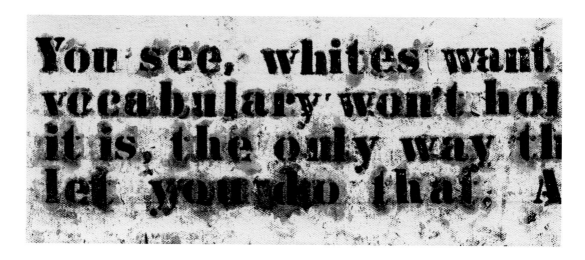

You see, whites want black artists to mostly deliver something as if it were an official version of the black experience. But the vocabulary won't hold it, simply. No true account really of black life can be held, can be contained, in the American vocabulary. As it is, the only way that you can deal with it is by doing great violence to the assumptions on which the vocabulary is based. But they won't let you do that. And when you go along, you find yourself very quickly painted into a corner: you've written yourself into a corner.

Glenn Ligon
American, born 1960
Untitled (James Baldwin), 1990

In his canvases, Glenn Ligon uses text as a material with presence in physical space. An avid reader, Ligon employs writings by authors who frequently engage issues of nationality, race, sexuality, gender, and the legacies of colonialism. In *Untitled (James Baldwin)*, he pays homage to Baldwin's reflection on the impossibility of creating a complete portrait of black identity through the English language. The chosen passage comments on the contradictions faced by African Americans and others who are bound to express themselves in a language used by their oppressors. To create the work, Ligon pressed an oil stick against a reusable, thin plastic letter stencil. Over time, the oil pigment stuck to the stencil and formed smudges, producing a trail that began to fill in the spaces between the letters. The visual complexity powerfully reflects Baldwin's message, and the viewer must make an active effort to decipher the text. The long, horizontal format makes reading a full-body endeavor—suggesting perhaps that with movement can come a shift in consciousness.

Oil on canvas
6¼ x 84 in. (15.9 x 213.4 cm)
Seth K. Sweetser Fund   1991.546

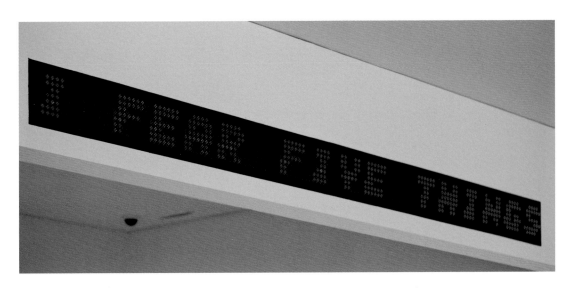

Jenny Holzer

American, born 1950

Selections from Truisms, Inflammatory Essays, The Living Series, The Survival Series, Under a Rock, Laments, and Child Text, 1991

Throughout her career, Holzer has created works that place ideas and words—her own and others'—into the sphere of everyday life. *Truisms* (1977), her first all-text composition, took the form of one-liners, printed commercially as posters, which she had pasted up on the streets of New York. Over time, Holzer began utilizing other familiar delivery methods, often linked to advertising: from billboards and T-shirts to stickers and electronic signage. Her first museum commission, this scrolling LED extends that medium's urban, commercial aesthetic to a more pristine, detached world. It combines selections from seven different text-based series Holzer created between 1977 and 1990; each selection appears in a different typeface and format. Words scroll by at varying speeds, and the tone constantly changes: from aggressive to mild, dogmatic to questioning, practical to fear-inducing. By turns comic, insightful, and hostile, the words and phrases express multiple viewpoints—and arouse multiple responses.

LED (light-emitting diode) electronic-display signboard in three colors (yellow, green, red)
9⅜ x 144⅛ x 2½ in. (23.8 x 366.1 x 6.5 cm)
Ernest Wadsworth Longfellow Fund   1991.1099

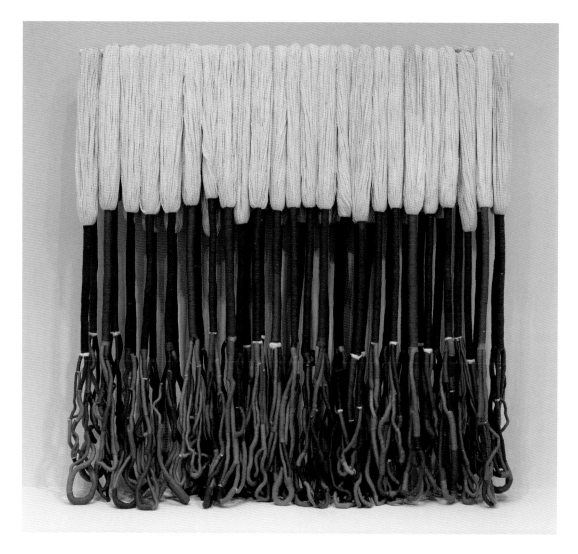

Sheila Hicks

American, born 1934

Bamian (Banyan), 1968

In her large-scale installations, Sheila Hicks has
pushed the sculptural possibilities of fiber as a
medium, creating monumental, architectural works
of art. Made from densely wrapped wool and acrylic
yarns, *Bamian (Banyan)* also exhibits the sense of
movement and softness inherent to textiles. The title
alludes to the artist's travels and lifelong interest
in non-Western cultures, whose textile traditions
she has studied and taken as inspiration in her own
works. Bamian (or Banyan), a town in Afghanistan,
was a trade hub on the ancient Silk Road; it's known
as well for the massive sculptures of the historical
Buddha that were carved into the side of a cliff nearby
(and destroyed by the Taliban in 2001). Banyan is
also a variety of tree that figures prominently in both
Hindu and Buddhist narratives.

Wool and acrylic yarns, wrapped
102⅜ x 102⅜ in. (260 x 260 cm)
Charles Potter Kling Fund and partial gift of Sheila Hicks
2011.474

Nick Cave

American, born 1959

Sound Suit, 2008

Nick Cave's *Sound Suits* blur the lines
between fashion, costume design, fiber art,
sculpture, and performance. Cave trained as
both a visual artist and a dancer, studying
with the Alvin Ailey American Dance Theater.
Movement is central to the meaning of his
works. His *Sound Suits* also connect to a long
history of dress as an element of ritual, from
the elaborate regalia associated with African
dance performances to the liturgical robes
of Christian clergy. This example comprises
two parts: an elongated headdress-suit that
sheaths and obscures the face and body, and
leggings. Cave made them from scavenged
textiles, which he bought at thrift stores and
flea markets and then dazzlingly embellished
with beadwork, stitching, and appliqué. Worn,
the work has both protective and transforma-
tive qualities, turning the body into a glittering, otherworldly apparition.

Fabric with appliqué of found sequined
material, beading, crocheted and knitted yarn,
metal armature
98 x 27 x 14 in. (248.9 x 68.6 x 35.6 cm)
Gift of Judith P. and S. Lawrence Schlager
2012.1358.1-2

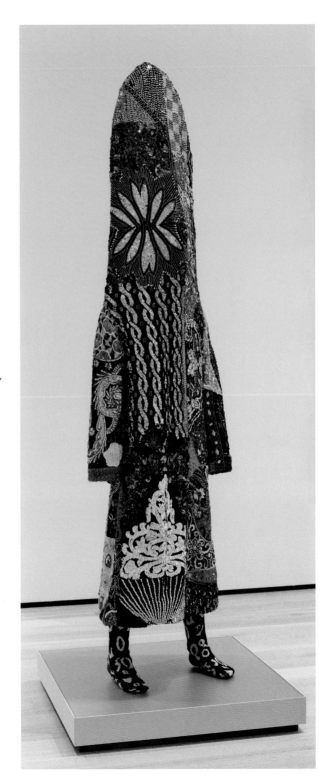

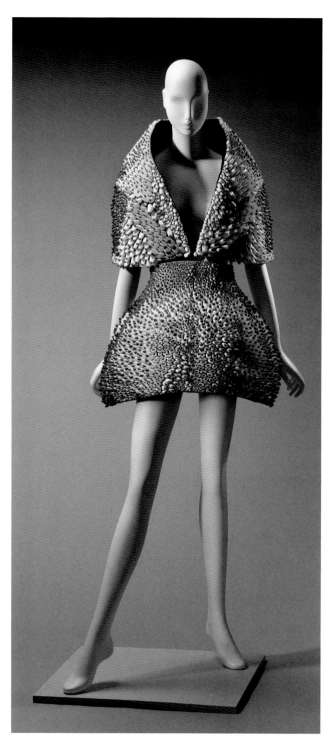

Iris Van Herpen and **Neri Oxman**
Dutch, born 1984; Israeli, born 1976
in collaboration with **W. Craig Carter**
American, born 1961
Anthazoa 3-D Cape and Skirt, Voltage
collection, 2013

Dutch designer Iris Van Herpen's avant-
garde creations blur the lines between art,
technology, and fashion. For this ensemble
from her Voltage collection, she joined
forces with Neri Oxman, an architect and
a professor at the Massachusetts Institute of Technology's Media Lab. Oxman's
work explores the interface between digital
design and natural forms — an interest
that resonated with Van Herpen's forward-
thinking approach to fashion. *Anthazoa
3-D Cape and Skirt* was the first 3-D–
printed garment made of both soft and
hard materials, a combination of polyurethane rubber and acrylic. Its rigid, tactile
"barnacles" are astonishingly flexible;
together, they form a futuristic fabric that
the designers shaped around a steel cage
to create the garment. Shown on the Paris
haute-couture runways in January 2013, it
represents a blending of forms that look to
nature with a process rooted in the twenty-
first century.

Polyurethane rubber and acrylic, steel cage,
cotton twill inner lining and silk satin lining;
printed on a Stratasys Objet Connex multi-
material 3-D printer
Skirt: 34 x 23 x 36 in. (86.4 x 58.4 x 91.4 cm)
Cape: 20 x 18 in. (50.8 x 45.7 cm)
Museum purchase with funds donated by the
Fashion Council, Museum of Fine Arts, Boston
2013.1487.1-2

John Cederquist
American, born 1946
How to Wrap Five Waves, 1994–95

California sculptor and studio furniture maker John Cederquist is known for his irreverent, trompe l'oeil works. In this playful chest of drawers, a large wave seems to crash out of a stack of packing crates. Cederquist takes as a reference point the eighteenth-century Japanese artist Hokusai and his instantly recognizable woodblock print *The Great Wave (Under the Wave off Kanagawa)*. In a nod across mediums, he used oil-based lithography inks, rather than paint, for the colorful wave itself. The object's name, *How to Wrap Five Waves*, is a riff on a classic book on traditional Japanese packaging design, *How to Wrap Five Eggs*; it's also a fond allusion to surfing, which Cederquist enjoys. Through these references, the artist makes a statement about the importation of Asian culture to the West, as with the popularization of Zen Buddhism in 1950s California, when Cederquist was a teenager. Above all, however, the chest is a humorous visual pun—blurring the lines between furniture, painting, and sculpture.

Baltic birch plywood, poplar, maple, Sitka spruce, pine, epoxy resin inlay, oil-based lithography inks, metal hardware
74 x 49 x 14 in. (188 x 124.5 x 35.6 cm)
The Daphne Farago Collection   2017.4774

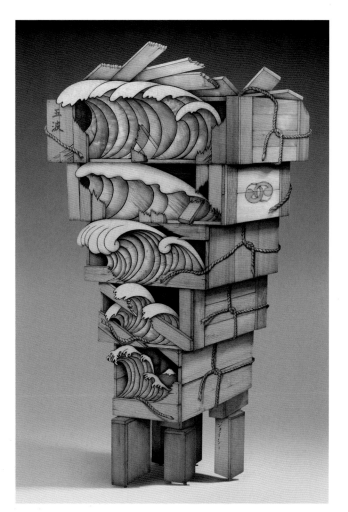

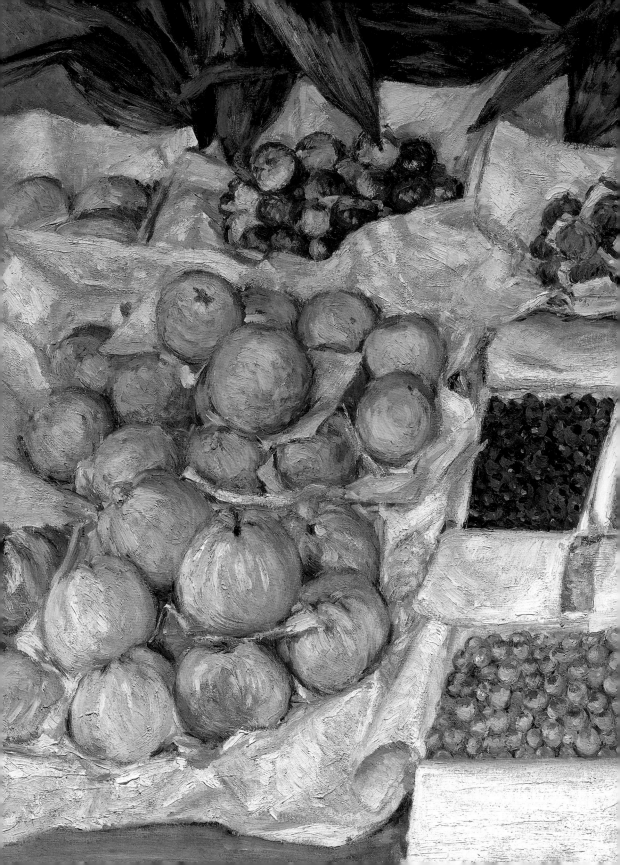

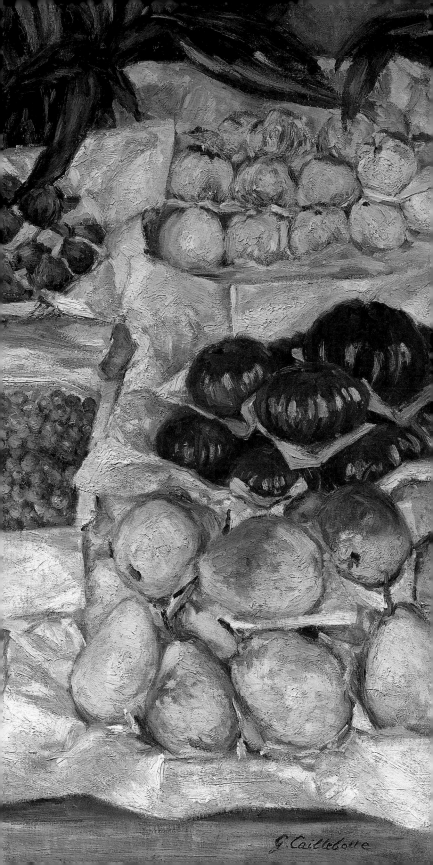

G. Caillebotte

Figure Illustrations

p. 6
The Huntington Avenue Entrance, Museum of Fine Arts, Boston

p. 8
Josiah McElheny
American, born in 1966
Endlessly Repeating Twentieth Century Modernism, 2007
Hand-blown mirrored glass, low iron and transparent mirror, metal, wood, electric lighting
94½ x 92¾ x 92¾ in.
(240 x 235.6 x 235.6 cm)
Museum purchase with funds donated by the Linde Family Foundation, 2007.600

p. 8
Face from mummiform coffin
Egyptian
Third Intermediate Period to early Late Period, 1070–660 B.C.
Wood
18.4 x 16.7cm (7¼ x 6⅝ in.)
Hay Collection—Gift of C. Granville Way, 72.4775

pp. 10–11
Visitors engage with:
Paul Gauguin
French, 1848–1903
Where Do We Come From? What Are We? Where Are We Going?, 1897–98
Oil on canvas
54¾ x 147½ in. (139.1 x 374.6 cm)
Tompkins Collection–Arthur Gordon Tompkins Fund, 36.270

p. 12
Joseph Mallord William Turner
English, 1775–1851
Slave Ship, 1840
Oil on canvas
90.8 x 122.6 cm (35¾ x 48¼ in.)
Henry Lillie Pierce Fund, 99.22

p.13
Night Attack on the Sanjō Palace (detail)
Japanese
Kamakura period, third quarter of the 13th century
Handscroll; ink and color on paper
Entire scroll: 41.3 x 699.7 cm
(16¼ x 275½ in.)
Fenollosa-Weld Collection, 11.4000

p. 15
Dish, 1740–67
Vietnamese
Le-Trinh period, Trinh Doanh government
Porcelain with underglaze cobalt blue
15 x 3.2 cm (5⅞ x 1¼ in.)
Gift of John D. Constable, 2007.401

p. 15
Possible bags, about 1890
Native American (Lakota [Sioux])
Tanned hide, lazy-stitch beadwork embroidery, sinew, and tin cones with tufts of dyed red horsehair
Overall: 33 x 53.3 cm (13 x 21 in.)
Gift of the Estate of David Rockefeller from the Collection of David and Peggy Rockefeller, 2018.250.1-2

p. 17
The William I. Koch Gallery

Details

p. 1
Edgar Degas
French, 1834–1917
Little Fourteen-Year-Old Dancer; original model 1878–81, cast after 1921
Bronze, gauze, satin; H. 40⅞ in. (103.7 cm)
Frederick Brown Fund and Contributions from William Claflin and William Emerson, 38.1756
Photograph courtesy of Tony Rinaldo

pp. 2–3
Kara Walker, *The Rich Soil Down There*, 2002, p. 401

pp. 28–29
Interior face of the outer coffin of Djehutynakht, 2010–1961 B.C., p. 35

pp. 62–63
Sarcophagus, about A.D. 215–25, p. 89

pp. 96–97
Heroine Rushing to Her Lover, late 18th century, p. 106

pp. 154–55
Bedcover, about 1900, p. 167

pp. 170–71
Henry Ossawa Tanner, *Interior of a Mosque, Cairo*, 1897, p. 233

pp. 270–71
Rembrandt Harmensz. van Rijn, *Artist in His Studio*, 1628, p. 300

pp. 396–97
David Hockney, *Garrowby Hill*, 1998, p. 404

pp. 426–27
Gustave Caillebotte, *Fruit Displayed on a Stand*, about 1881–82, p. 368

Index of artists and works

Credits

Josiah McElheny, *Endlessly Repeating Twentieth Century Modernism*, 2007. © Josiah McElheny 2007

Archibald Motley, *Cocktails*, about 1926. © Valerie Gerrard Browne

Takashi Murakami, *If the Double Helix Wakes Up . . .*, 2002. © 2002 Takashi Murakami/Kaikai Kiki Co., Ltd. All Rights Reserved.

Alice Neel, *Linda Nochlin and Daisy*, 1973. © The Estate of Alice Neel. Courtesy David Zwirner, New York/London

Emil Nolde, *Irises*. © Nolde Stiftung Seebüll

Georgia O'Keeffe, *White Rose with Larkspur No. 2*, 1927. © 2019 Georgia O'Keeffe Museum/Artists Rights Society (ARS), New York

Oscar Heyman Bros., Marjorie Merriweather Post brooch, 1929. Reproduced with permission.

Pablo Picasso, *The Bull*, December 18, 1945. © 2019 Estate of Pablo Picasso/Artists Rights Society (ARS), New York

Pablo Picasso, *The Bull*, December 26, 1945. © 2019 Estate of Pablo Picasso/Artists Rights Society (ARS), New York

Pablo Picasso, *The Bull*, December 28, 1945. © 2019 Estate of Pablo Picasso/Artists Rights Society (ARS), New York

Pablo Picasso, *The Bull*, January 2, 1946. © 2019 Estate of Pablo Picasso/Artists Rights Society (ARS), New York

Pablo Picasso, *The Bull*, January 5, 1946. © 2019 Estate of Pablo Picasso/Artists Rights Society (ARS), New York

Pablo Picasso, *The Bull*, January 17, 1946. © 2019 Estate of Pablo Picasso/Artists Rights Society (ARS), New York

Pablo Picasso, *Standing Figure*, 1908. © 2019 Estate of Pablo Picasso/Artists Rights Society (ARS), New York

Pablo Picasso, *Portrait of a Woman*, 1910. © 2019 Estate of Pablo Picasso/Artists Rights Society (ARS), New York

Pablo Picasso, *Rape of the Sabine Women*, 1963. © 2019 Estate of Pablo Picasso/Artists Rights Society (ARS), New York

Amalia Pica, *Now Speak!*, 2011. Reproduced with permission.

Sigmar Polke, *Lager*, 1982. © 2019 The Estate of Sigmar Polke, Cologne/ARS, New York/VG Bild-Kunst, Bonn

Jackson Pollock, *Troubled Queen*, 1945. © 2019 The Pollock-Krasner Foundation/Artists Rights Society (ARS), New York

Robert Rauschenberg, *Breakthrough II*, 1965. © 2019 Robert Rauschenberg Foundation/Licensed by VAGA at Artists Rights Society (ARS), NY

Diego Rivera, *Self-Portrait*, 1930. © 2019 Banco de México Diego Rivera Frida Kahlo Museums Trust, Mexico, D.F./Artists Rights Society (ARS), New York

Viktor Schreckengost, Punch bowl from the *Jazz Bowl* series, 1931. Reproduced with permission.

Charles Sheeler, *Doylestown House — The Stove*, 1916–17. © The Lane Collection.

Cindy Sherman, *Untitled #282*, 1993. Courtesy of the Artist and Metro Pictures Gallery

Stephen Shore, *Trail's End Restaurant, Kanab, Utah, August 10, 1973*. © Stephen Shore

Lorna Simpson, *She*, 1992. Reproduced with permission.

Art Smith, necklace, about 1958. Reproduced with permission.

Kiki Smith, *Lilith*, 1994. Reproduced with permission.

Josef Sudek, *Labyrinths*, 1969. © Anna Fárová

Kara Walker, *The Rich Soil Down There*, 2002. Courtesy of Sikkema Jenkins & Co.

Andy Warhol, *Red Disaster*, 1963, 1985. © 2019 The Andy Warhol Foundation for the Visual Arts, Inc./Licensed by Artists Rights Society (ARS), New York

Vivienne Westwood, Woman's shoe, 1991. Reproduced with permission.

Kehinde Wiley, *John, 1st Baron Byron*, 2013. © Kehinde Wiley Studio

John Wilson, *Dr. Martin Luther King, Jr.*, 1985. © Copyright Agency. Licensed by Artists Rights Society (ARS), New York, 2019